Administering
Data Centers:
Servers, Storage,
and Voice over IP

Administering Data Centers: Servers, Storage, and Voice over IP

Kailash Jayaswal

WILEY

Wiley Publishing, Inc.

Administering Data Centers: Servers, Storage, and Voice over IP

Published by
Wiley Publishing, Inc.
10475 Crosspoint Boulevard
Indianapolis, IN 46256
www.wiley.com

Copyright © 2006 by Wiley Publishing, Inc., Indianapolis, Indiana

Library of Congress Control Number: 2005026258

ISBN-13: 978-0-471-77183-8
ISBN-10: 0-471-77183-X

Manufactured in the United States of America

10 9 8 7 6 5 4 3 2 1

1MA/QZ/RR/QV/IN

About the Author

Kailash Jayaswal (Campbell, CA) is currently a project manager for Cisco Systems, Inc. He has more than 18 years of technical experience as a systems and storage administrator at various companies, such as Caterpillar, Inc., Roche Bioscience, IBM, Navisite, Siebel, KLA Tencor, and Cisco Systems, Inc. He has worked extensively with operating systems, servers, networks, and storage products from Sun, EMC, IBM, VERITAS, Intel, Microsoft, Network Appliance, and Hewlett-Packard. He has a wealth of hands-on and project-management experience in deploying storage architectures, large data-center consolidations, capacity planning, and disaster-recovery design and implementation. Throughout his career, he has taught several classes on systems administration (HPUX, Solaris, and AIX), data-center best practices, and server and storage capacity planning and architecture, using industry-leading products.

Credits

Executive Editor
Carol Long

Development Editor
Kevin Shafer

Production Editor
William A. Barton

Copy Editor
Publication Services, Inc.

Editorial Manager
Mary Beth Wakefield

Production Manager
Tim Tate

Vice President & Executive Group Publisher
Richard Swadley

Vice President and Publisher
Joseph B. Wikert

Project Coordinator
Ryan Steffen

Graphics and Production Specialists
Denny Hager
Stephanie D. Jumper
Melanee Prendergast
Alicia South

Quality Control Technician
Leeann Harney
Jessica Kramer
Brian H. Walls

Media Development Specialists
Angela Denny
Kit Malone
Travis Silvers

Proofreading and Indexing
TECHBOOKS Production Services

Contents

Preface

This book explains technologies deployed within data centers. This includes facility setup, network configuration, power layout, servers, storage, data-center consolidation, disaster recovery, and voice over IP (VoIP). It describes data-center management, such as security, server administration, capacity planning, clustering, and fault tolerance. The book covers architecture, implementation, and management details. Implementing high-availability systems, one of the key topics in this book, is an essential step toward achieving any "always-on" service.

The book can be used in various ways:

- It can serve as an introduction to the myriad of technologies deployed within a data center.

- It can be used as a reference by various professionals such as Information Technology (IT) managers, data center facilities teams, system administrators, database administrators, network managers, security implementers, and general data center personnel. The chapters can be chosen in any order and read at any time.

- It can be used as material for various Masters in Business Administration (MBA) courses on IT Management or IT Operations management. All basic, evolving, and advanced IT technologies are covered here. This material can be used with more specific information to challenge the highly experienced MBA student.

- This book can be used by system and storage administrators, as well as IT managers, to build resiliency and high-availability into their environment.

When I started this book, I was challenged with trying to convey more than 18 years of experience as a hands-on IT administrator in a way that is easy to understand and implement. This book is not a programmer's manual. It has no low-level protocol descriptions or code. This book is about concepts, and most of the material is fairly generic across operating systems, server platforms, and industry-leading products. I have tried to stay away from mentioning vendors and their products. Several figures in the book provide end-to-end complete designs. Therefore, there are some repetitions of concepts illustrated by figures.

The book contains descriptions of what makes a well-designed data center, storage and network architecture, VoIP implementation, and server and storage consolidation. It provides generic (and sometimes specific) guidelines on day-to-day data center operations. It explains good security, capacity planning, and system administration policies. However, none of the solutions fall in the one-size-fits-all category. Some will work for you, and some will not. That is for you to decide.

If this book can help you build reliable and secure designs and data center policies that can withstand human fallacies and technical breakdowns, I think I have done my work.

As an IT architect, you will find your reputation and job at stake if the server, network, or storage architecture that you helped design cannot keep services running in the event of some hardware/software failures.

Acknowledgments

While writing this book over the last 5 years, I have had the truly exceptional opportunity to work with many, many bright and wonderful people. They have all contributed to this book by providing thoughts for new chapters, technical materials, and detailed reviews. At the same time, I am moved to elation and tears by the amount of work performed by people who deal with the arduous basics of a book such as editing, page layout, and printing — all of which finally make it possible to present a book.

Sometimes an author is inspired by a few special people to undertake an onerous work. In my case, I cannot limit myself to a few. For the past 5 years, there have been many, many who have pulled me out of writer's block and provided suggestions for new concepts and time to write the book.

Foremost, my gratitude goes to my family. With the love and sacrifice of my wife, Archana, and my sons, Vatsal, Sabal, and Kushal, this book has reached completion and exceeded my initial expectations. Thanks for your encouragement and endless support. Thanks to my friends who understood when I missed important events in their lives. Thanks to my parents, Prakash and Brinda, and parents-in-law, Basant and Suprabha, who stayed with us time and again to help me tirelessly with all they could to provide me valuable writing time. I can go on and on. It just took a whole *lot* more help than what anyone signed up for.

I would like to thank the entire editorial team at John Wiley and Sons. Carol Long drove the proposal across several boards for approval and got many, many people to contribute to this book. My development editor, Kevin Shafer, worked tediously across each page to increase the flow of ideas. Many thanks to Adaobi Tulton, Erica Weinstein, Tim Tate, Mary Beth Wakefield, Bill Barton, Jennifer Theriot, Lorie Donovan, Ryan Steffen, Shelley Lea, Barbara Moore, and Eileen Bien Calabro for helping at various stages of editing and development. They all have provided priceless suggestions to improve overall readability and presentation. You have been a first-rate team and I owe you a lot of gratitude for standing by me for the last five years.

I also want to thank various people for enlightening me on various technologies and providing suggestions to improve what I wrote: Seth Mason, Sunil Battu, Param Connur, Yatin Wadhavkar, Chris Phama, Phil Lowden, all from Cisco Systems, Inc.; Sridhar Deuskar from EMC; Shyam Kumar and Dilip Gupta from Verizon; Rajiv Kumar from Microsoft; Arun Saha from ECIL; Pamela Lacey from VERITAS; and Sanjeev Choudhary. They gave me new ideas and continually provided genuine feedback.

Introduction

Live like you were going to die tomorrow;
learn like you will live forever.
— **Gandhi**

In information technology (IT), infrastructure is the physical hardware used to interconnect computers and users. Infrastructure includes the network equipment, servers, storage media, cables, wired and wireless media, antennae, routers, switches, and other devices that make up the transmission paths and devices at both ends. Infrastructure also includes the software used to store, manage, send, and receive the data and signals that are transmitted.

In some context, infrastructure refers to interconnecting hardware and software and not to computers and user-end devices. However, in this book, infrastructure includes the IT users, servers, data storage subsystems, and everything that supports the flow and processing of information.

Infrastructure companies have played a momentous part in building the software, network, and devices that connect users in homes and offices around the world.

The servers have undergone radical metamorphosis in the last 40 years. Figure I-1 shows the changing face of servers and related IT equipment over time.

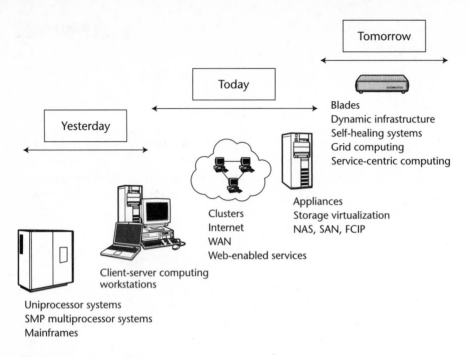

Figure I-1   Past and future technologies in the computing world.

How This Book Is Organized

This book covers several IT infrastructure-related topics that may appear unrelated at first glance. Although the chapters are in an ordered sequence, they can be read independently if you have a high-level idea about the topic. The book starts with the importance of service availability and data center design and maintenance. It covers systems capacity planning, fault tolerance, server administration, and clustering. The discussion then focuses on NAS, SAN, and ways to design a resilient and high-performance SAN. Emerging technologies such as SoIP, FCIP, and iSCSI are also covered in fair detail. The section on networks covers IP addressing, network devices and protocols, LAN and WAN topologies, network design, and network security (such as VPNs and firewalls). The book ends with disaster-recovery recommendations and models and a look at what the future data center holds, such as converged networks.

Throughout the book, there are some sidebars, called "Tales from the Tech Turf." These are engaging and true. Some are painful, while others are funny, but they all have a lesson. I hope you learn from the mistakes and examples that I have read about, seen happening to others, and sometimes suffered through.

Here is a brief outline of each chapter:

- *Chapter 1: No Time for Downtime* — This chapter explains the primary causes of service outage, associated costs, and why businesses cannot afford it.

- *Chapter 2: The High-Availability Continuum* — This chapter describes high availability (HA) terms, metrics to measure HA, the five HA levels, and how they can be achieved.

- *Chapter 3: Data Center Requirements* — This chapter is the first of six chapters that describe data center architecture. This chapter details the physical area, cooling, HVAC, weight, power, and bandwidth requirements that must be considered before building a data center. The financial and geographic constraints are other factors.

- *Chapter 4: Data Center Design* — This chapter explains the features of and guidelines to designing an outstanding data center. It describes various structures such as plena, aisles, raised floors, and so on.

- *Chapter 5: Network Infrastructure in a Data Center* — This chapter presents a modular design for cabling, points of distribution (PODs), and WAN connections from ISPs.

- *Chapter 6: Data Center Maintenance* — This chapter explains what is required for day-to-day maintenance of a data center, including physical security and equipment monitoring.

- *Chapter 7: Power Distribution in a Data Center* — This chapter helps you understand and plan the power requirements for equipment in a data center.

- *Chapter 8: Data Center HVAC* — This chapter focuses on environmental requirements (such as temperature, humidity, air circulation patterns, and rack placements).

- *Chapter 9: Reasons for Data Center Consolidation* — This chapter and the next focus on needs and procedures for consolidating resources (such as storage, servers, network equipment, applications, staff, and process).

- *Chapter 10: Data Center Consolidation Phases* — This chapter details the steps for data center consolidation (such as evaluation of current environment and architecting, implementing, and managing a consolidated environment).

- *Chapter 11: Server Performance Metrics* — This chapter describes the various benchmarks (such as SPEC, Linpack, and TPC) required for server capacity planning.

- *Chapter 12: Server Capacity Planning* — This chapter focuses on the process of estimating the resources required for a server to meet an anticipated workload.

- *Chapter 13: Best Practices in IT* — This chapter explains industry best practices for systems, as well as storage and network management and documentation.

- *Chapter 14: Server Security* — This chapter lays out basic host and Internet security guidelines.

- *Chapter 15: Server Administration* — This chapter describes various best practices in system administration and various needs, types, and tools for work automation.

- *Chapter 16: Device Naming* — This chapter is a vital issue in any IT environment and has far-reaching effects on making the environment easier to understand and manage. This chapter explains best practices for naming devices and common name management technologies (such as NIS, NIS+, DNS, and LDAP).

- *Chapter 17: Load Balancing* — This chapter explains the various advantages (such as improved performance and service availability) as well as software- and hardware-based methods for distributing incoming service requests among two or more servers. It also reviews a few common load-balancing algorithms.

- *Chapter 18: Fault Tolerance* — This chapter explains what it takes for a host or subsystem to recover from a component failure without incurring any outages. They increase the availability of a server or stand-alone device.

- *Chapter 19: RAID* — This chapter details the various RAID levels (such as RAID 0, RAID 1, RAID 0+1, RAID 1+0, and RAID 5) and their relative advantages and performance.

- *Chapter 20: Data Storage Solutions* — This is the first of five chapters that focus on data storage technologies (such as direct attached storage, NAS, SAN, FC over IP, and iSCSI). What are the reasons for rapid increase in storage needs? It compares DAS, NAS, and SAN and their relative merits and demerits.

- *Chapter 21: Storage Area Networks* — This chapter explains the various SAN hardware components (such as hubs, switches, and directors), topologies (such as point-to-point and loops), and switched fabrics (such as mesh, ring, star, cascaded, and core). It provides the advantages/disadvantages and situations where you should deploy a particular topology.

- *Chapter 22: Configuring a SAN* — This chapter details the SAN design phases and steps for implementing a SAN.

- *Chapter 23: Using SANs for High Availability* — This chapter provides guidelines for designing a fault-tolerant and scalable SAN that has redundancy at various levels (such as path, switch, and fabric). It describes the steps that must be taken to increase resiliency and redundancy in a SAN environment. It also provides guidance on SAN-based campus and metropolitan clusters designed for future disaster tolerance.

- *Chapter 24: IP-Based Storage Communications* — This chapter examines the growing trend toward using an IP-based network for transporting block-level data. Common techniques are iSCSi, fibre channel over IP (FCIP), and Internet fibre channel protocol (iFCP). It also explains how to deploy a geographically dispersed SAN by extending it across an ATM, SONET, or IP-based network to enable disaster recovery.

- *Chapter 25: Cluster Architecture* — This chapter looks at host cluster types and types of failover clusters. It lists a myriad of cluster configurations. It describes the components and the myriad of different failover configurations (such as symmetric and asymmetric clusters), as well as the benefits, requirements, and issues with three-or-more-node clusters.

- *Chapter 26: Cluster Requirements* — This chapter examines the hardware and software requirements for designing and deploying a cluster.

- *Chapter 27: Designing Cluster-Friendly Applications* — This chapter looks at application requirements for suitability in a clustered environment.

- *Chapter 28: Network Devices* — This is the first of ten chapters on network design, implementation, and security. This chapter reviews network devices (such as hubs, switches, and routers), security devices (such as firewalls and access servers), and network cable types.

- *Chapter 29: Network Protocols* — This chapter examines the seven-layer OSI model and network ports.

- *Chapter 30: IP Addressing* — This chapter describes IP version 4 addressing scheme, Class A, B, and C networks, subnets, and netmask calculations. It introduces IP version 6 and how it resolves certain limitations in its predecessor.

- *Chapter 31: Network Technologies* — This chapter reviews industry technologies (such as ATM, Ethernet, FDDI, and optical networks). It also details common WAN types (such as T-1, DSL, and fiber-optic links).

- *Chapter 32: Network Topologies* — This chapter looks at various logical arrangements for local, metropolitan, and wide area networks.

- *Chapter 33: Network Design* — This chapter explains the hierarchical network design made up of the access, distribution, and core layers. It reviews campus designs, network backbones, and what is involved in architecting an enterprise-level network design.

- *Chapter 34: Designing Fault-Tolerant Networks* — This chapter looks at how different services such as voice and storage data are now using the

IP network, the importance of building a resilient network, and how various levels of redundancy can be architected for different network topologies.

- *Chapter 35: Internet Access Technologies and VPNs* — This chapter and the next two look at ways of securing the network. It introduces various types of virtual private networks (VPNs) and different types of VPN security mechanisms (such as symmetric and asymmetric data encryption, digital signatures, IPSec, and authentication mechanisms such as AAA servers).

- *Chapter 36: Firewalls* — This chapter covers types of firewalls, rules, filters, DMZ areas, and network area translation (NAT).

- *Chapter 37: Network Security* — This chapter reviews common threats (such as Internet worms and viruses) and protection methods such as traffic- and user-based security and the AAA (authentication, authorization, accounting) model.

- *Chapter 38: Disaster Recovery* — This chapter explains the need to configure a DR environment for critical IT servers and data. It outlines the phases for evaluating whether you need DR and creating and testing the procedures.

- *Chapter 39: DR Architectures* — This chapter discusses three types of DR models based on the distance between the primary and remote DR data centers.

- *Chapter 40: Voice over IP and Converged Infrastructure* — Most corporations have an IP network for data, PBX-supported telephone network, and a fibre channel–based storage network. This chapter describes the trend toward using a single infrastructure for voice, data, and storage.

- *Chapter 41: What's Next* — This chapter forecasts what the future of computing holds for us. It explains a few emerging technologies that have the potential to shape the way we build data centers and IT infrastructures.

- *Appendix A: Storage and Networking Solutions* — This appendix contain a series of diagrams that do not readily fit into any chapter. They illustrate IT solutions explained in more than one chapter.

As I mentioned in the Preface, this book describes technical concepts. It is not a programmer's manual. It does not cover industry products. Products and vendors change rapidly, and I prefer not to make judgment calls. However, there are several questions to ask your vendor when selecting a product. The goal in this book is to describe a few (but complete) solutions and samples so that you can use them to build your own architecture.

Key Points

Every chapter in this book will end with a few important points that have been discussed therein. The book covers significant areas of a typical IT infrastructure. It focuses on general concepts, design, and implementation, but not on industry products.

Data Center Basics

In This Part

No Time for Downtime

We gain strength, and courage, and confidence by each experience in which we really stop to look fear in the face . . . we must do that which we think we cannot.
— **Eleanor Roosevelt**

The need for high availability did not originate with the Internet or e-commerce. It has existed for thousands of years. When Greek warships or merchant ships sailed to discover new lands or business, the captains carried spare sails and oars on board. If the primary sail failed, the crew would immediately hoist a replacement and continue on their way, while they repaired damaged sails. With the advent of electronic sensors, the spare parts employed in industrial systems did not need human intervention for activation. In the early twentieth century, electric power-generating plants automatically detected problems, if any, in the primary generator and switched to a hot standby unit.

With the recent explosive growth of the Internet and our dependence on information systems, *high availability* has taken on a new meaning and importance. Businesses and consumers are turning to the Internet for purchasing goods and services. People conduct business anytime from their computer. They expect to buy clothes at 2 a.m. on the Web and expect the site to function properly, without problem or delay, from the first click to the last. If the Web site is slow or unavailable, they will click away to a competitor's site. Business globalization caused by the Internet adds another layer of complexity. A popular online store, with business located in Bismarck, North Dakota, may have customers in Asia who keep the seller's servers busy during quiet hours in the United States. Time zones, national borders, and peak and off-peak hours essentially disappear on the Web.

As computers get faster and cheaper, they are being used for more and more critical tasks that require 24-7 uptime. Hospitals, airlines, online banking services, and other service industries modify customer-related data in real time. The amount of online data is rapidly expanding. It is estimated that online data will grow more than 75 percent every year for the next several years. The rapidly increasing demand for placing more and more data online and the constantly decreasing price of storage media have resulted in an increase of huge amounts of critical information being placed online.

Employees and partners depend on data being available at all times. Work hours have extended beyond the traditional 9-to-5, five days a week. Intranet servers such as e-mail, internal applications, and so forth, must be always up and functional for work to continue. Every company has at least one business-critical server that supports the organization's day-to-day operation and health. The unavailability of critical applications translates to lost revenue, reduced customer service and customer loyalty, and well-paid, but idle, workers. A survey of 450 Fortune 100 companies (conducted by the Strategic Research Division of Find/SVP) concluded that U.S. businesses incur about $4 billion of losses per year because of system or network downtime.

In fact, analysts estimate that every minute of Enterprise Resource Planning (ERP) downtime could cost a retailer between $10,000 and $15,000. Systems and data are not expected to be down, not even for maintenance. Downtime literally freezes customers, employees, and partners, who cannot even complete the most basic daily chores.

The requirements for reliability and availability put extreme demands on servers, network, software, and supporting infrastructure. Corporate and e-commerce sites must be capable of processing large numbers of concurrent transactions and are configured to operate 24-7. All components, including both the server hardware and software, must be configured to be redundant.

And what happens when no one can get to the applications? What happens when data is unreachable and the important servers do not want to boot up? Can you shut down your business and ask your employees to go home? Can you tell your customers to go somewhere else? How is it that no one planned for this scenario? Is it possible to recover from this? How long will it take and how much will it cost? What about reputation among customers? Will they ever come back? Why doesn't this happen to your competitors?

As you can see, it happens all the time and all around us. Following are some events that have occurred over the last few years. They expose our total dependence on computer systems and utter helplessness if critical systems are down.

- In April of 1998, AT&T had a 26-hour frame relay-network outage that hurt several business customers. In December of 1999, AT&T had an 8-hour outage that disrupted services to thousands of AT&T WorldNet dial-up users.

- In early 1999, customers of the popular online stock trading site ETrade could not place stock trade orders because the trading sites were down. At the same time, there were a few outages at The Charles Schwab Corporation because of operator errors or upgrades. Schwab later announced a plan to invest $70 million in information technology (IT) infrastructure.

- In June of 1999, eBay had a 22-hour outage that cost the company more than $3 million in credits to customers and about $6 billion (more than 20 percent) in market capitalization. In January of 2001, parts of the site were again down for another 10 hours.

- In August of 1999, MCI suffered about 10 days of partial outages and later provided 20 days of free service to 3,000 enterprise customers.

- Three outages at the Web retailer `amazon.com` during the busy holiday-shopping season of December 2000 cost Amazon more than $500,000 in sales loss.

- Denial-of-Service and several virus-induced attacks on Internet servers continue to cause Web site outages. On July 19, 2002, a hacker defaced a page on the U.S. Army Research Laboratory's Web site with a message criticizing the Army's organization for bias to certain nations.

- Terrorist attacks in Washington, D.C., New York, London, and cities around the world in recent years have destroyed several data centers and offices.

Businesses everywhere are faced with the challenge of minimizing downtime. At the same time, plans to enhance service availability have financial and resource-related constraints. Taking steps to increase data, system, and network availability is a delicate task. If the environment is not carefully designed and implemented, it would cost dearly (in terms of required time, money, and human resources) to build and manage it.

To increase service availability, you must identify and eliminate potential causes of downtime, which could be caused by hardware failures, network glitches, software problems, application bugs, and so forth. Sometimes, poor server, application, or network performance is perceived as downtime. Service expectations are high. When someone wants to place a phone call, he or she picks up the phone and expects a dial tone within a few seconds. The call must connect within one second of dialing and there should be no dropped connections. When surfing the Web, users expect the first visual frame of a Web page within a few seconds of accessing the site. All systems, especially those related to consumers and critical operations, should always be ready and must operate with no lost transactions.

But potential causes of downtime abound. The entire IT infrastructure is made up of several links, such as user workstations, network devices, servers, applications, data, and so forth. If any link is down, the user is affected. It then does not matter if the other links in the chain are available or not. *Downtime,* in this book, is defined as an end user's inability to get his or her work done. This book examines ways to enhance service availability to the end user and describes techniques for improving network, data, server, and application uptime.

Availability is the portion of time that an application or service is available to internal or external customers for productive work. The more resilient a system or environment is, the higher the availability is. An important decision is the required availability level. When you ask a user or project manager how much uptime he or she needs for the application, the reflex answer is "One-hundred percent. It must always be available at all times." But when you explain the high costs required to achieve 100 percent uptime, the conversation becomes more of a two-way negotiation. The key point is to balance downtime cost with availability configuration costs.

Another point is the time duration when 100 percent uptime is necessary. Network Operations Center (NOC) and 24-7 network monitoring applications and e-commerce Web sites require 100 percent uptime. On the other extreme are software development environments, used only when developers are accessing the system. If, on occasion, you take development systems down (especially at night or on weekends), and if you warn your users well in advance, downtime is not an issue.

Table 1-1 illustrates how little time per year is afforded for planned or unplanned downtime as availability requirements move closer to 100 percent. Suppose a server, "hubble," has no special high-availability features except for RAID-1 volumes and regular backups and has 98 percent uptime. The 2 percent downtime is too high and, therefore, it is clustered with "casper," which also has 98 percent uptime. Server "casper" is used only 2 percent of the time when hubble is down. The combined availability is 98 percent plus 98 percent of 2 (0.98×2), which is 1.96 percent. These add to a theoretical service uptime of 99.96 percent for the two-node cluster.

Table 1-1 Total Allowable Downtime for Planned or Unplanned Events

PERCENTAGE UPTIME	PERCENTAGE DOWNTIME	DOWNTIME PER YEAR	DOWNTIME PER MONTH
98%	2%	7.3 days	14 hours 36 minutes
99%	1%	3.65 days	7 hours 18 minutes
99.9%	0.1%	8 hours 45 minutes	43 minutes 45 seconds
99.99% ("four nines")	0.01%	52.5 minutes	4 minutes 22 seconds
99.999% ("five nines")	0.001%	5.25 minutes	26 seconds

In reality, several other factors affect both servers, such as downtime during failover duration, power or network outages, and application bugs. These failures will decrease the theoretical combined uptime.

As you move down the table, the incremental costs associated with achieving the level of availability increase exponentially. It is far more expensive to migrate from a "four-nines" to a "five-nines" (99.99 percent to 99.999 percent uptime) configuration than to move from 99 percent to 99.9 percent uptime.

Causes of Downtime

About 80 percent of the unplanned downtime is caused by process or people issues, and 20 percent is caused by product issues. Solid processes must be in place throughout the IT infrastructure to avoid process-, people-, or product-related outages. Figure 1-1 and Table 1-2 show the various causes of downtime. As you can see, planned or scheduled downtime is one of the biggest contributors (30 percent). It is also the easiest to reduce. It includes events that are pre-planned by IT (system, database, and network) administrators and usually done at night. It could be just a proactive reboot. Other planned tasks that lead to host or application outage are scheduled activities such as application or operating system upgrades, adding patches, hardware changes, and so forth.

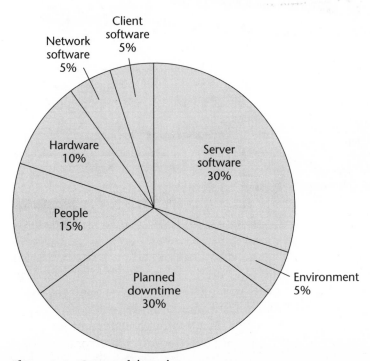

Figure 1-1   Causes of downtime

Table 1-2 Causes of Planned and Unplanned Downtime

CAUSES OF PLANNED DOWNTIME	CAUSES OF UNPLANNED DOWNTIME
Backup	Extended planned downtime
Replace or upgrade hardware	Human error
Software or application upgrade	Application failure
Software maintenance or reconfiguration	Operating system failure
Operating system upgrade	Hardware failure such as disk, CPU, memory
Patch installation	Incompatibility/conflict between application parameters

Most of these planned events can be performed without service interruption. Disks, fans, and power supplies in some servers and disk subsystems can be changed during normal run-time, without need for power-offs. Data volumes and files systems can be increased, decreased, or checked for problems while they are online. Applications can be upgraded while they are up. Some applications must be shut down before an upgrade or a configuration change.

Outages for planned activities can be avoided by having standby devices or servers in place. Server clustering and redundant devices and links help reduce service outages during planned maintenance. If the application is running in a cluster, it can be switched to another server in the cluster. After the application is upgraded, the application can be moved back. The only downtime is the time duration required to switch or failover services from one server to another. The same procedure can be used for host-related changes that require the host to be taken off-line. Apart from the failover duration, there is no other service outage.

Another major cause of downtime is people-related. It is caused by poor training, a rush to get things done, fatigue, lots of nonautomated tasks, or pressure to do several things at the same time. It could also be caused by lack of expertise, poor understanding of how systems or applications work, and poorly defined processes. You can reduce the likelihood of operator-induced outages by following properly documented procedures and best practices. Organization must have several, easy-to-understand how-tos for technical support groups and project managers. The documentation must be placed where it can be easily accessed, such as internal Web sites. It is important to spend time and money on employee training because in economically good times, talented employees are hard to recruit and harder to retain. For smooth continuity of expertise, it is necessary to recruit enough staff to cover emergencies and employee attrition and to avoid overdependence on one person.

> **TALES FROM THE TECH TURF: ON-CALL WOES**
>
> One organization I worked at rebooted their UNIX servers every Sunday morning at 4 a.m. to clear memory, swap, and process tables. Of course, sometimes the boxes would not boot up all the way and the NOC had to call someone at a weird hour. Later, the reboot time was moved to 6 a.m. This was done to avoid application-related problems on systems with high uptime. This was initially implemented due to a Solaris problem on Suns that had not been rebooted in the last 350 days and were running an old release of Oracle Database.

Avoiding unplanned downtime takes more discipline than reducing planned downtime. One major contributor to unplanned downtime is software glitches. The Gartner Group estimates that U.S. companies suffer losses of up to $1 billion every year because of software failure. In another survey conducted by Ernst and Young, it was found that almost all the 310 surveyed companies had some kind of business disruption. About 30 percent of the disruptions caused losses of $100,000 or more each to the company.

When production systems fail, backups and business-continuance plans are immediately deployed and are every bit worth their weight, but the damage has already been done. Bug fixes are usually reactive to the outages they wreak. As operating systems and applications get more and more complex, they will have more bugs. On the other hand, software development and debugging techniques are getting more sophisticated. It will be interesting to see if the percentage of downtime attributed to software bugs increases or decreases in the future. It is best to stay informed of the latest developments and keep current on security, operating system, application, and other critical patches. Sign up for e-mail-based advisory bulletins from vendors whose products are critical to your business.

Environmental factors that can cause downtime are rare, but they happen. Power fails. Fires blaze. Floods gush. The ground below shakes. In 1998, the East Coast of the United States endured the worst hurricane season on record. At the same time, the Midwest was plagued with floods. Natural disasters occur mercurially all the time and adversely impact business operations. And, to add to all that, there are disasters caused by human beings, such as terrorist attacks.

The best protection is to have one or more remote, mirrored disaster recovery (DR) sites. In the past, a fully redundant system at a remote DR site was an expensive and daunting proposition. Nowadays, conditions have changed to make it very affordable:

- Hardware costs and system sizes have fallen dramatically.
- The Internet has come to provide a common network backbone.
- Operating procedures, technology, and products have made an off-site installation easy to manage remotely.

TALES FROM THE TECH TURF

In 1995, a building in downtown Oklahoma City was destroyed by a terrorist. Many offices and data centers lost servers and valuable data. One law firm had no off-site backup of its data and lost its records. The firm was in the business of managing public relations for its clients. It was unable to restore any data pertaining to its customers. Sadly enough, it went out of business within three months. Another commodity-trading firm had a remote mirror site just outside the city and was able to bring up its applications on standby servers at the remote site. It quickly transferred its operations and business to the secondary site.

To protect against power blackouts, use uninterruptible power supplies (UPS). If Internet connection is critical, use two Internet access providers or at least separate, fully redundant links from the same provider.

Cost of Downtime

Organizations need to cost out the financial impact caused by downtime. The result helps determine the extent of resources that must be spent to protect against outages. The total cost of a service outage is difficult to assess. Customer dissatisfaction, lost transactions, data integrity problems, and lost business revenue cannot be accurately quantified. An extended period of downtime can result in ruin and, depending on the nature of the business, the hourly cost of business outage can be several tens of thousands of dollars to a few million dollars. Table 1-3 provides some examples of downtime costs.

Table 1-3   Average Cost of Downtime per Hour for a Variety of Industries

INDUSTRY	BUSINESS OPERATION	DOWNTIME COST RANGE (PER HOUR)	AVERAGE COST OF DOWNTIME (PER HOUR)
Financial	Brokerage operations	$5.6M to 7.3M	$6.45M
Financial	Credit card/sales authorizations	$2.2M to 3.1M	$2.6M
Media	Pay-per-view TV	$67K to 233K	$150K
Retail	Home shopping (TV)	$87K to 140K	$113K
Retail	Home catalog sales	$60K to 120K	$90K
Transportation	Airline reservations	$67K to 112K	$89.5K
Media	Telephone ticket sales	$56K to 82K	$69K

Table 1-3 *(continued)*

INDUSTRY	BUSINESS OPERATION	DOWNTIME COST RANGE (PER HOUR)	AVERAGE COST OF DOWNTIME (PER HOUR)
Transportation	Package shipping	$24K to 32K	$28K
Financial	ATM fees	$12K to 17K	$14.5K

Source: Computer Economics, Inc., Irvine, California, www.computereconomics.com

It is important to arrive at reasonable estimates of financial losses that could be incurred during an outage. The total cost is calculated by the sum of losses in areas of labor, revenue, and downtime. A good starting point is to collect employee-related statistics from human resources and accounting departments regarding salary, duration of past outages, number of employees in each group, and annual gross revenue from online or telesales.

Employees continue to receive full pay even during planned or unplanned outages. The productivity of the employee is rated to be higher than the salary. Labor cost during an outage is calculated using the following equation:

$$\frac{\text{Labor}}{\text{Cost}} = \frac{\text{Number of}}{\text{Employees}} \times \frac{\text{Hours of}}{\text{Outage}} \times \frac{\text{Average Hourly}}{\text{Pay Rate}}$$

Several employees within a department and with similar salary can be grouped together. A department with 50 employees that cannot function for a week (assuming 40-hour weeks and average employee expense of $100 per hour) incurs a loss of $200,000 for the week. Then there is the cost of overtime that must be paid to catch up on the work. That doubles the loss to $400,000.

If you estimate the loss of revenue to a company whose sales rely on server and application availability, the lost revenue is calculated using the following equation:

$$\frac{\text{Lost}}{\text{Revenue}} = \left(\frac{\text{Gross Annual Revenue}}{\text{Annual Business Hours}}\right) \times \frac{\text{Percentage}}{\text{Impact}} \times \frac{\text{Hours of}}{\text{Downtime}}$$

The first two elements of the equation provide the revenue generated per hour. The percentage impact allows you to scale the hourly revenue based on whether the lost customers can be partially or entirely recovered, or whether they would cause more damage by creating negative publicity among those who never witnessed the downtime firsthand. During a downtime, customers call in and the operator politely tells them, "Our systems are down. Please call back after a few hours." Some customers prefer to complete the purchase sooner. They will go to a competitor, buy what they want, and do not need to ever call back. Some will call back. If 75 percent do call back, then the loss and percentage impact is only 25 percent. One way of collecting data on the percentage of customers who called back is to look at the amount of revenue generated above and beyond the normal orders immediately following the outage. If it is 50 percent more, that means 50 percent of the people called back.

Several other effects of downtime are impossible to quantify. Some customers who were merely inconvenienced may tell the story to friends and recommend to them never to shop at that place. Percentage impact is difficult to estimate and is different during different outages.

The results from the equations convey only part of a company's losses. Satisfied customers become loyal customers and dissatisfied customers do not. Let's say a customer would have made a $100 purchase and would have repeated that just once a year. Using a discounted cash flow rate of just 15 percent, the present value of those purchases over a 20-year period would have been $719. The company, therefore, suffered a total loss of more than seven times the first lost sale value.

Downtime causes several other losses that are difficult to predict. Companies that host applications or servers for customers have strict service level agreements (SLAs) that require them to credit customer accounts upon incurring any service disruption. Downtime also causes missed deadlines and penalties. It adversely affects stock price, goodwill among customers and partners, and employee morale.

For servers connected to the Internet, the greatest cause for concern is security. Hackers are quick to take advantage of vulnerabilities. Malicious code attacks have significant economic impact. Table 1-4 shows the adverse economic impact caused by cyber attacks.

Table 1-5 shows the economic impact of specific incidents. To date, the "I Love You" Bug outbreak in 2000 has caused the highest financial damage.

TALES FROM THE TECH TURF: THE WEEKEND MUSIC

On July 25, 2002, the Recording Industry Association of America (RIAA, www.riaa.com) openly backed the U.S. Peer-to-Peer Piracy Prevention Act proposed by Congressman Howard Berman. The bill enables music copyright holders to "block, divert or otherwise impair" networks believed to be involved in music piracy. The bill was criticized for various reasons. On the Internet, it is nearly impossible to tell good computers from bad. Many innocent servers on the Internet are "stolen" for file sharing and participating in "distributed denial of service" (DDoS) attacks. On July 26, 2002, the RIAA Web site was buried under a flood of DDoS attacks from hundreds of computers. The attack continued until 2 a.m. on July 29. The bill allows RIAA and music copyright owners to engage in precisely this kind of denial-of-service attacks against networks that distribute illicit copies of music.

Table 1-4   Annual Economic Impact Due to Cyber Attacks

YEAR	WORLDWIDE ECONOMIC IMPACT ($ U.S.)
1995	0.5 billion
1996	1.8 billion
1997	3.3 billion
1998	6.1 billion
1999	12.1 billion
2000	17.1 billion
2001	13.2 billion

Source: Computer Economics, Inc., Irvine, California, www.computereconomics.com/

The use of the Internet is rapidly expanding around the world and across cultures, and it spans a wide range of economic and educational strata. With such widespread use, cyber attacks will only become more frequent. Server downtime and adverse economic impact will become more pronounced. Law enforcement agencies around the world face the challenge of investigating, prosecuting, and combating cyber crimes. The liberal use of the Internet has sparked discussions and laws at the highest government levels in almost all countries. The Internet conflicts with local laws governing commerce and openly accessible content. Many countries (such as France, Saudi Arabia, and China) have attempted to control the use of the Web.

Table 1-6 shows the number of Internet users by continent for 2002 with projected growth through 2006. Internet users are those who are connected via LANs, dial-up modems, DSL, cable modems, ITV, wireless connections, and so forth.

Table 1-5   Economic Impact Analysis per Incident

YEAR	CYBER ATTACK CODE NAME	WORLDWIDE ECONOMIC IMPACT ($ U.S.)
1999	Explorer	1.02 billion
1999	Melissa	1.10 billion
2000	I Love You (Love Bug)	8.75 billion
2001	SirCam	1.15 billion
2001	Code Red(s)	2.62 billion
2001	Nimda	635 million

Source: Computer Economics, Inc., Irvine, California, www.computereconomics.com/

Table 1-6 Internet Users by Continent

CONTINENT OR REGION	2002 (MILLIONS)	2003 (MILLIONS)	2004 (MILLIONS)	2005 (MILLIONS)	2006 (MILLIONS)
North America	212	223	234	244	256
South and Central America	25	32	43	59	80
Europe	163	196	225	240	257
Middle East/Africa	9.2	10.7	11.6	12.6	13.6
Asia and Pacific regions	151	204	238	273	313
TOTAL WORLDWIDE	560.2	665.7	751.6	828.6	919.6

Source: Computer Economics, Inc., Irvine, California, www.computereconomics.com/

Key Points

Following are some key points discussed in this chapter:

- With the fast-growing dependence on computer systems, availability is a requirement for the entire IT infrastructure. Businesses view availability as the single metric of overall system performance.

- Unplanned service outages are expensive and are caused by hardware and software failures, human errors, Internet viruses and attacks, natural disasters, and human-caused crises.

- Financial losses incurred by downtime depend on the business operation.

The High-Availability Continuum

In all chaos there is a cosmos, in all disorder a secret order
— Irish Proverb

The levels of continuity described in this chapter are not discrete. They do not have well-marked separations, but rather blend into each other. Cost is another important consideration. Just as downtime incurs financial losses, protecting against downtime costs money. You must examine your environment and build a list of likely failure causes. Strive to protect against the most serious scenarios and work your way toward the least-critical ones.

These are some common high-availability terms that appear to be similar at the outset. However, a good understanding of these reveal undeniable distinctions that further help in explanations of service availability:

- *Reliability* — Reliability represents the probability of a component or system not encountering any failures over a time span. Reliability is a measure of "not breaking down, once it is put in use." The focus is on making the component or system unbreakable.

- *Resiliency* — Resiliency is the property of a component that allows it to continue with full or partial functionality after one or more faults. Highly resilient components are able to detect and quickly compensate for faults. The compensation is done by utilizing alternate resources of correcting the error. An example is error-correction code (ECC) memory. If errors are detected, the bad area is taken out of service, and memory addresses are moved to another area that is properly functioning.

- *Availability* — Availability measures the ability of a system or group of systems (cluster) to keep an application or service up and running. Designing for availability assumes that systems will fail, and the systems are configured to mask and recover from component or server failures with minimum application outage.

- *Serviceability* — Serviceability is the probability of a service being completed within a given time window. If a system has a serviceability of 0.98 for 3 hours, then there is a 98 percent probability that the service will be completed within 3 hours. In an ideal situation, systems can be serviced without any interruption of user support. This is possible by using hot-swappable components such as power supplies, fans, disks, and system boards.

- *Fault-tolerant systems* — These are systems that have redundant hardware components and can operate in the presence of individual component failures. Since the cost of individual components continues to drop, several non–fault-tolerant systems have built-in component redundancy. Therefore, the distinction between fault-tolerant and non–fault-tolerant systems has become increasing blurred.

- *High availability (HA) clusters* — These clusters consist of two or more nodes with a number of external interconnections such as shared disks and private heartbeat network and are managed by special software with a goal of providing uninterrupted service despite node failures. If a node running one or more applications fails, one or more of the remaining nodes in the HA cluster take over applications from the failed server. Ideally, the only downtime is the time it takes to stop the application on the failed host and start it on another. In a HA cluster, the focus for availability changes from hardware components or servers to applications. It does not matter which server is running the application. What matters is that the application is running and available for clients and users.

- *High-performance clusters (HPC)* — These are also called *parallel computing clusters*. Each cluster has a group of computers, tied together to work at the same time on a problem, not as backups to each other. The movie *Titanic* could not have been done without several clusters of computers doing the animation and graphics. Technical computing requires huge files and applications that can slow down most computers. Performance clusters assign a small piece of the task to each computer, so it can perform quicker than a single computer.

- *Disaster recovery (DR)* — Disaster, in the context of online applications, is an extended period of outage of mission-critical service or data, caused by events such as fire and terrorist attacks that damage the entire facility. A DR solution requires a remote, mirrored site where business and mission-critical applications can be started within a reasonable period of time after the destruction of the primary site.

High-Availability Metrics

Simple engineering methodology suggests that before you begin to control something, you must devise a way to measure it. The same applies to service availability. A slight increase in the required level of availability will cause a several-fold increase in the cost required to design and implement an infrastructure that meets the increased availability level.

Following are some key terms:

- *Mean time between failures (MTBF)* — MTBF is an average time interval (usually in hours) between two consecutive failures of a certain component or system. MTBF is often confused with a component's useful life, although they are not related. A battery may have a useful life of 10 hours and an MTBF of 50,000 hours. This translates into one battery failure every hour during its 10-hour life span in a population of 50,000 batteries. Another common misconception is to assume that MTBF value is higher if there is a high degree of component redundancy. While it does increase overall system MTBF, the component failure rate is increased because of several, similar components.

- *Mean time to repair (MTTR)* — MTTR is the average length of time required to complete a repair action.

- *Availability* — This could be calculated as follows:

Availability = MTBF/(MTBF + MTTR)

As you can derive from this simple equation, the secret to high availability is using very reliable components (high MTBF) or designing components and systems that can recover from failures rapidly, can be quickly serviced preferably without having to take the application offline, or can be changed by hot-swapping (very low MTTR).

There is another way of measuring availability:

Availability = Uptime/(Uptime + Downtime)

As downtime approaches zero, availability approaches 100 percent. If uptime is very high, the effect of downtime is lessened.

Availability Choices: How Much Availability Is Enough?

This section describes different levels of availability. The appropriate availability level of a server depends on the critical nature of the applications and data. A server storing high-school inter-class hockey scores has different uptime needs than one that stores medical records of patients for use by hospital doctors and nurses.

This section describes ways to enhance availability of standard configurations. The levels described are not discrete, and several levels are often combined in any single high-availability architecture.

Level 1: Depend on Built-in Hardware Reliability

This level is also called *base availability*. It is achieved with a single system and basic system management practices in place. Systems have some built-in resiliency. Some come with hot-swappable redundant power supplies, disks, and fans. Operating systems mask memory, disk block, network, and CPU failures in a multi-CPU server, thus preventing a host crash. No special steps are taken except to configure backups. All data updates (since the last backup) are lost upon disk failure.

Reliability is a component of availability but the two are not synonymous. Reliability is a measure of how rarely a component or system breaks down and is expressed as the MTBF. The longer the MTBF, the more reliable the component or system is.

Today, most servers and components are very reliable. But is that good enough? A server that has 99 percent reliability will be down for 3.65 days every year (see Table 1-1) and that can happen anytime — probably when you can least afford it. Also understand what reliability of a component represents. If a CPU has 99 percent reliability, that does not mean the system has 99 percent reliability. The system is composed of disks, I/O buses, memory, network cards, power supplies, system boards, and so forth.

Let's consider a system that has 10 components, where each can fail independently but have 99 percent reliability. Statistically, the entire system reliability is 0.99 raised to the tenth power, or 90.44 percent. Then you would expect a downtime of 9.56 percent or 34.9 days each year! If a server provides any critical services or contributes to revenue generation, this level of protection is clearly unacceptable.

Moreover, hardware reliability problems cause only 10 percent of the downtime (see Figure 1-1). The other 90 percent is software-, maintenance-, people-, or process-related. That's why there is reason to look at other ways to enhance availability.

Level 2: Data Protection

Data is protected using RAID volumes. RAID-5 protects against disk failures but not against controller or subsystem failure. If data is mirrored using a separate disk subsystem attached to a different *host bus adapter* (*HBA*), the subsystem, HBA, or controller are no longer single points of failure. Backups must still be used to protect against data corruption, accidentally deleted files, and system crashes that damage the operating system.

Level 3: Fault-Tolerant Servers

A fault-tolerant server provides a fully replicated hardware design that allows uninterrupted service in the event of a component failure. Most components have an active redundant partner. The recovery time or performance loss caused by a component failure is close to zero, and all memory-based information and disk contents are preserved. Fault-tolerant servers are expensive. The problem with a fault-tolerant system is that the system itself has a *single point of failure* (*SPOF*). Any software faults (such as application bugs or operating system problems) can render the entire system unusable and result in service outage.

Level 4: Server Redundancy or Clustering

The Standish group predicts that the clustered server deployment will grow at the rate of 160 percent annually. Clustering protects applications against any server-level problems. Two or more systems are clustered together using failover management software. One of the early architects of clustering technology, G. Pfister, defined a cluster as "a parallel or distributed system that consists of a collection of inter-connected whole computers, that is utilized as a single, unified computing resource." Industry-leading implementations of clustering include VERITAS Cluster Server, Microsoft Cluster Server, Hewlett-Packard (HP) MC/ServiceGuard, and IBM High Availability Cluster Multi-Processing (HACMP). Hardware or software problems on a node in a cluster trigger a failover of applications to other healthy servers within the cluster.

Service outage is only for the duration required to switch or failover the application. It is recommended (but not strictly necessary) for the backup server to have the same hardware resources as the primary. Moreover, the secondary server need not be an idle standby, dedicated for backup protection. It can host applications and provide services. Scheduled activities such as hardware reconfiguration or software changes or upgrades can be done on a server with minimal service disruption by migrating all services from one server to another.

There is a certain degree of complexity in configuring and maintaining clusters. Another problem is that cluster members located in the same general vicinity are affected by a local disaster, potentially damaging all nodes of the cluster. To protect against such mishaps, you must plan for disaster recovery.

Level 5: Disaster Recovery

Many organizations may find the cost of building and maintaining an off-site facility with duplicate hardware and software highly prohibitive. Various companies such as IBM's Business Recovery Services, Sungard, and Comdisco provide third-party backup facilities at prices that are affordable because the cost of maintaining the site is shared by several companies that subscribe to the service.

Set up near real-time data synchronization at a third-party or dedicated recovery site. That way, an organization can be quickly up and running at the recovery facility after a disaster at the primary site.

Commercial Cluster Management Software

Several clustering or node failover management software packages are available. Following are a few market-leading software packages:

- *VERITAS Cluster Server (VCS)* — This is available for Solaris, Linux, AIX, HP/UX, and Microsoft Windows 2000 and NT platforms. By far, it is the market leader on Solaris. It supports several third-party software packages such as Apache, Iplanet, Oracle, Sybase, and Informix. It also supports hardware from IBM, EMC, Network Appliance, and Hitachi. Up to thirty-two nodes can be configured in a single cluster. It is easy to customize VCS for new applications.

- *IBM's High Availability Cluster Multiprocessing (HACMP)* — This is available on AIX platforms and dominates the IBM AIX server market.

- *Microsoft Cluster Server (MSCS)* — This software owns the Microsoft platforms. It is simple to install and manage. It is available for Microsoft operating systems only.

- *Sun Cluster (SC)* — This is developed and sold by Sun Microsystems, Inc., and is available only for the Solaris operating system. It supports several third-party disk subsystems and works well with Solstice DiskSuite, as well as VERITAS Volume Manager.

- *Hewlett/Packard's MC/ServiceGuard* — This is available only on the HP/UX operating system and is developed and marketed by HP. It is complex to install and manage and has several advanced features not available in competing products from other software vendors.

Key Points

Following are some key points discussed in this chapter:

- Protecting against failure is expensive, as is downtime. It is important to identify the most serious causes of service and build cost-effective safeguards against them.

- A high degree of component reliability, data protection via redundant disks and adapters, fault-tolerant servers, clustering, and disaster recovery decreases the odds of service outage.

Data Center Architecture

In This Part

Data Center Requirements

Nothing will ever be attempted if all possible objections must first be overcome.
— Samuel Johnson

Most of the principles and lessons learned for designing and building data centers have accrued over the last 50 or so years. Nevertheless, a modern data center shares several aspects with ancient structures. The purpose of any building (be it a fort, cathedral, or house) is to provide a set of services. The data center's primary service is to provide care and feeding for all equipment housed within it. The practical requirements of a data center are as follows:

- Provide a physically secure location for servers, storage, and network equipment.
- Provide 24 × 7 network connectivity for equipment within the data center to devices outside the data center.
- Provide necessary power to operate all equipment.
- Provide an environment where the temperature and humidity are controlled within a narrow range and air is exchanged at an adequate rate.

Data Center Prerequisites

This chapter describes what a data center must provide in order for the equipment to operate. This is a list of prerequisites for the design process.

Understanding the manufacturer's requirements is without doubt the most significant criterion for the design.

Required Physical Area for Equipment and Unoccupied Space

Physical capacity is defined as available space for servers, storage, network devices, HVAC (heating, ventilation, and air conditioning), power panels, breakers, and floor to support the weight of the equipment. The immediate need could be to house, say, 100 servers and storage. Some equipment such as small servers and storage devices are placed in racks. Large equipment such as EMC Symmetrix Storage Array (height, width, and depth of $75 \times 9 \times 36$ inches), IBM Enterprise Storage Server (also known as Shark, with height, width, and depth of $75 \times 55 \times 36$ inches), and Sun Fire 6800 Server are not designed to fit within racks but rather stand alone on the floor.

Rack dimensions, as shown in Figure 3-1, vary in size. The external height, width, and depth of a typical full-height rack are 84, 22, and 30 inches; internal dimensions are 78, 19, and 28 inches. The height of equipment placed in racks is measured in Us, with 1 U being 1.75 inches. The usable height of 78 inches translates to 45 Us. When you are calculating how many devices fit in a rack, you must know the height of each device in Us.

Note that approximately 50 percent of the space is occupied by racks or stand-alone hardware. The remaining physical area is used for aisles, ramp, space next to walls, breaks between rows of racks, perforated tile spaces to let cold air from subfloor plenum to the racks, and open space to let exhaust air from racks to the HVAC plenum.

Figure 3-1   Cabinets and racks in a data center.

Space required for new servers and storage in the coming years must also be accounted for in the initial plan. It is very difficult to add more space to a live data center. It requires ripping up tiles, walls, electricity, and HVAC.

The number and type of devices (servers, storage, and network equipment) to be placed in the data center have the most impact on its design. The area (square meters or square feet) in the data center must be large enough to accommodate servers and storage for the coming years. Although initial designs may not include servers and storage, it is still necessary to know the equipment to make prudent design decisions.

Required Power to Run All the Devices

To protect against power failures, uninterruptible power supplies (UPSs) must be present in every data center. They kick in when electricity fails and can provide power for up to an hour (some UPSs can run longer). If the utility company has frequent long-duration outages, generators are required.

The first thing you must know is the power requirement of the devices. That will, in turn, help decide your power needs: the number of breakers, outlet types, single-phase or three-phase, layout of data-center wiring, and watts per rack. Since power conduits and wiring are difficult to retrofit, you must install with future requirements in mind.

The unit of power (for each piece of equipment) is watts. Power (or watts) is the product of volts and amperes. A circuit that draws 2 amperes of electric current when 100 volts is applied will dissipate 200 watts of power.

A volt, in turn, is the unit of electric potential between two points and is the product of resistance (Ohms) and current (amperes). Voltage is the electrical equivalent of water pressure. Just as excess water pressure can burst pipes if the pressure is too high, excess volts to equipment will damage it. Below certain voltage levels, no damage will occur. But above certain voltage levels, the hardware device will be destroyed.

Required Cooling and HVAC

HVAC is required to keep the devices cool and maintain low humidity within the data center. Like power, the HVAC system is very difficult to retrofit. Therefore, the HVAC system must have enough cooling capacity to meet present and future needs.

Cooling requirements are measured in British thermal units (BTUs) per hour. The HVAC manufacturer provides this. What you must know is the combined BTU-per-hour requirement for all of the equipment in the data center. For example, an IBM ESS Storage Subsystem requires 16,000 BTUs per hour.

Add the BTUs of all equipment. Let's assume that is 200,000 BTUs. If the HVAC delivers cold air at 80 percent efficiency, it must have a rating of 250,000 BTUs per hour.

The air-flow pattern is very important in cooling the equipment. It is controlled by the under-floor pressure, which, in turn, depends on the HVAC unit and relative placement of solid and perforated tiles on the raised floor.

Required Weight

It is critical to know the weight of each rack without any content (server, storage device) inside it and the combined weight of all the racks. Add the weight of all devices (approximate estimate) that will be placed in the racks. That will give you an idea of the weight that the data-center floor will be subjected to. You can estimate if the existing floor is strong enough for the weight. If it is not, you must change the tile quality, pedestals in the plenum, and support grid.

There are a few different types of loads that the floor must be able to support:

- *Maximum weight that the entire data-center floor can support* — This data helps decide if the raised floor is strong enough for the present and future loads. This is especially critical if the data center is on an upper story (rather than the ground floor) in a multistoried building.

- *Maximum weight that a single tile can support* — The maximum weight that a tile can support depends on the tile material (concrete, aluminum, and so forth) and whether the tile is solid, perforated, or grated. (Tiles made of cast aluminum are not weakened by perforation or grating.)

- *Maximum point load that a tile can support* — Standalone equipment or racks are usually supported on four casters or rollers. The *worst-point load* is a quarter of the weight of the heaviest stand-alone equipment or rack in the data center. Each tile supports either one or two casters from two different racks or from the same rack. The *maximum-point strength* of any tile should be half the weight of the heaviest equipment or rack in the data center.

In recent times, high-end servers and high-capacity storage subsystems have had a lot of weight packed into a smaller size and footprint (floor area occupied by the equipment). As this trend of putting more in less space continues, the per-tile maximum strength becomes a restriction.

This equipment can cause strain on the data-center floor. A fully configured IBM p630 server weighs 112 pounds. Six of those in a 100-pound rack would weigh 772 pounds, and each of the four casters would support $772/4 = 193$ pounds, which would be a point load on a tile. An EMC Symmetrix 8830 Storage Subsystem with 384 disk drives weighs 3,796 pounds, which causes a point load of 949 pounds per caster. If a tile supports two such casters, its point load strength must be 1,898 pounds or higher.

It is common for data centers to have the same strength tiles throughout. If there is not enough money and some areas must have low-rated floor (for lighter racks of low-end servers and PCs), these must not be placed close to the entrance. If low-rated floor is between the entrance and the high-rated floor, they would be damaged when heavy equipment is rolled over them. Low-rated floor and light racks must be placed further from the entrance.

Load capacity of the floor tiles must be accounted for before rolling equipment into the data center. It is impractical to replace floor tiles in a live data center.

Required Network Bandwidth

The bandwidth offered by the Internet service provider (ISP) should at least be equal to the data center's inbound and outbound bandwidth specifications. Since the cost of bandwidth, network switches, and ports goes down over time, it is worthwhile to provision only the amount required and add more if and when needed. If business-critical servers must be connected to the Internet, reliable and redundant ISP links to the Internet are mandatory.

Most of the requirements can be met using Category 5 (Cat5) copper or multimode fiber. Single-mode fiber links may be needed for WAN connections, network attached storage (NAS) heads, and network-IO bound servers. You must calculate the number of copper and fiber connections needed for all the equipment in the data center.

There are several other optional elements within a data center. They add convenience to the work and include things such as overhead lighting, loading dock, windows, fork lifts, security cameras, card readers, and so forth. These components are secondary in importance and not essential to the existence of the data center. However, most data centers have these.

The requirements for the equipment are that it must be available all the time (that is, it must have almost 100 percent uptime). Most data centers have mission-critical servers and need 24×7 service uptime. The connection to the Internet must be redundant with two or more feeds from different ISPs. Also, network devices, sources of backup power (UPS or generators), and cooling units must have built-in redundancy.

Table 3-1 shows the requirements of three equipment sets in a data center.

Table 3-1 Equipment Requirements That Must Be Provided by the Data Center Facilities

EQUIPMENT	IBM P690 COMPUTER SERVER	IBM ENTERPRISE STORAGE SERVER (OR SHARK)	A RACK WITH FIVE PCS AND TWO RACKED-STORAGE SUBSYSTEMS
Physical space (inches)	80 inches height × 31 inches width × 59 inches depth	75 inches height × 55 inches width × 36 inches depth	Occupies entire rack. Height, width, depth: 84, 22, and 30 inches
Power (watts)	13,000	6,400	4,000
Cooling (BTUs)	51,000 BTU/hour	16,000	12,000
Weight (pounds/kg)	2,666 pounds (1,209 kg)	2,200 pounds (998 kg)	800 pounds (including 100-pound rack)
Required network bandwidth	12 multimode fiber	2 Cat5 Copper	10 Cat5 Copper 2 multimode fiber

Budget Constraints

In theory, you can get more than enough money for constructing a data center, but in practice, this rarely or never happens. You will find that the toughest thing about designing and constructing a data center is staying within the allocated budget.

The amount of money allocated for designing, building, and initial deployment of a new data center is called its *build budget*. Here is a list of budget-related considerations:

- What is the budget amount?
- Is the amount adequate to design and construct a data center, given the set of expectations such as capacity, uptime requirements, building codes, and so forth?
- Is there enough money to set up all mandatory elements? Should the UPS, generators, HVAC, and Internet connectivity have built-in redundancy?
- Do you need redundant links to the Internet via different ISPs?
- At what stages will the funds be released to pay for incurred expenses?

You will have to make certain compromises, such as not having generators or redundant HVAC units. Each compromise reduces the cost but adds some risk, and you must weigh the risk of each decision. You can also look for features or areas that can be added or upgraded later.

A *run budget* is the allocated amount for on-going operations, maintenance, and upkeep of the data center. It is money used for recurring expenses such as hardware and software supplies, expenses for cleaning and upkeep of the data center, and utility costs such as phone, electricity, and network connectivity charges.

For an existing data center, these requirements (such as power, network bandwidth, floor space, and HVAC cooling) determine the number and type of devices, servers, and so forth that can be placed there. This is called the *equipment capacity* of the data center. On the other hand, if you know in advance the number of and requirement for the devices that must be placed in the data center, you can then determine the required floor size, cooling capacity, network bandwidth, and budget to build one that suits the needs. The equipment thus determines the data-center capacities.

Selecting a Geographic Location

In early 2003, a large customer relationship management (CRM) software corporation in San Mateo, California, decided to relocate its data center to Salt Lake City, Utah. Around the same time, another biotechnology firm in Palo Alto, California, moved most of its enterprise-level servers to New Jersey.

When deciding on a geographic location, several factors must be weighed, including those described in this section. After selecting a site, the next question is whether to build a data center in an existing building or buy suitable land and construct a building and data center. If you must buy a building, ensure that it has adequate space for equipment, HVAC, and generators, preferably on the first or second floor. However, the build-to-suit option has more flexibility. Here are some factors to consider.

Safe from Natural Hazards

Ideally a data center must be located in an area with no possibility of floods, fire, tornadoes, strong winds, or earthquakes. Since it is impossible to find such an area, you must identify the hazards that are most likely to occur within the data-center lifetime (10, 20, or even 30 years) and make provisions to mitigate their impact.

Areas near a river, in a valley, or at the bottom of a hill are prone to floods.

In an earthquake, the entire building should be built so that it will gently rock but will not get warped or cracked. One data center in Northern California had rollers below the outer walls of the building.

Fires can be caused deliberately by humans. Dry areas in New Mexico and southern California, aided by strong and hot winds, can ignite and spread a fire. In October of 2003, a fire in Southern California, shown in Figure 3-2, ravaged for several days, burned 800,000 acres, and caused 22 deaths.

The California Department of Forestry and Fire Protection reports most fires are started by humans (90 percent to 95 percent). Arson accounts for 10 percent to 15 percent of them, and the remainder start accidentally — caused by a cigarette, a spark from a weed eater, and so forth.

The fire suppression agent used over equipment should not leave behind any oily residues, particulates, water, or corrosive materials, or cause any collateral damage in the event it is activated.

Safe from Man-Made Disasters

Nature is not the only cause of an ill-suited site for a data center. Many human-caused hazards are equally liable.

A data center should not be located very close to an airport, electrical railways, or telecommunications signal center. They create a high level of radio frequency interference (RFI) and electromagnetic interference (EMI) that hamper computer network and hardware operations. Avoid selecting a site too close to a mine, quarry, highway, or heavy industrial plant whose vibrations may disrupt racks and servers within the data center or utilities outside the data center.

Figure 3-2   Fires can get out of control and take days to extinguish.

Keep away from locations that are close to sources of industrial pollution such as farms, sewage treatment plants, and chemical factories. Their chemical waste, dust, and so forth can get inside the controlled areas of the data center and adversely impact equipment and health of data-center employees. If you have no choice, install a filtration system that can remove local contaminants.

Availability of Local Technical Talent

The "Silicon Valleys" of the world (such as the Bay Area in northern California, or Bangalore in India) have a good pool of technical talent, but these people are expensive to hire and even more difficult to retain. Ideally your location or city is attractive enough for new hires to relocate and live there for several years to come. Many companies in the United States are migrating their data centers to Colorado and Utah. Although these are beautiful states, the primary reasons for the move are low cost of property and a less-expensive work force.

Abundant and Inexpensive Utilities Such as Power and Water

This is an important consideration if you wish to pick a site in a rural area. Redundant feeds for electrical supply and Internet connection from ISPs are expensive to install and operate.

Selecting an Existing Building (Retrofitting)

Once you have selected a geographic location, you can construct a building. Use the first floor (also called the ground floor in some countries) or second floor of your building for the data center. Ensure that there is adequate parking space and easy access for emergency vehicles such as ambulances, fire trucks, and large delivery trucks. There must be a large-enough unloading and docking area. There should also be plenty of room for vehicles to pass one another, turn around, and get in and out without damaging the facility.

The luxury of constructing a new building is not always an option. Sometimes you have no choice but to select and rent a floor in an existing building. Although you have to make necessary internal modifications required for data-center operations, there are some conditions that make a floor or building an outright impossibility. Such conditions are overhead water or gas pipes, no access for large trucks and equipment, and security problems (that is, no control of who enters or leaves the floor). There are several pressing and upcoming considerations when selecting a room or floor that will become the data center. Here is a list to help you decide:

- There must be enough space for a raised floor. The height between the floor and ceiling must be adequate so that after constructing a ceiling plenum and at least a 2-foot subfloor plenum (the area below the data-center tiles), you have enough remaining height for 7- or 8-foot racks or equipment and space above the equipment for hot air to return to the HVAC units. The space in the subfloor plenum must be just enough to channel cold air. Too little space cannot carry enough cold air for the entire data center. Too large of a space will make it inefficient.

- If network and electrical cables will be run in the subfloor plenum, they must not obstruct the flow of cold air.

- It must be easy to set up redundant T1, DS3, fiber-optic, and other high-bandwidth network links.

- The building must have adequate power and redundant electrical grids to guarantee high 24×7 operations. Power outages must not be more than a few (three or four) times a year.

- The room or floor must be large enough for present and future equipment. Think of needs 15 or at least 10 years from now. It should be possible to remove walls and construct new ones without causing structural weakness. The floor must be strong enough to bear all the weight.

- The data center must be isolated form contaminant-producing areas within the building.

- The exhaust from generators and other sources should not be allowed to enter the data-center air intakes.

- The gas and water pipes must be safe and leak-free. Pipes or mains can leak or burst and, therefore, should not be running above the equipment. The occupants of floors above the data center should not create water leaks. Make sure there is an emergency water shut-off valve for emergencies and that all your data-center personnel know how to use it.

Key Points

Following are some key points discussed in this chapter:

- The functional requirement of a data center is to provide a safe and secure place for servers, storage, and networking equipment.

- The data center must also provide the required power, a well-controlled environment (with regard to temperature and relative humidity), and network connectivity to other devices within and outside the data center.

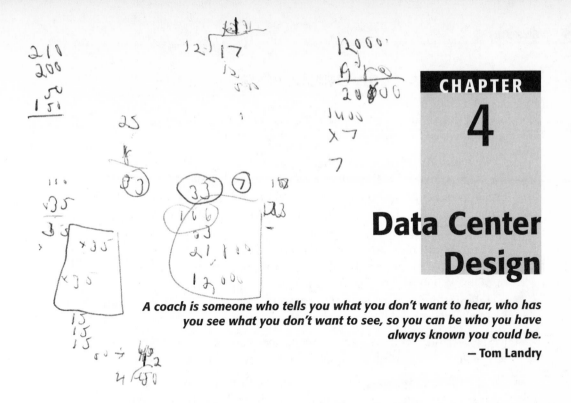

Data Center Design

A coach is someone who tells you what you don't want to hear, who has you see what you don't want to see, so you can be who you have always known you could be.

— Tom Landry

This chapter discusses guidelines for building a data-center facility. The process appears to be simple on the inception but has several aspects that must be done correctly. "If you cannot get it right the first time, learn your lessons and aim again" is a great motivator, but data-center architecture and construction must be done right from the get-go. Modifications and retrofitting a data center would involve ripping up floors, walls, HVAC, and electricity, and that is very difficult, expensive, and cumbersome.

An important distinction must be made between the data center itself and contents within the data center. The data center is the physical site, facility, the raised floor, UPS (which kicks in if power from the utility company fails), power generators (if installed to provide power for extended blackouts), network infrastructure (Internet connection, routers, switches, terminal servers), and air-conditioning units. On the other hand, the contents include servers, data storage subsystems, and shared monitors (if required). Both the data center and the contents are important. Without the contents, the data center is a big, expensive, cold room. Without the data center, the servers have no power or connection and are nothing but expensive boat anchors.

Characteristics of an Outstanding Design

The following are some features for design of an outstanding data center (although they would serve well for any other building):

- *Design must be simple* — Simplicity makes it difficult to err. To make the work simpler for those using the facility, all cables, circuit breakers, servers, storage devices, network ports, and power outlets must be labeled. The grid location of the tile (where the equipment is located) must be kept online so it can be readily accessed by others. No one should have to guess. In today's data centers, guesswork on the part of humans is the leading cause of network and system outages. When tiles, ports, and outlets are all labeled, it is easy to install new equipment. It is also simple to service or replace existing hardware.

- *Design must be scalable* — The design, once finalized, must work for any size of data center — 50,000, 5,000, or even 500 square feet.

- *Design must be modular* — Ancient Greeks, Romans, and Zoroastrians built large complex structures using small, manageable units that could be designed and manufactured easily. Data centers must also be constructed with small building blocks that can further be divided into smaller blocks for higher granularity.

- *Design must be flexible* — It is impossible to predict the technical requirements for the data center 10 (or even more) years out. To build a successful data center for long-term use, it must be easy to upgrade and to change layout or components.

A data center design that has these four characteristics will be less expensive and far easier to use, maintain, and expand.

Guidelines for Planning a Data Center

Following is a list of the key guidelines for design, construction, and deployment of a data center:

- *Plan in advance* — The sooner you start planning, the quicker you will discover potential problems and have time to think of and implement solutions. It removes the "Oops, I didn't see this coming!" factor.

A man in my neighborhood once told me, "I am not afraid of getting hit by the truck racing toward my face. I am afraid of ones racing toward my back."

- *Plan for the worst* — At least you will have thought of solutions to any impending problems.

- *Plan for growth* — The data center most probably will be in use longer than originally planned. Relocation is cumbersome and companies do not relocate unless absolutely necessary.

- *Simplify your design* — If it is complicated, changes will take more time and money and cause financial losses and emotional upheaval.

- *Plan for changes* — Design must be modular and flexible to accommodate changes and growth.

- *Label all equipment, especially cables and ports* — Maintenance and adding servers or devices will take less time. More importantly, they will be less likely to create unwarranted problems.

Data Center Structures

This section describes the essential elements within each data center. Together they compose the essential framework and prepare it for the HVAC, network connections, servers, and storage.

No-Raised or Raised Floor

No-raised floors are common in ISP and co-location (CoLo) data centers that have cages for different customers. These have no subfloor space for cables or air conditioning, but they have certain advantages. The wire-fenced cages go from floor to ceiling and each cage is rented to a customer. The absence of floor tiles removes the possibility of illicit access by someone removing a tile and crawling below the tiles to a neighboring cage rented by another company. Another advantage is the even distribution of cold air throughout the data center. With raised floors, it is possible for areas close to HVAC units to have too many open or perforated tiles, thereby decreasing the cold air pressure in other areas. Figures 4-1 and 4-2 show data centers with no raised floors. All cables and HVAC ducts are overhead — that is, above the cabinets and cages.

Figure 4-1   Data center with locked cabinets and\cables but with no raised floor.

A *raised floor* has about 2 feet of space (called *plenum*) below the tiles. The space provides a good mechanism for network cabling, power distribution, and air conditioning. All cables are neatly arranged along wireways and cable trays in the subfloor plenum. For these advantages, a number of modern ISP and CoLo data centers have raised floors.

Figure 4-2   Data center with no raised floor. Cabinets and stand-alone equipment are in cages.

Aisles

Aisles refer to the space between two rows of racks. Aisles and open space around corners and walls must be wide enough for moving racks and large, heavy equipment (movement that involves a forklift and few people). There must be enough space to remove and roll out a broken rack and roll in a new rack. Also, a large number of racks should not be placed in a continuous manner. There must be gaps after a set of continuous racks. Long rows of continuous racks make maneuvering from aisle to aisle, as well as from front to back of a rack, a time-consuming process. An optimally populated data center will have slightly more than half its area used by racks and stand-alone equipment.

Ramp

Constructing a *ramp* is the most common and practical way to get equipment in or out of a data center. The ramp must support the weight of the equipment, people, and mechanical devices used to lift the equipment (such as electrical-powered pallet jacks). Ramps that must support heavy weight are made of poured concrete.

The gradient or slope of ramps must be gradual. A gradient of 1 in 10 (a vertical rise of 1 inch for a horizontal length of 10 inches) is steep; 1 in 20 is a gradual ramp and a 3-foot rise in length would require a length of 60 feet. There must be at least a 6-foot level platform at the bottom and top of a ramp. That makes the total length to be 72 feet. It must be wide enough for cabinet-sized equipment such as IBM p690 (whose base dimensions are 2 1/2 feet × 5 feet) or EMC Symmterix storage devices. An 8-foot-wide ramp would be 72 × 8 = 576 square feet in area. Constructing a ramp is a considerable task.

Compulsory Local Building Codes

The local city authorities have codes (or a set of specifications) that must be met by the design. Also, the insurance companies require the data center to adhere to certain specifications that would decrease the extent of damage by natural disasters. In many countries, the city authorities must approve twice: First they endorse the plan or design on paper and later inspect the constructed facility to verify compliance with the plan. Detailed code knowledge and continuous involvement of city authorities and insurers will help prevent last-minute changes.

Raised Floor Design and Deployment

A raised floor is constructed on a grounded framework of vertical pedestals and stretchers that support floor tiles (2 feet × 2 feet in size). The space below the tiles is called the plenum. The raised floor provides for the following:

- A place for the equipment to sit. The tiles must be strong enough to support the weight of the equipment.

- Grounding for the equipment.

- A means to channel cold air from the HVAC units throughout the plenum in an optimal manner and direct it up to the data center to cool the equipment.

- A place to route network cables and power outlets and cables for equipment on the tiles. Since they are under the floor tiles, the data center looks less congested. The cables are also safe from being accidentally unplugged or kicked around by data-center people.

Despite the advantages of raised floors, some data centers do not use them.

Plenum

The word *plenum* (pronounced PLEH-num) means "full" in Latin. It is the space between the data center subfloor and the floor tiles and is usually between 1½ to 2 feet in height. The HVAC must be capable of pressurizing the plenum. The open structure in the plenum contains a floor grid system (pedestals and stringers) that must be strong enough to support the tiles and maximum-expected weight on the tiles (such as equipment-filled racks), HVAC units, dollies, forklifts, and people in the data center. The plenum contains the power outlets and network cables for equipment in the racks.

Floor Tiles

The raised floor consists of tiles or floor panels that provide a supporting base for the racks and equipment. They are generally 2-feet squares. Tiles are usually made of metal such as cast aluminum. You must choose tiles whose maximum load specifications exceed your requirements. Cast aluminum tiles can support a load of up to 1,500 pounds, even if they have a 50 percent pass-through. Tiles made of concrete or compressed wood can support only up to 500 pounds and, therefore, should be avoided. Tiles with inadequate strength or ill-fitting size warp or crack under the load and then pose a risk to equipment and people.

Tiles can be solid (that is, with no holes) or perforated (with holes for cold air to enter the data center). Tiles provide a great deal of flexibility in controlling air-flow patterns between the plenum and equipment. Solid tiles redirect air flow and help preserve pressure in the plenum or subfloor. Perforated tiles are used next to equipment racks and below bottom-cooled heavy equipment to redirect some cold air into the room or directly to equipment racks. Figure 4-3 shows the placement of racks, solid and perforated tiles, and aisle locations. Tiles with cutouts are used for passage of cables. Equipment racks are usually arranged in alternating rows: back-to-back or face-to-face.

□ Solid tile   ▦ Perforated tile   ⊓ Equipment rack

Figure 4-3 Equipment rack, aisles, and tile location on the data-center floor.

Sometimes it is necessary to cut and modify tiles to accommodate odd shapes of the room, edges of the floor, and around columns. The exposed cut edges of the tiles must be capped with protective trims to avoid particles entering the air stream. Exposed edges can damage cables and injure people lifting and repositioning tiles in their slots.

Equipment Weight and Tile Strength

One of the central issues impacting data center design is the weight, power, and cooling requirements of the equipment located therein. This section discusses the effect of size and weight of the equipment on design of floor tiles. Chapter 7 covers the effect of power requirements on the design of data-center facilities.

First, it is important to assess the present and future load on the raised floor. Once the data center is functional, changing the raised floor is close to impossible and rarely done in practice. It is an arduous and expensive task in terms of both time and money. Knowing the approximate weight of equipment is a prerequisite to a good design of the stretcher system in the subfloor plenum and quality of tiles. There are two types of load:

- *Point load* — Most equipment or racks sit on four rollers, casters, or feet. The load on any one of these four feet is called *point load*. For example, an IBM p690 server weighing 2,600 pounds has a point load of 650 pounds on each of its feet. If its feet rest on 1 square inch, the tile must be capable of bearing 650 pounds on 1 square inch without deflection of more than 1 or 2 mm.

- *Static load* — The sum of all point loads on the tile. If each of two racks (or stand-alone equipment) with point loads of 700 pounds per feet have one foot on a particular tile, that tile will be subjected to a total of 1,400 pounds. The tile must therefore be rated for 1,400 pounds of static load.

Historically most tiles are made of concrete with a steel shell. Perforations in the concrete weaken the tile. When equipment is rolled along the aisle, the perforated tiles are temporarily subjected to static load and, therefore, must have adequate static load rating. Strength of cast aluminum tiles are not undermined by perforations and are, therefore, preferable to concrete tiles.

Electrical Wireways

A *wireway* is a long metal box containing electrical wiring and power outlets for equipment. It is usually located below the tiles (or panels). The power cords from servers and devices in the data center are routed through cutouts in the tiles to these power outlets. The outlets are, in turn, connected by electrical wiring to circuit breakers and subpanels. Alternatively you can run power cables directly from each breaker (in a subpanel) to the floor. But this would create two problems: They obstruct air flow in the plenum (thereby decreasing air pressure), and they create a mess of cables.

Electrical wireways help centralize power distribution to few areas. Additionally they help secure power outlets (otherwise, they would be swinging around in the air). The smaller the electrical wireway, the less is its blockage to air flow. But electrical wireways must also meet city electrical codes.

Cable Trays

It is common practice to route the power cables from equipment in the data center through cutouts in the tiles to outlets in the under-floor plenum. A large number of such cables create disarray. It is difficult and time-consuming to trace bad cables. The pandemonium of cables obstructs air flow and decreases air pressure in the plenum.

Cable trays help reduce the cable mess. They are U-shaped wire baskets that usually run parallel to the wireways and contain the length of the cables. The cable lengths snake along the cable tray to the power outlets. Besides power cables, the trays also contain network and storage cables. Cable trays are not necessary but are useful.

The cable tray should not be placed very close to the bottom of the raised floor tile. Optimally cable trays must be at least 2 inches below the bottom of the tile. It is also important that the wireway and outlets be accessed by removing only one or two tiles.

Design and Plan against Vandalism

For most organizations, online data is one of their most expensive assets. All business-critical information is stored online and must be protected from sabotage, vandalism, and so forth. The data center must be selected in a building or neighborhood where it is easy to control access. Check for existing doors, windows, or ventilators that open to the outside and uncontrolled areas. If they are not necessary, replace them with walls. If they are necessary, you must install alarm systems and motion detectors. However, it is best to locate the data center in the interior of a building so that it has no exterior doors or windows. When designing a new area, plan for one (or, at most, two) entrances to the data center.

The design must include various monitoring devices. Install surveillance cameras at various locations, especially at entrances, such that they record the facial view of those entering the area. Motion detectors and alarms must be installed at various locations. If data-center space is shared with other companies, each company must have separate areas with physical barriers.

Make provisions for emergencies. Keep equipment-safe fire extinguishers at a few locations.

You must protect the equipment and data not only from external intrusions but also from internal elements. Disgruntled employees are a common cause of vandalism. Only employees who need access must be granted it. Untrained personnel can create security risks, and they must be kept away from critical areas of the data center.

Best Practices

When designing a data center, plan ahead. New factors unfold and must be resolved before starting the construction phase. Keep the design simple. It is easy to set up and manage. Root causes of problems are easy to identify and resolve.

Following are some hints:

- *The design must be modular* — Use patch panels for Cat5 and fiber connections. Segment the data center with sets and keep them independent of each other. Each set must have its infrastructure equipment in a single rack called the *point of distribution* (POD).

- *Label everything* — This includes ports, cable ends, and devices. Also, label the physical grid locations in the data center. If the north-south side is labeled with alphabets, the east-west side must be labeled as numbers.

- *Document everything* — This includes device details, location, and software components. Equipment location in the data center must be documented online.

- *Isolate cables* — Keep all cable bundles either in the subfloor plenum or ceiling plenum.

- *Use cast aluminum tiles* — They are strong and will be able to handle increasing weights of future equipment and densely packed racks.

Data-Center Design Case Studies

This section discusses data-center design cases. The process of determining the requirements and final suggestions must be changed for other situations.

Celebrity Travels

Celebrity Travels is a full-service travel agency that must keep all its data online. It also provides travel- and vacation-related services to several other agencies. It has recently acquired Castro Services, another long-established travel agency. Celebrity Travels wants to provide independent travel agents with the ability to use Celebrity's reservation system remotely for a certain fee.

Requirements

Because of shrinking profit margins, Celebrity Travels has decided to reduce expenses. Most of its 400-person workforce operate out of their homes, anyway, and have no need to visit the data center. The only people who must physically work at the data center are the NOC, equipment installers, and maintenance and security personnel. Celebrity Travels has decided to relocate its data center from Boston to Kansas, where space and local help are far less expensive.

The company has purchased a large plot of land for its data center. It engages a data-center design consultant from the beginning to plan all the details. Unknown future expansion plans require the need for a flexible and scalable design that must provide high availability and servicing without equipment downtime.

The consultant must make final determination regarding all aspects of the design and construction of the data center including size, raised floor design, rack layouts, HVAC systems, UPS, generators, electrical and mechanical distribution, fire suppression and detection, and network and electrical cable design.

Solution

The consultant determined the approximate base load of the equipment in the proposed data center and suggested a raised floor design. The floor area was divided into functional areas such as NOC area, equipment staging area, network room, and data center area, which would have rack rows containing servers, storage, and other devices. Some floor area near the entrance was marked for large floor-standing servers and storage subsystems (which are not designed for racks).

The consultant suggested a redundant three-phase UPS system and power-distribution unit, backed by a diesel generator. The generator was located just outside the data center with exhausts facing away from the building. For redundancy, the data center had two power feeds from different grids.

The HVAC unit was designed to be redundant. It had two units and sub-floor air distribution systems. The return-air ducts were located in the ceiling plenum. The two units were located on diagonal sides of the data center. The electrical and mechanical infrastructure was designed in such a way as to be able to double the amount of UPS protection and precision cooling seamlessly should it become necessary.

The network room had switches connecting the servers to the intranet and ISPs. The racks in the data center were grouped into sets. Each set of racks had POD racks that contained patch panels, terminal servers, and subswitches. The POD patch panels were connected to the patch panel in the network room.

The fire-suppression system included a preaction sprinkler system, smoke detectors at various locations and plenum areas, and temperature-based fire-sensing devices.

The entire data-center construction project took 8 months from concept to completion. The close cooperation and partnership of all critically involved parties (such as the customer, engineers, and contractors) was vital to the accomplishment of the overall project.

Designer Dresses

Designer Dresses, Inc., has several off-line stores around the state. The owners have decided to establish an online presence to be able to allow anyone in the country to order dresses. They have acquired services from a software-development firm to place their catalog online. They have rented a building in the state of New York.

Requirements

Designer Dresses has engaged a data-center consultant to architect and build a 1,000-server data center that must have no downtime for network devices, servers, or any facility services (such as power and air conditioning).

Solution

The data center was architected with raised floor. There were two redundant HVAC units and subfloor plenum chilled-air distribution. Two separate power feeds came from different utility companies. Two 50-kilowatt three-phase UPS units with 30-minute batteries backed the grid power, which, in turn, were backed by diesel generators.

Separate areas were allocated for different functions (such as NOC, loading area, network room, and racks). All the devices in the data center were designed for racks. However, a part of the data center had no racks and would be used for future, nonrackable equipment.

The rack rows were laid out, along with hot and cold aisles. Only cold aisles had perforated tiles. The equipment had front-to-back cooling, and each rack front faced a cold aisle.

Key Points

Following are some key points discussed in this chapter:

- It is important to get the design right because retrofitting a data center is too expensive and unwieldy.
- A data-center design must be simple to modify and manage, scalable to accommodate future needs without any changes, and modular and flexible so upgrades can be made if necessary.
- Common structures within a data center are raised floor, aisles, floor tiles, subfloor plenum and ceiling plenum, electrical wireways, and cable trays.
- All equipment, cable ends, and grid locations must be labeled in an orderly manner.

Network Infrastructure in a Data Center

Only by going too far can we possibly find out how far one can go.
— Jon Dyer

This chapter describes the network cabling that must be set up to connect the data-center servers to the intranet and Internet, a modular cabling layout, and Internet access.

A large number of cables (such as Category 5 or 5e, copper or fiber) are required to connect a set of servers to other devices and the network. Let's say your data center has 50 servers. That may be a small number, but it makes the calculation easier. Each server is connected to two storage devices, using two fiber cables (for performance and redundancy). Each storage device is also connected to the administrative network using Cat5 cables. This facilitates console-based storage administration. Each server has redundant connections to the production network. Here is an estimate of all the cables required:

- *Server to storage fiber cables* — 50 servers × 2 storage devices × 2 cables = 200 cables.

- *Storage to admin network* — 100 cables.

- *Server to console server (out-of-band or remote console access)* — 50 cables.

- *Server to production network* — 50 servers × 2 = 100 cables.

That makes 450 cables for only 50 servers. Most data centers have several hundred servers. In addition to the mentioned cables, storage devices, and servers, you must account for yet more connections (such as power). Ideally the storage devices would be in close proximity to the servers, but that rarely happens and you need to run cables under the floor.

Modular Cabling Design

In the past, a data center had a few large, networked mainframes and cabling requirements were limited. All cables were run from the data center to a central location (such as the network room). Since then, the number of connections has increased by a few orders of magnitude. You can still run all the cables from the data center to your network room, but that would be too cumbersome to install or manage. It also goes against the "keep it simple" principle.

A set of racks contains servers, terminal servers, and so forth that need Cat5 or fiber cable connections. There are two ways to do this:

- Cable hosts directly to the switch ports.
- Use patch panels.

If you use patch panels, all hosts and other devices that need network connections are cabled to ports in a patch panel located close by in the data center. Ports in this patch panel are cabled to ports in another patch panel (say, in the network room), which, in turn, are connected to switch ports. Figure 5-1 shows a copper Cat5 cable's ends and a Cat5 patch panel. Figure 5-2 shows two patch panels.

Patch panels offer several advantages. They keep connections and cables localized within each physical area. However, you must determine the number of Cat5 and fiber ports needed in each section of the data center and install appropriately sized patch panels. Since patch panels are very difficult to replace, you must also have extra, unused ports for future use. Figure 5-3 illustrates how patch panels are used to connect servers in the data center and switches in the network room or closet.

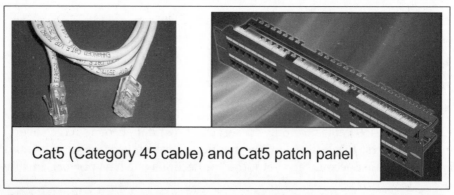

Cat5 (Category 45 cable) and Cat5 patch panel

Figure 5-1   Cat5 port connections and a patch panel with 96 Cat5 ports.

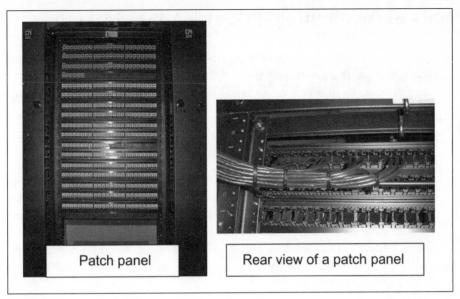

Figure 5-2 Patch panels.

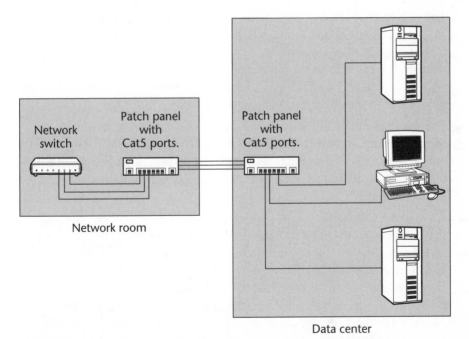

Figure 5-3 Use of a Cat5 patch panel to link computers in a data center to a switch in the network room.

Points of Distribution (PODs)

A point of distribution (POD) is a rack with devices, network switches, terminal servers, and patch panels that together provide the infrastructure required for a number of racks filled with servers and storage. PODs allow you to group cables and networking equipment required for a set of racks into a single manageable location.

Let's consider an example. A data center with 1,000 racks of servers and storage devices can be divided into 50 sets, each set containing 20 racks. Each set must have a dedicated rack or POD containing all required patch panels, network switches (if any), and terminal servers. The POD is located within the data center. Network cables connect servers within the 20 racks to patch panel ports located inside the POD rack. The patch panel is, in turn, wired to the network room. When a new server is added, you do not need to run another cable all the way from the machine to the network room. All you need is a short cable from the machine to the POD.

A POD rack contains the following three items:

- *Cross-patch ports* — Cat5 and fiber connections can be cross-patched. The POD has several ports that are wired to ports in the network room. Each port in a POD must be labeled with the same identifier as its corresponding port in the network room. The wires connecting the POD ports to the ports in the network room must be bundled and run in separate cable trays, preferably in the ceiling plenum. Figure 5-4 shows the process on installing fixtures and wirings for a POD.

  The patch panel installer must test all connections using a cable tester. Since the number of network connections increases and it is very cumbersome to replace patch panels, you must install patch panels with the highest available port density. Port density is number of ports per U (1 U is 1.75 inches) of rack height.

- *Network terminal servers* — A *terminal server* is a device on the network that allows you to log in to a server's console port, which is usually a serial port. The terminal server is sometimes known as a *portmaster* and contains up to 100 or so ports. It can be accessed over the LAN. Each port within the terminal server is cabled via patch panels to console ports in racked servers. Console access helps in installing OS, viewing bootup messages, and working at the open boot prom (OBP) level from a remote location.

Figure 5-4 Laying fixtures and cables for data-center PODs.

- *Network subswitches* — Small switches used to connect servers to a certain network, such as the administrative or backup network, can be located inside a POD. These switches must be connected to the master switch via a link with higher bandwidth than the subswitch-to-host links.

Internet Access

Access to the Internet is provided by an Internet service provider (ISP) such as UUNet, AT&T, Sprint, and Nippon Telegraph and Telephone (NTT). There are two components that an ISP provides: its network infrastructure and its WAN links.

ISP Network Infrastructure

There are several reliable vendors for network equipment, and Cisco is the undisputed market leader. However, because of several new and nimble players in the field, there are many vendors to choose from. If the ISP uses equipment from several vendors, it must verify interoperability. A router may have very high reliability, but its performance may suffer when connected to a switch from another vendor. The ISP must have a test lab to verify intervendor compatibility before deploying a production architecture, to recreate field problems, and to plan maintenance and upgrade windows with no service disruption.

Other important features of an ISP infrastructure are reliability and tolerance to hardware failures. Providers should have redundant switches and routers at every network layer. The network should withstand at least one failure in each layer and continue to function at full performance. The backup systems should not consist of inferior-capacity hardware. If it is so, a failure at peak times will cause perceptible performance degradation.

ISP WAN Links

The second part of the network is the ISP's wide area network (WAN) connection. The WAN link is composed of two aspects: "transport" and "transit."

Network "transport" is the path that carries the data and has a certain maximum bandwidth, while the "transit" is the actual data. Let's consider an analogy to explain these terms. The "transport" is like a water pipe that comes to your house from the city water supply corporation. You may have a narrow or wide water pipe. The water pipe is connected to one or more sources of water. The water is the "transit." A wide pipe carrying a thin stream of incoming water is not useful. You need a wide pipe and a large flow rate of water supply. Many ISPs have OC-12s or OC-48s to the Internet, but these fast, high-bandwidth circuits are a waste without adequate transit. It is, therefore, important to know the actual transit bandwidth and to which service providers you're connecting.

Figure 5-5 shows part of the world's IP network, used to carry data over the Internet.

The ISP must also have reliable and redundant circuits. Having all the transit on a single pipe is not reliable. A circuit can have many problems such as a misconfiguration at the central office (CO) or a physically cut fiber in the street. Therefore, an ISP must have several fiber providers and several transit providers. There must be a minimum of three of each, and any two should be able to handle the maximum network traffic. An ISP with three T1s (at 1.5 Mbits/second) and one T3 (at 45 Mbits/second) does not have redundant circuits, because if the T3 fails, the provider loses more than 90 percent of its capacity.

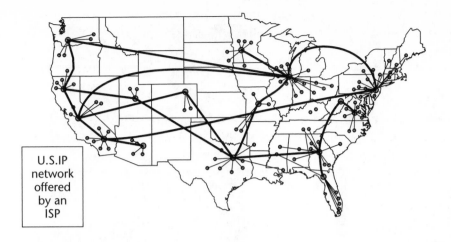

U.S.IP
network
offered
by an
ISP

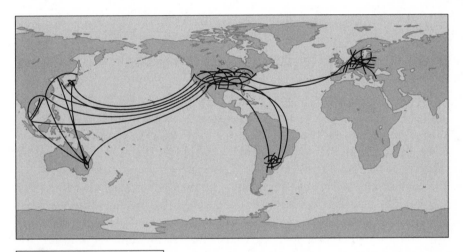

Worldwide OC-192 fiber-
optic backbone network

Figure 5-5   Portion of the U.S. and worldwide IP network.

Best Practices

Several best practices must be followed to ease configuration and maintenance:

- *Label your equipment* — Label both cable ends and all devices such as switches, routers, and electric breakers. Figure 5-6 shows two clearly labeled cable ends.

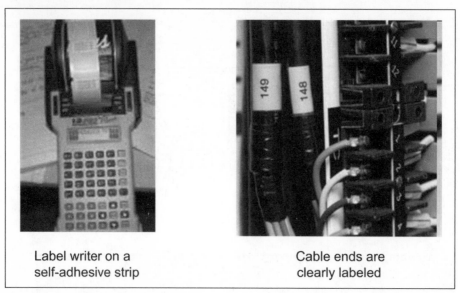

Label writer on a
self-adhesive strip

Cable ends are
clearly labeled

Figure 5-6   Label maker that prints the text on a self-laminating label that is easy to wrap around wires.

It takes the least effort and time when done during installation. Thereafter, it is a cumbersome task to trace a cable inside a wireway or under the tiles. If a device is having network problems, it is easy to substitute a cable if both cable ends have similar labels. Remember that several ports (such as patch panel ports) and cable ends (such as electrical, network, and storage cables) must be labeled. To provide a unique label designation for any type of cable, you may use a two-alphabet and two-digit nomenclature such as AX25. This gives you 6,084 unique labels ($26 \times 26 \times 99 = 6,084$).

■ *Color code cables* — At one company, the data-center crew had a policy of using yellow Cat5 cables for connecting servers to the back-end network and white Cat5 cables for the front-end network. If you have a backup network, production network, DMZ network, and administration network, you can have cables of four colors.

■ *Avoid a tangle of cables* — Figure 5-7 shows a group of messy cables around a patch panel. Figure 5-8 shows a neatly arranged bundle of cables connecting data-center devices to the patch panel. It takes deliberate effort to reduce the cable tangles and mess. Always use correct length of Cat5 or fiber cables to avoid coiling the extra length. Use cable ties to group similar cables. Route cable in cable trays under the tiles to minimize obstruction of air flow. Do not leave loose cables on the floor, as shown in Figure 5-7. That will trap dust and will be a hazard to people and equipment.

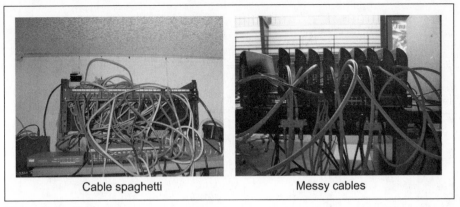

Cable spaghetti · Messy cables

Figure 5-7   Cable mess.

All data line terminations must be punched using proper termination tools. Electric punch equipment ensures proper termination and maximum bandwidth over copper cables.

■ *Patch panel ports and connections must be verified by the installer* — Use Cat5 and fiber cable testers. They can test up to 1,000-foot-long cables for cable continuity, bad wiring, and open, short, straight-through, or cross pinning. Note that a cable tester should never be used on a live connection. Figure 5-9 shows Ethernet cable testers.

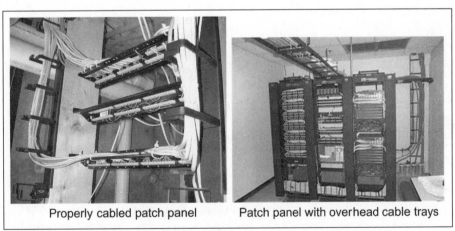

Properly cabled patch panel · Patch panel with overhead cable trays

Figure 5-8   Patch panel with neatly tied cables.

464

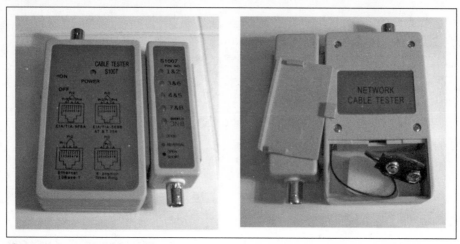

Figure 5-9 Cat5 cable testers.

- *Remote console access* — Remote console access for system administrators (SAs) is required to maintain 24 × 7 service uptime. SAs can reboot hosts or troubleshoot host problems from a remote location even if the login services are not running on the host. Like all remote accesses, security must be tightened around terminal services. The terminal services must be on an internal administrative network and not on the DMZ. Everyone must be required to log in to a server (where accounts and logins must be tightly controlled and monitored) from where they can get on to the terminal server.

- *Cable bending radius* — Cables must be placed with sufficient bending radius so as not to shear, kink, or damage jackets, binders, or cables, including where cables are coiled for future use or slack.

Key Points

Following are some key points discussed in this chapter:

- The network and cabling infrastructure within a data center must be modular, which is possible using patch panels and points of distribution (PODs) containing cross-patch ports, network subswitches, and terminal servers (optional).

- All cable connections must be well labeled.

- Internet access from ISPs must be redundant and reliable.

Data Center Maintenance

*Now, here is my secret, a very simple secret. It is only with the heart that one can
see rightly; what is essential is invisible to the eye.*
— Antoine de Saint-Exupery (from *The Little Prince*)

This chapter discusses day-to-day maintenance and usual upkeep of a data center, including NOC monitoring, security practices, and data-center cleaning.

Network Operations Center (NOC)

The network operations center (NOC) is a dedicated facility staffed with people (usually at all hours) who monitor the availability of all devices and services within the data center and respond to any data-center problems. The NOC has servers, consoles, and network monitoring software such as HP OpenView, BMC Patrol, IBM Tivoli, and Computer Associate's UniCenter. The software is used to monitor the health, status, and load of each piece of equipment and communication between all devices.

A NOC serves as a central logging point for all alarms and a location for evaluating the present status of the data center.

Simple network monitoring protocol (SNMP) agents can be used with storage devices such as UPS systems, HVAC, and storage devices such as NAS filers and storage area network (SAN) switches to get reports on their status and health on the monitoring software.

Network Monitoring

A critical requirement for data centers is the ability to proactively monitor the availability of all server and network resources. This section discusses the concepts of network monitoring so that network and IT managers can understand why this is such an important topic in today's enterprise.

At a high level, network monitoring is knowing what is happening within your environment. In some ways, it is like the smoke alarm in your house. Whenever there is fire or smoke, the alarm warns you. But, network monitoring software is also proactive. It can be tuned to warn you of impending problems that you must be made aware of such as a sudden burst of network traffic, file systems filling up to a certain threshold, and symptoms of Internet attacks on your edge routers.

Monitoring Requirements

Without network monitoring, you would be stuck in a reactive world. If a problem occurred, you would be notified by one of your clients, and you would fix the problem. Despite best efforts by all parties, this still happens, but network monitoring moves you (to some extent) into a world of proactive management of your IT hardware and software.

Network monitoring gathers real-time data and classifies it into performance issues and outages. Performance issues are used to predict the need for future scaling of the environment. Outages are alerted to on-call staff as a page or an urgent phone call from the NOC. Figure 6-1 shows a NOC.

SNMP

Simple network monitoring protocol (SNMP) is the most helpful tool in resource monitoring. It lets you discover what resources are out there and their status. It is used to send information about the health of resources to a central collection host. It enables various tools to organize incoming information in a logical and graphical manner. Operators are needed not for gathering data, but for evaluating the reports and relaying problems to those who can fix them.

SNMP is a protocol that runs over user datagram protocol (UDP). The daemon is typically called snmpd or snmpdx and runs over port 161. SNMP consists of a number of object identifiers (OIDs) and a management information base (MIB). A MIB is a collection of hierarchically organized OIDs. An "object" can be a network interface card, system board temperature, httpd daemon, or router. By extending the SNMP daemon, any server event or hardware can be monitored.

Figure 6-1 A network operation center (NOC) is used to resolve problems or escalate them to the appropriate personnel.

SNMP assigns unique prefixes to vendors in a nested fashion. For example, Cisco Systems owns all numbers under the 1.3.6.1.4.1.9 address for their products.

The SNMP language is composed of three main actions: GET, SET, and TRAP. GET fetches an OID value from the resource (for example, disk full percentage). SET configures a value (for example, number of processes allowed for an application). TRAP watches for an event, and if it occurs, performs some action (for example, restart application).

The SNMP daemon is insecure by default. It allows for reconfiguration of devices and, if a server or network device is incorrectly configured, data can be exposed. Therefore, many data centers have SNMP SET operations disabled. Security is also compromised because of a "community string" and a "private string," which equate to passwords. The public string is used for polling and the private string for setting configurations. Many vendors use the value "public" for public string. You can check to see if a device is SNMP-aware. If you do not have a login name and password, you can still poll the device and extract SNMP data using an SNMP toolkit and "public" as the public string. If the device times out, that means someone has changed the public string. SNMP version 3 supports advanced security such as encrypted sessions and stronger authorization such as Message Digest 5 algorithm (MD5) or data encryption standard (DES) hashes.

In-Band and Out-of-Band Monitoring

In-band monitoring is the capability to change system status through the existing network infrastructure.

Out-of-band monitoring is the capability to control systems not through existing network infrastructure but via a different data network or via a dial-in capability for individual devices. Several vendors have phone-line modems connected to their devices in customer data centers. These send device alarms to the vendor support personnel.

It is important to get immediate alarms from equipment. It has been found that mean time to repair (MTTR) contributes more to service outage periods than mean time before failure (MTBF). The sooner you are alerted to a problem, the sooner it can be resolved. Critical systems must have no downtime.

Besides monitoring the devices, servers, and storage subsystems, several other data center–wide features must be monitored, such as

- Power from the utility provider
- UPS status and usage
- Generator status and usage
- Leak detection from HVAC and air ducts and from liquid in the HVAC units
- Temperature in the data center
- Relative and absolute humidity in the data center
- Intrusion in the facility

Several systems and networked devices can be monitored over the network. The devices or the NOC monitoring software can be programmed to call a cellular telephone or pager upon finding certain preset alarms.

Data-Center Physical Security

A critical component of server and data security is the security of the data center itself.

All entry points and doors to the data center must be controlled by card readers or persons who are physically present to monitor and restrict access of those entering the data center. Recently biosensitive readers have been installed at various data centers. After swiping his or her badge, the employee must place a palm on a biosensitive reader, which matches the palm prints against an earlier recorded image. Cameras must be installed not only at the data-center doors but also at the corporate entrances.

Badge access to the data center must not be given to all employees. Only those who must access the data center must be allowed to enter. Various data centers have a policy for one-time accesses, where security personnel verify and record if anyone needs to enter.

Functionally there are two types of data centers: co-location (CoLo) data centers and managed-hosting data centers. There are significant differences in security needs between them.

- *Co-location data centers* — Hundreds or thousands of customers pass or visit a co-location data center each day. It is therefore vital to control and monitor the visits and list of people who have access to the data center. Despite all precautions and security, visitors can damage other customers' equipment.

- *Managed hosting data centers* — In a secure managed-hosting data center, only a few employees have access to the data center. Customers do not have badges or passes to go inside. If they must go inside, they must be escorted and given temporary badges. Also, large groups of visitors are not allowed to go in. Most of these data centers use a biometric system to control access. The advantage of these systems is that the activity is logged, it is not possible to use someone else's card to go in, and any employees who are no longer entitled to go inside the data center can be instantly removed.

  Despite the best physical security, servers can be attacked over the network and that can be far more expedient than gaining physical access. Therefore, it is critical to have an up-to-date OS image and patch set. OS and security patches and bug fixes are released daily. Managed hosting providers should have experts who evaluate these patches. It is often not practical to update the OS proactively on production servers because enterprises want to test the OS on development and stage servers first, and because updates may cause unforeseen application problems.

All data centers must use closed-circuit television (CCTV) to monitor and record activities in all areas of the data center, especially at all entry and exit positions.

Data-Center Logical Security

All valuable information of almost all organizations is stored online. It is, therefore, mandatory that the data and servers be protected from people with malicious intent. Preventing illicit access to the data is of utmost importance. It is important to keep out people who have no business being physically there (physical security) and to prevent unauthorized access via the network (logical security).

Logical security is making it more difficult for intruders to reach a login prompt on the hosts or other devices. The telnet port should be closed. Use ssh instead to log in to UNIX servers. Protocols using low-number ports (less than 1,024) should be allowed only if necessary.

Console-level access over the network is convenient because it enables remote diagnosis of boot-up errors experienced before network services are started in the boot process. However, this creates a new path for intruders to break in. You must construct more than one layer of authentication before presenting the login prompt and must also allow only a few and necessary users the capability to go beyond these layers. These users must be forced to authenticate themselves to a central login server, which should be the only machine having direct access to the consoles.

Data-Center Cleaning

There are many stories on how the cleaning crew knocked power off the storage array because the aisle was narrow or the crew was unaware of the environment. A data-center setting is different from an office area and, therefore, does not require regular cleaning or vacuuming. You must get a cleaning crew in the data center once every 3 or 6 months or as needed, such as after structural (floor, tile, wall, and so forth) changes.

It is common practice to have a vendor company do the work. The vendor and its cleaning crew must be qualified to do the work. The cleaning crew must be given a data-center map that designates electrical outlets they can use. They must know and follow all rules: no food or drink in the data center, no interfering with ongoing operations, no leaving doors propped open, and no unbadged/unauthorized personnel. Safety cones must be placed around open tiles and areas that are being damp-mopped.

Approved Cleaning Supplies

A prespecified list of equipment and supplies must be used by the cleaning crew. It is important not to leave particles and debris that could enter the air circulation. Triple-filtration high-efficiency particulate air (HEPA) vacuums capable of removing 99.97 percent of particles 0.3 micros or larger must be used.

Electrical cords used by the crew must be in good condition and have three-pin ground configuration. The cleaning chemicals must be pH neutral and static dissipative. The mops must be lint-free with nonmetal handles and sewn ends to prevent snagging, and the mop heads must have looped (and not stringy or open) ends. Only lint-free and antistatic wipes must be used. Threads from the mop or pieces of wiping paper must not be left behind on the equipment or racks.

Floor Surface Cleaning

When cleaning the raised floor, care must be taken to avoid disturbing cables routed through the openings in the floor tiles. The cables should not be accidentally pulled. Use HEPA vacuum cleaners to clean accessible floor areas, including notched, perforated, and solid tiles.

Use an approved solution to treat black marks, stains, and smudges on the floor, and scrub them with a medium-grade scrub pad. Use a HEPA vacuum cleaner to remove dirt and particles from the top of all accessible floor areas. Trying to clean below equipment or racks can disrupt operations. Finally the floor must be mopped with a damp (not wet) mop using clean, warm water.

Subfloor and Above-Ceiling Plenum Cleaning

For data centers with raised tiled floors, the space below the tiles must be cleaned. For data centers without a raised floor, most power and data cables run above the lowered ceiling. When removing tiles to access the subfloor areas or removing ceiling tiles to access the above-ceiling space, no more than 10 percent of the tiles should be detached at any one time, and they must be removed in a checkerboard pattern starting in one corner of the data center.

Large debris must be manually disposed of. Vacuuming in necessary areas must be done around cable bundles, walls, and base columns. Explicit care must be taken not to impact cable bundles adversely or unplug any cable.

Equipment Cleaning

Chemicals should not be sprayed directly on any equipment surface. Instead, a lint-free cloth treated with antistatic cleaners must be used to wipe racks, cabinets, and external surfaces of all equipment such as servers, storage devices, and network devices. HEPA vacuum cleaners must be used to clean horizontal surfaces of equipment. Keyboards must not be touched during cleaning.

Any unusual floor conditions (such as loose floor pedestals, cracked tiles, condensation, wet areas, or loose brackets) must be either corrected immediately or reported to the data-center team.

Best Practices

Several best practices must be followed to ensure trouble-free data-center maintenance:

- A high level of physical, network, and host-level security must be enforced at all times. A data center needs 24×7 dedicated professional security staff and multiple layers of hard-line physical security such as biometric scanners, electronic-coded badges, and video surveillance through the data center and the facility. A digital copy of the video-recorded events must be archived for future post mortems.

- Regular cleaning of the data center is important to remove all dust and dirt, which can damage devices. A live data center must be cleaned with extreme caution. Keyboards should not be touched. Antistatic cleaning and machine scrubbing is necessary for high-pressure raised-floor surfaces. The removal of floor tiles to perform work in a raised-floor environment creates serious safety hazards. It is easy to fall or drop equipment in an unmarked open floor tile. You should use safety cones to demarcate open tile work zones. Floor tiles that have been removed must be kept within the well-demarcated work zone.

- Quarterly preventive maintenance must include power systems checks, HVAC and generator servicing, and so forth. All service visits must be coordinated and tracked. Service plan must include the following:

  - UPS systems and batteries
  - Generator and automatic transfer switch (ATS) equipment
  - Power cables, outlets, subpanels, and circuit breakers
  - Static-switching equipment
  - Free-standing and rack-based power distribution equipment
  - Fire suppression and detection equipment
  - Overhead sprinkler systems
  - Air-conditioning and HVAC units, air ducts, and filters
  - Inlet-air blockages near perforated tiles

- Physical site inspection must be done every month. Coordination and communications should be done online via e-mails. A copy of all documents and standard operating procedures must be maintained at a central Web site.

Key Points

Following are some key points discussed in this chapter:

- Network monitoring makes it possible to be a proactive network or system administrator.

- Network monitoring identifies potential issues, devices that are down, and trends that can lead to problems.

- It is crucial to provide a predetermined level of service uptime to clients and reduce (or avoid) outages, embarrassments, and financial losses.

CHAPTER 7

Power Distribution in a Data Center

Nearly all men can stand adversity, but if you want to test a man's character, give him power.
— Abraham Lincoln

This chapter discusses the system that provides power to equipment in the data center and the building in general. The system includes electrical transformers, power distribution panels, circuit breakers, wiring, grounding mechanism, power outlets for the equipment, and backup sources of power such as an uninterruptible power supply (UPS) and generators.

A well-designed electrical system for a data center has the following characteristics:

- It must provide reliable and sufficient power to hardware in the data center.

- It must have adequate redundancy and no single points of failure to avoid disrupting services during power outages.

- It must conform to city, state, and national safety standards.

Estimating Your Power Needs

There are three categories of equipment that need power in the data center. You must add the three to get your total requirement. The total requirement must be less than the amount of kilovolt amperes (kVA) or kilowatts (kW) available for the data center. For DC power, watts equal the product of volts times amps. Let's assume that the amount available for the data-center floor and equipment is 6,000 kVA or 6,000 kW. A data center's requirements would be as follows:

- *Power for racks and stand-alone equipment* — You must add the requirements to power all the servers, devices, and network equipment that are stand-alone or racked. That is generally specified in amps, volts, or watts for each outlet. An outlet for small rack-mounted devices would be 15 amps, 120 volts, and require 1,800 watts (or 15×120). Large stand-alone equipment requires 30 amps, 220 volts, and L6-30R power outlets, each needing 6,600 watts (or 30×20). If you have 500 and 200 of each of these, respectively, your power requirement would be calculated as follows:

  - For 500 of the 15 amps, 110 volt outlets — 900 kW (or 500×1800)
  - For 500 L6-30 outlets — 1,320 kW (or 200×6600)

  Your total equipment requirement, therefore, is 2,220 kW (or 900 + 1320).

- *Power for the HVAC system* — A common rule of thumb is to allocate 70 percent of the equipment power for the HVAC requirement. In this example, the HVAC would consume 1,554 kW (or $0.7 \times 2,220$).

- *Power for lighting, monitoring systems, NOC servers, fire control devices, and so forth* — Let's assume that 100 kW of power is required for these provisions. The total data center requirement, therefore, is 3,874 kW (or 2,220 + 1,554 + 100).

The outlets must provide this amount of power, but circuit breakers have a diversity factor of, say, 0.9. That means they will trip and stop electric flow once it reaches 90 percent of the rated amps. A 30-amp, 220-volt outlet with 0.9 diversity factor will trip when current reaches 27 amps. The maximum power that can be drawn from that outlet is therefore 5,940 watts (or 27×220). In order for the data-center equipment, HVAC, lighting, and so forth to receive 3,747 kW of power, the outlets must be wired for a total of 4,304 kW (or 3,874/0.9), or 4.3 megawatts (MW).

Here are common data-center power estimates:

- *Data rooms, labs, small data centers* — 1 to 12 kW
- *Medium data centers* — 12 to 200 kW
- *Large data centers* — 200 to 10,000 kW (or 10 MW)

You must also consider future upgrades. If 20-amp wiring is sufficient for now, but you expect to need 40- or 50-amp circuits in the future, you should consider installing 50-amp wiring from the start. Once the higher-gauge wiring is in place, it is easy to change to higher-amperage outlets. The cost of dismantling and rewiring even for some parts of the data center is far greater than that for a new installation. Data centers must be wired for single-phase and three-phase. If you have only single-phase, consider the cost for retrofitting three-phase wires and outlets.

Power companies must make information on major outages available to their customers as soon as possible. Your contract with the power company must include a clause to this effect.

Power production differs from country to country and state to state. Some countries and states produce excess power that they sell to their neighbors, while others have to purchase power to meet their needs. During power shortages, those with excess power will obviously fare better because they can reduce their power exports to meet internal demand. Each data-center maintenance team must be familiar with the local power structure and be prepared to react quickly to information received from the power company.

Even the most reliable power company cannot guarantee $24 \times 7 \times 365$ supply. Each data center must, therefore, have an independent power infrastructure that consists of the following:

- A UPS that conditions the power and can maintain the load for a short period of time

- A generator that can replace utility power for extended periods of time

- A distribution system that provides power to the individual servers

Uninterruptible Power Supply (UPS)

A 24×7 data-center availability requires a continuous and reliable source of power. If power from the grid fails, the UPS system should be able to provide power for all equipment, HVAC, lights, access readers, and so forth for some period of time or at least until the source of power is transferred to other alternatives such as backup generators. That period of time could be 15 minutes to a few hours. The battery in the UPS should be capable of providing the initial power-on peak load, which is higher than normal run-time load. A device with a run-time load of 1,000 watts may require 1,500 watts of peak load.

The UPS usually has batteries that maintain the load while the generator comes online. That process usually takes between 15 seconds and 1 minute. One problem with batteries is that they must be replaced every five years or less. An alternative to batteries is to use systems that have flywheels instead of batteries to transition from grid power to generators. Flywheel systems can function indefinitely and have lower ongoing costs, but batteries are still preferred because of their popularity, simplicity of usage, and lower installation costs.

The UPS must be reliable, redundant, and able to provide enough power. The UPS is not only used to cover power outages but also to perform maintenance on the primary power system.

A basic, single-phase UPS unit would suffice for a few racks, but a scalable, sophisticated three-phase UPS is needed for large data centers. The UPS can be a tower or rack-mounted model. It must be easy to add or remove battery packs. Figure 7-1 shows the block-level view of the internal UPS design. Figure 7-2 shows the front and back of a UPS box.

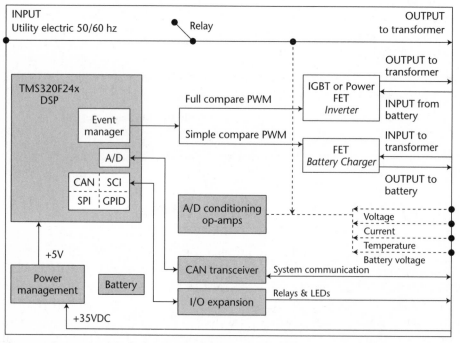

Figure 7-1 System block diagram of a UPS.

Figure 7-2 Redundant three-phase UPS system for data-center equipment and front and back views of a small UPS box, adequate for one rack or a few servers.

Generators

Generators must be installed if power outage durations are expected to be more than 15 minutes. Buying and installing a generator is expensive and a single 20-minute power outage every year cannot justify its return-on-investment (ROI). However, it is common for data centers with 24 × 7, mission-critical servers to have power generators.

There are several government code requirements. You must have a contract with diesel supplier who will regularly check and fill the tanks if necessary. It is a jeopardizing face-off to find the fuel tank almost empty when you must switch to it during a power outage. The diesel exhaust must not be allowed to enter the data-center HVAC system. Figure 7-3 shows a diesel-powered generator to supply electricity in the event of a blackout.

The generator is composed of

- An engine to produce power
- A generator coil to convert the power to electricity

The most popular generators utilize a large diesel engine with six to twelve cylinders and up to six turbochargers. Large diesel engine manufacturers include Caterpillar, Tata, Stuart, and Stevenson. Another alternative is to use a turbine engine. It is similar to those used in airplanes. Turbine engines are manufactured by General Electric (GE) and Rolls Royce. These engines usually run on natural gas or diesel and produce far more power than a similar-sized diesel engine. However, turbine engines are expensive and designed to run continuously. They are, therefore, rarely used for data-center emergency power. A data center should carry up to 24 hours of fuel at full load on-site.

Figure 7-3 Redundant generators located outside a data center.

Power Conditioning

Just as a *blackout* is a power outage, a *brownout* is when the voltage and amps from the grid are less than normal. The equipment cannot function properly with the reduced power. Persistent brownouts damage the equipment. If there are frequent durations when power is less than what is required by the equipment, you must use power-conditioning devices. They can be attached to or integrated within UPS systems.

Voltage spikes, on the other hand, are sharp rises in the voltage. They can originate at the power grid or within the power distribution system because of devices such as HVAC compressors turning on or off. Some UPS systems have power filtration units to smooth voltage spikes. If such a UPS is not used, a surge protector such as a transient volt surge suppressor (TVSS) must be used. Power outlets often have built-in surge suppressors.

Single-Phase and Three-Phase Power

The power feeds coming from the main supply grid into the building are three-phase. Transformers convert the three separate single phases. Some equipment in the data center requires single-phase supply and large equipment requires three-phase supply. Single-phase and three-phase power each use different circuit breakers, wiring, and outlets.

Your electric wiring must have the flexibility to change between single-phase and three-phase power, as well as high and low amperage. Let's say you need single-phase 15-amp wires now, but in the future it is possible that larger equipment will be rolled in that requires 40-amp, three-phase power. If you use standard-gauge wire, it will suffice for single-phase, 30-amp power. If your three-phase power requires up to 30 amps, this wire need not be replaced when you change to three-phase power. But, if the three-phase power requires 40 or 50 amps, you must change the wire, and that is a lot of work, time, and expense.

To get around the issue, you can use larger gauge wire from the start (even with single-phase power) because that works for 50 amps or less. This can be safely used for single-phase or three-phase supplies for up to 50 amps of current. If you must upgrade later from single-phase to large-amperage three-phase power, your wiring is already in place and you must replace only two items: outlets and circuit breakers. This is a relatively simple task.

Power Distribution Units (PDUs)

In a small data center, there are one or more power feeds from the power grid or utility company. The power feeds send electricity to transformers, which, in turn, send it to various subpanels. Each subpanel contains many circuit breakers. Power cables from the breakers run under the floor tiles to power outlets. This three-layered layout (subpanels with circuit breaker, cables, and outlets) make changes cumbersome and time-intensive, especially in a live data center. Pulling tiles causes cooling air-pressure problems.

One way to solve the problem is to use *power distribution units (PDUs)*. A PDU is a way to combine circuit breakers, cables, and outlets in a central place in the data center, from where it is easy to power several racks and equipment. Each circuit breaker has wires that feed power outlets. A three-phase, 90-amp feed to a PDU can supply 10 single-phase, 15-amp circuits or 3 three-phase, 30-amp circuits. Since the circuit-breakers, wires, and outlets are all within the PDU, it is easy to work on them.

In 2002, while working at a data center in California, all power outlets connected to circuit breakers in a PDU tripped. This brought down all equipment in a number of racks. The initial guess was a bad circuit breaker or subpanel. When the subpanel was reset, it powered the racks, but it soon tripped again. We recorded the voltage and amps across all racks. We found a faulty power supply in one server. Whenever the server powered up, it caused a voltage spike and tripped the circuit breakers. We had to unplug the server to bring up the subpanel and racks.

A PDU increases the ease of maintenance and upgrades, but there are some downsides. It must be designed to strict city and state electrical codes. PDUs are often custom-made and may take a few weeks or months to manufacture.

PDUs must be designed for reliability and safety. All switches and devices on the front panel must be recessed. Breakers and switches must be guarded or covered to avoid them being accidentally turned off or on. A PDU must have built-in surge suppressors and input EMI/RFI filters to protect against input surges and noise. It must be possible to work on any single circuit breaker without taking down the rest of the PDU.

Electrostatic Discharge (ESD)

Electrostatic discharge (ESD) is rapid discharge of static electricity between two objects that are at different electric potential. It can damage electronic components by changing their electrical characteristics.

There are several ways to dissipate electrostatic charges. Tiles must be properly grounded and have a static-dissipative surface to provide a safe path for static electricity to the ground. Electrostatic mats that are built into the floor and located near data-center entrances force everyone to step on them before they get to the equipment. Do not use any material that generates electricity in the data center. Before touching electronic devices, operators must dissipate charges on their fingers by touching metal doors or racks, and they must (at a minimum) use antistatic wrist wraps.

Key Points

Following are some key points discussed in this chapter:

- You must estimate the power requirements for equipment and HVAC.

- Power in a data center is provided by one or more power companies. They must be reliable and keep you posted on impending outages.

- Power conditioning is required, especially when power from the grid is less than normal.

- Each data center must have its own independent power infrastructure that is composed of a battery-based UPS and generator that are usually diesel-based.

Data
Center HVAC

The sun, with all those planets revolving around it and dependent upon it, can still ripen a bunch of grapes as if it had nothing else in the universe to do.
— **Galileo Galilei**

The equipment in a data center produces a lot of heat. A typical data center uses anywhere from 4,000 to 40,000 kW of power. Most of this power is divided between the equipment (such as servers, storage, and so forth) in the data center and the heating, ventilation, and air-conditioning (HVAC) systems used to keep the data center cool and dry. Temperatures and relative humidity (RH) outside a narrow operating range or extreme swings in conditions lead to device failures and unreliable behavior.

Since data centers expend tremendous amounts of electrical power, it is important to optimize HVAC usage. Because HVAC units operate at all times and require scheduled maintenance at regular intervals, it is critical to have redundant units available in case of HVAC failures and during maintenance windows.

Table 8-1 shows the optimal and acceptable temperature and RH ranges that HVAC must maintain within the data center. Although the acceptable ranges for the equipment are wide, the data center must be kept close to the optimal level to increase the life expectancy and reliability of the equipment. A temperature of 72°F is best because it is easy to maintain a safe RH level at that temperature. Uptime Institute, an organization that measures data-center downtime, says that it has measured upwards of 100°F in racks. A rule of thumb is that long-term reliability of electronics is reduced by 50 percent for every 18°F increase in temperature above 70°F.

Table 8-1 Temperature and RH Requirements within a Data Center

ENVIRONMENTAL FACTOR	TEMPERATURE	RELATIVE HUMIDITY (RH)
Optimal range	70°F to 74°F (21°C to 23°C)	45–50%
Acceptable range	50°F to 90°F (10°C to 32°C)	25–75%

RH is the amount of moisture in the air at a given temperature in relation to the maximum amount that the air can hold at that temperature. If the air holds the maximum amount of moisture it possibly can, its RH is 100 percent (that is, it is saturated). Since warm air expands, its ability to hold moisture increases with a rise in temperature. Since the air in the data center is warmer than the air in the subfloor plenum, its RH will be lower. As shown in Table 8-1, the RH must be kept between 45 percent and 50 percent. High RH will cause condensation and subsequent corrosion of the equipment and low RH (dry air) reduces the capability to dissipate ESD. At RH levels below 35 percent, ESD problems are more prominent. If RH is maintained within the optimal range, it also provides the best time buffer in case of HVAC failures.

Reasons for Strict Environmental Requirements

The inlet air temperature to a rack must be maintained within the temperature specifications required by the equipment manufacturer. It is important to understand the factors inherent in data centers that can lead to severely high internal server temperatures. The cabling, rack doors, and high equipment density decrease the air-flow rate through the servers. There is uneven temperature in front of each rack, depending on the proximity to the nearest cooling tile, and air pressure and temperature disparity below the raised floor. The impact of uneven inlet temperature depends on the HVAC system, aisle width, and tile perforation. A server at the top of the rack may be at 95°F (35°C), whereas another server at the bottom of the rack may be at 75°F (24°C), and that is a difference of 20°F (11°C). The servers on the upper half of the racks are prone to thermal damage.

Therefore, the HVAC system and air flow must somehow maintain the temperature and RH within a narrow range for the following reasons:

- *Servers and storage generate substantial amounts of heat* — The HVAC system must cool the equipment and the air around it to prevent over-heating, abnormal behavior, and damage.

- *Certain areas require more cooling* — Racks with densely packed equipment and areas with large servers and storage devices require more cold air from the HVAC. Manufacturers are making increasingly powerful servers that fit into incredibly thin slots within a rack. They vent more and more hot air.

- *The weather is unpredictable* — If it gets very hot or wet outside, the HVAC system must increase its cooling capacity to be able to maintain the data-center environment within the strict temperature and RH range.

- *Equipment changes within the data center* — If more heat-producing servers and devices are added to the data center, the HVAC system must adapt itself and provide more cooling.

- *Numerous air exchanges* — An office area requires an air exchange every half-hour and air conditioners for office comfort pass about 350 cubic feet per minute (CFM) per ton. On the other hand, a data center with full racks requires an air exchange every minute, and the precision air conditioners must pass at least 500 CFM per ton. If air is not exchanged at a very brisk pace, the cold air from the HVAC will warm up before reaching the racks and servers.

- *High RH causes corrosion and short circuits* — High humidity causes condensation inside or outside the devices. The condensation reacts with metals and corrodes the components. Condensation on dissimilar metals in close vicinity leads to electrolytic or galvanic corrosion. High amounts of moisture react with gases in the air to create corrosive compounds. Water also creates conductive paths and creates short circuits.

- *Low RH causes ESD problems* — ESDs are easily created and cannot dissipate in dry air, especially when RH reaches below 35 percent.

- *Data center activities that can disrupt the temperature profile* — The door may be left open. Tiles are removed for cabling. Some parts of the HVAC system may fail and shut down for maintenance. If the temperature is kept stable at an optimal level, activities in the data center will have less overall impact on the environment and equipment.

Need for Energy-Efficient HVAC Systems

While HVAC is a mandatory requirement in data centers and serves a critical function, it is also one of the most costly operational expenses. Indeed, HVAC has been estimated to account for between 40 and 60 percent of power use in data centers, while servers and all other equipment usually account for another 40 to 50 percent. In normal commercial buildings, HVAC systems consume only one-fourth of the building's energy requirements.

With energy prices climbing, cost-cutting measures in energy consumption are becoming common. It is important to pay attention to inefficient energy consumption rate by HVAC, server, and storage systems. Data centers must consider implementing energy-efficient HVAC systems, smarter temperature- and RH-control devices, and well-designed cooling layouts as essential components of the infrastructure strategy. All this will help lower operational overhead and energy expenses by 15 to 25 percent.

Figure 8-1 shows redundant HVAC systems used at separate data centers.

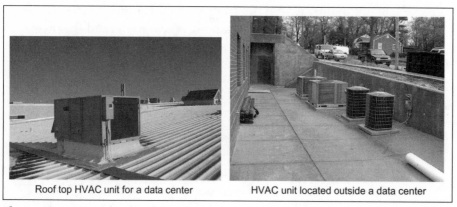

Roof top HVAC unit for a data center   HVAC unit located outside a data center

Figure 8-1   Two redundant heating, ventilation, and air-conditioning (HVAC) systems for two different data centers.

Air-Conditioning Systems

HVAC systems are large, precision air-conditioning systems with a highly effective air-flow mechanism. The efficiency of the system is determined by the capability to cool the air and deliver it to racks and equipment where it is needed. This section describes two common air-conditioning systems in use for large HVACs.

Cold-Liquid Air-Conditioning Systems

This type is useful in hot, desert regions such as Texas and New Mexico in the United States, and in Egypt and the Middle East. Air to be cooled goes into the HVAC unit through an intake. The intake air goes through the following stages before it is sent to the data center:

- The air passes through a set of electrically charged filters that trap dust, certain chemicals, and contaminants.

- The air then passes through a set of coils with very cold liquid. The liquid absorbs the heat from the air, thus lowering the air temperature. The fluid in the coils is sent to cooling towers to release their heat.

- The air goes through a humidifying chamber, which adds an atomized mist of water to the air to adjust the RH.

- Fans are used to force the cold air into the plenum below the raised tiles at a high pressure and velocity.

HVAC units have set target temperature and RH levels. The sensors located at various places within the data center record and transmit the environment temperature and RH level to the HVAC. This feedback helps the HVAC unit adjust its extent of cooling and humidification to reach the target levels.

Dry Air-Conditioning Systems

This type of air conditioning is suitable for humid regions such as Florida and Alabama in the United States, in Singapore, Hong Kong, and in coastal cities such as Kolkata and Mumbai in India. The primary function is dehumidification and, in the process, it cools and cleans the air and removes many airborne bacteria.

Dry-conditioning technology reaches its temperature and humidity targets more rapidly and with far less energy than other equipment. Since it reduces both temperature and humidity, it can be used instead of air conditioning either in warm or cool humid regions where air conditioning is necessary for dehumidification purposes only.

There are three stages in the dry air-conditioning cycle:

1. Collection
2. Heat exchange
3. Regeneration

Collection

The HVAC system utilizes a concentrated and cool solution of lithium chloride, applied as a continuous stream to a soaked, cellulose honeycomb substance. As the solution flows down the surface of the material, it comes in contact with a stream of air flowing in from the outside.

The water molecules in the incoming moist air react with the lithium chloride solutions, thus removing the water content of the air and cooling dirt, particles, and bacteria. An innovative feature of this type of HVAC system removes most of the air-borne dirt, smoke, bacteria, and other particles. The dryer and cooler air flowing out of the air-conditioning system is delivered back if it requires more cooling. Finally the cold, dry air is pumped into the indoor space.

The salt solution that absorbs the moisture and heat becomes diluted and warm. It is then pumped into the heat exchanger.

Heat Exchange

Some portion of the lithium chloride solution is sent to the heat exchanger and a filter, where a heat pump transfers the heat from the salt solution to a regenerator.

Regeneration

Here the lithium chloride salt solution is heated to remove the moisture. The warm solution is then sprayed as a continuous stream over a honeycomb material. As it flows down in a thin film, a stream of air is passed through the media (as in the collection stage). The air picks up the moisture and heat from the salt solution and is then expelled. The salt solution is thus dried and cooled. It is then pumped back to the collection side.

Figure 8-2 shows the stages in a dry air-conditioning system.

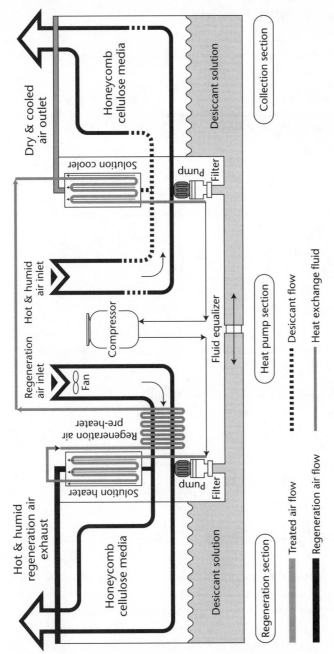

Figure 8-2   Schematic diagram of a dry air-conditioning system.

Air Circulation in a Data Center

The air-flow pattern in a data center decides the equipment and rack layout. Following are some common air-flow patterns:

- *Airflow pattern with subfloor supply and overhead return vents* — The air flow follows the basic convection principles: "Hot air rises; cold air sinks." The pattern is common in data centers with raised floors and has the following stages:

  1. The HVAC unit takes in air, which is cooled and dried.

  2. The air is forced into the plenum (between the subfloor and the tiled floor) and then directed into the data center and racks via cutouts and perforated tiles.

  3. The chilled air goes through the equipment and racks, where it mixes with warm air. As it cools the components, the air gets warmer.

  4. The warm air from the racks rises toward the ceiling.

  5. From the ceiling, the warm air is drawn back into the HVAC unit, where it is cooled and dried, and then forced back into the subfloor plenum.

- *Airflow pattern with overhead supply and return vents* — Data centers without raised floor pump cold air from overhead supply vents. The cold air mixes with warm air that is trying to find its way to the return vents, which are also located above the racks in the ceiling plenum or on the side walls. The contact warms the cold air before it can reach the equipment. The contact also creates minor turbulences above the racks.

Placement of Hardware Racks

Equipment from different manufacturers has different air-flow requirements. However, all equipment placed within a rack must have the same requirement. If two pieces of equipment have conflicting requirements and were placed in the same rack, hot exhaust air from one would enter the other.

Each stand-alone equipment or rack has a *physical footprint*, as well as a *cooling footprint*. The latter is the amount of area a rack or equipment needs to be cooled. Vertically cooled racks (top-to-bottom or bottom-to-top air flow) require less cooling footprint than horizontally cooled racks (front-to-back or side-to-side). The cooling footprint depends on how densely devices are packed within the rack and their heat-generating characteristics. Newer devices pack more electronic components within smaller boxes, thus increasing the heat generated within each device.

It is straightforward to understand the air-flow pattern of cold and hot air if you think of the data center as a closed cocoon. The relative locations of racks within the closed space should be primarily based on the rack's cooling requirements. The secondary factors are the location of the available power connections, as well as breaks in rack rows and structures (such as aisles, columns, entrances, and ramps).

Bottom-to-Top Cooled Racks

This is the most efficient cooling strategy. The cold air enters the rack from the bottom. In raised-floor data centers, the forced air is directed to the equipment via cutout or perforated tiles, placed below the racks. The cold air mixes with the warm air and cools the devices. It is then drawn out through the top of the racks into return vents in the overhead ceiling.

Once the lower portions of the rack get the chilled air, the upper portions do not receive any chilled air from the perforated tiles in the floor. It then draws warmer air from other portions of the room such as the rear of the rack. This leads to a recirculation cell near the top of the rack. Air inlet temperatures near the rack top can be 50°F (10°C) to 68°F (20°C) higher than the chilled air near the perforated tiles. To reduce the rack top inlet temperature, it is necessary to use high-flow rate racks (which have a higher air-flow rate between the front and back of the racks) and tiles with higher larger perforated areas (up to 60 percent).

When racks are added or moved around, it is simple to reposition solid and perforated tiles to direct cold air from the subfloor plenum to the new rack locations.

Figure 8-3 shows an example of this design.

Top-to-Bottom Cooled Racks

For racks in nonraised-floor data centers, the chilled air comes from overhead supply vents in the ceiling plenum. The air is supplied usually from the top into the rack. The air near the lower portions of the rack is much warmer.

Front-to-Front Cooled Racks

As Figure 8-4 shows the air-flow direction in each rack row is opposite to that of its adjacent row.

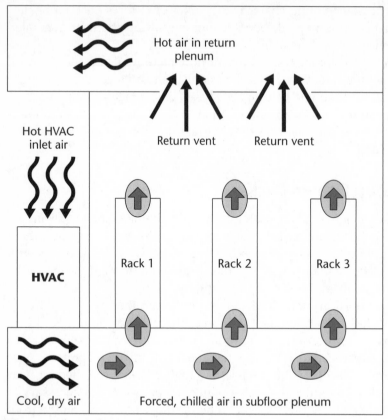

Figure 8-3 Air-flow cycle from HVAC to data center in bottom-to-top or horizontally cooled racks.

The chilled air enters the front of each rack (cold aisle in Figure 8-4) over the entire height of the rack. The air takes away the heat from the equipment as it flows around and inside it, and is later ejected into the other side (hot aisle). The equipment must be facing toward or away from the forced air, as required for optimum cooling.

The racks can be located next to each other with small inter-rack gaps that must be large enough for them to be removed or serviced. The cold and hot aisles alternate. Each cold or hot aisle is shared by two adjacent rack rows.

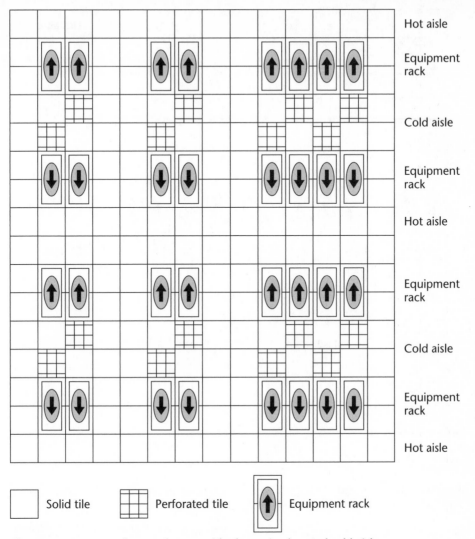

Hot aisle

Equipment rack

Cold aisle

Equipment rack

Hot aisle

Equipment rack

Cold aisle

Equipment rack

Hot aisle

☐ Solid tile   ⊞ Perforated tile   Equipment rack

Figure 8-4   Front-to-front rack rows with alternating hot and cold aisles.

Front-to-Back Cooled Racks

In this design, the airflow direction is the same in all rack rows, as shown in Figure 8-5. This is necessary if the cold air on one aisle cannot be shared by adjacent rack rows. The aisles must be wide enough to prevent hot exhaust air from one row from entering the adjacent row and warming the inlet air in a cold aisle.

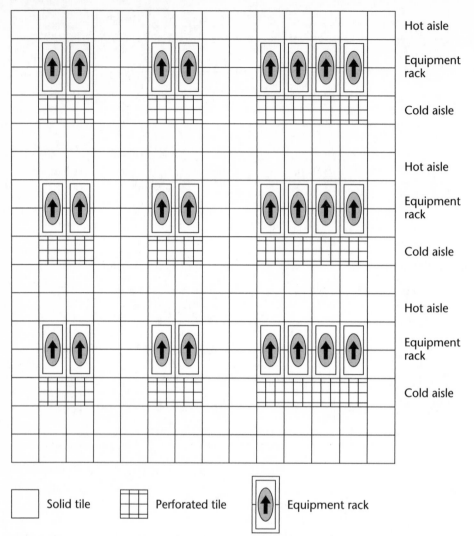

Hot aisle

Equipment rack

Cold aisle

Hot aisle

Equipment rack

Cold aisle

Hot aisle

Equipment rack

Cold aisle

☐ Solid tile   ▦ Perforated tile   ⬚ Equipment rack

Figure 8-5 All racks (front-to-back) have forced air flow in the same direction.

Best Practices

This section contains some general guidelines for optimizing cooling within a data center:

- Data centers should be configured with hot and cold aisles, and racks should be set up back-to-back pointing to the hot aisle and front-to-front facing the cold aisle.

- Devices are designed to expel their own heat in an optimal manner. Your air-flow pattern must be placed to pick up the expelled hot air and transport it to the HVAC.

- Different perforation levels (for example, 25 percent and 50 percent) for tiles in the cold aisle balance air-flow patterns within a data center. Hot aisles should not contain perforated tiles.

- Devices that have lower temperature requirements must be placed on the lower half of the racks, and high heat–generating devices must be placed on the upper half.

- Incoming air-flow rates must be balanced to maintain a uniform temperature along the rack height. Since hot spots are most likely at the rack tops, they must be eliminated by properly directing air flow through the perforated tiles.

- Since additional rack fans or fan trays mounted on rack tops usually impede server cooling, you must have as few of those as possible. If they are used, you must ensure that they contribute positively to cooling efficiency.

- Since cables impede air flow, they must be bundled properly and correct sized cables must be used to keep air-flow passages as open as possible.

Key Points

Following are some key points discussed in this chapter:

- The heat loads within each data center continue to rise at a brisk rate.

- The main objective of an HVAC system is to provide enough cold air flow to maintain a temperature that meets the equipment requirements.

- Cold-liquid and dry air-conditioning systems are two systems commonly used for data-center cooling.

- Data centers are arranged into cold and hot aisles. Since most racks use front-to-back cooling, this arrangement separates the cold air, coming from the perforated floor tiles (in case of raised floor designs) or from overhead chilled air vents (for nonraised-floor designs), from the hot air exiting the rack rears. The rack fronts must face each other in the cold aisle and the rack rears in the hot aisle.

Data Center
Consolidation

In This Part

Reasons for Data Center Consolidation

To achieve the impossible, one must think the absurd — to look where everyone else has looked, but to see what no else has seen.
— **Chinese proverb**

A little history of data center evolution will provide the reasons for its need for consolidation today. Data centers were first commercially deployed in the early 1960s for mainframe computers. There were many mainframe vendors such as IBM, Digital Equipment Corporation (DEC), Univac, NCR, Control Data, Honeywell, and Burroughs. Since then, data centers have evolved steadily. Today, IBM remains the most significant mainframe vendor. Mainframes have their strong points: stability, high utilization rates, capability to host several applications and users, and capability to deliver high service levels and a highly optimized workload management system.

However, because of high costs and the perils of being locked to a single vendor for hardware and software, many organizations migrated to minicomputers (minis) in the 1970s and 1980s. The key players were HP, Data General, Prime, and DEC. Mini-computers were cheaper and did not always require traditional data center facilities, therefore providing more freedom and flexibility to system administrators and application developers. However, the minis, too, had shortcomings. The flexibility led to too many informal procedures and a chaotic IT environment. But, the main cause of the end of minis was the difficulty in porting applications between different minicomputers.

After minis came the world of the distributed computing environment. The servers were rapidly getting smaller and cheaper and could be placed in offices instead of data centers. The leading players were Sun Microsystems, HP, IBM, Silicon Graphics, Inc. (SGI), and DEC. UNIX was the preferred operating system for all of these vendors. For IT organizations, it was easy to administer these servers and port applications between them. Soon, desktops and small workstations were used to develop mission-critical programs and even execute them for business benefits. The low-cost UNIX boxes doubled up as critical servers. All this freedom led to server sprawl and complexity, which have become the foremost reasons for data center consolidation.

Reasons for Data Center Consolidation

Consolidation is defined as the process of bringing together disconnected parts to make a single and complete whole. In the data center, this means replacing several small devices with a few, highly capable pieces of equipment to provide simplicity.

The key reason for consolidation is the sprawl of equipment and processes to manage them. It is absolutely crucial to understand the function of each piece of equipment and related processes before consolidating them. But, entering a data center is like entering the rabbit's hole in *Alice in Wonderland*. Nothing is what it seems to be.

It is also critical to understand the key reasons for consolidation:

- *Reduce the number of servers* — With distributed computing, each server hosted one application and users logged on to the application from their desktops. One application per server made it easy for each group or department to buy, own, and manage whatever it needed. The servers were cheap and small, and it was easy to buy one every time an application was needed. Actually, each application required more than one server. They needed a development server, staging server (to verify application compatibility before moving code to production servers), training servers (for classes and self-learning), and disaster recovery (DR) servers at a remote site. Up to seven or eight servers, therefore, were necessary for each application.

- *Increase usage of storage* — Each server has its own set of direct-attached storage creating storage islands. If a server runs out of disk space, more must be added to that server, even if other servers in the data center have lots of free storage.

- *Reduce IT processes* — There are sets of processes that must be written and followed by everyone for each server and application. Less equipment means fewer processes.

- *Reduce support staff* — All the individual equipment needs support staff to ensure it is humming properly. The servers and applications must be tuned, backed up, patched, upgraded, and protected from internal and external threats. In all metropolitan cities around the world, skilled system administrators, database administrators, and network engineers are hard to find and expensive to retain. Equipment consolidation in a data center will let you get by with fewer support staff.

- *Reduce IT expenses* — Replacing several pieces of equipment with fewer and more capable hardware components helps reduce expenses in several ways. It makes the environment simpler and easier to manage, reduces hardware maintenance expenses, takes up less of the costly data center floor space, and needs fewer processes and staff.

- *Increased service reliability* — With equipment and process consolidation, it becomes easier to centralize management of the IT environment. With fewer processes, the environment can be managed more effectively, which, in turn, gives higher service reliability and uptime and reduced fines caused by missed service level agreement (SLA) commitments. This is one of the most important reasons why several organizations have started consolidating their hardware and processes.

Consolidation Opportunities

The initial and obvious target for consolidation is the number of servers and storage devices. However, as the consolidation process starts off, several other equipment and processes seem ideal candidates. At a high level, you should think of consolidation as a way to reduce the number of devices and number of ways to manage the devices.

Server Consolidation

Some organizations have hundreds and others have thousands of servers. Whatever the number, it is too many for the in-house team to manage. Consolidation is necessary and there are two ways to do so: vertical scaling and horizontal scaling. *Vertical scaling* specifies how you can reduce the server count by running multiple applications on fewer but well-beefed-up servers. *Horizontal scaling* allows you to bear increased workload by distributing it across several replicated servers.

Once you are aware of these consolidation techniques, you can further refine the consolidation by grouping the servers into three broad categories. It is crucial to use the right consolidation technique within each category to ensure adequate performance for random load patterns in the future. Following are the three categories:

- *Front-end servers* — These servers are closest to the user community. The most common technique here is horizontal scaling, where incoming load is distributed among the servers by a load-balancing switch. The architecture calls for many low-end, easy-to-replace servers that have access to the same data on shared or dedicated storage. It is not possible to reduce the numbers of servers, but simpler management practices can be standardized for the set of servers to result in lower total cost of ownership.

- *Application servers* — These run applications and middleware. In most cases, it is possible to replace a large number of application servers with fewer large servers (vertical consolidation).

- *Back-end database servers* — These are high-end servers that run mission-critical databases or applications. They have a large amount of compute resources and are clustered to ensure almost 100 percent uptime. These are ideal candidates for vertical consolidation.

Storage Consolidation

In 2003–2004, a company I was working with in California wanted to consolidate about 40 terabytes (TB) of distributed data into a single high-end storage subsystem for two primary reasons: performance and utilization. The CPUs on servers connected to individual, local storage were running at 70 percent I/O wait. Despite best practices, their storage islands had a utilization of around 35 percent.

It is estimated that the amount of storage doubles every two years. The ever-increasing volume of data and its management has made the cost of storage a significant portion of the total cost of ownership of an IT environment. All this has led to various ways to consolidate storage.

Following are important advantages of storage consolidation:

- *Increased storage utilization* — A recent study showed that an average about of 20 percent to 40 percent of storage space is utilized if it is accessible by only one server. If a server requires more storage, it is a lot easier to buy new storage and add it, rather than migrate storage connected to another server (although other servers may contain a lot of unused, free space). The utilized percentage is higher if storage is accessible by several servers.

- *Easier data backup and recovery* — Backing up disparate storage devices requires more configuration and time than the same quantity of storage within a subsystem.

- *Affordability* — It is easier and more affordable to increase the reliability, availability, and serviceability (RAS) and remote data replication for a single high-end storage subsystem than for several small disconnected storage devices.

Following are four types of storage consolidations:

- Storage consolidation by consolidating servers
- Various servers linked to a single storage subsystem
- Consolidation with storage area network (SAN)
- Consolidation with network attached storage (NAS)

Storage Consolidation by Consolidating Servers

As applications (previously running on separate hosts) are moved to a single host, the storage must also be moved. The consolidated storage is now available to all the applications, as shown in Figure 9-1.

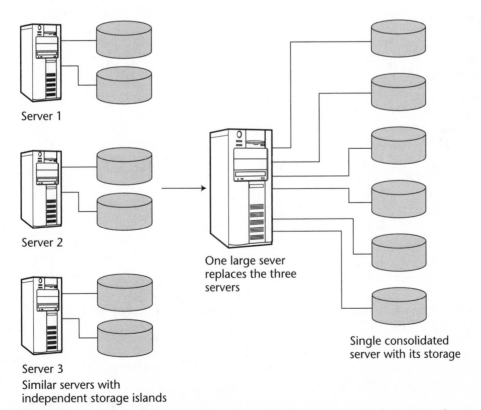

Server 1

Server 2

One large sever
replaces the three
servers

Server 3
Similar servers with
independent storage islands

Single consolidated
server with its storage

Figure 9-1 Consolidation of servers and associated storage to a single server and storage pool.

Various Servers Linked to a Single Storage Subsystem

This form of storage consolidation is the most popular type. Applications from various servers can be migrated to a single server if the servers are of the same platform (UNIX, Windows, and so forth). IT organizations rarely run enterprise-wide applications on one vendor's platform, but rather have a mix of Windows, Linux, and other operating systems. Instead of providing storage islands for each platform, a single, large storage subsystem can be used for all platforms (see Figure 9-2). It is important to ensure that storage drivers are available for various platforms.

Consolidation with Storage Area Network (SAN)

SAN is a set of storage-switching devices that connect a set of servers to a shared storage pool. SAN could be one or more switches or hubs. In Figure 9-3, the SAN fabric is composed of one switch. Any server connected to the SAN fabric can access and use any of the storage devices connected to it.

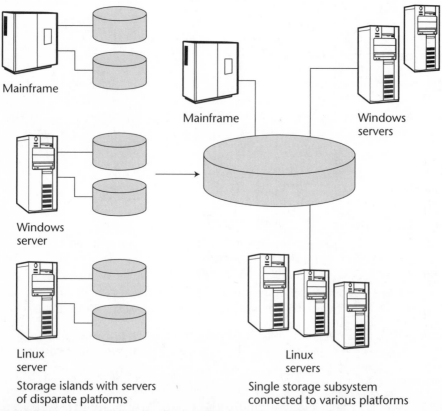

Mainframe

Mainframe

Windows
servers

Windows
server

Linux
server

Linux
servers

Storage islands with servers
of disparate platforms

Single storage subsystem
connected to various platforms

Figure 9-2   Consolidation to a direct-attached single storage pool.

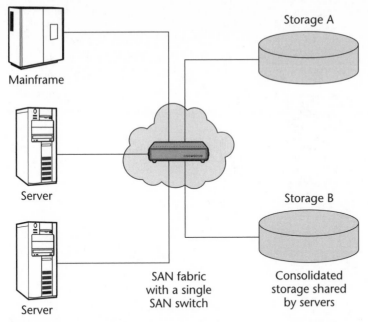

Figure 9-3   Consolidation of storage to a SAN-attached single pool.

Consolidation with Network Attached Storage (NAS)

Unlike the previous three consolidation forms, NAS allows servers to access storage over the network using networking protocols such as Network File System (NFS), Server Message Block (SMB), Common Internet File System (CIFS), Hypertext Transfer Protocol (HTTP), and File Transfer Protocol (FTP). Historically, NAS has its roots in department-level applications such as file and Web servers (see Figure 9-4). Now it is commonly used in enterprise-wide mission-critical applications.

Network Consolidation

Consolidating a heterogeneous network into a robust, homogeneous environment requires good process and people management. When faced with several heterogeneous networks, any one of the following three approaches can be taken to combine the network topologies and processes:

- The first strategy is to maintain a diverse network and consolidate people. There are no equipment or network topology changes. However, the headcount is reduced and a combined team is tasked to manage all the existing networks. All the networks compete for the reduced personnel time and the result is inferior network management and support.

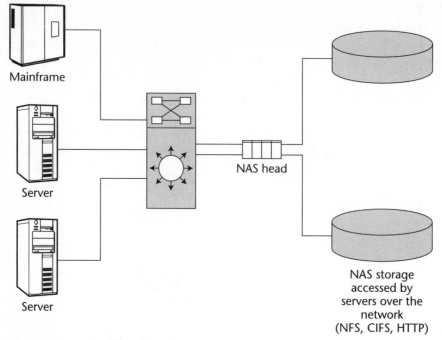

Figure 9-4 Consolidated storage accessed by server using network protocols such as NFS, CIFS, and HTTP.

- The second strategy is to select a pre-existing network and expand it to provide services to the entire organization. Servers and devices from other networks are slowly migrated to the selected network. It is important to select the network on technical merit and not on prior ownership or political pressures. Even otherwise sagacious and well-run corporations are guilty of not doing so. Because of the high business dependence on network services, a poor selection or consolidation plan will result in chaos, upheaval, reduced availability, and unplanned outages.

- The third strategy is hybridization. It involves a review and unit-cost analysis of all existing networks and new candidate solutions. The goal is to architect a solution that is a either a hybrid of the existing networks or a completely new network. The next step (after review) is to create a detailed, stage-by-stage migration from the existing network to a new solution. The plan must pay attention to application dependencies and acceptable latencies for users.

Small-scale testing must precede network conversion. Despite successful tests, each conversion stage from the existing network to a consolidated network must have a back-out plan. Applications that perform well in tests may suffer from application time-outs and failures and may cause user frustration when subjected to real-life loads.

A new set of best practices must be written and evangelized for those who will manage the new network.

The impact of server and storage consolidation on network devices can be adverse or favorable. The consolidation of servers and applications to fewer physical locations will require a higher network bandwidth in those locations if traffic is mostly from users and applications outside the consolidated applications. The amount of traffic could also remain unchanged, since applications or users are not altered. In certain cases, there could be a decrease in required network bandwidth since the applications are now on the same server and do not need the network to inter-communicate.

Application Consolidation

The first task is to select applications that are right for consolidation and those that are not. It is easy to identify and earmark applications that will not be consolidated. These include the following:

- Geographically dispersed servers configured for disaster recovery purposes

- Security servers such as gateways, terminal servers, firewalls, and virtual private network (VPN) servers

- Servers whose access is highly restricted because they contain sensitive data or logs

- Software whose vendors have definite needs of a dedicated server for proper functioning

Now identify applications that can be consolidated:

- *Database instance* — A common consolidation technique is to place several instances of a particular database on the same server. However, you should not place different databases (such as Oracle, DB2, Sybase, or Informix) on the same server because of their kernel and patch requirements.

- *Application sets* — It is important to identify a pattern in the applications usage. Which set of applications send data to or receive data from another group of servers? Because applications process data sequentially and often do not simultaneously compete for the same server resources, the applications can be consolidated to fewer servers. The net result is decreased network traffic and improved communication between applications.

It is important to distinguish between two types of bindings between applications: active and loose. In *active binding*, the applications have a two-way and prompt interaction. Examples are the communication between Web and middleware applications and between ERP applications and database servers. If these tightly bound applications are moved to one high-end server, the result would be decreased network load and faster interaction.

In *loose bindings*, the applications receive and process data and then transmit it to another server. All these happen at predetermined times. An example would be a database server that transfers its data to the reporting server once every night. The reporting server processes and forwards it to a data warehouse server, which in turn updates several data mart servers. All these applications are interdependent but do not occur at the same time, and communication does not persist throughout the day. Consolidating actively bound applications to a single server decreases the network load and has better payoff.

Service Consolidation

This is another popular consolidation used in corporations with several departments. Historically, every department implements its own services (such as file, print, and authentication) using software from vendors it is most conversant with. Soon there are too many such services in the organization. The complexity and cost of administration increases dramatically. Users from different departments cannot share information and services because of software incompatibilities. A common example is authentication services such as Lightweight Directory Access Protocol (LDAP).

The solution is to configure a single enterprise-wide service and deploy it across all departments. Many corporations have consolidated authentication services to a single sign-on application for all Web-based applications that require user login and password. Printers on some campuses have also been consolidated to a single print server that manages all network printer queues.

Process Consolidation

Some environments within a data center are chaotic, with servers rebooting all the time, high CPU, swap and disk usage alerts, low service quality, and reduced data availability. When such an environment is compared with another environment that runs in a problem-free and smooth manner, it is easy to see that the missing ingredient is a set of well-followed standards and processes. To improve service quality and availability, and to reduce operational costs, you must consolidate processes and train support staff on those processes.

Staff Consolidation

One important outcome of well-consolidated resources and processes is standardization and ease of management. This, in turn, leads to reduced requirement of the number of support staff.

Another aspect of staff consolidation is that staff must be well-trained on the data center processes. It is estimated that 80 percent of service outages are caused by staff negligence or process breakdown, and 20 percent is caused by hardware or technical faults. It is necessary to address people and standards issues to avoid low service quality and reduced availability.

Key Points

Following are some key points discussed in this chapter:

- The key objective of consolidation is to stop equipment proliferation, reduce IT costs (staff and equipment-related), and increase resource utilization levels.

- Most corporations start with the goal of consolidating servers, but it quickly expands to targeting other areas such as storage, network devices, applications, services, IT processes, and staff.

CHAPTER 10

Data Center Consolidation Phases

Three grand essentials to happiness in this life are something to do, something to love, and something to hope for.

— Joseph Addison

Consolidation is a complex project that spans over several months, or even a few years. The process must be split into several phases, and each phase must be managed by a dedicated, detail-oriented, and experienced project manager. It will impact several IT teams, user groups, and business units. Getting each party to agree to the same goals, agenda, and action items and, at the same time, maintaining executive sponsorship for the project is a tall order.

It is therefore necessary to break the giant task into phases and each phase into subphases, which is the main theme of this chapter. Assign enough time and human resources to each phase.

Following are the main phases discussed in this chapter:

- Phase 1: Study and document the current environment.
- Phase 2: Architect the target consolidated environment.
- Phase 3: Implement the new architecture.
- Phase 4: Control and administer the consolidated environment.

Phase 1: Study and Document the Current Environment

This is the first and the most important stage. During this stage, you understand all facets of the IT environment that are targets for consolidations, as well as collect and document all technical information. What are the servers, storage, networking, and application requirements? How do these intercommunicate and how do they depend on each other?

This phase can be very detailed and time-consuming. Therefore, it is vital to decide on the amount of details required and then stick to the requirement. If the evaluation is cursory, then significant details will not be understood, which will later lead to service outages, user frustration, and possible failure of the project. At best, it would lead to expensive rearchitecture and failure to remain within the allocated time and budget. If too much data is collected, portions of the data would be irrelevant. It requires an in-depth technical and business know-how to judge the extent of information required for the entire project.

Evaluate Application Requirements

The purpose of this step is to understand the function of each application, as well as the flow of data from server to server and process to process. There are several information sources. The best source, however, is speaking with system administrators, application managers, and developers. Another way is to delve into existing documents, if available. Whereas third-party applications usually have documentation, home-grown processes and applications have very little. In such a situation, you are left by yourself to use OS and application tools to collect requirements.

Following are the important tasks that help you in understanding applications:

 Data flow — Document all software components, their inter-dependencies, and how they communicate with other servers or applications. Figure 10-1 shows an example of data flow. The front-end Web servers receive requests from the end-users through a load-balancer. The Web servers communicate with the application servers, which, in turn, talk to the database servers.

Besides the data flow for providing services, you must understand the communications required for administrative upkeep (such as access from central login or gateway servers, monitoring stations, and backup servers). At some stage, you will wonder if you should dig deeper for more information. The right question to ask yourself is, "Do I have enough to rearchitect the environment?" For simple physical consolidations, details are unnecessary. For logical application consolidations, details about port numbers, network access control lists (ACLs), and intervening routers and load balancers are required.

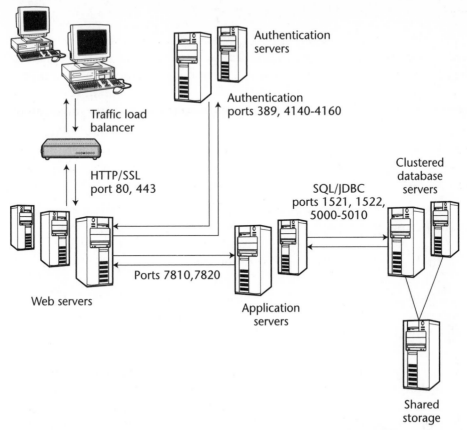

Figure 10-1   Sample data flow in an environment.

 Interview architects, developers, and system administrators (SAs) — The objective of speaking with these people is to get details on configuration and server dependencies for the next two phases (Phase 2 [design] and Phase 3 [implementation]). Various areas must be covered, such as applications release levels, operations, code development, service level agreements, previously determined downtime windows, user expectations on uptime, testing, planned software and hardware upgrades, and expected increase in user load. Ensure that you understand and document at all points. If, after the meeting, you come out thinking, "I do not know what he or she was trying to explain," the meeting was a waste of time.

Also consider how the future software upgrades and changes in user load will impact the application infrastructure. You must make provisions in the new consolidated architecture for all foreseen changes.

Evaluate Hardware Infrastructure

After applications have been profiled and documented, it is time to assess the hardware platforms. Several OS and third-party tools are available to help with this assessment. The important task at hand is to verify the current inventory along with the configuration and to estimate the resource utilization. The depth of these investigations must be limited to the server and applications that will be consolidated.

Verifying current inventory — Get a list of all servers, network devices, and storage subsystems that provide the infrastructure for applications on the consolidation list.

For servers, document the machine make and model, as well as details about resources (such as the number and type of CPUs, memory, attached disks, and access to NAS, and peripheral cards such as HBAs). Also, get a list of software components such as OS release, application versions, a list of home-grown scripts and programs, and kernel patch levels. This process is detailed, but it is also the easiest to automate via a script. You must have enough information to recreate a similar operating environment on another server during Phase 3 (implementation).

For network devices, list the number of ports, router port configurations, and load-balancer incoming traffic and outgoing traffic settings. In the new environment it is necessary to open ACLs for required ports for traffic to communicate.

Estimating hardware resource utilization — There are several OS commands and third-party applications to estimate the server utilization such as CPU, memory, and I/O and network bandwidth. A commonly used tool on UNIX platforms is System Activity Reporter (`sar`). It records the utilization of CPU, memory, swap, and disk I/O rate at regular intervals such as 5- or 10-minute intervals. The system collects data over the time interval and records it in a file at the end of the interval.

It is true that OS tools are free and expedient, but they are limited to text-based reports on utilization. Third-party monitoring software and performance suites have graphical display capabilities, which certainly provide a great deal of ease compared to manually scanning many pages of numbers. Performance suites have a modeling component that uses the historical utilization data to predict performance for systems with different resources when placed under differing loads. This feature is particularly useful for server sizing and consolidation.

Evaluate Storage Requirements

Over the last few years, the demand for more and more storage has far exceeded the demand for more servers or network bandwidth. Adding storage to existing servers was least disruptive and, consequently, it was added whenever needs arose. Because of all the factors listed earlier in this chapter, storage consolidation has become a key project in most data centers.

While assessing storage requirements for the subsequent phases of consolidation, you must document the following:

- *Storage hardware* — What is the quantity of direct-attached, SAN, and NAS storage for each server? Are the logical units (LUNs) or devices configured as hardware-RAID volumes? Is there cache on the storage subsystem? Is the data replicated to a remote site for disaster recovery, and, if so, how is it copied over and how frequently?

- *Logical configuration* — What are the volumes set up? Are they RAID or logical volume management (LVM)–based volumes? Are the volumes used raw, or are they file systems?

- *Data* — What is the type and quantity of data that resides on the storage devices? What percentage of the storage is actually used up by data? Is the data copied from another server, and, if so, how frequently is it refreshed?

Like server data collection, storage data gathering can be automated. There are also many third-party applications for this purpose. They provide the percentage used, usage trends, predicted data usage (based on historical trends), and data categorization by size, type, or access data.

Evaluate Networking Requirements

Network assessment is necessary to make provisions for enough bandwidth in the new architecture. The network is used not only for server communication but also for NAS and for storage over IP (SoIP). There are two important areas within network evaluation: setup and performance.

- *Setup* — This refers to the LAN topology, link speeds, and technologies used for the network such as 100baseT Ethernet, gigabit Ethernet, fiber distributed data interface (FDDI) and asynchronous transfer mode (ATM). For WAN topologies, the setup comprises a number of T1, E1, frame relay, and integrated services digital network (ISDN) links, as well as pattern and amount of usage.

- *Performance* — Network performance is the amount of network bandwidth that is actually used by the traffic. You must be aware of the maximum throughput of the links, the percentage utilization at different times of the day, and the allowable network latency for the users.

If you are consolidating several servers within a single data center, you do not have to worry about anything more than the client-server LAN configuration. But if you are consolidating servers currently located at different data centers around the world, you must document the current link speeds between servers and users and provide for enough throughput between the new consolidated server(s) and users around the world.

It is also critical that the network reliability and speed from the consolidated server to administrative networks (such as NAS and backup networks) are not negatively impacted after consolidation.

Evaluate Operations Requirements

Staff and the processes they follow are always an important, and yet overlooked, part of an assessment process. Studies have shown 80 percent of data-center and service outages are caused by people or process mishaps, and only 20 percent are caused by purely technical problems. It is essential to identify the processes and make suitable updates to make them pertinent to the post-consolidation environment. It is also important to update the staff skills regarding various data center activities (such as server, storage, and network management, security, disaster recovery, asset management, and hardware resource utilization management).

During one DC-consolidation project at a customer site, the client deployed a third-party application to facilitate server auditing and administration. The software reduced the time and effort required by SAs, and they were able to get by with fewer SAs.

Evaluate Risk

Consolidation, like any other IT project, has its fair share of risks. Like all risks, the main risk is looking the other way when it is staring you in the face. You do not have to like it, but you have to understand all the risks and implement ways to alleviate them.

The first step is to identify all the risks. The risk could be financial. It may be difficult to keep expenses within the allotted budget. The initial estimate of the project duration could be at risk if the parties you rely on do not respond or complete their parts in time. The level of expertise within your staff members could be inadequate for the work as it unfolds. Also, the scope of the project must be kept within the predetermined bounds. Your executive support might wither if the champion or main sponsor were to leave the corporation or division.

Once you have looked at the risks in the face, you must make a list of dos and don'ts to reduce their brunt. For example, to get a constant and high degree of executive support for your project, keep management posted on all happenings. Ensure that all parties are aware of deadlines, and give them as much notice as possible. One way to mitigate risk is to use common sense.

Phase 2: Architect the Target Consolidated Environment

In this phase, a consolidated design is architected using data from the evaluation phase.

What are the features of a good design? First of all, it must contain solutions to most of the key problems identified earlier. The design must specify overall organization of servers, storage devices, and network equipment, as well as the relationships between them. This stage does not specify specific hardware models, server resources, equipment details, or software versions or patches. These will be specified in the implementation phase.

There are several steps in design:

1. Analyze the collected data.
2. List architectural requirements.
3. Create an initial architecture.
4. Size all equipment.
5. Create a prototype of the proposed solution.
6. Test the prototype.
7. Revise the proposed architecture.
8. Document the proposed architecture.

Design Step 1: Analyze the Collected Data

A good way to analyze the data is first to classify it into various broad categories, such as

- Availability data
- Maintenance-related data

■ Data center and equipment support processes

■ Staff skill set information

■ Performance data for servers, storage, or network equipment

Data gathering (in Phase 1) is different from analyzing.

Design Step 2: List Architectural Requirements

The information must now be used to create architectural requirements. Table 10-1 shows the various architectural necessities that must be included in the proposed solution and is derived from data gathered in Phase 1.

A central problem in any consolidated environment is keeping traffic and applications from negatively impeding others that must share the same environment. Another problem is that a single failure would bring down many services. A good architecture must therefore identify and have enough resiliency to mitigate such issues.

Table 10-2 shows a few inherent problems with consolidation and suggested remedies.

Table 10-1   Important Data and Required Architectural Configurations

DATA	ARCHITECTURAL REQUIREMENT
Equipment failure does not cause outages of Web services.	New consolidated design must have redundant Web servers with two front-end load-balancing devices.
Database server contains 5 TB customer data and 6 TB of of unused storage space. It is expected to grow at 20 percent per year. The database services must have 24 × 7 and high-service uptime.	You need two high-end clustered servers for database with storage of about 30 TB.
Database must be backed at the end of each day. There must be a full database backup once a week for off-site tape storage.	The backup server must be capable of high throughput. Schedule online, hot backups every weekday and a cold, offline backups every Saturday night.
Because of financial constraints, NAS storage must be used for database server. However, the performance must be high.	Set up an isolated network that is dedicated to NAS storage devices and servers that use the NAS.

Table 10-2   Problems with Consolidated Environment and Remedies

PROBLEMS CAUSED BY CONSOLIDATING APPLICATIONS AND RESOURCES	REMEDIES
Failure of the central hardware would cause outage for many applications.	Several critical applications rely on the central hardware, which must have redundant hardware. Fault tolerance is increased by having redundant components such as power supplies, fans, mirrored cache, and RAID storage. Most high-end servers, storage subsystems, and network equipment already have built-in redundancy.
Network communication for different applications contend for bandwidth on the same network pipe.	Provide a dedicated network for certain traffic. Examples are a dedicated network for backup, NAS access, and production. For certain lightweight traffic that can be grouped together for easier management, build a network with high bandwidth and fault tolerance.
Server failure causes all applications to fail.	Keep applications on separate servers. If you have a high-end server (for example, SunFire 15K, HP Superdome, and IBM p690), partition the server into independent domains, each running an independent OS instance. Cluster two or more servers that must run critical applications.
Management of security configurations for different applications becomes a nightmare in a single consolidated network.	Use virtual local area network (VLAN) configurations to separate different network interfaces within one or more servers.
Applications within a server are subjected to unwanted resource contention.	Use OS tools (such as the `nice` command on UNIX) or commercial scheduling software (such as BMC Software's Control-M or CA's Maestro) to intelligently schedule and allocate resources to interactive and batch jobs. Grid computing uses server profiles, user requests, and preconfigured policies to schedule workload to different servers. This is ideal for compute-intensive and number-crunching applications.

(continued)

Table 10-2   *(continued)*

PROBLEMS CAUSED BY CONSOLIDATING APPLICATIONS AND RESOURCES	REMEDIES
Since more network ports and users need access to applications in the centralized subnet or VLAN, several servers are impacted by a single security breach.	Security must be tightened at the OS and application level via strict user access controls. This is done by using `sudo` and `ssh` on UNIX, activity logging, encrypting all network traffic, and providing the minimum file access for users.

Design Step 3: Create an Initial Architecture

During this step, a solution is created. The main components are server, storage, and network architecture. General guidelines, policies, detailed technical operating procedures, training needs, and staff consolidation must be identified and documented. It is important that the initial design address all requirements identified in Design Step 2. A high degree of fault tolerance is necessary for centralized areas that support multiple services.

- *Server architecture* — Each application is assigned a server with enough direct-attached, SAN-, or NAS-based storage. At this stage, it is enough to say that the server will be a high-end, medium, or low-end server. CPU, RAM, and network interfaces will be detailed in Phase 3. It is important to specify if the servers will be standalones, clustered, or a load-balanced farm.

- *Storage architecture* — All application data must be placed on a centralized SAN- or NAS-based storage. Local and direct-attached storage devices must be used only for OS, application binaries, and swap space. The overwhelming benefits of using centralized SAN- or NAS-based storage have been detailed earlier in this chapter.

- *Network architecture* — Set up dedicated networks for high-traffic communications such as backup, production, and NAS storage. Some networks where traffic from different servers must co-exist (such as administrative network) must have adequate bandwidth.

Design Step 4: Size All Equipment

Once you have listed all the requirements for the consolidated environment, you are now ready to size the servers, storage, network equipment, and other devices. The proposed capacity must be enough to meet the minimum acceptable performance levels during peak load periods. It is therefore important to use these two data (expected performance and peak loads) actively at this stage.

Design Step 5: Create a Prototype of the Proposed Solution

A *prototype* is a scaled-down version of the actual proposed design. It is created to discover potential problems in the proposed design, especially compatibility issues between applications when they are centralized to a few servers and networks. It is helpful to keep the prototype environment until the implementation (Phase 3) is complete.

The servers and storage used to build the prototype environment need not be the same models with the number of CPUs and memory that will be used in the production environment. If you have an IBM p690 server with six domains, you can use an IBM p650 server and build six domains. The size of the storage, database, and workload need not be the same as production. However, it is important that the versions of the operating systems, application binaries, and software fixes are the same as the production environment.

In short, the prototype environment used for testing has scaled-down hardware but has software, network ACLs, and VLAN set up like the production environment.

Design Step 6: Test the Prototype

Once a test prototype is built, it must be tested. The goal is to discover fallacies that may be very expensive before going to the next phase. Testing must cover the following vital areas:

- *Setup* — Test whether all servers, storage devices, applications, device drivers, and network settings work well together. It is important that the applications coexist in harmony.

- *Security* — The wide range of open ports and users in the same environment should not reduce the security.

- *Functionality* — Application, backup, monitoring, and access from and to various networks (backup, administrative, storage) must work. Test that the results from the applications are correct.

Most of the testing must be automated via commercial packages or scripts. These tests will be necessary to verify setup during implementation.

Design Step 7: Revise the Proposed Architecture

At this step, you tune the proposed solution based on the test outcome. It is expected that some tests will fail and some will pass marginally. A failed test may point to serious problems in the proposal and may warrant a complete design redo.

Beware of marginal failures. Some may point to deep, systemic problems, while others can be ignored as having been caused by the use of scaled-down hardware. It is difficult to gauge how much you must change due to a marginal failure. Even if you make design changes, you must be aware of the failure modes during the implementation phase (Phase 3) and be on the lookout for their reoccurrence.

Design Step 8: Document the Proposed Architecture

A clear documentation of the following areas is necessary (and must include these areas):

- Important assessments from the gathered data
- Architectural requirements
- Proposed architecture
- Prototype layout and its hardware, network, and software components
- Test results
- Design modifications prompted by the test results

The documentation will assist others within the organization to rearchitect and consolidate their IT environment.

Phase 3: Implement the New Architecture

After evaluating the existing environment, creating a design proposal, and testing a prototype, and with the revised documentation in hand, it is time to start building the consolidated design. Following are the main steps in the implementation phase:

1. Draft all low-level specifications.
2. Construct the new environment.
3. Create a data migration process.
4. Back up data in the old environment.

5. Migrate data and application services to the new environment.

6. Train the operations staff.

Although all this work seem like a tall order, it is easier than Phases 1 and 2.

Draft All Low-Level Specifications

Write a detailed layout of the environment that will be configured. If equipment will be installed in a to-be-built data center, you must write out the physical environment specifications. For applications that will be migrated to a new server, you must decide and write out the server model and resources, storage configuration, and software to be installed. Nothing can be left out. Think as if someone else will take the documents, build it as outlined, and deliver it to you after a month. The design specification must contain some or all of these:

- Physical environment such as power circuits, floor space in the data center, racks, and environmental requirements (such as cooling and humidity).

- A description of the servers, including manufacturer, model, amount of memory, CPUs, adapters, and attached storage.

- Network specifications for administration, backups, NAS, production, and so forth.

- Operating system, including patches, network management, and backup software.

- User applications such as Web server software and databases. Specify the vendor and software release numbers.

The specification document will depend on the type of consolidation, but the more detail you provide, the better, because most of the work may be performed by others.

Construct the New Environment

This is the first act of constructing the target environment and preparing it for data to be migrated over. The building blocks are as follows:

1. *Build the physical environment* — Ensure that the data center area allocated for the new environment has adequate floor space, electricity outlets, cooling, and patch panel ports, and enough space to bring in the equipment from the docks. After the equipment is relocated here, there must be enough space around it for staff to work while installing OS and connecting cables.

2. *Build the servers and install the operating environment* — Once you have the servers in their respective tile locations, it is time to install the OS. Once, at a customer site, I was involved in installing about 20 servers. Five of those did not boot past their power-on self test (POST). I had to call the vendor, and they had to replace several faulty components over the next three days.

   Use automated OS install programs. They save time and effort. Popular technologies are Linux Kickstart, Microsoft Unattended Installer, Solaris Jumpstart, HP-UX Ignite, and IBM Automated Install Manager (AIM).

   Ensure all the network connections are working well. Set up all routing tables. You must be able to access the server from the backup, administrative end-user networks.

   Mirror the operating system to another local disk. It is a common best practice and saves you from an OS installation and setup after an OS disk failure. Also, install and configure administrative applications such as network management client software and backup client software. It is best to take a full backup. During the ensuing installation and reconfigurations, it may be necessary to revert a few files or the entire OS.

3. *Attach storage subsystem* — NAS- or SAN-based storage should be used for storage consolidation. Check storage vendor documentation for the order of installing device drivers (if applicable) and connecting the storage subsystem.

   Like the servers, the storage subsystem must be thoroughly tested and burned-in before configuring logical volumes on the devices and migrating data.

4. *Install application software* — Now that the OS and devices are set up, it is time to install and configure the applications. It is best to install them from vendor distribution CDs. Although the same version may be installed on the old server, avoid the temptation to copy entire application directories or configuration files from the old server. But, you must use the old server configuration as a guide. When you must configure several instances of the same application (for example, four Apache instances or two database instances), use non-default names, directory locations, and filenames for each configured instance.

Create a Data Migration Process

Now that the servers, storage, and applications are ready and tested in the new environment, it is time to move all data from the old to the new servers. Data integrity, ease of migration, and minimum time taken and service outage are key objectives.

Data migration is simple if you have a large downtime window or a small data set for a non-database application. NFS mounts, common backup utilities (such as `cpio`, `dump`, and `tar` on UNIX) and transfer programs (such as scp, FTP, and tape backups) work well in such scenarios.

Complex migrations are those where the available downtime to transfer data is very small and for databases that reside on raw logical volumes. Application managers and database administrators must outline the migration process because it usually requires application-specific utilities provided by the vendor.

Database export/import programs are often used to back up an entire instance of a database and later import it on another instance. This is a well-tested, versatile procedure when moving data to a different server, OS, or database version, or another platform.

The migration process must be tested at least three times on a part of the new environment, part of the old servers and storage, or on the prototype. Each test must be monitored and timed, and results must be noted for communicating to staff involved in data migration and administration of the environment.

It is also imperative to create a backout process, should something go wrong. The backout process must include two items:

- The conditions under which you should stop progress and initiate the backout action plan
- The steps required to put services back to the old environment

Back Up Data in the Old Environment

After building the new environment and deciding on the migration process, you must make a full backup before going ahead with the service migration. The backup must be made just before you migrate the data and services. It is important that you also test the backup media to verify that you can retrieve data from it. The backup tapes will be required if the same storage media is being attached to the new environment and it gets damaged during migration.

Migrate Data and Services to the New Environment

There are certain prerequisites before data migration. The data and service migration time must be during off-hours and all teams (network, application, database and system administrators, and facilities) must be involved and available within short notice. The time period should be one when no other large-scale work or network activity is scheduled. Network and systems monitoring must all be in place. Migration of data entails three steps:

1. Migrate data.
2. Cut-over services to the consolidated environment.
3. Test services and tune services.

The data migration steps outlined earlier should be followed. The team that tested the steps must be involved in actual migration. OS utilities can be used to transfer files and small directories. It is faster to transfer the database export files over the network, unless the data must come from a remote location. In that case, backup tapes must be shipped in advance and data can be copied to the target environment before the scheduled downtime. Once the data is copied over, test the environment. Tune it as best as possible before directing services over to the new, target environment. Tuning parameters (such as network and I/O settings, kernel parameters, and shared memory settings) must be configured now.

Migrating services involves changing the IP addresses of consolidated servers to those that are used by users. This can be host-based services. Alternatively, you can change service IP addresses in DNS to be the IP addresses of the consolidated servers. This is preferred for services that go to a virtual IP address on a load balancer or a cluster of servers.

Testing and tuning the consolidated services are critical and should be done within the scheduled migration downtime. Monitor server and network load, application behavior, and result integrity. Test the new applications for functional accuracy. If any of these are not up to the desired level and cannot be remedied within reasonable time, it is imperative to start the backout process.

Train the Operations Staff

Training is critical to ensuring high uptime of services from the consolidated environment. However, good documentation is a prerequisite for proper training of personnel that must support the services and hardware. There are two important questions: What level of training should be provided, and when should it be provided?

The level of training should match the environment's setup. Modern servers, storage arrays, and network devices are feature-filled and have layers of complexity, various applications, and their exclusive management interface. Basic training of the hardware configuration, OS, and applications must be supplemented by group meetings and formal knowledge-exchange sessions. Low-level how-to's are more important than architectural concepts.

When should the training be held? Not too soon before the consolidated environment is deployed for live production use. It is ideal to schedule the training sessions about one month before the migration. People will forget the material if taught too much in advance before hands-on usage, and if training is held too close to migration, say a week before, they will not have time to review the training material before delving into the trenches.

Phase 4: Control and Administer the Consolidated Environment

Sticking a new environment within an otherwise smooth operation is annoying. A consolidated set of applications sharing the same servers, resources, and infrastructure is an added nuisance. It requires diligent planning and tough operational processes to allay the impact.

The Sarbanes-Oxley Public Company Accounting Act of 2002 (www. sarbanes-oxley.com) requires publicly traded U.S. corporations to set up and follow strict access controls and change-tracking policies, especially for servers containing financial data.

Formal policies and tight change management is far from the world of distributed client-server computing. Application developers and administrators do not like to work by someone else's rules. Policies, used by some within data centers, have no following among system and data administrators in the UNIX and Windows world. Tools are created, and servers and storage are provided as and when necessary. Such behavior gravely impairs smooth operations within a centralized environment.

It is crucial to develop a set of robust policies and operational procedures to improve the following:

- *Increase accountability* — Each person's activities on important servers can be easily tracked. This is necessary to undo commands if necessary and make each individual liable for his or her work. At one client site, all UNIX administrators were forced to log in as themselves and use sudo for root-level commands to force work logs.

- *Increase availability* — A recent Gartner report has shown that only 20 percent of service downtime can be attributed to hardware failures, 40 percent is caused by application and software errors, and 40 percent is caused by operational errors made by humans. To increase service uptime, it is therefore necessary to make the staff follow preset policies and a set of well-documented, technical procedures.

- *Increase security* — When a set of rules is accepted and followed by all levels of IT management, there is less temptation to ignore the rules and do tasks that would compromise security.

To maintain an acceptable level of accountability, service availability, and security, it is necessary to identify and prioritize areas that can most negatively jeopardize required service levels. The following are important categories to manage an environment shared by many applications and users:

- *Execution control* — This covers policies for scheduling various data center resources among the users of the consolidated environment. The resources include staff time and hardware such as servers, network, and storage. It also includes formulating and enforcing business processes that impact several user groups.

- *Problem management* — This is about identifying and resolving problems, hopefully before they flare up. Most corporations have a 24×7 network operations control room or a help desk that serves as a first-step in problem resolution. They have a list of internal staff members that they can tap into for problems outside their technical capabilities. They also have access to folks who can manage the relationship with customers during the sensitive period of "why can't anyone get the server up right now?" Problem management is crucial to delivering promises service levels.

- *Change control* — This includes things such as scheduling activities or changes in the environment, performing the work, and documenting the results of the change. These changes include hardware changes, reboots, software upgrades, configuration changes, and user account changes. Being able to perform such tasks effectively and quickly, while adhering to all the required policies, is a critical factor determining the delivery of the promised services levels.

  Many corporations have a change-control board that must review and approve all scheduled changes. The board must ensure that no stakeholders in the consolidated environment are negatively impacted by the proposed change.

- *Asset control* — In an environment that is not centralized, there is a one-application-to-one-server relationship. Each user group knows of the servers that it uses. In a consolidated environment, the asset control team (or person) must set up a computing model to determine the resource usage by each user group. This is necessary for hardware and IT staff charges that must be based on usage.

  Another important work for the asset control team is to acquire and track all used hardware and decommission hardware that is not being used. Every piece of equipment must have an asset tag identification (that is, a unique corporate-wide number assigned to it). It eases documenting details for a wide range of devices in a database.

■ *Personnel management* — This includes staff recruitment, training, and proper use of the staff-at-hand. Staff consolidation is an important goal for centralizing services. You must ensure that the right number of employees, with the correct skill sets, are assigned to each work.

Key Points

Following are some key points discussed in this chapter:

■ The high-level consolidation phases are assessment of the current environment, architecting the target consolidated environment, implementing the environment, and managing the environment.

■ Consolidation phases are assessment, architecture, implementation, and administration.

■ Assessment is a critical phase where you must evaluate servers, applications, dependencies, HA deficiencies, resource (storage, server) utilization, performance bottlenecks, redundant processes, and the pain points that you hope to alleviate.

■ In the architecture phase, you draft an initial solution, create a test prototype, test the migration process, and make final changes to the solution.

■ The implementation phase requires execution of the detailed step-by-step plan, often during a scheduled downtime.

■ The administration phase requires training, setting up robust policies, documenting all operating procedures (such as problem and change management), training the support staff, and handing over control to them.

Data Center Servers

In This Part

Server Performance Metrics

A moment's insight is sometimes worth a life's experience.
— Oliver Wendell Holmes

This chapter describes several criteria for determining server benchmarks, as well as methods used to decide on the right amount of server resources required to meet certain workloads. On the one hand, there is no need to buy the fastest and most expensive equipment. On the other hand, you must avoid getting caught with servers that cannot keep up with the growth of your environment, servers on the vendor's end-of-life list, and those that have a high maintenance expense.

As network and computer hardware become faster and less expensive, it is expected that everyone will try to get the best. It is human nature to want the fastest that can be afforded. But, how do you know if your existing toy is good enough? Enter performance metrics — an incessantly evolving set of parameters (or benchmarks) that describe the current utilization and maximum capabilities. They have been developed by various organizations.

What Is a Benchmark?

A *benchmark* is a standard of measurement. A *computer benchmark* is a set of programs that performs work or operations on a system and returns back the capability of the tested configuration. It defines the speed and throughput of the system. *Speed* is how fast the system can complete a predetermined set of activities. *Throughput* is the amount of workload that can be done per unit time.

The advantage of a benchmark is that it allows us to run the same set of operations (or workload) on different configurations, thereby providing a comparison. Since no two applications are the same, it would be ideal to test different configurations with your own applications to compare them. But, that is very difficult in the real world because of lack of expertise, time, money, feasibility, and other constraints.

Benchmark Organizations

The leading general benchmark organizations are Standard Performance Evaluation Corporation (SPEC) and Transaction Processing Council (TPC). Proprietary benchmarks established by these two nonprofit organizations have been widely accepted by most hardware and software vendors to provide performance numbers for their products. Table 11-1 lists various benchmark organizations.

Table 11-1   Benchmark Organizations

ORGANIZATION	WEB SITE
GPC (Graphic Performance Characterization)	www.spec.org/gpc/
Linpack	www.netlib.org/linpack/
NotesBench Mail	www.notesbench.org/
Pro/E	www.proe.com/
SPEC	www.spec.org/
STREAM	www.cs.virginia.edu/stream/
TPC	www.tpc.org/
VolanoMark	www.volano.com/

Aspects of System Performance

To understand performance units, it is important to identify important performance aspects. The most important ones are latency, throughput, utilization, and efficiency.

Utilization

Utilization is the fraction or percentage at which a particular resource is being used with respect to its maximum. A 10-Mbits/s network link delivering data at 2 Mbits/sec has a utilization of 20 percent. Utilization is interesting because it tells us if the resource is over-configured, which in itself is not a problem unless you have users complaining about high latency.

If utilization is high (for example, the disk I/O is always at 60 percent or 70 percent), that could be a problem. Most server resources such as CPU, memory, disk, and network links cannot deliver at the rated throughputs at high utilization.

Latency

Latency is the amount of time that a user must wait for response from the system. Data over fiber cables has a latency of 5 microseconds per kilometer. A DR site that is 1,200 km away would, therefore, have a latency of 6,000 microseconds, or 6 milliseconds (1200×5) to receive data from the primary site. Latency is of prime importance to users because they immediately feel the adverse impact of high latency.

Throughput

Throughput is the amount per second. Examples are NFS operations per second (NFSops/sec), transactions per minute (tpm), disk data transfer rate of megabytes per second (MBps), and network transfer rate of megabits per second (mbps). Such units are widely used in industry to specify transfer rates.

It is interesting to compare throughput and latency. A system with a high throughput would provide low latency (or quick responses) if the load is low. But, if the system is bogged down with too much work, latency would be high and users will feel the delayed responses. IT architects and sizing teams are mainly responsible for recommending systems that can meet organizational needs and have adequate throughput. Users, on the other hand, need an environment with low latency so that they do not have to sit around waiting for responses.

One way to illustrate this is through the example of a water pipe with a diameter of 2 feet that gives you a throughput of 20 gallons of water per second if no one else is tapping out water before it reaches you. That's good throughput and you will get 100 gallons in 5 seconds. But, if there are several others before you who are tapping out water, the decreased water pressure may get you only 2 gallons/second, and your latency is 50 seconds. Now that's a long wait for a user.

It is intuitive to say that systems with high throughput will have low latency. This is usually true, except when the load on the system is so high that, despite the fact that the system is working at high throughput, users have to wait for their submitted jobs to complete. Users, therefore, are subjected to high latency.

Efficiency

A system that expends fewer resources to accomplish a quantified amount of work is more efficient than another that must expend more of its resources to do the same work. You may have enough network and disk bandwidth to service 1,000 users, but if each user session uses CPU resources in an inefficient manner, you may run into high-CPU-utilization problems with only 100 users.

Factors Impacting CPU Performance

The processing speed of a CPU depends on cache and clock speed.

A cache is a special high-speed storage device made of static RAM (SRAM) instead of slower and cheaper dynamic RAM (DRAM, which makes the main system memory). By keeping as much information in the SRAM, the computer avoids accessing the slower DRAM. Memory caching is effective because most programs access the same data or instructions over and over.

Following are common types of memory caching:

- *Level 1 (L1) cache* — This is on-board cache for data and instruction. These are built into the CPU architecture. Sun Sparc processors have 64 KB of data cache and 32 KB of instruction cache. Intel Pentium CPUs have 32 KB and 64 KB of data and instruction cache. IBM RISC processors have 256 KB and 128 KB of data and instructions cache. L1 cache is faster than L2 cache, and L1 is the first place the CPU looks when searching for data. If data is not found in L1, it searches the contents of L2 cache.

- *Level 2 (L2) cache* — This is external SRAM and sits between the CPU and DRAM. The Level 2 cache is larger in size than the Level 1 cache.

- *Level 3 (L3) cache* — This exists on some models of high-end servers. Some IBM servers have up to 512 MB of L3 cache.

Clock speed (MHz or GHz) of the CPU is the frequency, usually in megahertz (MHz) or gigahertz (GHz). IBM p690 servers have 1.9 GHz CPUs.

SPEC Benchmarks

Standard Performance Evaluation Corporation (SPEC), a nonprofit consortium, was formed in 1988 by a group of server and workstation vendors. Its members include several hardware manufacturers and software developers, universities, consultants, and customers. Their objective is to ensure that the industry has a set of metrics to evaluate computer systems. To that end, the consortium develops and maintains a standardized set of relevant benchmarks that can be used by vendors to measure and compare their high-performance, latest-generation computers.

SPEC CPU benchmarks are designed to compare compute-intensive workloads on different computer systems. Table 11-2 shows some of the SPEC-architected and endorsed CPU metrics. The SPEC CPU2000 and CPU2004 are designed to provide performance measurements that can be used to compare compute-intensive workloads on different computer systems.

Table 11-2   CPU Benchmark Suites Developed by SPEC

BENCHMARK SUITE	BENCHMARK	DESCRIPTION
SPEC CPU 95 (has been retired since June 2000)		The integer performance was measured by SPEC int95, SPEC int_rate95, and SPEC int_rate_base95. Floating point performance was measured by SPEC fp95, SPEC fp_rate95, and SPEC fp_rate_base95.
SPEC CPU 2000	SPECint2000 or CINT2000	Used to measure and compare compute-intensive integer performance.
	SPECfp2000 or CFP2000	For measuring and comparing compute-intensive, floating-point performance.
SPEC CPU2004		As of 2004, SPEC is working on identifying applications that could be used for the next CPU-intensive benchmark suites, SPEC CPU 2004.

The following SPEC benchmarks reflect microprocessor, memory architecture, and compiler performance of the tested system (*xxxx* is either 2000 or 2004). The ratio for each SPEC integer and floating-point benchmark is calculated using a SPEC-determined reference time and the run-time of the benchmark. A higher score for the same workload indicates "better performance."

SPECint*xxxx* (CINT*xxxx*) and SPECfp*xxxx* (CFP*xxxx*) are used to measure CPU-level (not system-level) performance. The "C" stands for "Component." Users running integer-based applications will find SPECint*xxxx* relevant. Those working with floating point computations such as mathematical simulations and scientific applications find SPECfp_rate*xxxx* and SPECfp_rate_base*xxxx* relevant.

There are two ways to measure CPU performance. The first is the speed to complete a single task and is measured as SPECint*xxxx* or SPECfp*xxxx*. The second is the number of tasks that the computer can accomplish within a certain time. This rate measurement is called SPECint_rate*xxxx* or SPECfp_rate*xxxx*. It is used for multiprocessor machines.

SPEC provides the test suite as source code, which must be compiled before it can be run. This gave rise to another discrepancy between server vendors. SPEC provided the nonbase and base options such as SPECint*xxxx* and SPECint_base*xxxx*. Compilation for nonbase benchmarks are flexible and you can use any number of performance or optimization flags during compilation. But, compilation for base benchmarks must have no assertion flags and a maximum of four flags that must be used in the same order for all benchmark runs. The base metrics are required for all reported results.

SPEC Integer Benchmarks

A few leading SPEC integer benchmarks are described here:

- *SPECintxxxx* — This is the SPEC component-level benchmark that measures integer performance and is abbreviated as CINT*xxxx*. The result is the geometric mean of 12 normalized ratios (one for each integer benchmark) when compiled with aggressive optimization for each benchmark.

- *SPECint_basexxxx* — This is the result of the same tests as SPECint*xxxx* but when compiled with conservative optimization for each test.

- *SPECint_ratexxxx* — This is the geometric average of 12 normalized throughput ratios when compiled with aggressive optimization for each benchmark.

- *SPECint_rate_basexxxx* — This is the geometric average of 12 normalized throughput ratios when compiled with conservative optimization for each benchmark.

SPEC Floating-Point Benchmarks

Following are SPEC floating-point benchmarks:

- *SPECfpxxxx* — This is the SPEC component-level benchmark that measures floating-point performance. These tests are included in the CFP*xxxx* benchmark suite. The result is the geometric mean of 14 normalized ratios (one for each benchmark) when the programs are compiled with aggressive optimization for each benchmark.

- *SPECfp_basexxxx* — This is the geometric mean of the same 14 tests as SPECfp*xxxx* but when compiled with conservative optimization for each benchmark.

- *SPECfp_ratexxxx* — This is the geometric average of 14 normalized throughput ratios when compiled with aggressive optimization for each benchmark.

- *SPECfp_rate_basexxxx* — This is the geometric average of 14 normalized throughput ratios when compiled with conservative optimization for each benchmark.

SPEC Web Benchmarks

A few leading SPEC Web benchmarks are:

- *SPECweb99* — This benchmark is used to evaluate the performance of Web servers by specifying the number of conforming, simultaneous connections the Web server can support using a predefined workload. The SPECweb99 test harness emulates clients sending the HTTP requests in the workload over slow Internet connections to the Web server.

- *SPECweb99_SSL* — This is the number of conforming, simultaneous SSL encryption/decryption connections the Web server can support using a predefined workload.

- *SPECweb2004* — This consists of SSL and non-SSL workload such as e-commerce and banking. The test configuration also includes a lightweight back-end application and database server that answers queries for the front-end Web server.

SPEC OpenMP Benchmark Suite

Following is the component of the SPEC OpenMP benchmark suite:

- *SPEC OMP* — This measures performance based on OpenMP (`www.openmp.org`) applications. The benchmark suite is adopted from SPEC CPU 2000 programs. It is used for needs of engineers and researchers to model large, complex tasks and places heavy demands on CPU and memory.

SPEC NFS Benchmarks

Following is the component of the SPEC NFS benchmark suite:

- *SPECsfs97_R* — In December 1997, SPEC released its new system file server (SFS) benchmark. It is used to measure the speed and request-handling capabilities of network file services (NFS) computers. It includes NFS protocol version 2 and version 3 and support for TCP, as well as UDP network transport.

SPEC Java Benchmarks

TPC has several JAVA benchmarks. This section describes a few leading ones:

- *SPECjAppServer200x (x is 1 or 2 or 4)* — SPEC Java Application Server is a multitier suite for measuring the performance of Java 2 Enterprise Edition (J2EE) servers. It measures the performance of Java Enterprise application servers using a subset of J2EE APIs in a complete end-to-end Web application. It exercises all major J2EE technologies and underlying infrastructure implemented by compliant application servers (such as the hardware, network, JVM software, JDBC drivers, Web container, EJB container, servlets, and JSPs).

SPEC Graphics Benchmarks

The following graphics benchmarks reflect the performance of the micro-processor, memory subsystem, and graphics adapter:

- *SPECapc benchmark* — The benchmark consists of a certain number of graphics-intensive and CPU-intensive tasks. The total number of seconds required to run each test is normalized based on a reference machine. The normalization process ensures a scoring system where a bigger score is better.

- *SPECviewperf benchmark* — This benchmark is a predictor of graphics subsystem performance (primarily graphics bus, driver, and hardware) and its impact on the overall system performance without creating a full overhead of an application. It is a good performance predictor of graphics applications that generate a similar OpenGL command stream when not bound by other component-level bottlenecks. Larger values indicate better performance.

■ *SPECapc Pro/Engineer 2000i2 benchmark* — PROE2000I2_2000370 was developed by the SPECapc committee to measure all areas of system performance relevant to Pro/E users on a UNIX or Microsoft work-station equipped with a three-dimensional display device. The bench-mark includes eight tests that are run to measure performance in five categories: CPU, I/O, wireframe graphics, shaded graphics, and file time. Scores are then compiled for individual tests and calculated as weighted composites for each of the five categories and as an overall composite. Larger numbers indicate better system performance.

SPEC Mail Benchmarks

Some widely used SPEC Mail benchmarks include the following:

■ *SPEC MAIL 2001 benchmark* — This benchmark is designed to measure the capabilities of a system to act as a mail server servicing e-mail requests based on standard protocols such as SMTP and POP3. The benchmark suite measures the throughput and response time of the mail server with real-world network connections, client workload, and I/O transfer rates.

■ *SPEC IMAP 2003* — This benchmark is designed to measure the perfor-mance of corporate e-mail servers for processing e-mail requests based on SMTP and IMAP4.

Linpack Benchmarks

The Linpack Benchmark is a measure of a computer's floating-point rate of execution. It is determined by running a computer program that solves a dense system of linear equations of different array sizes. It is a numerically intensive test that has been used for many years.

The Linpack Benchmark report is entitled, "Performance of Various Com-puters Using Standard Linear Equations Software." The report lists the perfor-mance in megaflops per second (Mflop/sec) of a number of computer systems. (One Mflop is 1 million floating-point operations. Each operation is a 64-bit addition or subtraction.) A copy of the report is available at www.netlib .org/benchmark/performance.ps.

- *Linpack DP (double precision)* — The results are measured in megaflops per second (Mflop/sec) or millions of 64-bit floating point operations per second. The computation array size is 100.

- *Linpack SP (single precision)* — The array size is 100 and the result is measured in Mflops per second. The operations are in 32-bit floating point.

- *Linpack TPP (toward peak performance)* — The array size is 1,000. The results are measured in Mflops.

- *Linpack HPC (highly parallel computing)* — The benchmark solves the largest system of linear equations possible. The results are measured in gigaflops (Gflop), which is equivalent to 1,000 million floating-point operations per second.

TPC Benchmarks

The Transaction Processing Performance Council (TPC) specifies benchmarks that control the database world. These benchmarks reflect the performance of the microprocessor, memory subsystem, disk subsystem, and some portions of the network.

The TPC consortium has provided the following benchmarks.

TPC-C

This was approved by TPC in 1992 and is a popular yardstick to measure the online transaction processing (OLTP) capability for a given hardware and software configuration. TPC-C is more complex than its previous OLTP benchmarks (such as TPC-A) and includes a mixture of update-intensive and read-only transactions in an OLTP environment with numerous transaction types and complex database format and execution structure. It simulates a complete computing environment where a group of users execute transactions against a database.

The TPC-C compliant database is composed of nine types of tables and a varied range of record and population sizes. The benchmark is centered around principal activities (or transactions) of an order-processing environment (such as entering orders, recording payments, checking status of orders, monitoring the level of stock at the warehouses, and delivering orders). Although this sounds like a wholesale supplier, it represents any business that must distribute, manage, and sell a product or service.

TPC-C includes a wide breadth of real-business components, such as the following:

- Concurrent execution of several complex transaction types
- Several online terminal sessions and users
- Online and deferred transaction execution modes
- Moderate system and application execution time
- Transaction integrity — atomicity, consistency, isolation, and durability (ACID) properties
- Intensive disk I/O rates
- Contention on data access and updates
- Database consisting of many tables with a broad mix of sizes, attributes, and relationships

All references to TPC-C results must include the tpmC, the associated price-per-tpmC, and the availability date of the configuration:

- *tpmC* — TPC-C is reported in transactions per minute and abbreviated as tpmC. It is throughput measured as the average number of transactions processed per minute during a valid hardware and software TPC-C configuration run.
- *$/tpmC* — TPC-C benchmark price/performance ratio is obtained by dividing the cost of buying and maintaining the hardware configuration by the measured tpmC for the system. The cost includes hardware purchase price and 3-year, 24×7 maintenance support for the system and software.

TPC-H

TPC-H is an ad hoc decision-support benchmark where users do not know which queries will be executed against the data (hence the "ad hoc" label). Preknowledge of the queries cannot be used to optimize the database and, therefore, execution times are expected to be very long. The queries and the data populating the database in this suite of tests have broad industry-wide relevance.

TPC-H is used for decision-support systems that scan large volumes of data, execute queries with a high degree of complexity, and provide answers to critical business questions. It includes the following:

- *QphH* — This is the TPC-H Composite Query-per-hour performance metric. It reflects several aspects of the system to process queries of TPC-H and is based on a mean of many TPC-H queries, insert tests, and delete tests. It measures the capability of the system to give a single user the best possible response time by harnessing all available resources.

- *QthH* — This is the throughput metric of TPC-H and is a classical throughput measurement characterizing the capability of the system to support a multiuser workload in a balanced way. A number of query users are chosen, each of which must execute the full set of queries in a different order. In the background, there is an update stream running a series of insert/delete operations.

- *$/QphH* — This is the price/performance metric for the TPC-H. The price includes the purchase price of hardware and software, and a 3-year, 24×7 support agreement for all hardware and software in the tested configuration.

TPC-R

Like TPC-H, TPC-R is a decision-support benchmark but allows additional optimizations based on advance knowledge of the queries. The test suite consists of business-oriented queries and concurrent data changes.

- *QphR* — This is TPC-R Composite Query-per-hour performance metric. It reflects numerous aspects of the system such as database size, query-processing capability when queries are submitted by a single stream, and query throughput when queries are submitted by concurrent users.

- *$/QphR* — This is the price per TPC-R performance metric for a tested configuration. The price includes hardware and software purchase price and maintenance support (3 years).

TPC-W

TPC-W is a benchmark for transactional Web-based e-commerce business-to-business and business-to-consumer environments. It was introduced in February of 2000 and specifies a workload that simulates customers browsing and buying products from a Web server in a controlled environment. The configuration includes security, shopping carts, credit card validation, and load balancing.

The workload simulates typical real-world features such as the following:

- Several client browser sessions
- Dynamic page generation with database updates
- ACID properties for transactional integrity
- Concurrent execution of several complex transaction types
- Contention on data access and updates

The primary TCP-W metrics are the Web Interactions per second (WIPS rate) and price per WIPS rate for the hardware and software configuration:

- *WIPS rate* — This is the performance metric reported by TPC-W. It is the number of browser interactions processed per second that can be sustained by the configuration under test. The interactions simulate the activity of a retail store and are subjected to a response-time constraint.

- *$/WIPS* — This is the associated price per WIPS rate for the tested configuration.

Obsolete TPC Benchmarks

This section describes a few previously widely used but now obsolete TPC benchmarks:

- *TPC-A* — This was issued in 1989 and made obsolete in 1995. It was used to measure update-intensive online transaction processing (OLTP) applications.

- *TPC-B* — This was issued in 1990 and made obsolete in 1995. It was used to measure database stress tests characterized by significant disk input/output and specified the maximum number of transactions per second (tps) that a system can process.

- *TPC-D* — This represents a broad range of decision-support (DS) applications that require long running and complex queries against large, complex data structures. This was approved in 1995 and withdrawn in 1999.

NotesBench Mail

The NotesBench Mail workload simulates users reading and sending e-mail. A simulated user will execute a prescribed set of functions four times per hour and will generate e-mail traffic about every 90 minutes. Performance metrics are as follows:

- *NotesMark* — This is the server capability measured in transactions/minute (tpm).

- *NotesBench users* — This is the number of client (user) sessions being simulated by the NotesBench workload.

- *$/NotesMark* — The ratio of total system cost divided by the NotesMark (TPM) achieved on the Mail workload.

- *$/User* — This is the ratio of total system cost divided by the number of client sessions successfully simulated for the measured NotesBench Mail workload. The total system cost is the price of the server under test and clients, including hardware, operating system, and software licenses.

Key Points

Following are some key points discussed in this chapter:

- A server benchmark is a measurement of performance or task execution speed.
- Factors such as amount of resource utilization, latency, throughput (amount/second), and resource efficiency impact overall performance.
- There are several industry metrics such as SPEC CPU, Web, NFS, Java, Graphics, and Mail benchmarks; Linpack benchmarks to measure floating-point computation speeds in megaflops per second; TPC benchmarks for database performance; and NotesBench Mail metrics for e-mail servers.

CHAPTER 12

Server Capacity Planning

If you take too long deciding what to do with your life,
you'll find out you've done it.
— **George Bernard Shaw**

I have been asked the following:

- How much CPU and RAM should I have in my database server to service 2,000 requests from front-end application servers?

- My world-wide e-mail server must service 10,000 clients. Could you let me know how my single Linux mail server must be beefed up?

- How many and what type of servers do I need to build a Windows 2000 Active Directory environment for 1,500 current users, soon to be 2,500 users?

Sizing one or more servers is an important portion of systems management. Once the characteristics of applications are understood, it is a relatively simple task. The key is to break the resource requirements into two categories: *system-wide category* and a *per-process category*.

People tasked with having to recommend a configuration for an environment must have two sets of information: *what service is required* and *what service a particular configuration can offer*. Given a set of goals such as predicted workload, acceptable end-user performance, and cost limitation, one must forecast a set of server resources that together are able to satisfy the goals. The task is complex and too prone to inaccuracies.

Server Sizing and Capacity Planning

Server sizing is an estimate of hardware requirements based on applications, anticipated activity, and satisfactory performance levels. For example, to meet the needs of 3,000 end users, you require two load-balanced application servers with four 1.3 GHz CPUs and 8 GB of RAM, and one back-end database server with 8 CPUs and 10 GB of RAM.

Capacity planning is a two-phase process. In Phase I, you run tests to measure utilization and performance given a certain amount of hardware resources and activity. In Phase 2, you project the amount of hardware resources required to support larger workloads. The distinction from sizing is that you have technical performance data to make a projection, rather than simply providing an estimated quantity.

Nevertheless, both sizing and capacity planning are difficult and prone to inaccuracies because of the following reasons:

- Sizing and capacity planning constitute a prediction of the future that has too many unknowns and variables. How will the users utilize the applications? How will the hardware, operating system, and applications work together? What will be the extent of performance tuning? The very foundation of the prediction is not accurately predictable.

- The technical landscape is changing constantly and rapidly. By the time a server configuration is sized up and understood, some component has changed before it can be deployed.

- The computing environment has become too complex. Gone are the days of one computer configuration with one application. New generations of hardware platforms and software products have layers of tuning parameters and complexities.

- It is impossible to put together a sizing team with experts in every subject matter. It has been found that sizing teams even in large corporations are made up of a few individuals and vendors. It is not possible to accurately size a server with high-level general information.

- The biggest unknown is the user community. An assumption such as "after 1 year, we will have 6,000 users accessing the application via a Web interface and another 2,500 using text-based interface" will rarely turn out to be true after 1 year.

Given all the vagaries, it is astonishing that capacity planning can be mastered and treated as a science. It is also true that most server estimates that work satisfactorily after implementation are those that are oversized in more than one way and therefore more expensive This happens because it cannot be said with conviction that a server with certain resources will meet all its needs, but it can be safely claimed that a particular configuration is too undersized to meet its objectives.

To perform a proper sizing estimate, the entire complex configuration of servers, networks, peripheral devices, operating system, applications, and user interfaces must be viewed as a chain of connected components. The server consists of CPUs, memory, disks, buses, adapters, and software. The network is composed of switches, routers, firewalls, links, and TCP/IP, which keep it humming.

A system's performance is calculated by that of its slowest link. In other words, data flows between the components at the speed of the slowest link, which could be a software application that processes one block of data at a time, even if the network is providing data from a remote file server at 10 MB/sec. In some cases, the disk I/O rate of 500 blocks per second could be the bottleneck for the system.

The methodology to identify the slowest link during server sizing is also used to tune an implemented environment. Network and server tuning is essentially an after-the-fact assessment and bottleneck investigation. Sizing and tuning are nothing but identification and remediation of the slowest link. The entire gamut of connected components, along with their capabilities and deficiencies, is system architecture.

The goal of server sizing is to remove bottlenecks and liberate the flow of data. This is sometimes attained by adding more and more hardware resources, but this is hardly an appealing way to solve problems. This chapter describes ways to help identify potential bottlenecks in an architecture and those that are not really cause for worry.

Identifying the Slowest Link

At an abstract level, a server processes and transfers data between various components such as disk, buses, memory, CPU, and the network. The data from disk is moved to cache and memory, where it is processed by the CPU and sent to the requesting client over the network pipe. Data must travel along several links such as fiber channel link to disk, backplane to memory bus, memory to CPU bus, and network pipe to another host. The slowest link must be identified and remedied during the sizing phase. After implementation and during system tuning stage, the performance must be studied to identify and increase the bandwidth of the slowest link.

Let's take a simple example. Let's say you have to measure the network-based data transfer rate from Server A to Server B, which are in a gigabit Ethernet subnet. You can use any software utility to transfer a set of files from A to B. There are several concurrent activities: A reads the files from disk, A processes the data, data is transferred over the network, B processes the data, and B writes the data to disk. The slowest operation is probably how fast Server B writes data to disk, unless Server B has very high CPU processing capabilities and high-speed high-cache disk subsystem with striped volumes. It is difficult to stress or fully utilize the gigabit link, and the transfer rate recorded is far less than the maximum potential of the connection.

Capacity Planning for Servers

This section describes ways to estimate the amount of hardware required within a server with a goal to satisfactorily meet forecasted loads. Specific examples are provided for CPU and memory because they are the most important variables. Other factors such as adapter speed, network link speed, and server backplane frequency have a few alternatives, and it is prudent to get the best available option. The quantity of disk storage depends on the data size and future data demands.

The entire capacity planning is divided into three phases:

- *Phase 1* — Define the customer's requirements.
- *Phase 2* — Measure or estimate current resource utilization.
- *Phase 3* — Size the new server.

Phase 1: Define the Customer's Requirements

The first task is to assess the workload for the new environment. The second task is to understand what the user expects to be a satisfactory latency (or response time). It is important to collect enough information about the business needs, applications that will be used, and type and amount of workload of batch jobs and acceptable response time.

CPU Requirements

When estimating CPU load, several assessments of intended load must be made. Will large sorts be done in memory or on disk? Will the users do a lot of parsing and complex form navigation? Will the extent of mathematical manipulation on the rows and columns be too taxing on the CPU?

Memory Requirements

Sizing memory is important. Adding generous amounts of memory is expensive, but it should not be undersized to cause swapping, which is a big performance deterrent.

For database systems, the system global area (SGA) must be sized correctly. The maximum number of application users determines the amount of required memory, I/O throughput, and CPU for the application and back-end database servers. The type of operation performed by users must be noted, especially the amount of shared images help privately and in memory, as well as the amount of sorting and SQL parsing. These impact the amount of memory captured by the user.

For application servers, memory is the most important factor determining the maximum number of concurrent users. The other two factors are disk access rate (measured in I/O operations per second, or iops) and CPU.

Disk Requirements

When estimating the number and size of required disks, a couple of factors must be considered:

- It is important to spread the I/O across several spindles. This is easy with several, small-sized disks attached directly or via a SAN fabric to the server. If the disk storage subsystem has a lot of cache and presents virtual disks that are not a direct 1:1 with the physical disks, spreading I/O across spindles may be difficult and unnecessary.
- For databases servers, tablespaces, binaries, and redo logs must be kept on separate disks. One disk for each redo log is especially helpful for database archiving.

Maximum Latency Requirements

Latency is the time duration that a user has to wait for answers. The goal of understanding CPU, memory, and disk requirements is to provide enough for low latency. One common cause of high latency is poor disk I/O rate. For database servers, high latency is caused by large disk sorts, lack of indexes, poor indexing techniques, number of rollback segments, and size of redo log buffer. It is important to identify the worst-case acceptable response time for various types of workloads.

Type and Amount of Current Workload

Identify the transaction types and their consumption of memory, CPU, and I/O usage. Also, get the peak and average number of application users. The workload must be quantified as light, medium, or heavy.

Future Requirements

A customer I once worked with was looking to migrate 2,500 application users from a text-based to a GUI interface. The migration would happen (if at all) after 2 years. Yet the customer needed enough free slots in the new servers for additional CPU and memory in the servers to avoid any replacement after the migration.

An environment, once set up, is usually in place at least for a year before it is upgraded and in use for several years before replacement. It is, therefore, necessary to provide enough resources for at least 1 year. To accommodate for increased usage beyond that, the server must be built to have enough free CPU and memory slots. If applications are going to be upgraded, make sure that the new requirements are included in the current sizing.

Be generous in allowing for errors in workload prediction. A key source of wrong data is the prediction of future requirements. Incorrect load estimations compromise all successive predictions. It is necessary to use the worst-case load scenarios for all estimates. Ensure that the future estimates provided by users are reasonable.

Phase 2: Measure or Estimate Current Resource Utilization

In this phase, we must estimate or measure CPU and memory use for each computation or user. The resources used are measured by testing existing applications under current workload. If applications are not available, the amount of resource used must be estimated from data available from vendors, independent test organizations, or in-house studies. It will be approximate, at best, but the factor of safety applied in Phase 3 does not require precise numbers.

CPU Workload

CPU workload caused by a particular computation is measured by multiplying the amount of used CPU capacity and the amount of time the CPU is under load. CPUs are rated by various industry-standard units. A convenient standard is SPECfp2000 (CFP2000) units. A set of computations that causes a 25 percent utilization of 1,800 CFP2000 CPU for a duration of 30 seconds causes a total CPU workload of 13,500 CFP2000-seconds units (0.25×1800 CFP2000 $\times$ 30 seconds).

Workload is measured in performance units-seconds (for example, CFP2000-seconds). Another feature of CPU workload is that it is not CPU specific. A set of computations that generates a workload of 15,000 CFP2000-seconds would take 15 seconds on a 1,000 CFP2000 CPU and take 30 seconds on a 500 CFP2000 CPU (both assuming 100 percent CPU utilization). The same workload on a slower CPU would take longer to complete.

Table 12-1 shows some CPU workloads. The server running computation load A has two SpecFP 1500 CPUs and the load causes a 30 percent utilization for 20 seconds. The product of number of CPUs, percentage utilization, CPU capacity, and usage duration is the total CPU workload (column 6). The total workload divided by the number of computations in the set is the CPU workload per computation (column 8). A server tested with computation set B has one SpecFP 1800 CPU, and servers for loads C and D have six and four CPUs, respectively.

The CPU performance metric used is SpecFP2000 in this example. It can be substituted by any other unit.

Memory Consumption

The goal of sizing for memory is to minimize paging. Whereas it is possible to eliminate paging by buying enough memory, the value of sizing lies in recommending just enough memory and not over-prescribing.

Like CPU, memory requirements fall into either a system-wide category or a per-user category.

The *system-wide memory requirement* is for OS and applications and is estimated from default or manually configured variables. There are several components of system-wide memory:

- *Operating system memory requirement* — This is the portion of memory consumed by OS processes. Examples of UNIX processes are `cron`, terminal manager, `sendmail`, TCP port listener (`inted`) Volume Manager, RPC registry, route discovery daemon (`in.rdisc`), NFS, SNMP, and mount daemons. These processes can add up to 100 or more megabytes of memory and are provided in vendor OS documents.

- *Kernel requirements* — This is the amount of memory used by the kernel and depends on tunable parameters such as Inode cache, directory lookup buffer, and so on.

- *System Library memory requirement* — This component of the used memory is fairly static and is actively used by libraries. On UNIX systems, the libraries reside primarily in `/usr/lib` directory.

- *Application and database requirement* — A large chunk of memory is used for background processes and associated with database engines and applications. This portion of the memory is initially occupied by the application and later shared by various user requests. The size of the shared memory segment is usually decided by application or database administrators as part of tunable parameters. This portion is independent of the number of users and can be sized separately.

Table 12-1 CPU Workloads (in CFP2000-Seconds) Due to Various Computation Sets on Different Systems

1 COMPUTATION SETS	2 NUMBER OF CPUS IN SERVER	3 % CPU UTILIZATION	4 CPU CAPACITY (CFP2000)	5 CPU DURATION USAGE (SECONDS)	6 TOTAL CPU WORKLOAD (CFP2000-SECONDS)	7 NUMBER OF COMPUTATIONS IN SET	8 CPU WORKLOAD PER COMPUTATION (CFP2000-SECONDS)
A	2	30	1,500	20	18,000	1,000	18
B	1	90	1,800	5	8,100	2,500	3.24
C	6	50	1,000	10	30,000	1,200	25
D	4	80	500	50	80,000	2,500	32

- *File system buffer memory requirement* — This is the amount of memory used to prefetch and cache file system data. One problem is that it is difficult to size. The more you provide, the better the performance. As a rule of thumb, at least 2 percent of the database size should be used for buffer cache. If a database is 20 GB in size, the buffer cache should be 400 MB. If your database is on raw volumes (not file systems), you should get an extra 10 percent memory for file system cache, which would be used for OS, log files, and other file system–based data.

Per-user memory requirement is applicable to most workloads such as database servers, middleware clients, and timeshare systems. However, if you are sizing memory for applications that are not dependent on number of users (such as NFS or CIFS servers, or threaded Web servers), then this section is not relevant.

The objective in this section is to estimate the amount of memory required for each user. This is done by testing the application when in use by a controlled sample of users. When a user activates an application on a server, the amount of memory used is rather steady (ignoring disk swaps), even if the user is idle.

In situations where an application is not available for testing and measurements, the system-wide and per-user memory must be estimated from vendor or third-party data.

Phase 3: Size the New Server

Here, the estimates made in Phase 2 are extrapolated to calculate the CPU and memory needed to support requirements specified in Phase 1 (such as the projected number of users, acceptable latency levels, and larger workload).

CPU Estimates

Table 12-2 shows an example of CPU estimates for a predicted number of users and workload.

The total CPU usage for each computation type is the product of the number of users, projected computations per second, and estimated CPU workload per computation.

Besides the user needs, include the following as well in your CPU estimate:

- CPU requirement for operating system and kernel processes
- CPU requirement for application processes
- System response time requirements

Table 12-2   Example of Projected CPU Requirements for a Predicted Number of Users, Assuming 100% CPU Utilization

COMPUTATION TYPE	PROJECTED NUMBER OF USERS (N)	PROJECTED COMPUTATIONS PER SECOND (R)	ESTIMATED CPU WORKLOAD PER COMPUTATION (C) (CFP-SECONDS)	TOTAL CPU USAGE (N × R * C CFP)
Application requests to database instance	200	0.2	18	720
HTTP hits	400	5	3.24	6,480
Database reports	60	2	25	3,000
SQL queries	800	0.2	32	5,120
			TOTAL	15,320

Notes: As a rule, you should consider peak-loaded time windows when calculating N and R. R is estimated by dividing the total number of transactions during peak-usage periods by the number of seconds during those periods. C = Estimated CPU workload in Phase 2.

Response time is the most important factor. It is the total time that an end user must wait at the keyboard after entering a query. Response time is made up of four main components: CPU service and wait times, and I/O service and wait times. A 60 percent to 100 percent used CPU will have an unacceptably high wait time for end users. Therefore, when planning a server, consider the end users' expectations and size enough capacity to provide a significant margin of idle time.

Once you have defined the required total CPU capacity to support the predicted workload, you must identify CPU models that will meet the requirement. Base your selection on the CPU rating criteria used to derive CPU workload per computation.

Adding CPUs in a symmetric multiprocessing (SMP) system does not scale linearly. Two CPUs will not give you 200 percent of the performance but about 170 percent. This is called the *SMP factor* and is 1.7 in this case.

Table 12-3 shows the overhead caused by adding more CPUs. A server with two 1800-SpecFP CPUs will effectively have 2880 SpecFP (1.60 × 1800) and a server with six such CPUs will have 7992 SpecFP (4.44 × 1800).

Memory Estimates

Let's use the Phase 2 requirements to illustrate an example server. Table 12-4 provides memory sizing for OS processes, kernel, file system buffer, application, and database-shared space (such as instance startup requirements). Table 12-5 is an example of user memory prediction for a server subjected to four different loads, each having its own set of users.

The memory requirements in Tables 12-4 and 12-5 are 5,450 and 24,400 MB. The server is hence sized to 29,850 MB of memory.

Table 12-3 SMP Factor for Adding CPUs

NUMBER OF CPUS	SMP OVERHEAD FACTOR	CPU/SMP FACTOR	PERFORMANCE FACTOR
1	1.00	1/1.00	1.00
2	1.25	2/1.25	1.60
3	1.29	3/1.29	2.33
4	1.31	4/1.31	3.05
5	1.35	5/1.35	3.70
6	1.35	6/1.35	4.44

Table 12-4 Memory Sizing Example for System and Application Requirements

ITEM	AMOUNT (MB)	COMMENT
Operating system memory requirement	200	This would be larger for high-end systems with large CPU counts.
Kernel requirement	200	Tunable kernel parameters such as directory lookups and OS-level shared memory segments.
System Library	50	Generally takes 50 MB on a server. Size is fairly static.
Application and database requirement	3,000	Application and database shared memory space required for starting applications or database instances.
File system buffer cache requirement	2,000	Required for buffering database on file systems. It is usually 2 percent of the dataset size. This assumes a dataset size of 100 GB.
TOTAL (MB)	5,450	

Table 12-5 Example of Memory Sizing (MBs) for Predicted Number of Users

COMPUTATION TYPE	PROJECTED NUMBER OF USERS (N)	ESTIMATED MEMORY PER USER (MB)	REQUIRED MEMORY (N × M * MB)
Application requests to database instance	200	10	2,000
HTTP hits	400	1	400
Database reports	60	100	6,000
SQL queries	800	20	16,000
TOTAL (MB)			24,400

Is Your Server Starved for Memory?

After implementation, each server must be checked for memory shortage. Detecting memory starvation is not as straightforward as measuring CPU or disk activity. The recommended steps to ascertain if there is memory deficiency are as follows:

1. Determine if the server is paging actively. Active paging is obvious on UNIX systems by positive numbers in the scan-rate (sr) and page-out (po) columns of vmstat command.

2. Observe activity on the swap device. Queued I/Os and lots of activity are sure signs of application paging.

3. Use OS tools to find the percentage of memory used for file system buffer cache. If this is small (say, less than 10 percent), the server is low on memory.

Key Points

Following are some key points discussed in this chapter:

- Both servers' sizing and capacity planning help you identify the optimum number of servers and resources within each server to meet the desired performance goals.

- Capacity planning is a three-phase process:

  - *Phase 1* — Assessing the application requirements, acceptable end-user response time, and overall business goals

  - *Phase 2* — Measuring the current resource utilization, bottlenecks, and user behavior in a real-world scenario or in a simulated environment

  - *Phase 3* — Extrapolating the measurements in Phase 2 to estimate enough resources to meet the goals in Phase 1

- Estimates are approximate. Therefore, after implementation, server performance must be measured, tuned, and monitored continuously.

CHAPTER 13

Best Practices in IT

You can learn little from victory. You can learn everything from defeat.
— Christy Mathewson

The term *best practices* refers to an established method of doing a task or an optimized way of performing something under a set of constraints. Most companies have internally developed and tested procedures that they adhere to and regard as best practices.

It must be pointed out that there is some challenge to laying out the scope and an agreeable definition of the term "best practices." Not every good idea qualifies as a best practice. A best practice is a procedure that is the result of lessons previously learned and the collective opinion of a group of subject-matter experts. These lessons are based on real-life experiences or conclusions deduced from well-controlled experiments.

This chapter discusses various systems and network-related topics that contribute to high availability.

TALES FROM THE TECH TURF: WHAT'S IN A NAME?

A few of us once visited a client to evaluate their IT practices on data storage before designing a new overall architecture. The customer had a few noteworthy and well-deployed IT practices. In their data center, all cables (network, power, storage, and so on) were descriptively labeled at both ends. A cable connecting a host to storage devices was labeled servername_controller# at both ends. For example, a cable with sys1_c3 labels connected a Sun server sys1 to disks with device names c3t#d#. Network cables were labeled oradev2_hme1_swtdc1_port7, for example, if they connected the network port hme1 of host oradev2 to port 7 of switch swtdc1. When it came to creating VERITAS logical volumes, the customer configured small volumes: 25 MB, 50 MB, and 75 MB each. Each database tablespace was made up of several small files, each residing on separate file systems. They used performance-monitoring tools to identify I/O hot spots and then relocated heavily used files to lightly used disks. These procedures formed a part of their corporate-wide "best practices."

Defining Best Practices

Best practices are procedures that have the following characteristics:

- They are based on consensus or suggestions of subject matter experts.
- They are lessons learned through experience in a production or lab environment.
- They are proven practices, whose adoption has provided the best results.

There are other things that, on the surface, appear to be best practices but do not have the just-mentioned characteristics. Several operating procedures, such as the following, do not qualify as best practices:

- Performance-tuning guidelines
- Installation and configuration how-tos and procedures (including cookbooks)
- Troubleshooting suggestions

The distinction between performance-tuning guidelines and best practices is often subtle. Best practices must be included in the overall system configuration, which, in turn, is designed to meet business objectives. They must be applied with a high degree of consistency during system deployment. Performance tuning requires repeated trial and error to arrive at appropriate values, which, in turn, depend on host and network resources, average load, and other environment-specific factors. Tuning sometimes reveals uncommon relation-ships between various factors. A performance-tuning step, known to enhance performance, may sometimes cause a detrimental effect. Best practices are designed to be independent of environment-specific idiosyncrasies. If they incorporate negative potential, rely on a hardware model, or apply to certain software versions, these must be clearly identified and documented.

Deploying Best Practices

Best practices are deployed at several levels. Proper planning before imple-menting a high-availability solution eliminates (or at least reduces) problems before they occur. This includes things such as system configuration, power planning, and facilities. At another level, best practices are incorporated into functional tasks such as system management, network monitoring, and backups. As the highest level, best practices are a set of consistent operational procedures.

The following is the priority order to be followed when designing and building a new environment:

1. *Supported configuration* — This should have a high precedence during the design or deployment phase. The system and environment must meet vendor-provided support criteria.

2. *Best practices* — They must be applied for proper configuration as long as supportability issues are not violated.

3. *Performance tuning* — Every supported and properly configured system must be tuned. Determining the optimum tuning parameters for a par-ticular configuration requires several iterations.

There are social and technical impediments to implementing best practices. Various folks in your company may resist assimilating knowledge and sug-gestion from outside sources. Organizations have some "rules of thumb," and "traditional wisdom" is easier to sell and deploy. There is resistance to yield to new knowledge and acceptance of a new set of best practices. Many DBAs and SAs believe that two-thirds of potential performance gains in an application come from the code developers. There is little that the DBAs and SAs can do.

Resistance to accepting new best practices could also be caused by a previ-ous miserably failed deployment of suggestions. Best practices usually apply to many cases, and possible downside potentials should be documented.

Discipline is a vital requirement for success. Good discipline includes imple-mentation of proper design, adequate testing, designing scaleable code, proper change control-procedures and contracts management, and sufficient training for those responsible for critical systems.

TALES FROM THE TECH TURF: BIAS DELAYS FIXES

We had a database instance with serious performance problems. The DBAs had the database and kernel parameters memorized. They had contacted the database vendors many times. They had reviewed the database setup and configuration parameters several times and were unable to provide more value. The SAs who had installed the OS and built the RAID volumes were long gone to greener pastures.

A quick look at the RAID setup exposed the problem. The Oracle tablespaces were using separate RAID-5 volumes built on 12 drives within the storage subsystem. However, all the RAID volumes were on the same 12 disks. There were two problems: First, 12 members per RAID array was excessive. RAID-5 performance increases and then decreases with the number of disks. Second, each volume (used for data, index, rollback, and redo logs) was actually hitting the same set of disks.

The lesson: Best results come from efforts coordinated on several fronts.

Benefits of Best Practices

At first glance, most best practices make good sense, and there seems to be no reason not to accept and use the suggestions. But, not all of their benefits are obvious or immediately attainable:

- *Uniformity* — When best practices become a standard, the uniformity makes it easy for system and network administrators to do their job.

- *Reduced downtime* — A system or network that adheres to best practices has reduced hangs and crashes and is fault-tolerant to component or host failures. This is important as systems are being deployed for business-critical tasks that must be available 24×365.

- *Consistent achievement of business objectives* — This is the overall benefit of deploying best practices.

- *Improved quality of vendor support* — First of all, there is less need for vendor support for a system that is well-implemented using best practices. When vendor support is necessary, vendors do not get distracted with other obvious problematic configurations.

- *Improved results from performance tuning* — Good tuning guidelines can adversely impact performance when applied to systems that do not comply with current best practices. They lead to incorrect conclusions, misdirected efforts, and wasted capital expenses. When an environment is built on best practices, tuning yields positive performance gains and there are no unpleasant surprises.

Systems Management Best Practices

Driving down a highway, I saw an advertisement on a large billboard for a data backup and recovery company saying, "Funny what an unreliable server can do to your business!" with a picture of a large screw next to it. That was in northern California, home to several hardware, software, and Internet-based businesses whose livelihood depends on information availability.

Every organization has begun to rely more and more on online data and applications. Businesses can quickly come to a halt if a critical server is down. If an e-commerce server or Web site is unavailable even at nights or weekends, customers will go to a competitor who is just a mouse click away. System availability is, therefore, tied to business continuance and revenue and, in some cases, survival.

Several factors (such as environment, hardware, software, and operations) are responsible for a system's uptime. The failure of any of these factors reduces uptime. Possible causes of downtime are power failure in the data center, a network switch failure, CPU or disk failure inside a system, an OS or application bug that causes a system crash, and operation mistakes such as a server technician who inadvertently disconnects the LAN cable of a server that is running fine.

The following section lists best practices for managing highly available systems.

Systems Deployment

Mission-critical clusters or stand-alone systems must be managed by highly experienced system administrators. Besides day-to-day management, administrators must also keep pace with the rapidly evolving technology.

Systems must be actively monitored using network and host management tools such as BMC patrol, IBM's Tivoli, and HP's Openview. Besides monitoring for availability, the software must be configured to analyze resource usage trends and predict impending scarcity. The information must be used to schedule upgrades before an application causes any service outage.

Uniquely label each component, including attached devices and network, power, and disk-subsystem cables. The labels on both cable ends must be descriptive enough to prevent a technician from disconnecting the wrong device. Tracing cables is very difficult, especially if similar ones are bunched together or they run under the tiled floor. It is best practice to have logical device names on both cable ends (such as eri1 or ge1 on Sun network cables and c3 on a disk cable that connects a Sun to a storage device with disks having `/dev/dsk/c3t#d#` logical names).

Power Sources

It is best practice to provide power (to racked or standalone servers) from separate power units or circuits. If one unit fails, all cluster members should not be impacted. If a server or storage array has redundant power supplies (most do!), ensure that they are connected to different circuits. This is common sense, but I am surprised how often it is overlooked in a production environment.

Mission-critical cluster servers must have power sources from different stations or grids to remove the potential of a SPOF. Critical devices and systems must be plugged into a UPS. The UPS battery must be able to supply power to the connected systems for a certain time period.

For systems with higher availability needs, it is important to have a diesel generator to cover extended blackouts. Since it takes time for generators to power up and be functional, a UPS is still necessary to cover the period immediately following a public utility power failure.

Beware of easy-to-overlook issues. Power cords must be secured to prevent cable damage. Circuit breakers and switches must be in places where they cannot be accidentally tripped.

Hardware Maintenance

Problems with loose hardware components or insecurely inserted computer components are not easy to track. Some defective components crash a system without leaving any trace in the log files. I once managed a Sun server for an Internet-based business. The Sun server crashed a few times a month and it was so fast that the syslog daemon probably got no chance or time to write to `/var/adm/messages` file. Only after studying crash dumps in `/var/crash` directory did we find the problem with the CPUs. What was never resolved was whether the problem was with the CPU card or the way it was inserted into the motherboard!

TALES FROM THE TECH TURF: AUTOMATED ALERTS

One of my clients had several Sun A1000 storage arrays. Most of these were connected to two-node Sun clusters. However, the battery in one of the A1000 arrays was completely drained. The battery is used in the event of a power failure to keep the cache alive until its data is flushed to disks. Because the battery was dead, the cluster data was not protected against power failures. The customer did not know about this problem because it did not have any automated procedure for notifications. Most system-management software can be used to scrape application logs to detect problems and send alerts.

Here are common rules to enhance hardware stability:

- Insert CPUs, memory cards, adapters, and so on, securely in their slots. It is easy to troubleshoot if a host fails to boot after adding a memory card, but loose components cause hosts to crash during normal run-time. The flaws are difficult to nail down.

- External cables must be fully inserted and secured. Use strain reliefs to reduce connector-weight strains on internal components. They are provided for a reason.

- Avoid mechanical vibrations near critical devices and servers.

Software Deployment

This section describes principles that must be followed for successful deployment of software such as a database or an application:

- Use high-quality hardware for critical applications with careful consideration to disk subsystems, network connections, and so forth. Monitor firmware updates for system boards, NVRAM, disk, and I/O controller.

- Carry out design and planning exercises with the software. Know all the hardware and OS requirements for the software and aim to deliver a problem-free environment for clients.

- Test the combination of OS version, patch set, third-party software, and client applications before releasing the software for production use.

- Monitor the system and software health in a disciplined manner. Scan system logs regularly. Use scripts to periodically scan OS and application logs and to send you alerts if certain events are logged. Proactively identify problems that may exist in the background. Run disaster-recovery tests in a regular manner.

- Train the operation staff so they can understand and properly react to logs that signify OS or application-related problems.

Server Cluster Best Practices

The following guidelines will help you effectively configure and use a cluster:

- *Assign each disk to a resource group* — Each shared disk and all partitions or volumes within it must belong to only one resource group. The disk moves as a unit between nodes.

■ *Back up shared-storage controller (host-based adapter) information* — The configuration of the shared volumes (RAID type, disks stripe sizes, volume sizes, and so on) must be backed up because it is a single point of failure. If the shared volumes are configured using a RAID controller (which is connected to cluster nodes), the RAID configuration must be saved in case the controller is replaced.

■ *There must be at least two heartbeat networks* — Failure of a network should not impact other networks. The components must be physically independent.

Data Storage Best Practices

Market studies have shown that data storage–related costs will account for two-thirds of the server's cost. The critical component in a clustered environment is the data and storage hardware it resides on. The other cluster components can be changed without noticeable impact to the environment.

The following are storage-related best practices that enhance data availability and reliability:

■ *Deploy storage subsystem with no single points of failure (SPOFs)* — Disks, power supplies, and fans must be redundant. The design must allow easy replacement without need to take the data offline.

■ *Use multiple controllers for host connection* — This provides data path redundancy and performance improvement using host software that does load balancing among various paths.

■ *Set up hardware RAID volumes* — The controller software must have procedures for configuring RAID volumes and hot spares.

■ *Implementing cluster connectivity to increase data availability* — Data accessibility from more than one host eliminates host as a SPOF.

TALES FROM THE TECH TURF: MISUNDERSTOOD RELIABILITY, AVAILABILITY, SERVICEABILITY (RAS)

I once worked on a storage subsystem that had all types of availability features: hot-swappable disks and power supplies, as well as redundant fans, disks, controllers, and electrically separate back-plane busses for each half of the disk subsystem. The single backplane was split into distinct halves to keep failures on one side from taking down the other. However, there were two serviceability problems: replacing the back plane or even the fan required powering off the entire disk subsystem. There was no serviceability.

- *Use snapshot or point-in-time image functionality* — The storage subsystem must support a quick point-in-time copy of the actual data without needing to take the data offline. The point-in-time copy can reside on the same or another storage subsystem. The software must track updates and requests for data resynchronization. The point-in-time copy is used for backups, testing, and so on, and it contributes to high availability because there is no need to take applications or data offline.

Network Management Best Practices

The network is a critical component when architecting a highly available computing site. If clients within the organization or customers from the Internet cannot get on a server because of network failures, it does not matter whether the servers, cluster, or applications are up or not. They might as well be down.

If an Internet connection is critical, you must subscribe to the Internet using two different service providers or, if forced to use the same provider, use two separate access points. This prevents the Internet connection from being a SPOF.

The following are best practices for corporate networks.

What-If Analysis

It is a best practice to perform a what-if analysis before a network or application change and before deploying any business application. The analysis helps everyone understand the impact of the change. There are several cases where a network change (related to ACLs, switch or router OS) resulted in a congestive collapse and several hours of production downtime. A what-if analysis must be done before introducing an application or making changes to an existing application or network setup. A wrong DNS change can make a Web site or server unavailable because users cannot resolve the URL or hostname to an IP address. Without a what-if analysis, there is significant risk to network availability or the success of a change. If a what-if analysis is not done before deploying an application, the application group would blame the network and LAN administrators for unacceptable performance or outright failures.

What does it take to do a what-if analysis? The first step is to assess the level of risk (high, medium, low) associated with the change. High-risk changes require a detailed impact analysis. A network what-if study determines the impact of network changes on network utilization, device resource issues, and current services. For high-risk changes, detailed analysis is required. It is best to build some representation of the production environment in a lab to test the desired feature, hardware, or configuration under production-like load, created using a traffic generator. Test requirements of the new environment with different traffic types such as compressed, encrypted, SNMP, multicast, and broadcast. An application what-if analysis determines the bandwidth requirement, traffic impact on existing network service, and resource issues with network devices. It is best to do the test in a lab with a server or workstation, a router, a WAN delay simulator (to simulate effect of distance), and a protocol analyzer.

Baselining and Trending

It is best practice to conduct *baselining* and *trending* processes. A baseline process helps you to identify and properly plan for resource limitation problems before the problem causes performance degradation or network outage. The current network capacity and rate of network load increase are compared to identify network usage trends and accurately predict upgrades. Baselining and trending allow you to collect and study the network performance reports at certain time intervals to make sure that everything is working as designed. The problem is that there is an overwhelming amount of information, especially in a large network. This problem can be overcome by dividing the trend information into groups and concentrating on high-availability and critical areas of the network (such as production LANs, data center LANs, or critical WAN sites).

The report helps you to understand the current health and utilization of network resources and to identify existing network problems. It also shows how fast the network load is increasing and helps in predicting network congestion and failure, assuming the same growth rate in the future.

TALES FROM THE TECH TURF: WHEN EVERY MOMENT COUNTS!

An Internet e-commerce and message board site (that I worked with for a short time) introduced an instant messaging (IM) application. They had tested it, but the test traffic was orders of magnitude below the real traffic volume. When the IM application was introduced, the site was able to function. As word got out, more users flocked to it. Within a few days, the network could not bear the traffic volume and congestion. The problem was diagnosed to be with the firewall. It was configured to handle a certain number of simultaneous connections. The number was bumped up and up. No help! Another firewall was dropped in to share the load in an active-active configuration. Again, no help! Finally, the hardware platform was changed to a different vendor, who was able to resolve the problem. That was a few days of downtime, when every moment counted.

Exception Management

This is a valuable process for identifying and resolving existing capacity and performance problems in the network. Network devices must be configured to send alerts or e-mails whenever capacity or performance thresholds are violated. If an administrator receives notification of high CPU usage on a router, he or she can then log into the router to determine the cause and perform remedial configuration to reduce the CPU usage. If the traffic that caused the CPU usage is not business-critical, it can be prevented using an ACL.

Exception management must be configured for critical issues using RMON on a router or using advanced tools such as Netsys service level manager. Most network management tools have the capability to set thresholds that trigger alarms on violation. The tool must be capable of real-time notification and attempt to correct the problem. If there is a delay in logging into the network device, the problem may have gone away.

Quality of Service Management

This involves creating and monitoring specific traffic classes within a network. The criteria for categorizing traffic types are performance SLAs, specific application requirements, and network bandwidth.

One organization had a slow 10-megabit VPN link between two rapidly growing branch offices. The connection was usually congested with noninteractive user sessions (FTPs, Web site downloads, and so forth), which degraded OLTP connections, and database synchronization between metropolitan cluster nodes located in both branch offices. The organization set up three different traffic classes for transmission over the interoffice VPN. Critical applications such as database were given the highest priority. FTP sessions were given the lowest priority. All other traffic was placed in the intermediate class. The organization monitored the amount of time taken by traffic in each class. This is necessary to ensure that adequate network bandwidth is available for all classes.

TALES FROM THE TECH TURF: KICKSTART

I was involved in developing scripts for automated install process for Linux clients. The Linux install (also called a *kickstart*) *server* was a Sun Netra T1. The install clients were PCs. The installation for the OS would go well, but after a certain stage in the install process, it would slow down. Each Linux RPM would take up to 10 minutes to install (instead of a few seconds). After a lot of work and troubleshooting, it was discovered that the switch port for the install client was having problems with the speed and duplex parameters. We were able to force 100-full duplex mode on the network adapter. This resolved the problem. What earlier took 4 to 5 hours now took only 5 minutes.

Network Port Auto-Negotiation

Auto-negotiation is an optional feature of IEEE Fast Ethernet (802.3u) standard that enables network devices to set their duplex and speed capabilities automatically by exchanging information over a link. The ports could get set to 10 or 100 Mbps, and half- or full-duplex capability. Auto-negotiation operates at layer 1 of the OSI Reference Model and configures link ports when devices connect to the network.

The most common performance degradation in a 10/100 Mbps Ethernet link is when one port on the link is operating at half duplex and the other at full duplex. It happens if administrators configure one port to be half or full duplex at 10 or 100 Mbps and forget to set the other port of the link with the same parameters. The performance degradation can also happen if one or both ports are configured to auto-negotiate and somehow get reset, but the auto-negotiation process is unable to set the same speed and duplex abilities for both ports. It is also a common misconception that one link can be set at a certain speed and duplex capability and the other port can auto-negotiate itself to the same configuration. For auto-negotiation to work, both ports of the link must be set to auto-negotiate. Typical speed and duplex mismatch symptoms are increasing FCS, alignment, CRC, or runt counters on the switch.

It is best practice to force *both* ports of a link to a certain speed and duplex capability or configure both ends to auto-negotiate. A common configuration is to "hard-code" both link ports (for example, the network switch port as well as the host NIC port) to operate at 100 Mbps full-duplex capability. This works well for fixed devices such as servers, workstations, and switches. Host ports are set to this in adapter or OS configuration files. Auto-negotiation works well for link ports configured for transient devices (such as employee laptops).

Documentation Best Practices

Documentation is a critical part of every IT environment. Like security, it is not a one-time task. It needs to be adapted to IT changes and IT changes will always happen (new products, new versions of existing products, new practices, or changes to existing environment).

Good documentation leads to quicker installations, configurations that are similar, faster troubleshooting, less support escalations, and, in general, more peace of mind for the IT staff. That's why support centers have internal FAQs. We can all remember times when we wished we had written down how we did a task or resolved a problem in the past. That could easily cut down troubleshooting time by a couple of hours or even days.

There are many other benefits that are less obvious. With a good set of easily accessible documents, you do not need highly experienced SAs for all day-to-day operations. Tasks can be initiated by junior SAs and forwarded to experienced SAs if necessary. Inventory documentation allows you to plan for future hardware and software upgrades without having to inventory existing resources repeatedly.

Following are some types of documentation.

Methodology Documents

This category includes the majority of IT documents such as technical how-tos, working guides, troubleshooting procedures, and installation and configuration guidelines. They help others do their work and teach them the ropes of the place. An educated staff leads to higher uptime and faster project implementations. An IT division I once consulted with had two sets of documents called Technical Operating Procedures (TOPs), dealing with technical how-tos, and Standard Operating Procedures (SOPs), dealing with change management, escalation processes, and so forth.

Usability is the prime goal. During the writing of a methodology document, you need to often ask yourself, "What does the next guy need to know to build and manage this environment effectively?" When documenting how to upgrade cluster software, you must specify the process for getting a new set of license keys, vendor contacts, installation directory, process of notifying users and backing up before software upgrade, the upgrade process, how to back out if the upgrade causes uncorrectable problems, and the process of starting up software, databases, and applications. As you can see, it can get very detailed. It is necessary to title every section properly so a reader can skip it if he or she already knows the steps.

Proposal Documents

Proposals are documents to suggest a course of action or sell consulting services or products. The following sequence will make for good proposals:

1. *Current status* — Describe the current status and point out the existing fallacies (also called *gap analysis*). Is it urgent to fix the shortcomings? Why? This analysis will lend credence to the proposed solution.

2. *Proposed new design, activities, or products* — A proposal to rearchitect the back-end LDAP servers must include the layout of the new servers, applications installed on each, and communication between the applications. A proposal to install and configure voice-over-IP (VoIP) phones must include a list of new hardware, number of traditional phones that will be replaced by VoIP phones, use of existing PBX, communication of new VoIPs with the old PBX-attached phones, branch office that can use

IP-based phone conversations, and integration with a public switched telephone network (PSTN). Consultants who sell only services also write proposals detailing the tasks they will do.

3. *Justification for the proposal* — This section lists the reasons for making the suggestions. For example, moving to VoIPs will help the company integrate the voice and data network administrators, reduce per-minute phone surcharges, and reduce the amount of administrative work.

4. *Cost involved* — This section describes the cost of new goods and services. Provide as much detail as the client wants. Excess can be a distraction.

5. *Cost/benefit analysis and return on investment (ROI)* — List all the benefits from the new solution. Divide them into two categories: *hard benefits* (those that have clear money savings) and *soft benefits* (it is difficult to put a monetary value to these savings). The time saved in doing tasks after the new implementation should be part of hard benefits.

6. *Risks and caveats* — Every solution has some level of risks. If you propose to install and configure Microsoft Exchange e-mail services for the entire enterprise, it will prompt hiring an Exchange administrator.

7. *Target completion date* — Target date helps the client plan follow-up activities and also helps the client work toward a deadline. This is a necessary component of the proposal.

By following this sequence, you can create convincing, well-documented, and powerful proposals.

Event Analysis Documents

Many organizations call this *post-mortem*. At other places, it is known as an *incident report (IR)* or *failure analysis (FA)*. Every time a fire flares up, there is an analysis on what caused the fire, how many people were affected, whether anyone got burnt, whether you called 911 or the doctors, what was done to contain the fire (why the entire place go down), and whether it can happen again. How can a recurrence be prevented?

IT administrators spend a lot of time fixing problems. Some of these get too high up the chain. Then someone must document the entire event and explain that in meetings. Such a document must include facts in the suggested sequence:

1. *Executive overview of the event* — This is a high-level statement of what happened and who was impacted.

2. *Chronological sequence of events* — This includes who first observed the problem; who reported it and when; who was paged; vendors who

were called; and case numbers opened with them. The list goes on and on until the problem is resolved.

3. *Root cause of the incident* — As an IT administrator or manager, you should get comfortable with the concept of root cause analysis.

4. *Impact analysis* — This includes servers, applications, and users who were affected by the problem.

5. *Steps taken to solve the problem* — What has been done and what can be done in the future to avoid recurrence of such events.

All IT administrators will be called to write IRs and asked to explain those at meetings. Following these steps will make the process easier for all.

Technical Documentation

Here are best practices on writing technical documentation:

- Document should be relevant to the topic. In the vast land of IT infrastructure, it is easy to wander around. Stick to the problem or subject at hand.

- It should be easy to change the documents. Certain employees and managers should have rights to update the documents.

- The document should be easily available, preferably via a Web browser.

- Senior management should make it clear that employees need to adhere to documented procedures. The danger is that documented steps often kill creativity, but standardization is important, and creativity must be fostered in a lab environment, not on production servers.

- Documents must be stored where they can be retrieved, even if there is a site-wide disaster. A disaster-recovery document is useless if the Web server on which it is stored is down during the disaster.

- Everyone must be encouraged to suggest changes to the documents and one or more should be assigned to collect and implement changes to the documents.

Network Diagram Documentation

Clear network diagrams are critical during troubleshooting and when requesting assistance from vendors or partners. Their readiness to help and technical prowess should not be underestimated. Three types of network diagrams are usually needed:

- *Overall diagram* — This shows end-to-end physical and logical connectivity. If the network is implemented in a hierarchical design (common for large networks), each layer is documented separately. However, it is still important to have an overall, high-level diagram that shows how the domains or layers are linked.

- *Physical diagram* — This shows the switch and router hardware cabling. Domains, MAC address, trunks, links, speed, port numbers, slots, chassis, and so on must be labeled.

- *Logical diagram* — This shows the layer 3 functionality. Routers are shown as objects and VLANs are shown as Ethernet segments. It is best to label IP addresses, subnets, access, distribution, or core network layers and routing information. However, avoid creating busy diagrams. If there is a lot of information to document, split it into two diagrams or do some diagram explanation in text.

Documentation Formats

As you decide to write a document, the first thing you must choose is a format. Often the format may be already decided or the client may have a preference. Following are some common documentation formats:

- *Text files* — This is a very basic format. Its main advantage is that it can be e-mailed to anyone in the e-mail body. No worries about virus checking, opening, and reading inside an application. Another advantage is cross-platform compatibility. A text file behaves the same on all OSs. However, it is not very popular because it does not support enriched text (bold, underlined, and so on) or figures.

- *Figures* — This is the best way to explain configurations such as network, storage, cluster, or phone connections. Microsoft VISIO is a popular tool that is widely used by IT folks. It is easy to save VISIO diagrams as portable network graphics (.PNG) or graphics interchange format (.GIF) and insert those within a Microsoft Word document.

- *Docbooks* — These are Standard Generalized Markup Language (SGML) documents. This has become popular because several consultants use it to document a software or hardware configuration that they built for a client. It is gaining popularity in the Open Source market. It is overkill for small documents but a good choice for large documents.

- *Productivity applications* — This includes spreadsheets, presentation software packages, and word processors. Examples include Microsoft Office, Sun's StarOffice, and IBM's Lotus Suite. They provide the tools necessary for effective documentation. Microsoft Office is very widely used and its MS Word viewer is freely available from the Microsoft Web site.

- *HTML (Hypertext Markup Language) documents* — This is the most popular choice for documentation because of increased accessibility. Several word processors such as Microsoft Word and Excel files can be saved in HTML format. Several product documentations and how-tos are stored online as HTML pages. HTML is flexible, easy to learn, and handles inlines images elegantly.

Key Points

Following are some key points discussed in this chapter:

- Best practices must aim at reducing the cause and effect of human error and providing a high uptime with the given constraints.
- To improve availability of systems, they must have stable hardware and be clustered, monitored, and managed according to an approved and well-understood set of policies.
- Proper documentation of network configuration and operating procedures reduces reliance on a person or group and provides a valuable tool to quickly troubleshoot problems. Maintaining easy-to-understand, correct, and up-to-date documentation conveys a message of professionalism and adds longevity and value to the document and service provider at large.

Server Security

Attach yourself to your passion, but not to your pain.
Adversity is your best friend on the path to success.
— Yehoshua Eliovson

The number of Internet users has quadrupled from 36 million in 1997 to more than 142 million in 2002. This is an average annual growth rate of more than 50 percent. The Computer Security Institute released a survey that indicated that 90 percent of the respondents detected cyber attacks against themselves and a total of 273 organizations incurred a combined loss of $260 million. If you log port-usage attempts, you will be surprised how many times your fringe devices are being queried for vulnerabilities. And you thought that you were safe and people do not have time for malicious deeds.

Long before the Internet age, data security was required by corporations and government sectors. Today, public Web sites are hacked on an almost daily basis. The threat that your Web site will get on the hacked list is real. Because of the e-commerce revolution, business-critical data about employees and customers are now exposed to hackers, viruses, automated attacks, data corruption, partial or complete Web site outages, and system crashes. These have the potential to cause the demise of well-established businesses.

Security practices that work are those that stand the test of time, not simply those that are taught. Trying to protect a server and data fully is not a practical goal. Instead, you should focus on making it so difficult for the attacker that he or she gives up and goes somewhere else. It is like putting bars and locks on our windows and doors. Can a burglar get in the house with locks and bars? Sure, but it is more difficult and more work for the burglar. There is also a higher likelihood of getting caught. The burglar will turn to the neighbor, confident of finding an open door or window to welcome him or her. This is true of Internet attackers who have automated tools to detect levels of system vulnerability.

General Host Security Guidelines

This section provides some fundamental procedures to protect a system against foreseeable threats:

- *Keep OS and applications updated* — Most server and desktop security threats are based on OS flaws. OS vendors create and provide fixes to cover these holes very soon after they are known. You must keep the OS up-to-date at least for security threats. The same applies to applications such as Web servers, e-mail, DNS, and authentication software, which must be available to those outside the organization. Watch for patches. Subscribe to security alerts from `www.cert.org/` and from your hardware, OS, and application vendors.

- *Install and update antivirus software* — All antivirus software contains a list of virus definitions that it can detect and resolve. When new threats are created or discovered, the antivirus software must be updated to include them.

- *Don't open or use unexpected attachments* — E-mail is the most common way to spread viruses, which come as attachments, often from those you know. Sometimes they have a random "From:" and "To:." Hackers can send e-mails that appear to be sent from your corporation's security department. If the attachment looks suspicious, do not open it.

- *Use secure programs* — Use programs that have strong built-in security mechanisms. They use encryption, hard-to-break authentication schemes, and are well constructed.

- *Install firewalls and customize them* — A *firewall* is a program that monitors your network connection and stops bad traffic from getting in. All firewalls have an initial, minimal configuration and a common password. These must be changed. More about this appears in Chapter 36, "Firewalls."

- *Use good passwords* — This is common sense, but it has become more important because all systems now are accessible remotely. Those with vulnerable passwords are susceptible to dictionary attacks and rapid automated guessing of passwords. Avoid automatic logins without being asked for passwords. Be aware of saved passwords that may be blank.

UNIX Security Guidelines

There are a variety of UNIX operating systems. Sun Microsystem's Solaris, RedHat's Linux, HP's HPUX, and IBM's AIX are the leading implementations. This section provides generic instructions for building a secure UNIX host. Here are some fundamental basic steps for securing any operating system, but examples here are for UNIX:

- *Install security patches* — It is critical to test patches on a development or test server before rolling them out to production servers. Many security exploiters prey on systems that are not kept up-to-date. Unpatched machines are frequently exploited within minutes of being attached to an open network.

- *Verify user account security* — Enforce strong passwords. There is an easily available password-cracking program called crack, which is used to identify vulnerable passwords on a UNIX system. Minimize the number of people with root access. Remove or lock individual accounts that have not been used for 3 or 6 months.

- *Use* sudo — Use sudo and log all sudo commands. Make a corporate policy not to ssh to UNIX system as root but as a regular user and use sudo for root-level commands. At many sites, system administrators log in as root using root's password, and many sites still use telnet. At one customer site, servers had several UID zero accounts with separate passwords. This avoided sharing the root password with other people, but it makes the server far more susceptible to hackers. Verify that UNIX servers have only a single UID 0 account.

- *Eliminate unnecessary applications and network services* — inetd is the master controller on UNIX systems for network-based applications. Most of the applications should be secure, such as kerberized telnet. Changes should be made to /etc/inetd.conf on most UNIX implementations. On Linux, it is in /etc/xinetd.conf file or files in /etc/xinetd.d directory. Changes in the configuration file should be reread by the inetd process by running kill -HUP <pid of inted>.

- *Install and configure necessary applications and network services* — Services such as Andrew File System (AFS) are not essential, but they allow an easy way to integrate users across various machines within an enterprise. It can be used to distribute binaries and compiled packages and uses a strong authentication for transferring files.

In a client-server world, it is necessary to have the same time on all servers. Use ntpdate on force the same time. This can be run from cron daily.

TCP wrappers is a UNIX program that allows you to control and record all incoming and outgoing traffic from a host. The software uses /etc/hosts .allow and /etc/hosts.deny files to allow or block connections at the application level.

■ *Configure system logging to record significant events* — The amount of logging is usually controlled by /etc/syslog.conf. While editing the file, remember that the columns are separated by tabs. If you use spaces, syslog will die a silent death. A typical /etc/syslog.conf file looks like this:

```
#save boot messages also to boot.log
local7.*                 /var/log/boot.log
# setup syslog for traping to remote systems
kern.* /var/log/kernel
auth.*;user.*;daemon.none        /var/log/login.log
*.info;mail.none;authpriv.none   /dev/tty7
authpriv.*      /dev/tty7
*.warn;*.err    /dev/tty7
kern.*   /dev/tty7
kern.debug  |/var/lib/psad/psadfifo
local2.notice   /var/log/sudolog
local2.notice   @server1.company.com
local3.info     /var/log/ssh.log
local3.info     @dmz-host.company.com
```

If the destination file does not exist, it must be created for logging.

Internet Security Issues

Why do hackers harm good people? Because they can! They think they are anonymous and safe because they are targeting someone in a far-away land, perhaps on the other side of the world or at least in another country. One incident involved a hacker getting write access to an FTP server with 400 GB. He configured it as a warez site, filled it up with MP3 files and other stolen programs, and exchanged that with other hackers. Hackers prefer not to use their own computers directly, but always step through another system to a target. This obscures direct evidence of activity. To satisfy their egos, they retrieve information, modify business data, put pornographic material on corporate Web sites, and embarrass the corporations. Others want financial profits from stolen online data. Every accessible host is, therefore, an attractive target for hackers.

All communication over the Internet uses the transmission control protocol/ Internet protocol (TCP/IP). Its flexibility, worldwide acceptance, and compatibility with many devices, hosts, and networks make it a primary protocol for most Internet communication. This fact makes it a familiar target for third parties to interfere in various ways:

- *Tampering* — This is modifying the in-transit information. There is plenty of interesting in-flight data on the Internet: the amount of money in your account, national security data, and so forth. Someone could change the receiving account number money wire-transfers.

- *Eavesdropping* — Data is not changed, but it is simply noted down for future use. The data could be personal or national classified security information.

- *Impersonation* — Someone else poses as the intended recipient of data and gets all the information. Such impersonation is done by spoofing or misrepresentation:

  - *Spoofing* — Spoofing is when a person or a machine pretends to be someone else. A person can pose as another user and send and receive e-mails that are meant for others. Machines pose as someone else's domain name and IP address to send out and receive e-mails.

  - *Misrepresentation* — A site will pretend to be and identify itself as some well-known retailer and collect credit card payments but never send out any material.

Sensitive personal and business data exchanges over the Internet must be protected from the threats. The industry has come up with a plethora of remedies. Most of these rely on cryptography based on a public key. Some of these techniques are as follows:

- *Encryption and decryption* — This is the most fundamental technique used in several data-protection mechanisms. It allows two communication parties to scramble the data before sending it over the Internet. Only the receiving party can unravel it and make sense out of it. No one else is able to comprehend the mangled or encrypted data.

- *Tamper detection* — This allows the recipient to verify that the data has not been modified during transit. If it has been tampered with, the recipient knows about it and requests the sender to resend the data.

- *Authentication* — This allows the recipient to verify that the data has indeed come from the real sender. If your bank requests personal information from you, you can verify that the requestor is actually the bank and not someone else pretending to be the bank.

- *Nonrepudiation* — This is used to prevent the data sender from later claiming that the information was never sent.

TALES FROM THE TECH TURF: WHO DO I BLAME?

One company spent copiously on architecting a robust and secure infrastructure, with router ACLs, firewalls, and separate DMZ areas for different categories of Internet servers. Later they hired a security expert to audit their site and attempt break-ins. Such a job is called penetration (or "pen") testing, which is an attempt to crack a system's or network's security layers to identify security risks.

After two weeks of work, the expert was ready with his report. All the systems, network, and security administrators, managers, and directors crowded in a conference room. There were good things to hear, as well as authentic security holes. The expert was even able to break in using someone else's login name and password from his hotel room across the street using his laptop and modem. Everyone looked around the room. Who would be blamed?

He explained that early one fine morning he had called the company phone operator and asked to be transferred to an employee. Then he called for another employee and another until he got Sam's phone greeting that said that Sam was on vacation. Later that morning, he called again. The operator had gone for lunch and there was a substitute. The expert pretended to be Sam and said he needed to log in. He said he was on leave, could not recall his password, and that he had changed it before leaving for this long-awaited family vacation. He needed a network login name and password. Crisis was mounting and a solution had to be quick. The operator knew only her own login name and password. "That would work!" Sam said. Within a few minutes, the pseudo-Sam was successfully logged into the network.

Everyone in the room, exclaimed "Molly! Where is she?" The expert said the organization did not have any procedures or training for account administration, security policy enforcement, or use of shared accounts. It was the management's fault, not Molly's!

Hackers are technically savvy. They have a big network of anonymous friends and message boards where they can discuss their how-to procedures and findings and proudly announce their achievements. They communicate with fake identities.

To complement their savvy online skills, there is another layer, called "social engineering," that hackers use to increase the vulnerability of the masses. Many still scoff at the notion that their systems would ever be targeted. Such apathy is the biggest cause of security breaches. Security should not be implemented by network and system administrators only. It should be everyone's business. Anyone can unknowingly allow hackers into the corporate network. For anyone who asks, "Why should I care? The hackers have so many other interesting sites and servers they can go to. Why would they come to me?", I remind them of something closer at hand. Would you go away for lunch leaving a login session unprotected. If so, what if an angry employee walks up to the room and decides to send a nasty e-mail from your laptop to the company's president. Would you explain to someone that you did not *really* send it?

Internet fraud can happen to you to hurt your online bank, e-mail, or other accounts. In the first four days of November 2004 alone, the consumer protection group FraudWatch International (`www.fraudwatchinternational.org`) posted fraud alerts for more than 100 schemes perpetrated against customers of companies such as eBay, Citibank, and America Online. Here are a few tips on how you can protect personal information and corporate data against cyber crooks:

- Proceed gingerly when asked for account information. Separately verify any request for information by calling the company or by opening a new browser and finding the Web site on your own.

- Fight back with your own technology. Use a firewall, antivirus software, and antispam software to protect your computer and network from trespassers.

- Hyperlinks in e-mails can take you to dangers. Verify the Web site and look for alternate ways to get to your destination.

- Familiarize yourself with the security measures adopted by all of the companies with whom you do business.

- Be in the know. Regularly visit security sites such as the Federal Trade Commission (`www.ftc.gov`), the Consumer Federation of America (`www.consumerfed.org`), and FraudWatch International.

Audit software tools can be installed by users on their corporate desktops. Many programs are freely available on the Internet and are not genuine. If a complete stranger came up to you and gave you a free sandwich to eat, would you eat it? You wouldn't! How about someone you know or have met before? You would still like to know why he is offering the sandwich and what type it is! How about a close friend? You would still ask if there are strings attached to the sandwich! Does the friend want anything in return and is it fresh? So, why would you accept software from a provider you know nothing about. The software could do something you want, but it may have auxiliary features such as sending virus-infected e-mails to all your group aliases (or just everyone in your company), damaging data, or creating an administrator-level account for the software provider.

The well-publicized *denial of service* (*DoS*) attacks against Amazon.com, CNN, eBay, Etrade, and Yahoo in the late 1990s foretell a worrisome future. Lessons should not be ignored. Attacks such as *distributed denial of service* (*DDoS*) attacks involve malicious, repetitive requests from several sources to a target to deplete its application and system resources. The attack does not jeopardize the data, but genuine users cannot get to your Web site because it is too busy responding to bogus packets. It, therefore, impacts site availability. Systems connected to the Internet may become unwitting participants in DDoS attacks.

Implement the following two steps to reduce the chances that your systems could be used as a partner-in-crime to damage other networks:

1. Stop spoofed or forged IP packets from leaving your network. Your routers and firewalls must forward packets only if the source IP address belongs to internal networks. Do not forward packets with source IPs that belong to private (see *RFC 1918*) or reserved IP addresses.

2. Stop your network from being used as a broadcast amplification site to flood other networks with DoS attacks. Configure all servers, routers, and workstations so they do not receive or forward network directed broadcast traffic. When you buy and implement new network hardware, ensure that receipt and forwarding of directed broadcast packets are disabled (see *RFC 2644*).

Hackers attack indiscriminately, scanning the Internet for vulnerable systems. Here are some best security practices for Internet-connected servers:

- Minimize the operating system. Install necessary packages or software sets.

- Place the server in a DMZ, and set the firewall to drop connections on all but the required ports. For Web servers, the firewall must drop all requests except those destined for ports 80 (HTTP), 443 (HTTPS), and certain, other preconfigured ports.

- Harden the OS.

- Keep up-to-date on patches, especially those related to Internet security.

- Install security chokepoints at all appropriate stations. *Chokepoints* are devices that inspect incoming network traffic and decide whether they should go through or not, based on source, destination, data type, and other factors. Routers and firewalls are some examples.

- Deploy security applications that detect attacks and send immediate alerts if necessary.

- Remove all services from the host except those that are required. Several services (started from `inetd` or `xinetd` on UNIX) are not required. These include `ftp`, `telnet`, `imap`, `pop3`, `fs`, `kcms`, `sadmind`, `login`, `echo`, `time`, `daytime`, `discard`, `sftp`, `systat`, `rexd`, `netstat`, `ypupdated` (except NIS servers), `rusers`, `sprayd`, `walld`, `exec`, and `uucp`. Unneeded services only serve as attack avenues.

- Use open secure shell (SSH): Install and run SSH daemon to permit logins. By default, it uses port 23.

- Review startup scripts and ensure that unnecessary daemons are not started at boot time. Depending on the system role, the following can be stopped on most Internet servers: `sendmail`, remote procedure call (RPC), NFS, SNMP, `autofs`, and volume manager for removable media.

- Permit administrative logins from a few trusted internal systems only. Remote administrators will need to log in to the internal system before they can get on to the Internet server.

- Limit the number of people who have accounts on the server. Only a few people need to know the root password.

- Disable all remote administration unless it is done over an encrypted link or using a one-time password.

- Log all user activity and keep an encrypted copy of the log files on the local system or another server on the network.

- Monitor logs for suspicious activity. Configure automatic alerts if certain messages are logged or critical files (such as user account or application configuration files) are modified.

- For Internet application software such as Apache, Iplanet, IIS, or ExAir, remove all "default" directories that are shipped with the Web server software.

- On UNIX systems, run Web or FTP server in a `chroot-ed` part of the directory tree. The services cannot be used to access the real system files.

- For external Web or FTP servers, maintain internal development and staging servers. All changes should be copied from the internal development server to the staging server. Every hour or so, push the updates from the staging to the external server. You will thus avoid corrupted or hacked data exposed for a long period of time.

- Scan the external servers periodically using tools such as `nmap` and Internet security systems (ISS) to look for vulnerabilities.

- Configure intrusion-detection software to monitor all client connections and send an alert when it sees any suspicious activity or log. Run Tripwire. It is free and can warn you of security breaches.

- Finally, stay up-to-date. Medical practitioners and doctors must be fully aware of the latest medical breakthroughs and new drugs. No matter how secure you initial setup is, if you do not stay current, you will eventually become vulnerable. Get on security and vendor patch-notification mailing lists. Read appropriate newsgroups.

Ostensibly it seems that data and system security is a daunting or even useless effort. The techniques and software tools used by hackers to tear down the network and system infrastructure must be focused and used against them to thwart their attempts. Several agencies have been established to increase awareness of threat and provide security guidelines. The National Infrastructure Protection Center by Presidential Directive, Computer Emergency Response Teams (CERTs), and the Sysadmin, Audit, Networking, and Security (SANS) Institute work together to discover security flaws and remedies. But, it is the collaborative effort of everyone (from those who configure intrusion-detection devices such as routers and firewalls to end users) and the stability of systems infrastructure that will protect from intrusion, evil intentions, and hackers.

Best security practices change and evolve. There is no sequence or order of effectiveness. It can be argued that one approach provides more protection than others, but the hard truth at the heart of protecting IT systems and data is that the war has to be fought continually on several fronts with different weapons.

It is best practice to impress upon everyone (including users, managers, supervisors, computer technicians, and peers) that information security is truly everyone's business.

It is best practice to implement layers of protection. Each component (such as firewalls, routers, server hosts, and data and network appliances) come with their own security-enhancing features, and they should be configured to do what they are best at. Thus, you have created a series of obstacles between the hacker and the data. Even if the attacker gets through a few levels, he or she will ultimately get to attack-resistant servers.

Despite all your best efforts, systems will get hacked. What are the most appropriate things to do if you are sure or suspect your Internet server to be hacked?

1. Disconnect the affected system from the Internet until you have identified what the event was and the exploited vulnerability in your system and have fixed the problem.

2. Make a backup of the system before you change anything. You can refer to the backed-up data to look at the system configuration and logs to understand the event and its cause.

3. One organization that I know about had a policy of disconnecting the system from the network and reinstalling the operating system and all applications on a hacked server. In the meantime, it would identify patches and other pertinent security fixes for the server. The patches and vulnerability fixes were applied on all similar systems. That is obviously the best step to eliminate the vulnerability.

4. Review all application and OS log files to see if the event has been logged anywhere. Validate all user accounts and ensure that they have strong passwords.

5. Look for suspicious files in `/tmp`, `/dev`, and `/etc` directories, the `cgi-bin` directories (for Web servers). If you find any, search all directories in the system for similar files.

6. Validate all open ports and services to ensure that there are no Trojan services.

If you know the source of vulnerability (OS, application, and so forth), contact the vendor and get all applicable security-related patches. Apply them on the hacked and similar Internet-application servers. Once you have identified suspicious files, accounts, logs, and so forth on the hacked server, validate other servers that could have been similarly targeted to see if they, too, have been hacked.

Sources of Information on Security

Here is a list of a few important Internet security Web sites:

- Computer Incident Advisory Capability (U.S. Department of Energy): `www.ciac.org/`
- Federal Bureau of Investigation (FBI): `www.fbi.gov/`
- Computer Crime and Intellectual Property Section: `www .cybercrime.gov/`
- Computer Emergency Response Team (CERT): `www.cert.org/`
- Computer Security Institute: `www.gocsi.com/`
- Microsoft Security Advisor Home Page: `www.microsoft.com/ security`
- SANS Institute: `www.sans.org/`

Key Points

Following are some key points discussed in this chapter:

- Security-related breaches are one of the biggest causes of unplanned downtime and financial loss.

- Security against Internet threats must be implemented at various layers (such as the router, firewall, host, and data-storage subsystem).

- Harden the OS. Remove software that is not required and software that is known to be prone to threats. Disable services that do not provide any business benefit.

- Be in the know. Subscribe to security bulletins and updates.

- Keep the OS and applications up-to-date, especially for software that strengthens security.

Server
Administration

Do what you feel in your heart to be right, for you'll be criticized anyway.
You'll be damned if you do and damned if you don't.
— Eleanor Roosevelt

Server administration is a journeyman's trade. Most of the skills and lessons learned are from on-the-job training. A large number of system administrators (SAs) have never taken a course, except for a few vendor-specific courses. Good system administration practices, unfortunately, are learned the hard way.

At a high level, *systems administration* is the installation and maintenance of computer systems. System administrators need to manage the operating system, applications, and hardware for the system. This includes kernel reconfiguration, security, backups, patches, networking, user accounts, printers, application installations and setup, performance, capacity planning, and anything else that is required to keep the system working and the users busy. To do this, the system administrator can assume super-user or root privileges to perform many tasks not available to the average system user.

Any IT infrastructure is made up of diverse equipment, platforms, operating systems, and user interfaces. Making all these work harmoniously together is one of the foremost goals of all system, network, application, backup, and storage administrators, who together make up the IT team. They are together responsible for the following:

- Set up and install equipment
- Monitor all hosts and devices to make sure they do what they are meant to do

- Monitor, record, and tune hardware and application performance
- Follow and implement corporate policies for design, security, and usage of the IT infrastructure

Expert skills, knowledge, and flexibility are required to perform these tasks. Although there is a lot of change, innovation and the unexpected do happen. It is also true that a lot of work is mundane and repetitive. If these are not automated in some way, there are two risks to the organization: There will be a waste of expensive talent in doing the same tasks over and over again, and these tasks done by humans will be prone to defects and errors (which will lead to all-around frustration and waste of time).

This chapter provides a list of best practices and "what-and-how" for automating repetitive system administration work.

Best Practices for System Administration

Given that IT environments are ever changing and systems are highly configurable, the list of best practices provided here is generic:

- *Pay attention to details* — Know your world. It is hostile. Do not ignore errors. If you cannot deal with it now, write it down for an easy reminder. Problems plot against you and will raise their heads on the same day, when your colleagues are on vacation and you have promised someone that you will leave work early.

- *Document* — Write down the steps or tricks that saved you today. You probably found it after lot of hair-pulling. Months and years later if you are still doing the same job, it will save you time and hair (whatever is left of it).

- *Check the simple, obvious things* — Is the cable bad? Is the unit powered up? After years and years of sys admin experience, you still overlook the obvious problem. When someone calls you to say his or her password is not working, ask, "Is your Caps Lock on?"

- *Keep your users informed* — If something could cause problems to users, let them know and tell them you will solve the problem when you get time to breathe. They will think of you as their omniscient protector. If changes are going to take place, schedule them as far in advance as possible. Also, inform everyone far in advance. You would be one of the few far-sighted folks they know. Even good events announced at the last moment do not seem funny. Leave surprise announcements for birthdays and baby showers.

TALES FROM THE TECH TURF: VACATION PAINS!

I was on a vacation by the beach. Work was far from my mind and whereabouts — 1,200 miles to be exact. It was mid-day, but who kept track of time? I had my cell phone with me, which was a mistake. It rang and a voice said, "`maildb` cluster servers are down. Looks like a bad `/etc/system` file! Did you change something?" I was jolted back all the way to the data center. The cluster systems were the back-end servers for our Web-based e-mail services. That meant our customers could not get to their e-mail boxes. Pain pangs! Should I admit guilt? I did! "Do you recall what you changed? I have just booted the cluster Sun box with Sun CDs. I can change the file." The file and its contents had not been the subject of my thoughts this morning. "Well, did you make a copy of the file, before changing it? I can just replace it." Pain pangs, again! Finally I had to walk him through the hand-edits. There are two lessons to be learned here: (1) Back up files before changing them, and (2) test the changes immediately or schedule downtime for testing in the near future.

- *Test, test, test* — For most of us, there is hardly enough time to do important things, and testing never gets to the top of the list of to-dos. Moreover SAs like their jobs because of the variety, challenge, creativity, and unwritten freedom. They are not the type to test and retest after applying patches or upgrades or after changing scripts. But then problems can cause so much downtime, and it takes so many people's efforts to identify and fix them. When someone asks, "Who changed what?" it is best to reply that you changed and tested the changes.

- *Projects take twice the time and resources* — Keep a straight face when asking for more. They will understand. Project planners always miss the small but important steps that could delay a project. A recent survey showed that 31 percent of software projects are cancelled before completion and 52.7 percent cost 189 percent of the original estimates. One cause for cancellation is that the project is predicted to fail its ambitious deadline and monetary constraint.

  Even if a project is completed but fails to meet its estimate deadline, its effect and value are less. If you have been to stores after the Halloween, Thanksgiving, or Christmas holidays, you know that everything that could not be sold and delivered to shoppers by the holiday is put on sale, often up to 75 percent off. The project you work so hard on deserves a better value.

- *Fix the root cause of problems* — Fighting system "fires" always wastes everyone's time. You will be surprised how seemingly unrelated things team together to create problems.

**TALES FROM THE TECH TURF: THE DIRECTOR WHO
ALWAYS GOT ENOUGH MONEY**

At the end of each fiscal year, all the directors at a place I once worked would
get real busy with departmental finances. They called all the managers and
tried to forecast expenses for the next fiscal year: hardware purchases, license
costs, maintenance, and so on. My director had his own "set of budget best
practices" (one of which was that software development ultimately costs twice
the initial estimates). He found out how much each director's budget would get
trimmed and added a safety of +20 percent for that amount. Simple! But it was
the only way he could be sure of getting enough for his division.

■ *Automate as much as possible* — Several OS features are turned off by
default such as log compression and rotation, automatic performance,
and system accounting data collection. Customize and activate them.
Have the backups e-mail you everything. VERITAS Cluster Software
has a NotifierMngr resource type that can be used within a group to
send e-mails of different levels of cluster events: information, warning,
error, and severe errors. If you can, script something and use `cron` to
run it instead of having a person routinely do the chore. It does not
mean that we do not trust our fellow human beings, but they will have
time for other productive things. Besides, people forget.

■ *Create backups* — This applies to full system-level backups before software changes and single-file backup (using the `copy` command) before
changing critical files. When I was helping an SA resolve boot-up problems on a Sun server, I backed up the `/etc/system` file and started
editing it. "Good thing you backed it. I would not have thought about
it!" he said. "Took me 15 years to get used to it!" I said. I have wasted so
much time in the past trying to undo my changes, when having a simple file backup would have helped. It is ironic that people do not back
up because they do not have enough time.

TALES FROM THE TECH TURF: FORGETFULNESS!!

At one IT shop, the backup operator was supposed to replace the set of tapes
on Saturday evening before leaving work. She forgot. Since the correct labels
on the tapes were not found, no data was backed up on Saturday or Sunday
nights. Murphy's law hit on Monday. The disks crashed. We had to go to the full
backup on the previous Saturday and restore until Friday, which meant there
were two missed days of backups. When the customer found this out, they
demanded credit on their bills for breaching the SLA on backups.

Lesson: Automate routine systems-related tasks to reduce the responsibility
on human operators.

TALES FROM THE TECH TURF: BROKEN GATEWAY

Back in my university days, I worked in a group that managed a handful of UNIX servers. We exchanged stories of sys admin events. One involved an incident where a person deleted some device files on a gateway-and-backup server. The backup was a secondary service. Research students and professors used the server to get on to a small, private LAN with some expensive machines, used for industry-sponsored research and development. During an intense-pressure troubleshooting session, a student deleted some kernel-level files and rebooted the machine with kernel reconfiguration, hoping that would generate the deleted files. It did not! They had to install the kernel files from the OS CD. The server was down for 2 days. Many in the department came to know him by his first name. The lesson: Do not try things for the first time on systems that affect the lives of others.

TALES FROM THE TECH TURF: MY WORKING-VACATION DAY

After months and months of keeping my home DSL modem powered up, I decided to give it a night's rest. I powered off my modem, router, switch, and all the PCs and Suns before I went to bed. Next morning, I powered up all the gear and sat down to send an e-mail that I was taking the day off. The Internet connection did not work. I logged into the router and checked all configuration settings, making some changes on the way. I power-cycled all the gear again in different permutations. I gave up and called my friend at work and asked him to send an e-mail to our group that I was on vacation. It was mid-day. I called my DSL provider and after 20 minutes of music and transfers, I spoke to someone who asked me to power off the modem and router, disconnect, and then reconnect all cables and power them on. Mysteriously, this time it worked.

- *Don't try new concepts on production servers* — We all learn by experimenting, especially in the SA land — but not in the production land. If you must try a new thought or troubleshooting step that you love (because you were the first to think of it), log on to a test box and try it. Then implement it on the production server.

System Administration Work Automation

This section provides a brief overview of automating frequent SA chores. It is meant for managers who need to understand what can be automated and what it takes to do so. As described earlier, failure to automate mundane tasks will lead to a waste of skilled talent, and manual tasks are highly prone to human errors.

What Should Be Automated?

System administration is a tough job and there is one truism about it: No task is fun more than twice. Repetition is mundane! Human involvement is prone to errors. The rule of the thumb is: If it has to be done twice, automate it! Chances are high it will be done again and again in the future. Simple tasks can be automated quickly. Time-consuming tasks will take longer to automate. Whatever the time required for automation is, it will be saved in the future. Corporations are now beginning to realize the value of automation. But there are guidelines (discussed later) that must be followed to make the automation worthwhile.

Sometimes you will do tasks that are repeated but do not seem worth automating, simply because the task outline is not well-defined or low-level. Their inputs vary wildly or they don't always perform a complete function. Now this is a very subjective decision. Of course, sometimes it's difficult to automate jobs, but you should at least think about the option and evaluate its advantages against the time spent on automation. Do not underestimate the shelf-life of a well-documented and easy-to-use tool. Others will use it after you.

At this stage, you must split the task into modules. Each module is a subroutine or function and is used only if certain conditions are met. Automating such an abstract work requires a sequence of code that is highly modular. It is easy to change it later based on user feedback and test results.

TALES FROM THE TECH TURF: THE MRTG STORY

Multi-Router Traffic Grapher (MRTG) software was developed by Tobias Oetikar in 1994 at a Swiss corporation that had a 64 kbit line to the outside world. Everyone was interested in knowing the line's utilization. So, Oetikar wrote a Perl script that shows the Internet link's traffic as a live, Web-based graph. It developed to be a configurable Perl script and was released as MRTG 1.0 in 1995.

Later Oetikar left MTU and joined the Swiss Federal Institute of Technology, where MRTG work was put aside. In 1996 he received an e-mail from Dave Rand asking why MRTG was so slow. Oetikar replied it was caused by certain inefficient subroutines within MRTG and because it was Perl. After a week or two, Rand wrote back saying that he had used Oetikar's suggestions, but it did not help much. Later he ported some time-critical sections of MRTG from Perl to C. The speed increased by a factor of 40! Soon Oetikar started working on MRTG-2 in his spare time.

MRTG was given out to many people. In return Oetikar received a lot of feedback, bug fixes, and enhancements. As of 2005, MRTG is at version 2.10.

Types of Automation

There are two types of software automation, based on how the automation was initiated and its goals:

- *Quick, efficient programs* — This is the most common type of automation done by SAs. You might hear something like this: "I wrote the program last night before I went home. It will output what Tim wants. I know it works on IBM AIX 5.2. I guess it should work on any UNIX platforms. But you need to test it. Well, it may work with our LDAP database, but I was not thinking about that when I wrote it and that would be too much work for me."

  As you can see, these scripts were developed to meet a sudden need. Many parameters are hard-wired and that's why they are fast. Porting the program to other environments is not an intention. They have a specific, narrow goal. For example, "we need this tomorrow by 10 a.m. to show the results in the meeting."

- *Well-planned programs with broad goals* — These programs or scripts exist because someone decides to dedicate certain resources, time, and funds to the program. Usually a team of people work on it for a brief or extended time. It has some level of resemblance to a software development life cycle (SDLC) project. There is an initial goal list, a framework, specific tools for program development, and a test plan. This type of automation, along with management commitment, has the greatest payback. It is well-documented and readily used by various teams within the corporation.

Automation Guidelines

This section contains some guidelines that, when followed, will help increase software effectiveness and adoption within the organization.

List All End-Users' Objectives

Find out and document the end-user base that will benefit from the script or program. Then list the actual goals that they have in mind. Typically the end-user is a group of employees, one or more managers, a division, clients, or the whole enterprise.

Let's take an example. You are writing a script to list down-rev software packages on all hosts. You need to get all SAs to provide you a list of OS packages, patches, applications, hardware PROM versions, and so forth, and up-to-date release numbers for each.

List Key Characteristics of the Target Environment

For the automation to have a significant impact, it is necessary to understand relevant characteristics where it will be used, such as hardware platform, operating systems, and applications. In the previous example, you need all server names where the script will be executed and what is installed on the system. This will help you select the right tools to develop the script. The tools used should be compatible with the server operating environment.

Get Feedback about the Automation

Keep in regular touch with the end-user community. Conduct official and written surveys. Discuss the automation with them. Have they forgotten about the automation? If not, is it doing what it is supposed to do? Is it easy to use?

Improve

Version 1.0 is not the last release. Use the feedback to add more features and improve existing functionality.

Simplify

Studies have shown that the key reason tools are left on the wayside and not used is because they are difficult to operate. The users should not have to "automate the automation" to make it easy to use.

Will the program be used by another program or by a human user? The interface should be natural to the user. If the user is another program, then your program should simply act like a filter that transforms input into output or takes a configuration file as input and output a text file. For human users, write a help section and easy-to-remember options.

Test Often

Testing is like drinking a glass of linseed oil. No one likes it, and it will never be high on any IT administrator's agenda. But testing still remains the best way to identify bugs before the code hits the production servers. Talking about production servers, I have come across many small IT shops where there are no production servers. If you develop and test scripts, programs, or even HTML pages on a production server, try to separate your work directory from the production tree.

When I first started coding, I wrote long chunks of code before running it for the first time. Bad idea! As you write, you should test along the way. Sometimes it is cumbersome because it requires compiling, linking, and so on, but it is worth its time.

Keep It Modular

Use functions or subroutines. Do not hardwire values into the code. Instead provide a way that the user can specify the value, such as a command-line argument. In our example of a program that deletes unused accounts, the following should be accepted as user input (and not assumed inside the code):

- Duration of inactivity for which accounts must be deleted or locked
- Host names to check for inactive users
- Whether to delete the account or simply lock the password
- Whether to delete the user home directory, archive it, or leave it untouched
- Whether to send the user an e-mail about what is being done

The rule is the more options, the better. Of course, it makes coding more complex. These are the items that must be decided in the initial phases with the user community. Remember, programs are not used because they have a cumbersome interface or lack features.

Test for Boundary Conditions

This applies to coding and testing. The program must be able to handle absurd values with grace. What if you enter a negative number where it expects a positive integer? What if an input directory name contains ? and ^? The program should point out the fallacy and provide a brief usage information. If the task cannot be completed, then the program should provide the cause and suggestion to the user.

TALES FROM THE TECH TURF: QUALITY COUNTS

A national bank in the U.S. (I do not name it for anonymity) launched a Web-based Travel & Entertainment (T&E) application. Within a short time, the T&E application became a heavily used application, with more than 25,000 registered users. The front end was handled by two load-balanced Web servers that interacted with the back-end SAP system. Some users had problems logging out of the system and some with their Web browsers. Some problems were even trickier. One user created an expense report with 45 different line items. When he tried to save the report, the entire report disappeared. This went against all expectations, since the application was supposed to save the report after each line item. After several attempts at recreating the problem, the developers discovered that the user was putting a comma in the amount field for credit card expenses, which made the SAP buffer disappear, and the report was lost. Discovering such a problem could take months during formal tests but only days in real-life usage. Application testing to a large extent is done by users during regular use.

Avoid Shortcuts

Once I was driving over the hills and saw a sign that read, "Shortcuts can cut short your life." In the land of automation, shortcuts can cut short the life of the program or sometimes the career of the programmer. The point is do not over-simplify and avoid an inflexible relationship with the current environment. How will the program behave if the infrastructure rules change? The program should be used in the future with minor or no code changes.

Choose Protocols That Are Open and Support Multiple Platforms

Protocols such as SNMP, HTTP, and SSL are well-tested and commonly used. Chances are higher that the target servers will have these software installed and necessary communication ports would be open. This makes it likely for you to leverage successful efforts of the past and lessen the chances of failure in the future.

Document Along with Code

One client had software that would go through the code and determine the percentage of comments. If the code had less than 30 percent comments, it would go back to the coder. IT administrators are more reluctant to write comments than professional software developers.

Documentation is of two types: in-code comments and a "how-to" document for the user. Both are important. Do not document unnecessary details that are obvious from the code statements, but explain the variables, input, and output parameters, and what each subroutine does and accepts as input. Also include a `-help` option with your scripts. Document the overall purpose of each logic.

Common Automation Tools

Tools must be selected that suit the target environment. Do not use Perl if your target server will not have Perl. Any of the following tools can be used to automate common chores. However, it is important to follow some guidelines and rules in the process.

UNIX Shell

A *shell* is a language and interface to an operating system. All UNIX operating systems ship with a few shells such as Bourne (`sh`), Korn (`ksh`), and Bourne Again Shell (`bash`). A shell and PERL are commonly used by SAs for scripting.

They are well-suited for small jobs and jobs that require calls to certain OS commands. They are glue that combines other tools.

They are popular because they are easy to learn, available on all UNIX servers, and require a short time to churn out a working piece of code. Unlike C, they require no compilation. However, they have several deficiencies such as a small set of features. They are not suitable for writing large, complex programs that require teams of developers.

DOS Batch Files

DOS batch files are text files that DOS and Windows use to run a set of commands. A well-known DOS file in older Windows versions was the autoexec.bat file. It is ideal for small jobs and can be written by knowing DOS commands.

C/C++ Languages

These are popular among software developers. They are commonly used among teams, whose code must finally be glued together as part of a larger, complex program. Most OSs ship with libraries that work well with C and C++. C is flexible, and C++ supports object-oriented principles.

Perl

This is actually an acronym for Practical Extraction and Reporting Language. It is popular and robust programming language commonly used for creating CGI programs on Web servers because it is faster than UNIX shell script programs. It can also read and write binary files, and it can efficiently process very large files. It was developed by Larry Wall and his motto was "to serve the programmer and not the language." Perl has a rich feature set, but mastery requires time. However, it is used by all levels of programmers. It has the power of C and the flexibility of the UNIX shell and is ideal for most automation tasks.

Expect

Expect is a language that is designed to talk with other interactive programs. It is a powerful programming language. It has been primarily used as a tool to interact with systems and run programs that require interaction with the user. Once the interaction is defined in a script, Expect will know what to expect from a program and what the correct response will be. One of the most widespread uses for Expect lies in the domain of testing.

TCL/Tk

TCL/Tk is a high-level scripting language that is used in a wide variety of programs. TCL is Expect's base, so any TCL program is also an Expect program. Therefore, Expect, like TCL/Tk, is considered to be a universal language.

Python

Python was invented by Guido van Rossum at CWI (National Research Institute for Mathematics and Computer Science) in Amsterdam, the Netherlands. Python is an interpreted, interactive, and object-oriented programming language. The Python implementation is copyrighted, but it is freely usable and distributable, even for commercial purposes.

Python has outstanding power and has gained popularity because of its clear syntax and readability. It has several modules, classes, exceptions, very high-level dynamic data types, and dynamic typing. It has interfaces to various system calls and libraries, as well as diverse windowing systems such as X11, Motif, and Windows 2000. It can easily be extended with modules or packages from C or C++. Python programs are portable, and they run on many UNIX implementations, Windows, Mac OS and several other OSs. It is used extensively by software developers at Google and other Internet firms. It is frequently compared to TCL, PERL, Scheme, or Java.

MySQL

MySQL is a popular Open Source database. By 2004, it had over 5 million installations worldwide. It is an attractive alternative to complex, high-cost databases. It is commonly used for Web sites, enterprise applications, and packaged software. It is fast, reliable, and available on several platforms such as UNIX, Windows, Mac OS, and Linux. The source code is readily available, and it avoids lock-in with a single vendor or platform.

Like other leading databases, it includes multiple storage engines and full transaction support with commit, rollback, crash recovery, and low-level locking capabilities. It query-caching feature improves performance.

It can be used to store data in a small or medium environment. It is useful for automation that has text-based criteria for queries and searches. MySQL has full-text indexing and searching, which allows for rapid searches for desired words or phrases. The search includes features such as relevance ranking, Boolean operators, and exact phrase matching.

PostgreSQL

This is Open Source database software. It had its beginnings at the University of California at Berkeley in 1986 as a research prototype. It has no licensing cost and is ideal for small or medium databases, even with high-volume traffic. It is ANSI-SQL compliant, has a set of open APIs, and includes native interfaces for ODBC, JDBC, C, C++, Perl, TCL, Python, and Ruby.

MRTG

Multi-Router Traffic Grapher (MRTG) was originally developed to monitor router traffic and generate HTML pages showing live, visual representation of the traffic. It supports SNMP, the most widely used protocol for network monitoring. MRTG is highly customizable and can be used to collect and graph data from various sources. It is free software, and no organization supports it. However, like many other high-profile applications, it has a wide and responsive user base. It can be used for monitoring the use and deployment of automated tools without having to worry about legal or proprietary issues.

Examples of Automation

This section lists some system and network administration tasks that are ideal candidates for automation. Some examples will just list the problem, and some may have automation hints. However they are all platform-neutral.

Example 1: Software Configuration Tracker

A corporation-wide policy would be to maintain all software versions to a minimum release. This is important for protocols such as HTTP, DNS, FTP, Sendmail, and SSH ports that are open to the outside world. If a security risk is discovered in a version, a newer release must be installed (after adequate internal testing, of course). If newer patch releases are available from the vendor and must be installed, this must go in the "required" list.

All SAs and application mangers in the corporation must upgrade the servers. The configuration tracker would simply get the software release numbers from servers and compare them against the minimum requirement.

A database can be kept in MySQL or PostgreSQL for server names to be tracked, software packages, and their minimum required versions. A script (written in Perl) would gather data every night and compare the version numbers. If a server has software below the required version, the script would send an e-mail to the system administrator.

Example 2: Log File Scanner

Hardware and software errors are logged in certain OS log files. Application errors would be recorded in application-related log files. You need to consult SAs, database administrators (DBAs), and application managers to get the list of log files and key words that flag errors and warnings. A script would be written to read these log files and send an e-mail to relevant person(s) if the file has an error or warning key word. The e-mail would include the filename and pertinent lines from the file.

Example 3: Usage Tracker

It is necessary for the various hardware resources not to be over-utilized. If this happens, you must either add more resources or identify and remedy the cause so it does not happen again. There can be a program to do this regularly:

- *Identify disk usage by users* — A variety of policies can be used to control disk hogging. Each user can be given a quote, which, if exceeded, sends e-mail alerts.

- *CPU, memory, swap utilization* — If a process takes up too much CPU, swap, or memory, the program would send alerts. The program simply looks at resource utilization data gathered over the course of the day and identifies high-resource processes.

- *Number of processes* — There can be a limit to the number of processes started by a user or by an application. If you have a misbehaving application or if a server is under denial-of-service attack, it can spawn hundreds of processes. Each user or application has a maximum number of allowed processes.

- *Trend analysis of usage* — This can be for disk utilization, number of processes, or CPU/RAM utilization. It is necessary to see how the usage increased or decreased over time.

Whereas disk space usage is static, other things such as CPU utilization and number of processes are transient. It is therefore necessary to log the activities in a file, which is later read by a program to determine if any alerts should be sent. Data of several days can be analyzed using a script to identify a pattern. Perl is a good choice for parsing text files.

Example 4: User Account Management

A corporation can have many policies about user accounts, passwords, user ID numbers, and so on. For example,

- Each individual is assigned a username and that username would be used on all accounts on hosts, applications, protected Web sites, and so on.

- A user's e-mail password would be used on all his or her new accounts.

- Host passwords would be set to expire every 4 months.

- Passwords need to be eight characters long with at least two numbers and cannot use a four-character string from any previous password.

- If a user has not logged in for 4 months, the account would be locked.

All this requires a central account server, which would have an account, management program. The program would take several options: create, delete, or lock one or more accounts; host names where action must be taken; user names who are impacted; and new home directories that must be used instead of the default /home/username. Again, Perl is ideal for such automation. It has a robust text-argument capability.

Key Points

Following are some key points discussed in this chapter:

- Systems administration is a learned skill.

- Attention to detail and caution before running any root and administrator-privileged command will save a lot of time in fixing any inadvertent problems caused by haste.

- IT automation is now being acknowledged as a major asset to an organization. It must be done in a preplanned manner, following guidelines such as modularity, extensive testing, meeting end-user goals, and simplicity of use.

- Scripting languages such as PERL, C, C++, MySQL, and Python are widely used for automation.

Device Naming

In real life, unlike in Shakespeare, the sweetness of the rose depends upon the name it bears. Things are not only what they are. They are, in very important respects, what they seem to be.
— Hubert H. Humphrey

While it is actually an easy concept to understand, device naming is one of the most important issues in any IT environment. The names selected for hosts, switches, routers, and so forth, the way they are stored, and the mechanisms needed to maintain order are crucial to scale the environment.

At one corporation, each employee had a three-character login name. It was usually a combination of their initials. Dan Jackowaski at that company would be `daj@somewhere.com`. While that is short, it is not possible to know if this login could be for another employee, for example, David Johnson. Another company had the full name of the employee followed by the employee's unique corporate ID number. Our Dan's e-mail address would then be `dan.jackowski.13912@somewhere.com`. While that is certainly inimitable, it is also unappealing and difficult to remember.

This chapter discusses certain practices for naming users, hosts, and other data-center devices, as well as common technologies used to store and manage the names and related data. The four naming technologies described are as follows:

- Network information services (NIS)
- NIS+
- Domain naming system (DNS)
- Lightweight directory access protocol (LDAP)

Naming Practices

In my university days, I worked with a team of Digital (DEC) Ultrix system administrators. Our lab hosts had interesting names: `shout`, `twist`, `dead`, `down`, `kick`, and `jump`. It lead to interesting conversation but difficulty in conveying the facts: "`down` is now up but `jump` is dead." After a trip to Hawaii, a colleague of mine named his servers after the islands of Hawaii. They were difficult to pronounce and gave no clue as to what they did.

Device names should make it easy to understand the function of the device. Here are tried-and-tested device naming practices:

- The name should reflect one or more of the following important facts about the servers:
  - Its primary application such as `mail`, `database`, `apache`, and so on
  - Its country, state, or city, such as `jp` for Japan, `fl` for Florida, and `tk` for Tokyo
  - Its purpose, such as `dev` for development servers, `stg` for stage servers, and `prd` for production
- If you will have more than one server of the same type, use `-1`, `-2`, and so on at the end of the name. Some customers have `001`, `002`, and so on. The leading zeroes usually can be dropped without any negative impact.

Based on the previous two rules, an Apache Web server used for production in a New York data center would be named `web-prod-ny-1`. A development Oracle server in a Hong Kong data center would be `ora-dev-hk-1`. Some operating systems allow up to 14 characters for hostnames.

Another client had a well-thought-out convention for servers:

State (or Country if outside U.S.A.) + City + Application + Purpose + Number

They had codes for all U.S. states (such as `MI` for Michigan), countries (such as `SK` for South Korea), cities around the world (such as `BLR` for Bangalore), a short code for application (such as `ORA` for Oracle), and a code for purpose (`D` for development, `DR` for disaster recovery, `T` for test, `P` for production, and so on). The codes were published on the intranet and employees around the world adhered to that convention. It took a month or so of getting used to, but then each new name you came across conveyed some familiarity. A production mail server in Brisbane, Australia, would be `aubrmailp1`. For desktops, the convention was as follows:

State (or Country if outside U.S.) + City + First few alphabetical characters of user's first name and last name

NIS

Network information services (NIS) is commonly used to store and share user login data (passwords, home directories, and account status), user groups, host IP addresses, and so forth.

NIS was developed independently of DNS and has a slightly different focus. While DNS focuses solely on simplifications that translate hostnames to addresses and vice versa, NIS focuses on simplifying network administration by providing centralized control over a variety of information. NIS stores data not only about workstation names and addresses but also about users, the network itself, and available services. This collection of network information is referred to as the NIS namespace.

Like LDAP and DNS, NIS uses a client-server arrangement that is shown in Figure 16-1.

The main server is the NIS *master server,* and, for increased scalability and robustness, there are *backup* or *slave servers.* If the master server goes down, the slave servers keep the NIS domain functioning, except that no changes can be made to the namespace until the master is up. If data in any NIS map is changed in the master server, the entire map is propagated to the slave servers.

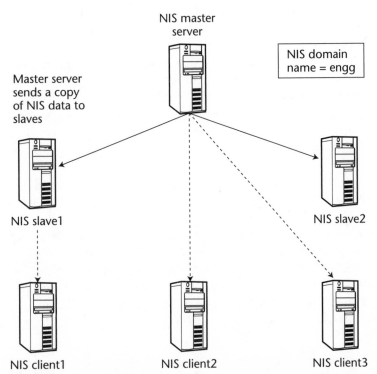

Figure 16-1 NIS master, slave, and clients. Slaves periodically get NIS tables from the master.

At bootup time, each NIS host within the NIS domain (named engg in Figure 16-1) connects to the master server or slave server. The command ypwhich is used to show which NIS server is being used by a host. Should that NIS server go down, the host connects to another server (master or slave).

NIS, like DNS, uses domains to arrange the workstations, users, and networks in its namespace. However, NIS namespace is flat. Note that DNS, NIS+, and LDAP have a hierarchical namespace.

An NIS domain cannot be connected directly to the Internet. Organizations that want to use NIS and be connected to the Internet use NIS to manage all local information and DNS for hostname resolution. NIS provides special client routines for this purpose, referred to as *DNS forwarding*. When a client needs access to any type of information except IP addresses, the request goes to the client's NIS server. When a client needs name resolution, the request goes to the DNS server. From the DNS server, the client has access to the Internet in the usual way.

NIS+

NIS+ extends the name service provided by NIS. NIS+ enables the storage of information about IP addresses, security, user accounts, mail information, Ethernet interfaces, network services, and so forth in central locations where all users and workstations on a network can access it. This configuration of network information is referred to as the *NIS+ namespace*.

The NIS+ namespace is hierarchical and similar in structure to a traditional UNIX directory file system. A NIS+ domain can have subdomains. The engg domain can have subdomains such as asia.engg and na.engg. The layout need not be physical, but can be based on functions, business units, or ownership. Each subdomain can be managed autonomously. Clients may have access to data in other domains, as well as their own if they have the appropriate permissions.

Another advantage of NIS+ over NIS is that changes to the tables (or maps) are propagated incrementally to the replica (or slave servers). Only the updates and not the entire map must be transferred from the master to the replicas.

NIS+ includes a more sophisticated security system to protect the data than does NIS. It uses authentication and authorization to verify whether a client's request for information should be fulfilled. Authentication determines whether the information requester is a valid NIS+ user and has the proper login credentials. Authorization determines whether a particular host or user is allowed to view or change any particular information.

DNS

The Internet is a gigantic field and growing by the day. There are 4.3 billion IP addresses, including reserved addresses. For humans, names are far easier to remember. DNS exists to translate Internet names to IP addresses, as well as IP addresses to names. DNS is like a massive phonebook of Internet names and corresponding IP addresses.

In the early days of the Internet and Arpanet, all machine IP addresses and names were kept in one master host file, namely `/etc/hosts` on UNIX servers. Every time a new host was added or moved to another IP address, someone had to manually edit the file on all hosts. There were several problems with IP/name conflicts and data synchronization.

In the early 1980s, NIS helped by maintaining a single copy of the hosts table that could be viewed and used by all nodes within the NIS domain. But, this still required each NIS administrator to change individual NIS tables.

In 1984 *RFC 1034* ("Domain Names: Concepts and Facilities") was drafted. It described a new way in which machine names and addresses could be managed, decentralized, and distributed. In 1987, *RFC 1035* ("Domain Names: Implementation and Specification") detailed the data types, functions, and protocol.

DNS uses a client-server configuration and lets any user resolve any address in the Internet. The DNS is made of the following components:

- *Namespace* — This contains the data names, IP addresses, and corresponding names.

- *Resolver* — This is the set of programs that allows anyone to query the DNS namespace to convert names to IP addresses and vice versa. When a client needs to convert a name to an IP address, the DNS resolver on the client machine sends the request to the local DNS server. If the local DNS server is authoritative for the requested domain, it provides the information. Often, the DNS server must get the answer from other DNS servers around the world. This is called *DNS recursive queries.*

- *DNS servers* — These are the machines on the Internet that can be queried to provide useful IP address and hostname information. Like LDAP, DNS is also an inverted tree-like structure, as shown in Figure 16-2.

  - *Root-name servers* — At the top of the inverted tree are 13 root-name servers called `a.root-servers.net.` through `m.root-servers.net.` These are managed and hosted by various independent agencies. Ten of these servers reside in the United States, one in London, one in Stockholm, and one in Tokyo. All these servers do is point the requests to the layer of machines below them, which, in turn, are the top-level domain (TLD) servers.

- *Top-level domain (TLD) servers* — Initially, there were seven top-level domains, namely .net, .com, .int, .org, .edu, .mil, and .gov. After that, several were added such as .biz and .tv. Several countries have country-level domains such as .de for Germany, .my for Malaysia, .jp for Japan, and .in for India. These are managed by Internet domain registrars.

- *Domain name servers* — When you register a domain such as thechavezfamily.org, you must provide the IP addresses of at least two DNS servers that will be considered as *authoritative servers* for the domain. The TLD servers will delegate control of your domain to these two DNS servers, hence called the new domain's authoritative servers. These two servers can be managed by you, your ISP, or by the domain registrar. These could be, for example, ns1 and ns2.thechavezfamily.org, and any client that searches for www.thechavezfamily.org will ultimately come to ns1 or ns2.thechavezfamily.org to get the correct IP addresses. It is therefore important that the DNS servers be highly available and contain correct data within their zone files.

Most domains on the Internet have the following name servers:

- *Master servers* — These servers contain the master data for each domain that it is authoritative for. Data for each domain is kept in a zone file. A *zone file* contains machine names, aliases, and corresponding IP addresses for all hosts within the domain.

- *Slave servers* — These servers contain copies of the master zone file. Periodically the master propagates all changes to the slave servers. These downloads are called *zone transfers*.

- *Caching servers* — These are hosts that can be queried to resolve DNS records. They return an answer from the local cache or contact the DNS authority chain to ultimately consult the authoritative server for the domain.

You can use the whois database to see the list of authoritative DNS servers and other information about any registered domain name:

```
www.internic.net/whois.html
```

```
www.gandi.net/whois?l=EN
```

```
www.whois.net/
```

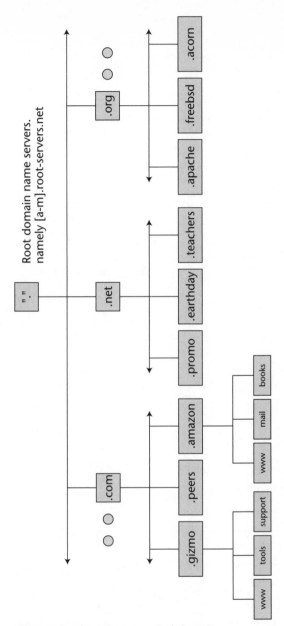

Figure 16-2   DNS servers and domains.

This is a typical result of a `whois` query for `pbskids.org` from `www.whois.net`:

```
Domain Name:PBSKIDS.ORG
Created On:09-Apr-1999 04:00:00 UTC
Last Updated On:23-Oct-2004 12:02:07 UTC
```

```
Expiration Date:09-Apr-2012 04:00:00 UTC
Sponsoring Registrar:Network Solutions LLC (R63-LROR)
Status:CLIENT TRANSFER PROHIBITED
Registrant ID:24737677-NSI
Registrant Name:Public Broadcasting Service
Registrant Organization:Public Broadcasting Service
Registrant Street1:1320 Braddock Place
Registrant City:Alexandria
Registrant State/Province:VA
Registrant Postal Code:22314-1698
Registrant Country:US
Registrant Phone:+1.7037395100
Registrant Email:hostadmin@pbs.org
Admin ID:24737677-NSI
Admin Name:Public Broadcasting Service
Admin Organization:Public Broadcasting Service
Admin Street1:1320 Braddock Place
Admin City:Alexandria
Admin State/Province:VA
Admin Postal Code:22314-1698
Admin Country:US
Admin Phone:+1.7037395100
Admin Email:hostadmin@pbs.org
Tech ID:19329813-NSI
Tech Name:Carlos Lacruz
Tech Street1:1320 Braddock Place
Tech City:Alexandria
Tech State/Province:VA
Tech Postal Code:22314
Tech Country:US
Tech Phone:+1.7037395100
Tech Email:hostadmin@pbs.org
Name Server:DNS1.PBS.ORG
Name Server:DNS2.PBS.ORG
```

DNS Caching

DNS caching allows hosts to hold on and use DNS information that it has queried for in the last 24 hours (default TTL, or time-to-live, value). The TTL value can be as low as a few seconds or as high as a week or more (24 hours is a typical value). That is why when you make a DNS change at your registrar, you are told that it will take 24 hours for the changes to be propagated worldwide.

This is how caching works. If you are the first one from your ISP to contact www.pbskids.org/, your browser contacts the ISP's DNS server, which does not find the domain in its cache. It then forwards the request to the root-name servers, and then contacts the TLD server and finally the authoritative DNS server for pbskids.org (either dns1.pbskids.org or dns2.pbskids.org). These servers return the IP address 149.48.192.139 for the name server `www.pbskids.org` and the TTL value. These are kept in the ISP's DNS server cache for the amount of time period specified in the TTL parameter. The next time someone at your ISP wants to contact `www.pbskids.org`, the DNS server will not reach out to the Internet but only to its local cache. This speeds operations and takes a lot of load off the Internet.

You can use the Microsoft `ipconfig` tool to view and to flush the DNS resolver cache. To view the contents of the DNS resolver cache at the command prompt, type the following:

```
C:\> ipconfig /displaydns
```

To flush the cache manually, type the following at the command prompt:

```
C:\> ipconfig /flushdns
```

Table 16-1 lists the common types of DNS resource records. These are specified in the zone file for each domain.

Table 16-1: Common DNS Resource Records in the Zone Files

RESOURCE RECORD DATA	DESCRIPTION	EXPLANATION
SOA	Start of authority	This record is usually the first resource record in the zone file but may be preceded by a TTL statement. The SOA record establishes this file as the authoritative source of information for this zone. It contains information such as the name of the zone, the e-mail address of the zone administrator, and configuration parameters that control how slave DNS servers update the zone data files.
A	Address	This is the key name resolution record. These lines look like `www.intlwidgets.com IN A 141.20.1.23`. Hostnames that do not end with a "." are automatically appended the domain name.
CNAME	Canonical name	These are also known as alias records. They specify an alternate or alias name for an existing hostname. They point to another name, which has an A record.
PTR	Pointer	They map domain names to IP addresses. These are used inside reverse lookup zone files. The reverse domain is named by reversing the IP address and appending `.in-addr.arpa` to the zone name.

(continued)

Table 16-1 *(continued)*

RESOURCE RECORD DATA	DESCRIPTION	EXPLANATION
MX	Mail exchanger	These servers are default e-mail recipients for hosts within that domain. E-mails are delivered to the IP address specified by the MX record. If a domain has no MX record, the mail transport agent will contact the host directly to deliver the e-mail.
NS	Name server	This record specifies the name server responsible for a given zone.

Registering Your Domain Name in DNS

If you want a domain name of your own, you can register a domain name with any domain registrar. Following are some of the popular registrars in United States:

```
www.godaddy.com/
www.register.com/
www.usacheapdomains.com/
www.easydns.com/
```

The annual fee is usually between $7 and $35 per year for each domain name. If you register for many years, you get a price break.

LDAP

The lightweight directory access protocol (LDAP) is a directory service that runs on a layer above the TCP/IP stack. It allows an organization to store and manage information in one or more directories. The function of LDAP is to enable access to existing directories.

LDAP was originally designed as a front end to X.500, the OSI-based directory services. The data model (data and namespace) of LDAP is still similar to that of the X.500 OSI directory service but with lighter resource requirements.

LDAP is based on a client-server model. One or more LDAP servers contain the data making up the LDAP directory tree. An LDAP client connects to an LDAP server and requests information or performs an operation. The server provides the information or performs the operation, or refers the client to another LDAP server for further processing. Regardless of the LDAP server to which a client connects, the client sees the same view of the directory.

Figure 16-3 shows the servers in an LDAP architecture.

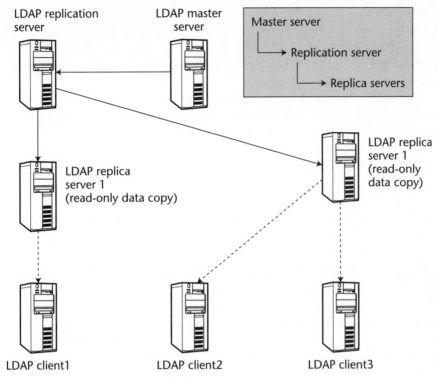

Figure 16-3 LDAP master, replication, and replica servers.

The following servers make up the LDAP server space:

- *Master server* — All modifications to the LDAP directory and contents are made on the master server. Most implementations have one master server, but it is possible to set up replica servers to become the master in case the master server fails.

- *Replication server* — This server has the task of pushing all data changes from the master servers to replica servers.

- *Replica servers* — These have a read-only copy of the data. LDAP clients can query or search the data.

- *LDAP clients* — These get data directly from the master or from replica servers.

It is important to note that LDAP is designed to allow quick and efficient access to an existing directory. Its streamlined (lightweight) design prevents it from being able to create a directory or to specify how the directory service itself operates.

In LDAP, directory entries are arranged in a hierarchical tree-like structure that reflects political, geographic, and organization boundaries. Figure 16-4 shows an example of a corporation LDAP hierarchy. The corporation name is International Widgets with offices in Boston, Los Angeles, New Delhi, and Hong Kong. Each site has a department. Entries representing continents are at the top of the tree. Below them can be entries representing business units (such as departments), devices (such as printers or hosts), or data types.

This is a good baseline for large corporations. Splitting up the directory at various levels makes it scalable, easier to manage, and quicker to replicate to other servers. But the problem is the size of the *distinguished name* (*DN*). Chris Bart's DN is `Cn=Chris Bart ou=Sales ou=Boston c=USA o=IntlWidgets`. This does not have to be typed as e-mail IDs because the LDAP remembers and expands it.

An entry's DN is constructed by taking the name of the entry itself, followed by the names of its ancestor entries. The name of the entry itself is called the *relative distinguished name* (*RDN*). Table 16-2 lists typical RDN strings and their Attribute values.

For example, the RDN for Eric Miller would be `cn=Eric Miller` and its DN would be `cn=Eric Miller, ou=Sales, ou=Boston, c=US, o=IntlWidgets`. An RDN could be other data such as `badge=12987`, in which case information about the person would be arranged around the badge number. Think of the RDN as the apartment and building number and the DN as the entire address.

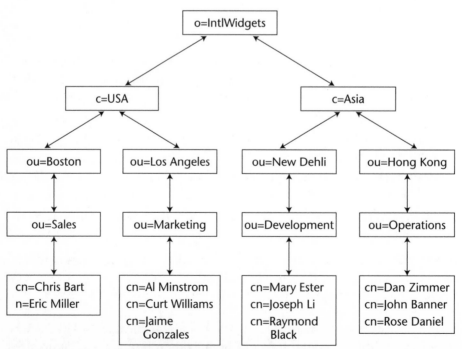

Figure 16-4 An example LDAP directory tree.

Table 16-2 Typical RDN Strings and Attribute Values

RDN STRING	ATTRIBUTE VALUE
DC	domainComponent
CN	commonName
OU	organizationalUnitName
O	organizationName
STREET	streetAddress
L	localityName
ST	stateOrProvinceName
C	countryName
UID	Userid

Too many subdivisions make for a long DN entry for each employee. Splitting at the city and department level means that if an employee moves to another location or department, his DN must be changed. Therefore, a good architecture of the directory information tree (DIT) is important.

Designing a Directory Information Tree (DIT)

A good understanding of the requirements and objectives of the LDAP implementation is crucial to making a resilient, scalable architecture. Let's classify the DIT design:

1. *Data* — List and understand all data types that will stay in the directory (such as employee HR records, employee login information, MD5 checksums, and performance data).

2. *Directory-enabled applications* — List requirements of all applications that need to access LDAP for information. Consider the interface and data format requirements.

3. *Topology* — Will data have different branches based on business units or geographical locations?

4. *Replication* — If LDAP data needs to be replicated to a remote server, it has an influence of DIT design.

5. *Scalability* — Regardless of how small the LDAP data currently is, it must be able to accommodate future data growth.

After designing an appropriate DIT and agreeing on a standard storage mechanism, it is time to implement the solution. Several well-tested industry implementations of LDAP are available. One popular implementation is

OpenLDAP, derived from the University of Michigan's LDAP v 3.3. It includes the following components:

- `slapd` — A stand-alone LDAP directory server
- `slurpd` — Replication server to send data to other read-only servers
- `ldapd` — An LDAP-to-X.500 gateway server
- `centipede` — An LDAP centroid generation and maintenance program
- `libldap` — An LDAP client library
- `liblber` — A lightweight BER/DER encoding/decoding library
- `in.xfingerd` — A finger-to-LDAP gateway server
- `rcpt500` — An e-mail-to-LDAP query responder
- `mail500` — An LDAP-capable mailer
- *LDAP tools* — A collection of shell-based LDAP utility programs

Other popular LDAP implementations are available from Microsoft, Novell, and Sun.

Key Points

Following are some key points discussed in this chapter:

- Device and hostnames must follow a corporate-wide standard.
- Despite initial hurdles and the getting-used-to factor, doing so has sustained, long-term payoffs.
- Names can be configured in NIS, NIS+, DNS, and LDAP.
- NIS (also referred to as yellow pages) and NIS+ are commonly used for user account management (such as user names, passwords, home directories, and groups).
- DNS has become the key IP addressing system. The Internet DNS system is an inverted tree-like structure with root-name servers at the top, followed by top-level DNS servers (for `.edu`, `.com`, `.net`, and so forth) and individual domains (such as `redhat.com` and `sendmail.org`). Each large domain has DNS master, slave, and sometimes caching servers.
- LDAP is gaining popularity for user authentication.

Load Balancing

It is only imperfection that complains of what is imperfect. The more perfect we are, the gentler and quieter we become towards the defects of others.

— Joseph Addison

The term *load balancing* implies distribution of disk I/O or network traffic over two or more active paths or channels. The advantages of load balancing are enhanced performance and service availability. This chapter describes how you can use load balancing to set up a highly available and scalable group of servers. Each server in the group can process all incoming requests. The group of servers is called a *server farm*. Any one server has limited resources and, at some point, will be overwhelmed by requests from clients. To avoid this problem, an optimizing algorithm is used on a front-end machine to distribute the load among all servers in the farm.

The protocol of choice for most Internet applications is TCP/IP. The term "IP load balancing" was coined in early 1997. *PC Magazine* published one of the first reviews on IP load-balancing products in February 1997. Since then, the term has become a standard for describing products that intercept and distribute IP packets among a group of servers or devices configured logically behind them. In other words, the term refers to forwarding each incoming request to the least-busy server, as selected by a predetermined algorithm.

Customers expect availability and refuse to accept latency or failure. If a Web site is slow or unavailable, users and customers will go somewhere else and possibly never return. Load balancers are used to guarantee service availability (regardless of server failures) and to make services scalable. A variety of network services, such as HTTP, streaming audio and video, FTP, NNTP (news), cache, firewall services, LDAP, and e-mail, can be load balanced. *Load* is the amount of incoming requests. However, the most common industry implementation of load balancing has been for Web services.

Load-Balancing Terminology

Following are some key terms related to load balancing:

- *Front-end machine* — A load balancer that distributes client requests to a group of servers, placed behind it.

- *Web server farm* — A group of Web servers hidden behind the load balancer (or front-end machine) that process incoming Web requests. They are also called *back-end servers*. To the Web client, the site appears as a single Web server represented by the front-end machine. The front-end machine has an Internet routable IP address (also called *public* or *external IP*), but the back-end servers do not need routable IPs.

- *Super farm* — A server farm consisting of two or more server farms.

- *Port* — Most servers or devices have only a few physical network interfaces or NICs for data communication. Various services communicating over the same physical NIC are distinguished by port number. Different port numbers are designated for different kinds of IP traffic. For example, port 21 is FTP, port 80 is commonly used for HTTP, and port 23 is used for telnet. Ports 1–1023 are the well-known ports and are defined in RFCs available at various Web sites such as www.faqs.org/rfcs/ and www.ietf.org/.

- *Network address translation* (*NAT*) — Load balancers use NAT to allow a public or external IP address to be assigned to a Web site. The individual servers in the Web farm can have private or internal IP addresses. The load balancer forwards incoming requests to the routable IP address (belonging to the front-end server) to servers in the Web farm.

- *Stickiness* — This is the capability of a load balancer to direct data flows from certain browser clients to the same server in the farm. One criterion to assign stickiness is a mathematical combination of the client browser IP address and TCP port of the requested traffic.

- *Persistent connection* — For many applications requiring session-specific information (such as a customer shopping cart on an e-commerce Web site), it is important that once a connection is established between a client browser and a back-end server, the connection remain intact for the entire duration of the transaction. For example, when a user purchases a book on a Web site, all requests related to the purchase must be directed to the same back-end server. This is enabled by persistent connection feature of load balancers. Persistent connections are based on various client- or server-side attributes such as IP bindings and cookies. It enables a client browser to download all page elements in one session from a single server in the farm. Persistent connections enhance performance because there is no need to round-robin to different servers to retrieve all the page elements (such as HTML, images, and frames).

- *Virtual local area networks* (*VLANs*) — VLANs allow networks to be logically or administratively divided into numerous separate LANs. Network switches use VLANs to provide flexibility and ease in changing network topologies.

Advantages

This section lists features and advantages of most load-balancing solutions. If the vendor and load-balancing solution you are considering does not provide this minimum set of features, keep looking.

Fault Tolerance

This is perhaps the most important reason to implement a load-balancing solution. With load balancing, the failure of a server does not interrupt services. Load balancers verify if back-end servers are available and check whether critical applications are running and responding correctly. If a back-end server or application is unavailable, the server is disabled and does not receive any incoming requests. It can be removed from the group and later added back without having to offline the service offered by the server farm. All remaining machines in the farm have to carry some extra load until the disabled server is repaired and added back to the group.

Service Availability

If you have only one server with 90 percent availability, the servers will be unavailable for 10 percent of the time (that is, 2.4 hours every day). This is an extreme example, and most servers have higher reliability, but it better illustrates the point. With two such servers, the probability of both servers failing at the same time is 0.1 * 0.1 = 0.01 (that is, services will be unavailable for 0.24 hours or 14.4 minutes per day). With six such unreliable servers in the farm, the probability of all the servers being down at the same time is 0.000001. Service availability is therefore 99.9999 percent of the time, an availability of "four nines."

Performance

Load balancing spreads the work among several servers. Without load balancing, all work must be done by a single server. The incoming client requests are distributed among servers in the farm. Response time to the client decreases, especially for CPU-intensive tasks. Each host in the farm runs an independent copy of the programs required by the load balancer

Scalability

If you add new services or applications, traffic to your Web site will undoubtedly increase. A load balancer makes it easy to add new servers to handle the increased traffic. Servers can be taken offline or put back in the farm transparently.

Flexibility

The load balancer must be able to manage a heterogeneous set of servers, hardware platforms, and operating systems. Ideally legacy hosts and latest servers should all work together in the server farm, and there should be no need to deploy only a certain platform or buy from a single vendor. Load balancers increase flexibility by enabling different traffic-distribution methods among servers in the farm. A Web farm could use round-robin method, while an e-mail server farm uses the least-connections method. (These methods are described in more detail later in this chapter.)

Cost Savings

It is cheaper to implement load balancing because the servers do not have to be fault tolerant. All you need are many small, low-cost servers. The alternative architecture using a high-end, high-performance server would be a more expensive option.

Security

When virtual servers are configured on the load balancer for sending traffic to server farms, certain ports are designated for the traffic. The load balancer drops requests sent to all other ports. This protects the servers from having to deal with malicious or unwanted traffic.

Types of Load Balancing

At a high level, the concept of load balancing is simple. When a request comes in, the load balancer must decide which server should be assigned the request. There are several methods for selecting the server, the most common of which are described in this section.

Software-Based Methods

Software-based methods require the load-balancing algorithm to be configured on a host. Servers in the farm may require some software. Some software solutions provide the capability of data synchronization between servers, thus guaranteeing identical content. Software solutions have some disadvantages, such as limited scalability, license costs, software tuning, and platform dependencies.

Round-Robin Domain Name Service (RRDNS)

RRDNS is a low-cost solution for configuring load balancing for Web farms that can be enabled via Berkeley Internet Name Domain (BIND) version 4.9 or later. BIND is the de facto implementation of DNS and is included in many operating systems. It is maintained by the Internet Software Consortium (ISC). With RRDNS, incoming requests are forwarded to each server in the farm in a cyclical manner. This method is simple and cheap to implement.

RRDNS has several shortcomings. Unless specifically disabled, DNS servers cache the resolved hostname and IP address mapping to reduce the load on DNS servers, thus eliminating the need to query the DNS server continuously. Thereby, DNS clients do not negatively impact the DNS server performance. However, this causes one load-balancing problem.

The Web server IP address that is resolved in the first query gets all the requests. This leads to reduced load balancing. This problem can be solved by disabling cache. But this, in turn, slows the DNS server, because all requests must be sent to the DNS server.

Another solution is to control the time-to-live (TTL) value appended to each piece of information by DNS servers. TTL resides in the start of authority (SOA) resource record of the DNS zone file, where the CNAME resource records reside. If TTL is set too high, there are fewer queries sent to the DNS server, but the DNS servers cache the information for too long, which again leads to bad load balancing over the server farm. If TTL is set too low, other DNS servers cause the information to expire faster, and more queries are sent to the DNS server. This leads to better load balancing but more burden for the DNS servers. In practice, a TTL value of 30–60 minutes provides a balance between load distribution in the server farm and the amount of DNS queries.

There is one more problem with RRDNS that is worth describing. Let's take a Web farm that is load-balanced by a DNS server. If a host in the farm fails, the DNS server is not automatically aware of the failure and will continue to forward requests to the failed server. Hitting the "reload" button on the browser does not help because the IP address that belongs to the failed server is cached on the DNS server. The problem persists until the failed server is manually removed from DNS. Even after that, users must wait until DNS times out the value in the cache before they can resolve the Web site to another server in the farm and successfully access the Web site.

Because of these shortcomings, RRDNS is rarely used for mission-critical or large Web farms. You can use RRDNS for a small Web farm of two or three servers or use it to distribute traffic among multiple Web farms, where each Web farm is, in turn, load-balanced by another more reliable solution.

Windows 2000 Network Load Balancing (NLB)

NLB is a clustering technology included with Microsoft Windows 2000 operating system (Advanced Server and Datacenter Editions). NLB is implemented using a network driver logically placed between the network adapter in the server and the high-level TCP/IP protocol. Each server in the farm has at least two IP addresses: a *cluster address* and a *dedicated address*.

NLB has several merits. As you can see, no additional hardware components are required. All you need is an additional component for the networking driver, which is easy to install or remove. Another advantage is that NLB can detect a failed server and stop sending requests to it. Performance of the farm depends entirely on the performance of the individual servers in the farm and network speed.

VERITAS Cluster Server (VCS) Traffic Director

VCS is used to increase application availability through failover. If a cluster service or the server itself fails, the applications and services running on the node are migrated to remaining cluster nodes.

The Traffic Director option is an extension to VCS. It increases performance, scalability, and availability by load balancing incoming TCP/IP and UDP/IP traffic among a group of back-end servers. Performance is enhanced because there are several back-end servers ready to accept incoming IP requests (see Figure 17-1). As the demand on a Web site or application increases, more servers can be added. There is no limit to the number of back-end servers in a farm. The Web site or application can, therefore, easily scale to meet increased demands.

If a back-end server fails, Traffic Director automatically stops directing incoming requests to the server. It is easy to remove back-end servers for maintenance and later return them to the farm. Server failures do not interrupt service.

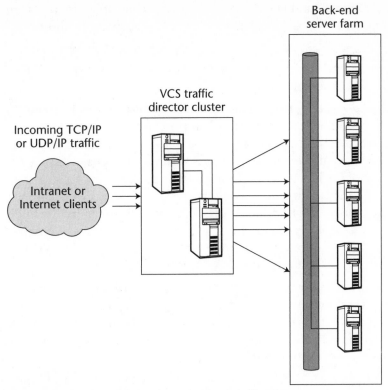

Figure 17-1   IP Load balancing using VCS Traffic Director option.

Another feature that enhances service availability is its ability to failover open connections. All members of the VCS Traffic Director cluster continuously share traffic direction and state information. If a member of the cluster fails while directing traffic, a healthy node takes over all open connections of the failed node and resumes operations from where they paused when the node failed. This is stateful failover.

Hardware-Based Methods

The load-balancing switch is the only hardware required. It is placed between the user community and the server farm. There are some distinct advantages to having a dedicated hardware. Mission-critical application servers can be transparently placed in or out of service, thus providing fault tolerance. The environment is independent of operating system, and heterogeneous servers can be placed in the same farm. The individual servers do not need any software. They continue to do their tasks as before. The entire setup is flexible and the overall maintenance is simple.

Hardware solutions have their disadvantages as well. All traffic to and from the farm goes through a single piece of hardware. This is a single point of failure

(SPOF), unless a standby load-balancing switch is set up. Incoming requests are distributed among servers in the farm, using one of the following methods:

- *Round-robin* — Incoming requests are distributed evenly to all nodes in the farm. When the load-balancing switch receives a new request, it is passed to the next server in line.

- *Weighted round-robin or ratio* — This is similar to the round-robin solution. The only distinction is that all servers are not considered equal. Servers that can handle a greater load than others are assigned a higher weight. They have more hardware resources and, therefore, accept a greater share of the incoming requests. If there are four servers in a Web farm and they are assigned weights of 5, 10, 10, and 15, the sum of these weights is 40. The first server gets 5/40 or 12.5 percent of the total incoming requests. The second, third, and fourth servers have weights of 10, 10, and 15, respectively, and therefore get 25 percent, 25 percent, and 37.5 percent of the total incoming requests.

- *Priority mode* — In Priority mode, you create groups of servers. Each group is assigned a priority level. All nodes in the highest priority group receive incoming requests via the round-robin method. If all the nodes in the highest priority group fail, the load balancer uses servers in the next-lower priority group.

- *Least-connections mode* — The load balancer passes a new request to the server handling the least number of connections at that moment.

- *Fastest-response mode* — The load balancer determines the response time of each server by measuring the elapsed time between sending a packet to a server and receiving a response packet from the node. The next incoming request is sent to the server with the fastest response time.

- *Combination of least-connections and fastest modes (Observed mode)* — Nodes are ranked according to a mathematical combination of number of current connections and response time. This is also called Observed ranking. The node with the best performance gets the next incoming request.

- *Predictive mode* — The load balancer analyzes the trend of the Observed ranking over time. The server with the best performance ranking that is currently improving gets the next request.

Figure 17-2 shows how a load-balancing switch serves as a bridge between clients and servers.

There are several other load-balancing methods. Some are based on client IP address, HTTP cookie header, HTTP Universal Resource Locator (URL) of the HTTP request, and so forth. Some load balancers have a limit on how many characters of the URL they can use to make a load-balancing decision (the number can range from 128 to 2,000 characters).

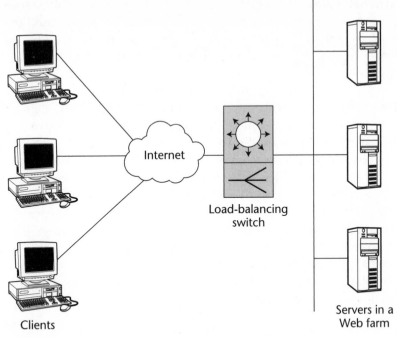

Figure 17-2   Load-balancing switch between Internet and servers.

Implementing a Network with Load-Balancing Switches

As we have already seen, load-balancing switches provide a reliable and scalable method for redirecting incoming requests to multiple, low-cost servers. Examples of hardware-based, load-balancing switches include Cisco's LocalDirector and Arrowpoint switches, F5 Networks' BIG-IP, and Nortel Networks' Alteon Content Director.

These switches sit between the Web farm and the connection to the Internet. All Web requests come to the load-balancing switch using the same IP address. Based on various algorithms, the switch forwards the request to different servers in the Web farm.

The switch frequently pings the servers in the farm to ensure that they are still up and to sense how busy they are. The switches are also highly scalable. The number of servers in the farm can be increased easily and with no downtime. Load-balancing switches are, however, expensive and business-critical Web farms need at least two for redundancy.

Load balancers have few ports. If servers are directly connected to the load balancer, you would quickly run out of ports. As shown in Figure 17-3, servers are connected to a network switch or hub, and the load balancer is connected to a router. Load balancers are connected to routers, hubs, or switches. Most load-balancing switches allow trunking (or multiplexing) of the connection between themselves and the network switch. Several links are grouped into a virtual, fault-tolerant channel. As you add more links to the virtual channel, performance increases.

Different interfaces on a load-balancing switch can be used to connect to multiple Web server farms, as illustrated in Figure 17-4. When two or more Web farms provide the same Web content, the group is called a super farm.

Use two load balancers to prevent this from being a SPOF. Figure 17-5 shows a network with redundant devices. Primary and secondary load balancers are interconnected by heartbeat cables (Ethernet crossover or serial cables). The switches also have heartbeat cables. At first glance, an environment with two load balancers seems to have enough redundancy. But what if a switch port in the load balancer or Ethernet cable fails? What if a switch fails in entirety? One solution is to use redundant switches and load balancers, which are able to detect and transparently resolve such failures. Under normal conditions, the secondary load balancer is a passive standby that waits for the primary to fail. Some vendors allow both load balancers to be active.

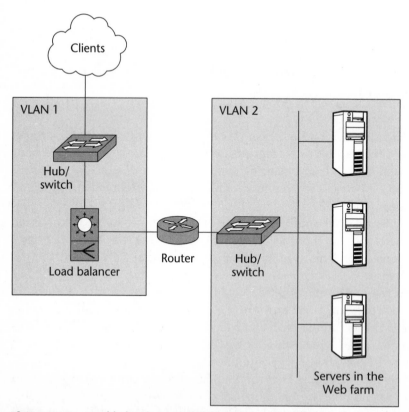

Figure 17-3 Load-balancing switch with hubs and switches.

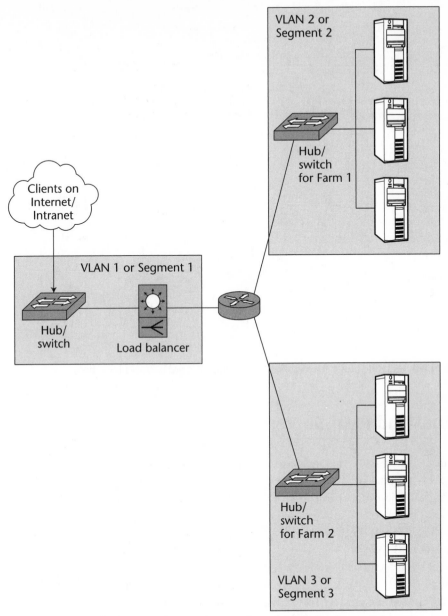

Figure 17-4 Multiple server farms connected to a load-balancing switch.

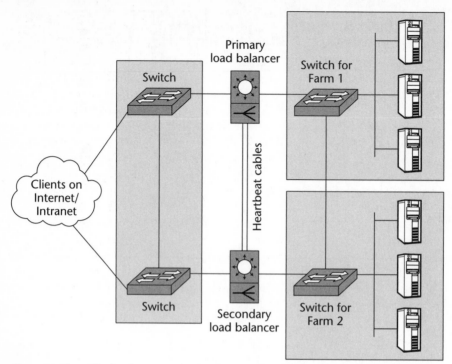

Figure 17-5 A fault-tolerant network with redundant switches and load balancers.

Virtual and Real Servers

Virtual IP addresses are configured on the load balancer. When a load balancer receives a request on a certain port on a virtual IP, it forwards the request to a specific port of a server in the farm. A virtual IP address and port combination on a load balancer is called a *virtual server*. If the virtual IP address is accessed from the Internet, it must be a legal IP address, allocated by the network information center (NIC).

A *real server* is the internal representation of a physical server in the farm and includes the IP address and port number. Just like a load balancer can have several virtual servers, a physical server can have several real servers.

Virtual and real servers can be mapped in the following ways:

- One virtual server mapped to one real server
- One virtual server mapped to multiple real servers
- Multiple virtual servers mapped to one real server
- Multiple virtual servers mapped to multiple real servers

TALES FROM THE TECH TURF: WHAT MATTERS MOST FOR HIGH-VOLUME WEB SITES

What really happens when traffic on Web sites reaches high levels is counterintuitive. Take the example of a company that conducted tests on its heavily accessed Web sites within a high-speed network. When it pitched successful television advertisements, the traffic from users increased. The users had low-speed, dial-up access to the Internet. The Web servers responded to browser connections, but the sessions would not end for a long time because of the slow network speed of the user's browser. Server resources such as memory, CPU, and network bandwidth were mostly idle, but the high number of simultaneous connections exceeded the limits allowed by the operating system and the Web servers crashed. Customers were surprised by the low-quality Web sites, resulting in a nonfavorable impression of the company (despite very successful television advertisements).

Figure 17-6 shows a single virtual server on port 80 mapped to three real servers on the same port. All traffic for port 80 on 30.40.50.60 is load-balanced across real servers with IP addresses 10.10.20.20, 10.10.20.21, and 10.10.20.22. Each real server resides on a separate physical server in the farm. The virtual address is a legal, Internet-routable IP address because the Web site must be accessible from the Internet. Only the virtual address must be configured in DNS. The real-server IP addresses can be nonroutable or private.

In Figure 17-7, all traffic destined for port 80 on IP address 30.40.50.60 is load-balanced across the three servers on port 1080. Similarly, traffic destined for port 80 on Virtual IP address 30.40.50.61 is load-balanced across the three servers on port 1081.

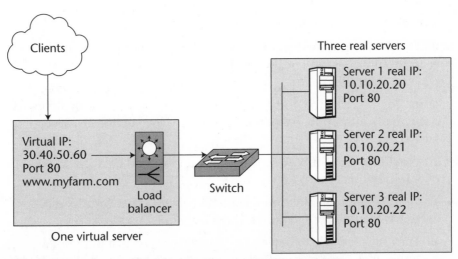

Figure 17-6   One virtual server mapped to multiple real servers.

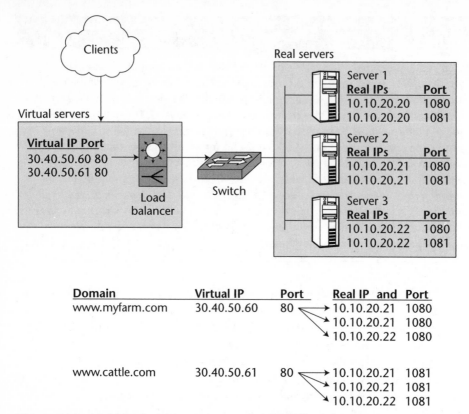

Figure 17-7 Multiple virtual servers mapped to multiple real servers.

Best Practices for Load Balancing

Following are some best practices for load balancing:

- Use load-balancing switches instead of software methods such as round-robin DNS or Windows NLB.

- Load-balancing switches are expensive and have a limited number of ports. To overcome the port-number limitation, connect the switches to a network switch, hub, or router. Set up VLANs to delineate server farms.

- To avoid a SPOF, set up a secondary or standby load balancer to take over if the primary unit fails.

- To improve fault tolerance and availability, verify that your load balancer has the following features and use them:

  - They must be able to detect the "health" of servers and remove a server that is not responding to requests. When a failed server is repaired and brought online, the load balancer must detect the host and start using it.

- Servers must be gradually taken out of service. Interruption of service because of a failed host must be transparent to users who have a live session with a server. Current users must be allowed to complete their sessions while no new requests are sent to a server about to be removed for maintenance.

- Servers must be gradually returned to service. When a server is introduced into a farm, the load balancer must allow the server software to stabilize and incrementally present user load to the server. The load balancer must be able to affirm that the server hardware and software are stable before using it to the full potential.

- Some load-balancing solutions enable specific servers in the farm to be configured as backup or standby servers that are used if any active server fails. Standby load balancers are analogous to hot spare disks in a redundant volume.

- Look for security features in your load balancer. Can it detect harmful attacks from the Internet community and protect the servers in the farm from such malicious requests?

- There are several load-balancing methods. Most vendors have round-robin or least-connections as the default method for load balancing. The optimum method depends on the amount of traffic and server resources.

Key Points

Following are some key points discussed in this chapter:

- Load balancers are network appliances that distribute incoming requests among multiple, low-cost servers. The group of servers is called a farm. A super farm is a group of farms where all servers provide the same service and content. A Web server farm is the most common implementation of load balancing.

- Load balancers reduce the cost of providing large-scale Internet services. They aggregate a group of low-cost servers into a highly redundant and fault-tolerant server farm. Individual servers can be transparently placed in and out of service without downtime, thus providing fault tolerance. Load balancers optimize the performance of the site by intelligently distributing client requests so that no server gets overwhelmed.

- Load balancing can be done using software such as the round-robin feature of BIND 4.9, Microsoft Windows 2000 Node Load balancing (NLB), and the Traffic Director option of VERITAS Cluster Server (VCS). The Traffic Director option has several high-availability features that enhance performance and scalability to meet increased demands.

- Hardware load balancing requires a dedicated switch. Industry-leading vendors for load-balancing switches are Cisco, Nortel Networks, and F5. With hardware load-balancing solutions, a second load balancer is often implemented as a passive standby device to provide redundancy. This avoids the active switch from being a SPOF.

- One or more virtual IP addresses and port numbers are configured on the load balancers. Each virtual IP address-port number combination in the load balancer is called a virtual server. Each IP address and port number combination on a server is called a real server. One virtual server could be mapped to one or many real servers. Multiple virtual servers can also be mapped to one or many real servers.

18

Fault Tolerance

Hope is the companion of power, and the mother of success;
for who so hopes strongly, has within him the gift of miracles.
— Samuel Smiles

This chapter describes fault tolerance and its role in improving service and data availability. *Fault tolerance* is the capability of a host or subsystem to recover from a component failure without service interruption. A fault-tolerant host or device has redundant components that monitor each other. All components work in lock-step, thus allowing the transition upon failure to occur almost instantly. The redundant components may be set up to work in parallel as an active-active pair. Alternatively, a component could be in a passive state and simply wait for its partners to fail or give inaccurate results before activating itself. A failed component is singled out of the system and the standby component starts providing the services of the failed partner. All the steps (namely monitoring, failure identification, and replacement) occur without user intervention and are transparent to the users and applications.

Vendors of fault-tolerant systems spend a lot of time and money on designing and testing the overall architecture. Fault-tolerant systems are expensive. You can configure component-level redundancy for storage devices. Explaining how is the objective of this and the next chapter.

There are certain things from which fault tolerance cannot protect your system — a bug in the operating system or application; loss of power to the entire building; fire, environmental problems, or disasters that cause downtime of the entire system — irrespective of the degree of fault tolerance.

Need for Fault Tolerance

In the past, a few large companies in industries such as telecommunications and finance used fault-tolerant servers for their business-critical applications. The high cost of implementation was a major impediment. Recently the cost of computing resources has decreased and new technologies (such as the Internet) have led to the introduction of several new applications. These new applications have improved productivity, have led to faster business transactions, and have provided critical information at all times.

However, customers and employees have become more and more dependent on availability of online information, 24 hours a day. Many businesses will halt if certain applications or servers are unavailable for even a short time. These servers, therefore, must somehow continue providing services despite failures of components such as disks, network devices, and power supplies. Fortunately fault tolerance can be enabled for servers and networks without incurring high expenses.

Component Reliability Terms

The terms described here represent statistical aspects of component reliability.

- *Mean time between failures (MTBF)* — This is a component's average time between failures. It is just a statistical figure. A CPU with a MTBF of 400,000 hours can fail after just 10 hours, or even after 800,000 hours of operation. A data center that has 500 such CPUs will experience a CPU failure on average every 800 hours (400,000 / 500).

- *Mean time to data loss (MTTDL)* — This is the amount of time that a system or subsystem can continue functioning before it encounters failures that are bad enough to cause data loss. For disks not protected by mirroring or parity, the MTTDL is the same as the MTBF. For mirrored disks, data loss will happen only if at least one disk fails from each of the two mirrored sets, which is less likely than a single disk failure and will have a longer MTTDL.

- *Mean time to data inaccessibility (MTTDI)* — This is the average time between data becoming inaccessible. There is no loss of data, but it cannot temporarily be accessed because of adapter failures or a server being down. Data that is accessed over the network such as NFS, Common Internet File System (CIFS), and HTTP cannot be accessed if the file server has lost its network links. MTTDI is increased by redundant adapters, clustered servers, and network trunking.

Fault-Tolerant Systems Versus Clusters

To recap, a fault-tolerant system is a single system with redundant components. A *cluster* is made up of two or more hosts that can withstand failure of an entire host or a software or hardware component within the host. Both fault tolerance and clustering have features that make them more suitable for certain applications than others, and both are effective ways to increase availability. The choice is determined by the applications, availability requirements, and financial constraints. Table 18-1 compares some important characteristics of both architectures.

The characteristics mentioned in Table 18-1 can help you decide whether to deploy a cluster or a fault-tolerant server for business-critical applications. A cluster is best suited for database servers where recovery models are based on transactions and high-end servers are required to run the applications. Since application failover for one host to another in the cluster can take up to a few minutes, the business needs must be able to tolerate such periods of downtime. Fault-tolerant systems are required if your environment cannot afford the downtime needed for applications to switch hosts and if the service-recovery model relies on in-memory data or state of application.

Table 18-1   Fault-Tolerant Systems and High-Availability Clusters

	FAULT-TOLERANT SYSTEMS	CLUSTERS
Operating environment	Single system.	Two or more systems.
Type of systems	Usually high-end.	Low- to high-end.
Configuration	Set up by vendor or configured in-house for critical components.	Host fail-over software is developed in-house or purchased from a vendor.
Ability to withstand OS crashes or bugs	No.	Yes. Applications failover to other healthy hosts in the cluster.
Protection for data on disk or memory	Data on disk and memory are protected.	Data on disk is protected.
Recovery time	A few milliseconds to a few seconds.	A few seconds to a few minutes.
Leading software products and vendors	All major system vendors try to build tolerance into their products. Price of server is proportional to the degree of fault tolerance.	VERITAS Cluster Server. Microsoft Cluster Server, M/C ServiceGuard from HP, HACMP from IBM.

Fault-Tolerant Disk Subsystems

This section explains various ways in which fault tolerance is implemented with a subsystem or host. The goal is to architect the entire system so that it continues to function despite component failures.

Arrays of disks have stringent cooling and power requirements, making them prime candidates for a fault-tolerant design. This section describes the factors that make a fault-tolerant disk enclosure or subsystem. The disks are connected to an internal bus and presented to the external controller ports as simple drives or RAID volumes. The external ports are, in turn, connected to hosts.

Following are some required factors of a fault-tolerant disk subsystem.

Hot-Swappable and Hot-Spare Drives

Disks in a fault-tolerant enclosure should be hot-swappable. *Hot-swappable* components are those that can be removed or replaced without interrupting server operations or data access.

Hot-spare components are those that are online and configured as standbys into the system and are used as automatic replacements for failed components. Hot sparing, unlike hot swapping, does not require a user intervention.

Hot swappable drives are useful only if hot sparing is also enabled either at the hardware or subsystem level or by the OS logical volume manager (LVM).

Cooling Systems

The flow of air inside servers or hosts is usually restricted. An array of disks inside a host enclosure increases the risk of overheating of disks and other server components. Placing the drives in an external enclosure allows for optimal cooling of disks and reduces the heat on server components. Several factors such as number of fans within an enclosure, fan velocity, path of air flow, and number and location of exhaust ports can be optimally designed to keep disks from overheating. Fans should be redundant. Any of them can fail without adversely impacting the overall cooling system. The chassis should be engineered so that a failed fan can be replaced without need to power-off the enclosure.

Power Supplies

Can you easily change them? There should be more than one power supply to eliminate single points of failure. As with cooling, each power supply should be capable of providing the necessary power to the entire enclosure. Power supplies within an enclosure should be cabled to separate power delivery units (PDUs). Whenever a problem with a power supply is detected, the enclosure should be able to isolate and disable the failed (or failing) power supply.

The chassis design should allow addition or replacement of a power supply without need to off-line data.

Robust Self-Monitoring Enclosures

In 1995, a standard called the SCSI Accessed Fault Tolerant Enclosure (SAF-TE) was drafted to design procedures to enable an enclosure to communicate its status (such as disk, power supply, and fan failure) to a management station or monitoring application. Environmental conditions such as chassis temperature can also be tracked through SAF-TE. Alarms and status lights within the enclosure must provide visual or audible indication of failures. Alerts can be sent via e-mail to a pager, cellular telephone, an operator, or technical support team. Monitoring applications can use SAF-TE status information from enclosures to provide critical details about the failing component or environmental problem.

This capability to alert or notify a failure is critical to system availability. For example, a failed power supply or disk may force the redundant components to become a SPOF. The online components are made to carry more load, which may make them more susceptible to failures.

Disk Redundancy Using RAID Levels

RAID originally was an acronym for redundant array of inexpensive disks. Later the word "inexpensive" was changed to "independent." RAID enables you to implement redundancy among a set of disks so that failure of a disk does not interrupt availability or cause data loss. Disks have moving parts and are susceptible to failures. The platters are rotating at speeds of up to 15,000 rpm. A broken head, a speck of dust, or a loose splinter on a platter quickly damages the magnetic surfaces.

Various RAID levels are described later in this chapter. Some disk enclosures have RAID controllers that let you configure a RAID group with drives within the enclosure. The RAID group can be divided into logical units (LUNs). The operating system on the attached hosts views each LUN as a single physical disk and usually does not know about the RAID configuration of the LUNs.

A disk in the enclosure can be assigned as a hot spare. Normally no data is written to the hot spare. If a disk in a volume fails, it is automatically replaced by the hot spare by the RAID controller. The level of data protection in the RAID group is regained. The failed disk can be replaced later (the sooner the better).

The good news is that we have built fault tolerance into the volumes using a single RAID controller, but we have introduced a new potential failure. A controller failure would disable access to the data. This is addressed by using redundant controllers, as described in the next section.

NOTE RAID is discussed in more detail in Chapter 19.

Redundant Controllers within a Disk Subsystem

The data paths could be active-active or active-passive. In an *active-active configuration*, each controller operates independently or in tandem with the other. Both controllers can be connected to the same host, which provides for faster access. The controllers verify each other's status. If one fails, the responsibilities of the failed controller are taken up by the other. The controllers can also be connected to different hosts. This would be necessary for setting up a cluster because disks must be accessible by all hosts in the cluster.

In an *active-passive* (or *active-standby*) *configuration*, a single controller is responsible for all I/O to all disks in the enclosure. The standby controller simply monitors the active controller. If a failure is detected, the standby controller takes over the I/O responsibilities.

The enclosure must be engineered so that controllers can be replaced without taking down the host or disk enclosure. Another concern is the upgrade procedure for the controller microcode version. Normally when you must upgrade the controller microcode, you must first stop all I/O through the controller. If the enclosure has only one controller, you must schedule downtime for off-lining the volumes and stopping all I/O. There is no choice. However, in a dual-controller enclosure, you can use the volumes in the enclosure via one controller when upgrading the microcode on the other. Thus, there is no interruption for server and data operations.

So far, we have focused on making the enclosure fault-tolerant by providing redundant fans, power supplies, controllers, disks, and so on. The next level of protection is the path from the server to the enclosure.

Host-Based Adapters (HBAs) within a Server

Servers should have two or more HBAs to prevent a SPOF from server to storage. Like dual controllers within an enclosure, the paths from server to disks can be configured to be active-active or active-passive. You must install and configure software on the server that would monitor the data paths for failure. VERITAS Volume Manager has a feature called dynamic multi-pathing, which helps set up active-active paths from server to storage. If a path fails, data is automatically rerouted to the other paths without interruption to users or services.

Cache in the Subsystem Controller

Cache boosts I/O performance and is included (often in generous amounts) from hardware RAID subsystem vendors such as EMC, IBM, and Network Appliance. To avoid the controller cache from being a SPOF, it should be mirrored and backed up by battery. There should be an easy way to check the battery status and determine if it must be replaced.

TALES FROM THE TECH TURF: WHO HIT THE POWER SWITCH?

A company purchased and deployed a large RAID subsystem with approximately 5 TB of storage. The employees who normally racked the servers were also asked to anchor the box to the data-center floor to prevent the box from rolling around in case of an earthquake. The goal was to prevent downtime in case of a real (or imagined) disaster. They needed to drill a large enough hole in the data-center floor. The drill gun accidentally hit the power switch and powered off the entire disk subsystem. In the ensuing chaos, they were asked to postpone their work. The second time around, the person inadvertently (again) hit the subsystem power switch. Again downtime. It took two outages to get the customer to buy and install a cover and lock for the switch.

Best Practices

There are some best practices for increasing fault tolerance:

- Server device components such as fans, power supplies, disks, and controllers must be designed so that they can be changed without having to off-line the data. These components should also not be SPOFs.

- Keeping spare parts on-site reduces the time required to recover from failures. If the hardware is covered under maintenance with a hardware service provider, the vendor must be able to replace a failed part quickly. Be aware of the turn-around time period specified in the service level agreements (SLAs) with your maintenance provider.

- When you have redundant disks because of mirroring or parity, and a disk fails, replace it as soon as possible. You may be asked, "Well, don't your volumes have disk redundancy? What's the hurry to replace failed drives?" The answer is "No! After a disk failure, there is no redundancy unless a hot spare can replace the failed disk."

- Disk redundancy does not replace backups. You still need backups for disaster recovery and retrieving corrupted or accidentally deleted files. Also, what about the chance of multiple disks failing at the same time in the RAID volumes? Yes, the probability is small, but real. If that happens, everyone will look to the systems administrator to pull a rabbit out of his or her hat.

- If you have parity or mirrored volumes, designate certain disks as hot spares to replace failed disks automatically. From time to time, check the status of hot spares to ensure that they are healthy. Implement some procedures so that the disk subsystem or host sends an alert when it experiences a disk failure. Because hot spares can only replace disks that are smaller or the same size as themselves, designate the largest disk as a hot spare.

- Implement SNMP traps so that the enclosures can send alerts to a network-management station in the event of critical component failures.

- When using hardware RAID, you may have cache on the RAID controller. Is the cache an SPOF? Is the cache mirrored and backed up by battery? Keep a tab on the status of the batteries.

Key Points

Some key points discussed in this chapter are:

- Components fail and you must plan for it.

- Understand the different ways that the various components, servers, applications, and so forth can fail and how a particular failure affects other healthy components. Build a what-if scenario. Implement redundancy for critical components.

- Both clusters and fault-tolerant systems are effective ways to increase availability.

- A cluster comprises several hosts that watch each other for application or hardware failures.

- A fault-tolerant system is a single server that is capable of providing services despite failure of certain individual hardware components.

- Your application requirements are the dominant factor determining your choice of which system to use. A combination of clustering and fault tolerance is usually the preferred solution.

CHAPTER 19

And in the end it's not the years in your life that count. It's the life in your years.
— Abraham Lincoln

In 1987, Gibson, Katz, and Patterson of the University of California at Berkeley published a paper entitled, "A Case for Redundant Arrays of Inexpensive Disks (RAID)." The paper introduced different RAID arrays, configured by combining individual disks.

This chapter covers various types of RAID volumes and how they can be built. The basic goal of RAID is to combine individual disks into an array to obtain performance, reliability, and capacity that exceed that of a *single large expensive disk* (*SLED*). Moreover, the entire array appears to the host operating system as a single device.

The mean time between failure (MTBF) of an array is equal to the MTBF of an individual drive divided by the number of drives in the array. If there is no redundancy in an array (as in the case of RAID-0 arrays), the MTBF is too low for mission-critical purposes. However, as we will see in this chapter, redundancy is provided by mirrored or parity-based arrays.

There are *hardware-based* and *software-based* RAID volumes. Hardware RAID is configured using device drivers for subsystem controllers or host-based adapters (HBAs). The vendor provides utilities to create and resolve problems with the RAID volumes. The advantage is lower host overhead, since RAID parity calculations are offloaded to the controller. But the RAID volumes are limited to the set of disks attached to the controller.

Software-based RAID volumes are created using special logical volume management (LVM) software installed on the host operating system. The problem with software RAID is the additional load that it places on the host CPUs and memory. However, it provides the flexibility of using any disk that the OS can detect. The hot spares can be located on different subsystems to protect data from entire subsystem failure.

There are five RAID levels, numbered from 1 to 5. (The number does not reflect a ranking in performance or availability.) There is also RAID-0. The "zero" means that there is no redundancy. Some of the RAID levels are combined to make new levels (such as RAID 0+1 and RAID 1+0). There are also other levels developed and marketed by some vendors. These unofficial levels are often only slight variations of the standard RAID levels.

RAID-0 (Striping)

This is simply disk striping. The data to be written is split into smaller chunks or stripe widths. Each chunk is written to a separate disk. Since the disks work in parallel to write the data, writes (as well as reads) are faster than I/O to a volume, where all data is written to a single disk. This is illustrated in Figure 19-1.

The only things to worry about are the size of the stripe width and the number of disks that would make up the RAID-0 volume. If you know the average I/O size of requests that would hit the RAID-0 volume, the stripe width would be the I/O size divided by the number of disks. Some hardware RAID controllers allow only a few choices for stripe widths (commonly 16 KB, 32 KB, 64 KB, and 128 KB). Some controllers may have their own cache, in which case the rules are now different.

It is important to understand that RAID-0 does not offer any redundancy or protection from disk failures. In fact, it decreases data availability. In order for the RAID-0 volumes to work, all disks must be available. If a single disk fails, all data is lost.

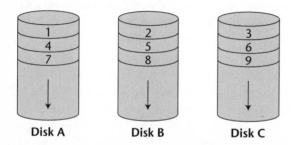

Data is striped on disks A, B, and
C in a round-robin manner

Figure 19-1   RAID-0 volume with three disks.

Let's suppose your disks have an MTBF of 100,000 hours. If all data were to reside on a single disk, the MTBF for the data would be 100,000 hours. If the data is striped over five drives, the MTBF for the data is reduced to 20,000 hours (100,000/5). One disk in the five-disk striped set will fail every 20,000 hours and cause data loss.

RAID-1 (Mirroring)

In a RAID-1 volume, there are two or more copies of the data. If a disk on one data copy fails, that copy is off-lined until the bad disk is replaced. However, the other copy (or copies) continues to operate without interruption.

If there are two copies of data, you are using twice the disk space. This is certainly a major disadvantage of mirroring data. If you have 100 GB of data, it takes another 100 GB to mirror it. This can get expensive.

Another problem is related to I/O performance. Any time a resync needs to occur (for example, when you first establish the mirrors or when a disk is replaced), each block needs to be copied. This takes time and places a lot of I/O load on the host OS (software mirroring) or on the controller (hardware mirroring). During this period of resync, user reads and writes are slowed down. For a RAID-1 volume, write performance during normal operation also suffers. The OS has to wait until data has been written to all mirror copies. Although this happens in parallel, the write operation is not complete until the slowest disk has completed writing.

All about RAID-1 is not gloom and doom. There are several advantages of RAID-1 and it is also a popular implementation. The primary advantage is superior I/O performance and data protection from disk failures. A hot spare can be used to automatically replace a failed disk in a mirrored set. Another advantage is related to read performance. Reads from mirrored volumes are faster because there is more than one data copy to service the read request. If there are more than two data copies, one can be split off from the volume for backups or for providing production-like data for development, disaster recovery, or QA purposes. Later, the split copy can be merged again to the mirrored volume and all updates (since the split) would automatically be synced to it.

There are no such concepts as primary and a secondary copy in a mirrored volume. The volume manager or RAID controller does not have a bias or ordering among the data copies. All copies are equal, unless a disk in one copy fails, in which case the copy obviously gets off-lined.

I was once asked: "Why should I back up data? It is mirrored!" Sure, mirroring protects against disk failures, but you still need backups. If some files are inadvertently deleted or corrupted, that will happen to all the copies of data. Your only recourse then is to retrieve the lost or corrupted files from a backup. In case of a local or site-wide disaster, all mirrored copies are destroyed or inaccessible. In such a case, backup tapes that have been stored offsite can be used to restore data at an alternate, disaster-recovery (DR) site.

RAID 0+1 (Mirrored Stripes)

RAID levels can be combined. A RAID 0+1 volume is made up of two or more striped (RAID-0) sets that are mirrored together. In Figure 19-2, the first stripe set and the second stripe set are each made up of three disks. The two sets are mirrored to make the RAID 0+1 volume.

If a disk in a striped set is lost, the entire stripe is disabled. In Figure 19-3, loss of disk A causes stripe set 1 to be off-lined. Now the entire volume is nothing but a simple RAID-0 volume. The bad disk should be replaced as soon as possible. After disk replacement, data must be synced to the striped set. Hopefully a member of the second striped set will not fail while all this is happening. Should any disk in the live stripe set fail before or while replacing a disk and syncing data, all information in the volume will be lost.

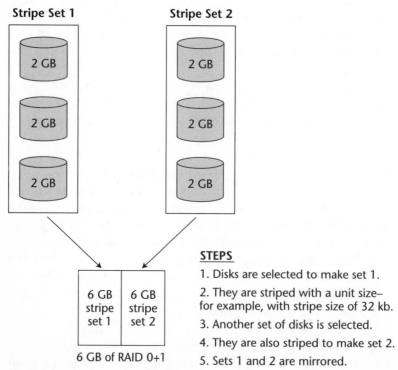

STEPS

1. Disks are selected to make set 1.

2. They are striped with a unit size– for example, with stripe size of 32 kb.

3. Another set of disks is selected.

4. They are also striped to make set 2.

5. Sets 1 and 2 are mirrored.

Figure 19-2 Constructing a RAID 0+1 volume.

Stripe Set 1   **Stripe Set 2**

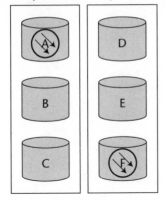

1. Drive A fails.
2. Stripe Set 1 is taken offline.
3. Before A is replaced, drive F fails.
4. Stripe Set 2 is taken offline. All data is lost.

Sets 1 and 2 are mirrored

Figure 19-3   How RAID 0+1 handles disk failures.

One way to automate replacement of a failed disk is to designate certain disks as hot spares. A hot spare normally has no activity and just waits for disk failures. It replaces a failed disk as soon as failure is detected by the operating system or RAID controller. The hot spare then becomes a new member of the RAID 0+1 volume. Data is synced to the entire stripe set. During the sync operation period, there is no redundancy.

RAID 1+0 or RAID 10 (Striped Mirrors)

The concept of RAID 1+0 is easy. However, many vendors of hardware and software RAID have found this difficult to implement or to implement it well.

Just like RAID 0+1, there is striping and mirroring, but the sequence is reversed. To create a RAID 1+0 volume, you first create mirrored sets (RAID-1). The drives in each set mirror each other. These sets are then striped (RAID-0). In Figure 19-4, there are three mirrored sets. Each set has two disks. The three sets are striped with a stripe size of 32 KB.

The distinction from RAID 0+1 is clear when you consider how disk failures are handled in RAID-1+0 and 0+1. In RAID 1+0, as shown in Figure 19-5, if any disk in a mirrored set fails, that set loses redundancy, but data is still online. If a disk in any other mirrored set fails, data remains online. Data will be lost only if both disks within a mirrored set fail.

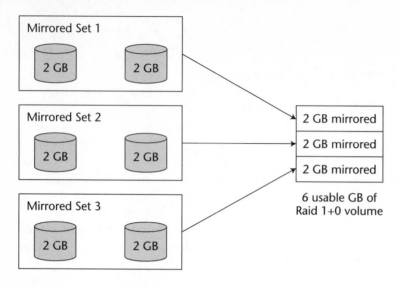

STEPS

1. Two disks are selected.

2. They are mirrored to form Set 1.

3. Sets 2 and 3 are similarly created,
each with two disks for each.

4. Set 1, 2, and 3 are striped together
with a certain stripe size.

Figure 19-4   Constructing a RAID 1+0 volume.

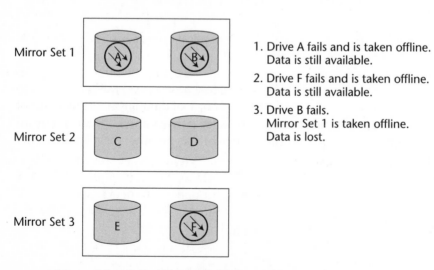

1. Drive A fails and is taken offline.
   Data is still available.

2. Drive F fails and is taken offline.
   Data is still available.

3. Drive B fails.
   Mirror Set 1 is taken offline.
   Data is lost.

Mirrored Sets 1, 2, and 3 are striped.

Figure 19-5   How a RAID 1+0 volume handles disk failures.

It can be argued that RAID 0+1 or RAID 1+0 volumes can safely withstand failure of half the number of drives. That's true. However, the chances of losing data are higher in a RAID 0+1 volume. In Figures 19-3 and 19-5, if disk A fails, data will still be available. That's good! Now in Figure 19-3 (RAID 0+1) data will be lost if D, E, or F fails out of the existing five disks. The chance of this occurrence is 60 percent (three out of five). In Figure 19-5 (RAID 1+0), data will be lost only if B fails out of the existing five disks. The chance of this occurrence is only 20 percent (one out of five disks).

There is one more advantage to Raid 1+0, related to the amount of time taken to recover from a disk failure. Because there is no redundancy during this time period, it is critical to keep it as small as possible. If disk A fails in a RAID 0+1 volume (Figure 19-3), the entire stripe set 1 is off-lined. After A is replaced, data must be synced to all three disks: A, B, and C. In case of a Raid 1+0 volume (Figure 19-5), only disk A needs to be synced to recover from its failure.

RAID-2

This RAID level checks for correctness of disk data using the Hamming encoding method. Certain disks in the RAID-2 array are dedicated to storing error-checking and correction (ECC) information. Since most disks embed ECC information within each sector, RAID-2 offers no advantage over other RAID architectures. It must be mentioned that you would be hard-pressed to find any software or hardware implementation of RAID-2.

Parity-Based RAID (RAID-3, -4, and -5)

When using parity-based RAID, data is striped among several disks. Redundancy is provided not by maintaining a full copy of data on an alternate set of drives, but by using space on one extra disk for parity values, calculated by an XOR or exclusive OR of corresponding data blocks on other disks in the RAID volume.

How are disk failures handled? If a disk is lost, the data on the lost disk is calculated from contents of all other disks in the volume. Therefore, read and write operations are very slow in a parity RAID volume with a failed disk. When the failed disk is replaced, the data for the new drive is calculated and written to the new drive after reading and doing an XOR of the contents of all other drives. Because this involves reading all data blocks of all disks, it is a very time-consuming process. The XOR calculation required to recalculate the data for the failed disk places a significant load on the server CPU, especially if RAID is software-based. Moreover, if two drives fail at the same time or a second disk failure occurs while the first disk is being rebuilt, all data on the RAID stripe is lost. It must be then restored from backups.

Write performance is slowed by a failed disk. But how is the write performance under normal conditions? It depends on the size of the write requests and stripe unit size. If there are full stripe writes (where corresponding strips on all disks are overwritten), there is no need to read old data. A parity value must be calculated for the new data, and the entire stripe gets overwritten. However, if the write requests are small, data from unaffected disks must be read in order to calculate the parity. This places a performance penalty on the server or RAID controller.

How about read performance? Reads are unaffected by parity calculations. Read performance is the same as for a RAID-0 volume with the same stripe unit size. Read performance is adversely affected only if a data (that is, non-parity) disk has failed and information on the failed disk must be calculated from parity.

A significant factor affecting performance is the number of disks in the parity-based RAID volume. Performance declines rapidly if you exceed six or seven members.

The primary distinction between RAID-3, -4, and -5 is the way parity information is stored.

RAID-3

RAID-3 uses a striped set of three of more disks. In most implementations of RAID-3, parity is written to a dedicated disk. Think of RAID-3 as a parity-based RAID with stripe unit size of 1 byte. In essence, virtual disk blocks are created; the virtual blocks are striped across all the disks in the RAID-3 volume. Regardless of size of the I/O request, all drives in the RAID-3 array need to be accessed to satisfy any I/O request. As a result, the array can process only one I/O request at a time.

What about performance? Again, it depends on the nature of the writes. RAID-3 delivers the best performance for a single-user, single-tasking environment where the I/O sizes are large and sequential. If the I/Os are random (all over the volume) and small, performance is poor. Hardware RAID vendors overcome this limitation by using memory-based cache.

RAID-4

Like RAID-3, RAID-4 requires a dedicated parity disk. However, the strip size is not 1 byte but can be set to large values (for example, 64 KB). In Figure 19-6, disks A and B are data disks. Disk C is used for storing the parity data for strips of the corresponding stripe.

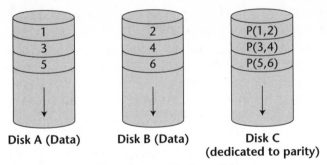

Figure 19-6 Raid-4 volume with three disks.

The most common implementation of RAID-4 has been done in hardware by network appliance for network attached storage (known as NetApp filers) and EMC Corporation. In RAID-4, one disk in the RAID volume is dedicated to parity. Whenever a partial or full stripe write is performed, the parity disk must be updated. Therefore, the parity disk becomes a bottleneck and performance (irrespective of I/O request size) suffers. This is a primary reason why vendors of software RAID refrain from implementing RAID-4. Hardware RAID vendors resolve performance issues by placing a large amount of memory-based cache logically in front of the RAID-4 disks. To increase fault tolerance, the cache is backed up by battery and sometimes mirrored by using two cache sets.

RAID-5

Like RAID-4, RAID-5 utilizes a set of striped disks, with parity of the strips (or chunks) being assigned to disks in a round-robin fashion. Figure 19-7 illustrates an example of a RAID-5 array using four disks marked A, B, C, and D. The first strip on disk D contains the parity for strips 1, 2, and 3. On each horizontal stripe, the parity for all corresponding data strips is designated by a $P(x,x,x)$ on one of the disks.

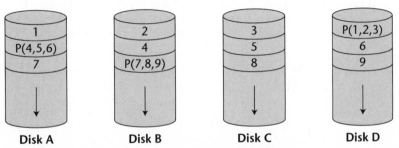

Figure 19-7 RAID-5 parity is distributed among all disks.

You can see that RAID-4 and -5 are similar, except that the bottleneck imposed by a dedicated parity disk in RAID-4 is eliminated in RAID-5. This advantage has encouraged various software RAID vendors to implement RAID-5. However, software RAID-5 is usually unacceptable for write-intensive applications. The general rule of thumb is that applications with more than 15 to 20 percent writes will suffer when using software-based RAID-5 volumes. However, if RAID-5 is implemented in hardware, cache in the RAID subsystem can be used to improve read/write performance.

If a RAID-5 disk fails, I/O performance is negatively impacted not only when data is synchronized to a new drive (the failed disk is replaced) but also for all run-time I/O requests. This is because the data on the lost disk must be calculated by reading all the other disks and doing an XOR. Besides the performance penalty, there is no protection against a second disk failure. Should another disk fail, all of the data in the stripe will be lost. Your only recourse then is to get the files from a backup. The moral of the discussion is that you should set up hot spares for automatic disk replacement or get to the problem as soon as possible.

Table 19-1 provides the advantages and disadvantages of each RAID level.

Table 19-1 Comparing RAID Levels

RAID LEVEL	ADVANTAGE	DISADVANTAGE	WHEN TO USE IT
RAID-0 (striping)	No reduction is usable disk space; increases performance.	No protection from disk failure.	Need high-speed access to storage, but do not need data protection.
RAID-1 (mirroring)	Performance improvement for reads; protection from disk failures; if a disk fails, there is no performance degradation for writes.	50% loss of disk space for a two-copy RAID-1 volume.	Use RAID-1 when data must be protected from disk failures.
RAID 0+1 (striped and mirrored)	Performance increases; protection from disk failures.	50% loss of disk space for a two-copy volume.	For applications that require high performance and data protection.
RAID 1+0 (or RAID 10, mirrored and striped)	Performance increases; high degree of protection from disk failures.	50% loss of disk space for a two-copy volume.	For situations where data protection is most critical.
RAID-4 (striping with single parity disk)	Disk redundancy; read performance enhancement because of striping.	The single parity disk in the volume is performance bottleneck.	For high read-only services.

RAID LEVEL	ADVANTAGE	DISADVANTAGE	WHEN TO USE IT
RAID-5 (striping with distributed parity)	Disk redundancy; good read performance.	If your application has a high percentage of writes, RAID-5 decreases I/O rates; if a disk fails, performance degrades when in recovery mode.	Applications are mostly read intensive; I/O requests are random as in databases; data protection is needed, but you cannot sacrifice half the disks.

Key Points

Following are some key points discussed in this chapter:

- Individual disks within a storage subsystem are used as *just a bunch of disks (JBOD)* or hardware RAID volumes. A RAID volume is a logical entity in which two or more physical disks are grouped together to provide data redundancy and enhanced performance.

- A RAID volume can be configured using hardware or software. Hardware RAID is enabled by HBA device drivers or an external disk subsystem controller. Software RAID requires you to install volume-management software on the host. You use the software to configure RAID volumes using internal disks or JBOD arrays.

- RAID-0 (striped disks) enhances performance, but it does not provide protection against disk failure.

- RAID-1 or mirroring provides protection against disk failure. It is the most expensive RAID level from a disk usage point of view.

- RAID-0 and RAID-1 are combined to make RAID 0+1 (mirror previously created striped sets) and RAID 1+0 (stripe previously created mirrored sets). RAID 1+0 is also called RAID-10.

- RAID-3 and RAID-4 have striped data. In that respect, they are similar to RAID-0. One dedicated disk is used for parity.

- RAID-5 is similar to RAID-4. The only difference is that RAID-5 assigns parity to all disks in the volume in a round-robin manner.

Data Storage Technologies

In This Part

Data Storage Solutions

You may be deceived if you trust too much, but you will live in torment if you don't trust enough.
— **Frank H. Crane**

It has been estimated that the cost of storage management and data security exceeds 10 times the purchase price of the storage hardware. Storage architecture is therefore a critical component for any server environment designed for high uptime. System and cluster administrators spend an inordinately large proportion of their work hours managing storage devices. The large number of vendors further confuses the issues of storage.

This chapter describes various storage architectures you can deploy in a highly available (HA) environment. Which one is right for you? The answer depends on several site-specific factors. It is your job to sort through the information and pick the storage solution that fits your short and long-term requirements, growth expectations, and budget. Are you setting up a storage device that is fault-tolerant or configuring a cluster with two or more nodes for application failover? Are you designing an environment for disaster recovery? What are the merits and demerits of using direct-attached (SCSI or fibre channel) or network-attached storage?

Here is a list of factors that you must think about before deciding on a storage solution:

- The quantity of current data and growth of storage needs. How will you store the endless information your users seem to come up with?

- The speed at which data must be accessed. Is SCSI and NAS good enough, or do you need a storage area network (SAN)? Both internal and external customers are becoming more dependent on the reliable and rapid access to company data at all hours.

- How will your disks be accessed from the server? Do you need multiple paths? Will all multiple paths be active, or will some act as hot standby (that is, waiting for primary data path to fail before activating themselves)?

- Do hosts require near 100 percent uptime? Do they need to be clustered? After all, your data must be created, stored, and delivered to users around the clock.

- How will the solution protect against network failures?

- How tolerant is the storage to disk, power supply, and fan failures? The answer must be built into the disk subsystem you select.

Rapid Data Growth

Studies have shown that storage-space requirements double every year. This is easy to accept knowing that information is the lifeblood of today's economy and almost all critical information is now online. The knowledge derived from online information is the core element that facilitates the rapid and unprecedented growth of our productivity. The use of the Internet has further entrenched information as the primary and permanent driver of our economy. Information must be stored as digital data and should possess a high degree of reliability and fault tolerance.

Storage now occupies a center stage in almost all enterprise-level IT planning. The large amount of important and sensitive data requires that the storage architecture be distributed yet secure and well-managed. Table 20-1 shows the rapid growth of required storage.

Table 20-1 Worldwide Disk Storage Shipments

YEAR	WORLDWIDE TOTAL DISK STORAGE SYSTEMS SHIPPED CAPACITY (PETABYTES)
2002 (Actual)	587
2003 (Actual)	839
2004 (Actual)	1,283
2005 (Forecast)	1,945
2006 (Forecast)	2,966

Table 20-1 *(continued)*

YEAR	WORLDWIDE TOTAL DISK STORAGE SYSTEMS SHIPPED CAPACITY (PETABYTES)
2007 (Forecast)	4,540
2008 (Forecast)	6,971
2009 (Forecast)	10,686

Source: "Worldwide Disk Storage Systems 2005–2009 Forecast and Analysis: Virtualization, Regulatory Compliance, and Cost-Optimized Storage – Pillars for Future Growth," IDC #33477, June 2005.

Here are some reasons for the growth of online data:

- *Internet site requirements* — Forget HTML and text files. Web sites today are bulging with images, audio files, news (you can listen to or watch), movies, and music. All corporate brochures and papers are online. These sites grow, and even if the Webmasters take some data off-line, you can be sure the files are saved or archived somewhere. The number of Web sites is increasing. In 1998, there were 2.6 million Web sites; in 1999, about 4.6 million. In 2000, there were about 7.1 million; by the end of 2001, there were close to 8.4 million Web sites. More important is the amount of data, either online or as backups, for each Web site.

- *Human habit* — Researchers estimate that in 2000, there were more than 900 TB of space required for storing e-mails only. E-mails today have audio and image attachments, and they are saved on local and server disks. The storage requirement for e-mails is expected to grow by 40 percent every year. If users find relevant or interesting material, they save it, especially if it is a big document. After all, there never seems to be enough free time to read documents. Users make a promise to use it in the future, but weeks and months go by and promises are forgotten.

- *Corporate data* — Enterprise resource planning (ERP) systems, data mining, data warehouses, and Internet downloads are some of the things that require large amounts of online data. They are paving roads toward a storage crisis.

Managing the growth of data is a huge challenge for IT professionals. Your choice of storage architecture must meet future requirements. Some people around you will help you by forecasting future requirements. Their estimates generally are as good as yours. No one knows future needs.

Data growth and scalability are not the only requirements. Data uptime must be guaranteed. If the data is unavailable to the users, it does not matter if the host systems are up or how well-designed the IT infrastructure is.

Data Storage Requirements

Developments in networking have had a profound influence on storage. When computers and mainframes were introduced in the enterprises, the focus was on making them faster, more applicable to everyday tasks, and cheaper. This led to the nimble, distributed, enterprise class servers that replaced large, centralized systems. When various networking applications began to gain widespread popularity, the focus changed to speed and technology employed for connecting computers. The maturation of networking and computing power, along with the hunger for large quantities of data, has enabled faster, more resilient, and accessible storage techniques. Enter storage networking. We will briefly look at some networking features that have helped the evolution of storage networking.

Developments in networking (mostly because of the Internet and its requirements) have brought high-speed networks. On the one hand, wide area networks (WANs) and metropolitan area networks (MANs) have come to have a high degree of reliability and speed. On the other hand, IT managers are still plagued with several stringent requirements for data storage and I/O transfer rates. IT managers must look for the following features that together enhance availability and I/O speed:

- *Host-level redundancy* — This means resistant to host failures and implemented via clusters.

- *Fault tolerance* — This means resilient to component (fans, power supplies, disks) failure.

- *Disaster tolerance* — Copies of data are kept across campus area networks, MANs, or WANs. You must ensure that all data copies are synchronized quickly.

- *High-speed access* — This is a requirement for all mission-critical applications.

- *Low latency* — This is required to serve real-time applications.

- *Interoperability* — Data and storage techniques must be based on open standards. Operating systems and storage technologies from several vendors must interact well with each other.

- *High scalability* — This is required to meet the insatiable requirement for more storage space.

- *Ease of management* — Installation and troubleshooting must be intuitive and not require special training.

Storage Access Modes

This section lists common ways for hosts to access storage devices. Except for direct-attached storage (DAS), the rest are network-based implementations, where storage devices are connected to an existing TCP/IP network or a dedicated SAN for access by several hosts.

The open framework of TCP/IP and its capability to communicate with products from various vendors and network protocols (ATM, SONET, and so on) have made it a compelling solution for supporting a number of initiatives on storage networking.

- *Direct attached storage (DAS)* — A disk subsystem is attached directly to HBAs in one or more hosts. This is also called *server-centric storage* because it is captured and physically cabled to the server.

- *Network attached storage (NAS)* — A NAS server is a network device that manages arrays of disks connected to it and shares the local volumes with hosts on the network using network-based protocols such as CIFS, HTTP, and NFS. NAS is discussed in detail later in this chapter.

- *Storage area network (SAN)* — This is a dedicated network where servers are connected via fibre channel switches or hubs to storage devices such as tapes or RAID arrays. SAN is easy to manage, flexible, and scalable. The servers are equipped with fibre channel (FC) adapters. As more storage devices are linked to the switch or hub, they too become accessible from all the servers. FC can transfer large blocks of data over long distances.

- *Internet SCSI (iSCSI)* — iSCSI is a networking protocol for SCSI-3 traffic over TCP/IP networks. IP connected hosts can use iSCSI to access storage over an IP network.

- *Fibre channel over IP (FCIP)* — Enables fibre channel SANs to be interconnected over an IP-based network.

The existence of high-speed networks and stringent requirements on data availability has provided a huge impetus to migrate to an IP-based storage environment. This is a shift from the past, where storage devices were directly attached or integrated within the servers (server-centric model). There is little doubt that in the near future a majority of enterprise data will be network-based.

DAS Versus SAN

As we have seen, SANs help to remove the tight association between servers and storage devices. Customer or application data should be placed on storage devices in the SAN. It is still common to place the operating system on internal or direct attached disks. Table 20-2 compares DAS and SAN.

Table 20-2 Direct-Attached Storage (DAS) versus Storage Area Networks (SANs)

CONSIDERATION	DIRECT ATTACHED STORAGE	SAN SOLUTION
Scalability	Complex and costly to add or remove storage devices from the server.	Servers and storage devices can be easily removed or added to the SAN. There is any-to-any connectivity. Storage administrators can easily change the amount of storage allotted to each server.
Use of host resources	Host resources are used for applications, I/O responsibilities, data transfers, and backups.	Storage functions and I/O responsibilities are done by SAN. Host is free to do application and OS tasks.
Availability of data	Storage is cabled to one or two servers. If the servers go down, data cannot be accessed.	Multiple servers can access the data. Each server can have several data paths. If one or two servers go down, data can be accessed via other servers.
Storage consolidation	There is no consolidation. Each server has its own dedicated storage.	There can be a large, shared storage device, portions of which can be allocated to different servers in the SAN.
Cost of storage administration	Expensive and time-consuming, each of the "islands of storage" must be individually maintained.	Servers and storage devices are grouped into one network, which simplifies administration and lowers time and cost of data management.
Distance	Limited to cable length, unless you use iSCSI for accessing data over IP. SCSI-3 is limited to 25 meters.	Single-mode fiber cable allows up to 10 kilometers. FC over IP or dense wavelength division multiplexing (DWDM) is used to extend distance.
Reliability	Copper SCSI suffers from electromagnetic interference (EMI).	Fiber cables are far less impacted by EMI.
Number of devices	SCSI has seven devices per target.	There are 126 nodes for fibre channel arbitrated loop (FC-AL) and up to 16 million for SAN fabrics.

NAS Versus SAN

The primary distinction between NAS and SAN arises from the different infrastructure used by them. NAS uses network infrastructure, which exists in all organizations. SAN requires you to set up a new fibre channel network to link servers and storage devices located within 10 km of the fibre channel network (unless switches are cascaded). Implementing a SAN is usually more expensive. Table 20-3 differentiates NAS and SAN based on their features and advantages.

Both NAS and SAN help consolidate storage. If you need more disk space, you just add disks to the common storage pool and let the servers access it. However, the extent of consolidation is greater with NAS. All servers in the network can access the increased storage space with NAS. With SAN, only the server that is configured to use a SAN volume gets the advantage of increased space in a volume.

Table 20-3 NAS and SAN Features and Benefits

CRITERIA	NAS	SAN
Network	NAS uses TCP/IP networks such as FDDI, Ethernet, or asynchronous transfer mode (ATM), and standard components.	SAN uses a dedicated fibre channel network and uses proprietary configurations.
Design	Defines a product or appliance.	Defines an architecture.
Protocols used	Any hosts on the network can access data on NAS devices using HTTP, FTP, CIFS, or NFS.	Encapsulated SCSI.
Performance	High latency caused by TCP/IP overhead.	Thin protocol and low latency.
Connection	Files are shared via an indirect (routed) connection.	Server accesses a volume via a direct (switched) connection.
Level of access and heterogeneous data sharing	NAS provides file-level access to UNIX and Windows servers and identifies data by filenames. NAS handles data security, user authentication, and file locking.	SAN provides block-level access to servers that are connected to the SAN. Data is transferred as raw disk blocks.
File system maintenance	NAS head unit manages the file systems.	File systems are created and managed by servers.
Compatibility among platforms	NAS allows simultaneous sharing of files between disparate operating systems and platforms.	File sharing is dependent on server operating system. There is little or no cross-platform compatibility.

Benefits of SAN

This section describes some business benefits of SAN. It must be noted that the advantage you derive from a SAN depends on several things. Do you have a lot of storage devices and servers that will use the SAN? Are you designing for disaster recovery or local clustering? How busy is your network traffic? Do your applications have lots of read or write functions to the disks?

Consolidation of Storage Resources

In a pure SCSI environment, you buy storage and attach it to one or two servers. Somewhere down the road, you may run into problems: Some servers may not need all the disk space they have; the free disk space cannot be connected to and used by other servers; you end up with the trouble of managing several small, disparate storage subsystems. Also, setting up mechanisms to protect the islands of data (for example, via hardware or software RAID, or data replication) for all of them could be time-consuming and expensive. With SAN, several dispersed storage devices can be consolidated into a few storage subsystems. These can be partitioned into sections. Each section can be assigned to a host, as shown in Figure 20-1. Changing disk allocation among servers is easy. The data on the few storage subsystems can be protected using RAID or data replication.

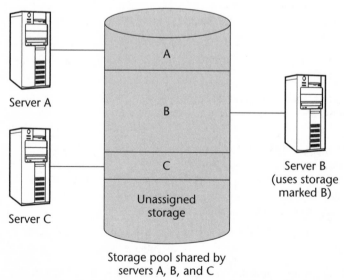

Figure 20-1 Each server uses preassigned storage from a shared pool.

Concurrent Access by Multiple Hosts

SAN allows several hosts to access the same set of storage devices. With appropriate software controls and applications, the same data can be accessed by two or more servers. Storage can be shared by many servers. This makes it easy to implement clusters with many servers. This also makes it easy to migrate data from one storage device to another to retire old disk arrays or to introduce new technology.

Reduced Total Cost of Ownership (TCO)

Costs related to buying and maintaining storage devices are the biggest portion of IT budgets. Gartner Group and IDC estimate that the volume of data will double every year. It is also estimated that the cost to maintain storage is about 10 times the cost to buy it. Experienced storage administrators are difficult to hire and expensive to retain.

SAN enables a centralized storage management. In a SAN, it is easier to maintain a few large disk subsystems (an outcome of consolidating storage). SAN administration takes less time and causes less pain for system administrators. Several vendors have SAN management software that provides an easy means to maintain storage subsystems and troubleshoot problems via a central, easy-to-access GUI.

SAN leads to reduced hardware costs. SAN provides a better utilization of storage space. If you allocated too much space to a server, it is easy to take the unused space and give it to another needy host in the SAN network.

The servers have less I/O and fewer storage responsibilities thanks to LAN-free and server-free data transfers in a SAN. The server resources can focus on applications running on them. This results in less expense for server purchases.

LAN-Free and Server-Free Data Transfers

Backup of the data on storage devices that are directly connected to server uses the IP network (LAN) and resources on the backup server and client. It is an arduous task, as shown in Figure 20-2. You also need to find a low-activity period for backups. Most backups can, however, be done without taking databases off-line. But at least once a week or every two weeks, you must take the database off-line, freeze all activity, take a snapshot, and bring the database online. The snapshot can later be backed to tape. The problem here is that there is no good time window. With the fast globalization of corporations, clients and employees all over the world will want to access the servers at all hours. What about e-commerce Web servers? When do your customers stop shopping? Your customers will be buying from your Web site at 3 a.m. while in their pajamas.

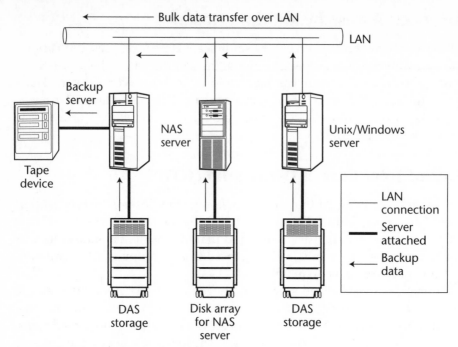

Figure 20-2 Traditional LAN-based backup.

In an ideal world, SAN can be used to remove the burden on the server and network caused by backups. A switch allows multiple simultaneous connections at full speed. Backups can be done directly from disks to tape (assuming both are connected to the switched fabric). The data never goes over the LAN. This is LAN-free data transfer, as shown in Figure 20-3.

A still-evolving backup SAN-based backup procedure is known as *server-free backup and recovery*. Data is transferred from disks to tapes, where both are attached to the same SAN topology. The load on the server is reduced. This concept, illustrated in Figure 20-4, is also called *serverless* backup.

The reality today is that the benefits are partially implemented. The backup server is the only one that knows about data to be backed up: names of files and blocks on the storage device that contain the to-be-backed-up data. This alone is a substantial part of the backup process, especially for incremental backups of small-sized files. Several vendors (such as EMC, Crossroads, and Pathlight) are developing products to enable SAN-based server-free backups.

Maximum Distance between Nodes and Use in Disaster Recovery Applications

The extended distance (10 km) between two nodes in an FC-AL loop, between a node and a switch, or between two switches in a fabric contributes to disaster-recovery solutions. The data transfer does not cause any LAN or

TCP/IP overhead because it is done in native storage protocol (FICON, FCP, or SCSI) over the fiber-optic cables in the SAN network and not over network infrastructure.

High Performance

This is attributable to the high bandwidth and low latency features of fibre channel. FC switches create physically discrete segments that further seem to help data-hungry applications such as decision support, image or movie manipulation, and data mining. As previously mentioned, the maximum bandwidth possible today with 1 Gigabit/second (Gbps) switches is 200 Mbps (transmit and receive cables each running at 100 Mbps), but 2 Gbps and 10 Gbps switches are currently under development.

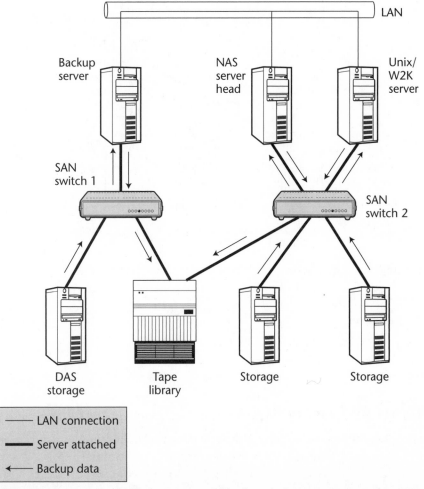

Figure 20-3   LAN-free backup: Storage and backup devices are connected to SAN.

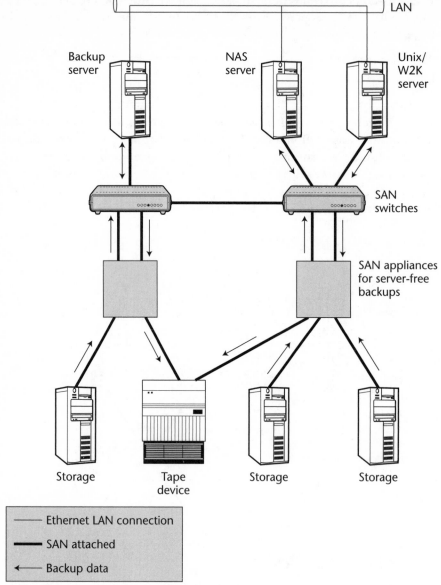

Figure 20-4 Server-free backup.

Scalability and Flexibility

This is probably the greatest benefit provided by SAN. Storage devices can be brought online or removed without disrupting servers. Similarly servers can also be added or removed dynamically. Any-to-any connectivity allows for allocating storage to any server. The allocation can be easily modified as storage needs for servers and applications change over time.

Server Clustering

SCSI generally allows no more than two servers to be physically connected to the same storage device. SAN provides a way for several servers to access the storage devices. Redundant data paths from each server to storage devices can be easily built. The number of servers and storage devices in the SAN can be increased or decreased dynamically without impacting any other device.

Applications Best Suited for SAN

Table 20-4 identifies applications that are well-suited for FC-based SANs.

Table 20-4   SAN Applications

APPLICATION	DESCRIPTION AND SAN ADVANTAGES
Video editing and distribution software	This application requires large files to be created, saved, and edited in real time. Also, several users and servers must access the files; some may be physically far from the storage area. The high rates of data transfer and large reliable RAID arrays in a SAN help meet the demands of video and imaging applications.
Clustering software	The servers and storage have any-to-any connectivity — a requirement for clustering applications. Also, in a SAN, devices can be added or removed dynamically and without any server downtime.
Disaster recovery	Traditionally data loss and local disasters were solved using restores from tapes. SANs allow automated data backup and "warm" availability of online data at a remote site to recover from a disaster at the primary site. The high bandwidth enables quick replication of data for mirrored copies. Because of long-distance connections (enabled by fiber-optic cables), copies of data can be stored across a campus or metropolitan area.
Dual pathing applications	SAN makes it easy for hosts to have multiple links to the storage devices. The links can be used for fault tolerance (data can be accessed even if one of the links fail) and load balancing.
Backup applications	Data can be backed up directly from disk storage to tapes (in the SAN) using SAN-aware backup software. Backup clients in the SAN need to do less work. Backup does not affect LAN traffic.

Considerations before Designing a SAN

The following are factors to consider when architecting and implementing a SAN for your client. Some of these general guidelines apply to every design.

Application Requirements

Will your SAN be used by database servers or for data-mining purposes? Will you have tape libraries for data backups, retrieval, and archiving in your SAN? Will you have Web sites bulging with graphics, full-motion video, and audio files?

Will the SAN be supporting mission-critical applications? Is downtime a no-no? (Sure it is.) Is disaster recovery part of the plan? Will your servers be clustered? If so, what are the requirements of the clustering software you intend to use? How many "nines" of uptime is expected?

Your single SAN design may have to accommodate several applications. After all, the IT department paid a lot of money for this. Fortunately there are a rich set of SAN building blocks — switches, hubs, HBAs, routers, and options for long and shortwave laser-based fiber-optic cables. Unfortunately details of these are complex and vendor-specific. You need to study and understand them.

What about the future needs of applications? Will more storage be required in the future? Sure! Your current plan should be able to accommodate future demands.

Know Your Site

Understand your company's business and the short- and long-term goals. What current hardware, operating systems, networking products, and backup procedures are in use? Do you already have SAN components such as hubs, switches, HBAs, servers, and storage devices that must be part of the new order? All this background information will go a long way toward ensuring success.

Type of Cables and Devices for Your Site

In the ideal world, you will only use fiber optic (rather than copper) cables. After all, it is more reliable, faster, and supports longer distances between nodes. Multimode fiber can support devices 500 meters away, and single-mode fiber up to 10 kilometers away. But the higher cost of fiber may be an issue. Your vendors, the products, and the HBAs and storage devices you need to use may only support copper interfaces. Parallel SCSI links can be up to 25 meters and support only up to 15 devices in each SCSI chain.

Need for Present and Future SAN Features

Is fibre channel over IP (FCIP) in the cards? Do you need to implement those protocols now or in the future? Keep in mind that the ability to use FCIP depends on your vendor and on the HBA device drivers you use.

Expected Traffic Volume

If your SAN has servers that provide full-motion videos and streaming media traffic, ensure that each port is capable of delivering 100 Mbps throughput by using hubs and switches. Beware of changes in application requirements and targeted customer base. Your traffic volume will change, and your design should meet the needs during peak traffic.

Distance between Nodes

Copper cables support a maximum distance of 25 meters and fiber-optic cables can run up to 10 kilometers (when using long-wave laser over single-mode fiber). But do not push it. Reliability of data transfer reduces once you approach the limits. Data and storage are usually very business-critical, and this is not the place to save money on hardware purchases.

In a FC-AL loop, the distance between two nodes can be 10 kilometers. You can have up to 126 nodes. Thus, the total cable length in a loop can theoretically be 1,260 kilometers. This is, however, one extreme. When connecting over long distances, propagation delay over the media factors into performance and network design. In practice, only a few ports may have devices as far as 10 kilometers away to protect against disasters. To further extend distances, you can use more switches or hubs (cascading), or use extenders to accommodate several 10-kilometer cable runs.

Most devices will be in the same room or data center. Copper connections will suffice for that. Most hubs and switches allow copper and fiber cables to be connected to different ports.

Number of Devices

In a switched fabric, you can have millions of devices. This is more than adequate for any enterprise and a nightmare to set up. Many devices can be attached to a fabric by using FC-AL hubs or switching hubs, or by cascading extensions to switches or hubs.

An FC-AL loop can have up to 126 devices. You may have to count the disks within an enclosure as well (for example, disks in a JBOD box) if the internal disks are cabled as an arbitrated loop and the internal loop is connected to the external port. In such a case, count each internal disk as a device in your external FC-AL. Typically a loop is set up to have three to ten nodes or devices. A small number of nodes per loop ensures high bandwidth and availability. For connecting more devices, it is a good idea to use a switch to get transparent activity between loop segments without sacrificing bandwidth within each segment.

Do You Need to Accommodate Existing Direct-Attached Components?

This can be an issue if your site has already invested money into SCSI tapes, disk subsystems, JBOD devices, and servers and wishes to migrate to a SAN. Companies do not like to get rid of old hardware as long as it is serviceable. To use SCSI devices in the SAN, you may need to deploy FC-to-SCSI bridges. They have FC and SCSI ports, and the microcode within the bridge handles the protocol conversion.

Cost

Besides the cost of hardware and software, the cost of training to learn skill sets for deploying and maintaining a SAN environment can be substantial.

NAS/SAN Hybrid

Portraying SAN versus NAS is a detriment to both technologies. This is unfortunate, because they have their places when designing for Internet services, high-stress database environments, server clusters, or a horizontally scaled Web farm. Most vendors today integrate SAN and NAS in what is called a "SAN backbone with a NAS frontbone."

An excellent example is the Web-based broadcasting sites. They offer more-or-less static content from multiple load-balanced Web servers. A NAS/SAN combination allows them to offer a NAS interface for streaming content to Web servers, where the storage is actually a SAN storage. The front-end Web servers get to use the caching capabilities of NAS with the scalability and fast speed of SANs. All raw audio and video files (gathered via satellite, news feeds, or reporters) are aggregated and stored on SAN storage devices. There are dedicated SAN servers to arrange, edit, and compose the incoming data into well-managed formats, taking advantage of the high throughput of the SAN. If there is demand for more storage space, it is easy to add a storage subsystem to the SAN fabric and make it available to all servers within the SAN fabric. It is also easy to add a hierarchical storage manager (HSM) to archive and retrieve audio/video files to a SAN-attached tape subsystem.

A SAN can be attached to a NAS head or filer that exports or shares the data via NFS or CIFS with load-balanced Web servers over the IP network. NAS eliminates the need to replicate content across many Web servers.

Key Points

Storage architecture is one of the most important factors in any highly-available environment. The main storage requirements are

- Ability to accommodate rapidly increasing data requirements
- Ease of management of the exploding amount of data while keeping expenses low
- Keeping data available at all times and protected from various software and hardware failures and disasters
- Providing data-replication and disaster-recovery applications that, in turn, require a large amount of bandwidth between storage devices and servers located at far-flung sites
- Compatibility between data format, storage hardware, and OS platforms

Following are some key points discussed:

- Direct attached storage (DAS), where the attached storage is held captive behind a server, is easy to implement but creates small, server-centric storage islands, spans short distances, and has low throughput.
- Network technology advancements have provided the storage industry with new ways to access data, such as NAS, SAN, iSCSI, and FC over IP.
- A NAS device has a file server (or *NAS head*) connected to fault-tolerant volumes that are shared with other network devices using file-sharing protocols such as NFS, HTTP, or CIFS.
- Fibre channel-based SANs have a distinct advantage over direct-attached storage due to better performance, flexibility of attaching to several hosts, ease of adding or removing storage, longer distances between servers and storage, and more storage devices that can be provided to each server.

CHAPTER 21

Storage Area Networks

It is a funny thing about life. If you refuse to accept
anything but the best, you very often get it.
— W. Somerset Maugham.

This chapter describes storage area networks (SANs), especially where they help build a highly available, high-speed, and clustered environment. The primary purpose is to speed access from servers to disk arrays and do so in a reliable manner so that applications have 24×7 availability.

SANs also help toward network convergence because I/O protocols can be used to transfer data over IP networks. This attribute has proven to be key in the fast acceptance of SANs.

What Is a SAN?

A SAN is a dedicated network that interconnects hosts and storage devices, usually via fibre channel (FC) switches and optical fiber media. A storage device is a disk subsystem or array with a set of disk drives. As more and more storage devices are added to the SAN, they become accessible to all servers attached to the SAN. Since any server can access the storage, more server power is available for applications and user data residing on the shared storage. SAN accesses data at the bock level; NAS accesses data at the file level.

Typically a SAN is part of the overall network of computing resources for an enterprise. Storage devices are usually located in close proximity to hosts but may also extend to remote locations for backups, disaster recovery, and so forth, using wide area network (WAN) carrier technologies such as asynchronous transfer mode (ATM) or synchronous optical networks (SONET). Hosts and storage devices can be connected using FC technology, SCSI, or IBM's Enterprise System Connection (ESCON). ESCON's fiber-optic links can extend the distance up to 60 kilometers with chained SAN directors or switches.

In a number of aspects, a SAN is similar to a local area network (LAN). A LAN consists of PCs, servers, printers, and workstations connected to each other using TCP/IP protocol, usually over Ethernet hardware. A SAN consists of servers and storage devices (RAID subsystems, tape libraries, JBOD, and so on) connected to each other. All storage devices and servers in a SAN are accessible to each other. In other words, instead of having little islands of storage devices that are tied to only one or two servers, a SAN provides you with a pool of storage devices and servers with any-to-any connectivity.

Figure 21-1 shows a typical LAN and SAN configuration. On the upper half is a typical network with clients, NAS storage, and servers with direct-attached storage. On the lower half is a LAN with servers and storage devices interconnected via a SAN.

Figure 21-2 shows a transition from a traditional direct-attached storage environment to an early SAN configuration. All storage devices and servers are connected to one or more SAN switches, thus providing any-to-any connectivity.

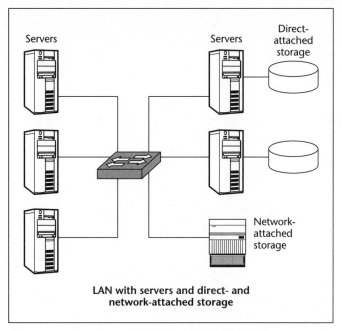

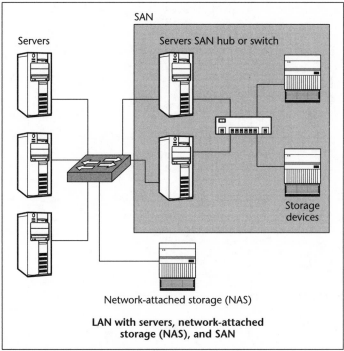

Figure 21-1 A typical LAN and SAN configuration.

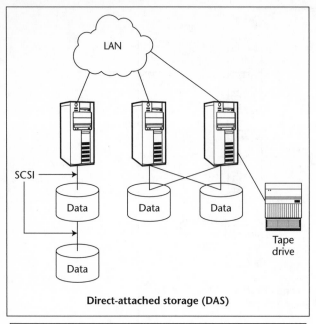

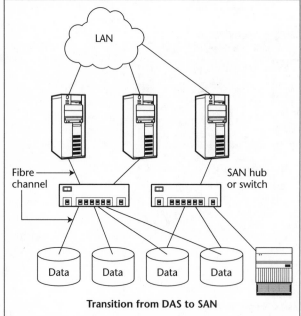

Figure 21-2 Transitioning SCSI or direct-attached storage to a small SAN.

Fibre Channel (FC)

FC is a high-speed data transmission technology used to connect multiple hosts and storage devices over fiber-optic or copper cables. *Fiber-optic* (or *optical fiber*) refers to the medium and the technology associated with the transmission of data as light pulses along a glass, fiber, or plastic wire. It carries much more information than conventional copper wire. It does not need to retransmit signals because optical fiber is not subject to electromagnetic interference (EMI). Most telephone company lines are made of optical fiber. Optical fiber wire requires repeaters at regular intervals. Also, the inner glass strands require more protection than copper-based cables. All this makes fiber optic deployment labor-intensive and expensive.

Most SANs are based on FC architecture. The initial objective of SAN is often to address shortcomings with SCSI protocol such as speed, resource-sharing capability, distance limitations, and maximum number of connected servers and devices.

Despite all these limitations in SCSI, there is no doubt that it is a mature, reliable, and well-tested channel-based protocol. As a result, SCSI is often mapped as a higher layer protocol on fibre channel (called FCP). Other I/O protocols such as serial storage architecture (SSA), Enterprise Systems Connection (ESCON), and high-performance parallel interface (HIPPI) can also be mapped on FC.

FC is capable of several peak transfer speeds. It is 1 Gigabit per second (Gbps), 532 Megabits/second (Mbps), 266 Mbps, or 133 Mbps. At 1 Gbps, FC has a theoretical peak throughput of 100 Megabytes per second (MB/sec) in each direction. Most connections are duplex (that is, there are two cables — one for transmitting and the other for receiving data), and each cable has a maximum throughput of 100 MB/second. Several companies are developing specifications and products for FC speeds of 2, 4, and 10 Gbps.

FC was originally designed to support fiber-optic cables only. Later, copper support was introduced and the spelling of the word "fiber" was changed to the French word, "fibre." This was done to reduce the association of the term with fiber optics. SAN topologies can also be built using copper cables. Since fiber optic cables are common, all examples in this book assume fiber as the media type. It has better noise immunity, scalability, performance, and support for longer distances.

Fiber Cable Connectors

The original FC standard specifies the DB-9 connector for copper cables and SC-type connector for optical cables. Now new connectors (such as LC and MT-RJ) are being used for high-density installations.

Duplex cables and connectors are used for point-to-point or switched topologies. Both transmitter and receiver cables are capable of carrying data simultaneously at 100 MB/sec. Simplex cables and connectors are used for arbitrated loop topologies. Figure 21-3 shows common fiber cable-end connectors.

Single-Mode Fiber or Multimode Fiber

Single-mode fiber is used for longer distances and *multimode fiber* for shorter distances. Single-mode fiber has a much smaller core than multimode fiber and is designed for transmission of a single ray or mode of light as a carrier. Multimode is designed to carry multiple light rays or modes concurrently, each at a slightly different reflection angle within the optical fiber core. Since the modes tend to disperse over longer distances (this is termed *modal dispersion*), multimode fiber is used over short distances. Figure 21-4 shows the layers within a fiber-optic cable.

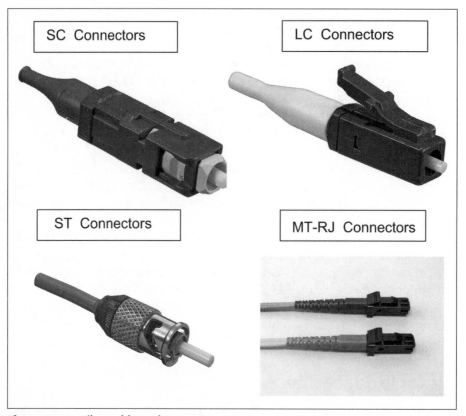

SC Connectors

LC Connectors

ST Connectors

MT-RJ Connectors

Figure 21-3   Fiber cable-end connectors.

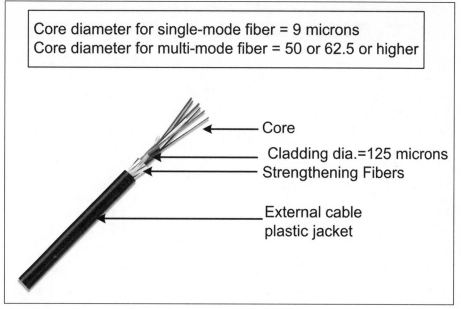

Core diameter for single-mode fiber = 9 microns
Core diameter for multi-mode fiber = 50 or 62.5 or higher

Core
Cladding dia.=125 microns
Strengthening Fibers
External cable plastic jacket

Figure 21-4 Layers within a fiber-optic cable.

The speed of each fiber-optic cable is also important. The speed ranges from 266 MHz to 4,250 MHz.

The active part consists of an optical core through which light passes. A *cladding* surrounds the core and keeps the light in the core. A *fiber coating* provides mechanical protection. The core is very thin and delicate and can easily be damaged. It therefore needs a protective coating in the form of an *external plastic jacket*.

Light travels in the core. Single-mode fiber has a single stream of photons. This cable requires finer optical fiber (9 microns in diameter) for better focusing. It has low dispersion. However, it is more expensive and used mainly for long-distance connections.

Multimode fiber has multiple streams of photons. It is cheaper and used for short distances (at most 2 kilometers). It is used where cost is a concern.

Wavelength Shortwave or Longwave

FC uses a carrier frequency modulated by the signal frequency. The carrier is defined by the wavelength. Short wavelengths are 780 and 850 nanometer (nm) and are used over multimode fiber only for short distances, as shown in Table 21-1.

Table 21-1 Various FC Media Types and Their Distance and Speed Limitations

MEDIA TYPE	PEAK TRANSFER RATE	DISTANCE RANGE
Copper media	1.0625 Gbps	25 meters to 100 meters
Long-wave laser over single-mode fiber (9 micron core diameter)	1.0625 Gbps	2 kilometers to 10 kilometers
Short-wave laser over multimode fiber (50 micron core diameter)	1.0625 Gbps	175 meters to 2 meters
Short-wave laser over multimode fiber (62.5 micron core diameter)	1.0625 Gbps	175 meters to 780 meters (usually for FDDI)

NOTES:
- 1 micron = 0.001 mm = 10^{-6} meters. A human hair is 75 microns thick.
- Short wavelength laser is 780–850 nm.
- Long wavelength laser is 1300–1550 nm.
- In FC-AL topology (discussed later), the distance is between two nodes, not the total distance around the loop.
- In switched fabric, the distance is from the fabric to the node, not the distance between nodes.

Longwave has wavelengths of between 1300 and 1550 nanometers (nm) and is usually deployed over single-mode fiber for long-haul connections. Note that 1 nm is one-thousandth of a micron.

SAN Components

The hardware needed to set up a SAN depends on your storage requirements and the topology you want to implement. This section lists various SAN components. The central component of a SAN is the switch or director. Table 21-2 compares a SAN switch with an IP-based switch.

The following components must work together to form a SAN:

- Host bus adapters (HBAs) are installed into hosts. Although these are FC adapters, they are like SCSI adapters. You may also need to install OS-specific device drivers for the adapter.

- Storage devices such as tape libraries, RAID subsystems, JBODs, and so forth.

- Interconnect devices such as fibre channel hubs or switches. Other special-purpose devices are SAN gateways, bridges, routers, and extenders, and fiber-optic cables to connect the hubs or switches to the HBAs and also to the storage devices.

Table 21-2 Difference between FC-Based SAN Switches and Directors

FEATURE	FC SAN SWITCHES	FIBER OPTIC–BASED IP SWITCHES
Type of Data	Transport storage data between servers, disk arrays, tape units.	Transports IP, IPX, Appletalk frames over LAN, MAN, WAN, and so forth.
Requirements	Adhere to strict requirements for low latency and high reliability. I/O bottlenecks have a severe impact of server performance.	IP networks ensure that systems can communicate with each other. Some protocols are less reliable than others.
Connectivity	Nodes connected to the same SAN fabric can access only each other. Zoning keeps the devices away from each other.	Once a server is online, it can access any other node on the LAN via proper routes.

A SAN management system ensures that all elements of the SAN network are configured and monitored properly.

SAN Topologies

SANs are implemented using any of the following three topologies:

- Point-to-point topology
- Fibre channel–arbitrated loop (FC-AL) topology
- Switched-fabric topology

Each one of these topologies is described in the following sections. Table 21-3 explains the requirements, benefits, and disadvantages of each topology.

Point-to-Point Topology

The connection type for point-to-point topology is similar to SCSI. A fiber HBA is installed inside a server and directly cabled to a fiber adapter within a disk enclosure, storage subsystem, or tape library. There are two links: one for transmitting and the other for receiving data. Each link can provide a peak throughput of 100 MB/sec or 1 Gbps speed, as shown in Figure 21-5.

Figure 21-6 shows the logical connection between the two node ports. The transmitter within a node is cabled to the receiver of the other node. Each FC port has two fibers. When operating in full-duplex mode, each fiber carries data at full speed: one for carrying data into the port and the other port for carrying information out of the port. The characteristics (speed, media, and protocols) of both ports must be compatible in point-to-point connection.

Table 21-3 Fibre Channel Topologies

CHARACTERISTIC	POINT-TO-POINT	FC-AL	SWITCHED FABRIC
Number of devices	Direct link between two nodes (host or storage).	Maximum 127 nodes per loop.	16 million devices with 24-bit address identifier (8 bits for domain, 8 for area, and 8 for arbitrated loop or port address).
Required components	Fiber-optic cables, HBAs on nodes.	A hub connected to server HBAs and storage devices.	Multiple interconnected switches, cables, and server HBAs.
Benefits	Simple to set up. Highest performance with full-duplex communications.	Low cost. Provides a beginning to a SAN environment. Ideal for small configurations with low-bandwidth requirements.	Any-to-any connectivity between nodes. Full bandwidth is concurrently available for all connections. Total throughput increases as you add more nodes.
Disadvantages	Storage is accessible by one server only and no storage sharing. Cannot dynamically or easily add or remove storage or servers.	Bandwidth is shared. Performance decreases as you add more nodes. If one node in the loop reboots, the node will temporarily break the loop. It is advisable to have few (for example, two or three) devices per loop.	A switch is expensive. Initial setup and maintenance are complicated. Most SAN hardware (switch, storage, HBAs) is proprietary.

The advantage of a point-to-point topology is that it is free from congestion or collisions and has the maximum bandwidth between the devices. However, it is extremely limited, with each storage unit tied behind a server. It has the same flexibility problems as an SCSI direct-attached topology.

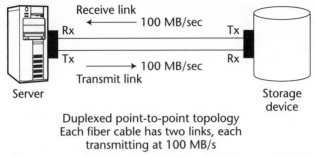

Duplexed point-to-point topology
Each fiber cable has two links, each
transmitting at 100 MB/s

Figure 21-5 Point-to-point SAN topology. Each link sends data at 100 MB/sec for a full-duplexed connection.

Fibre Channel–Arbitrated Loop (FC-AL)

In an FC-AL, the servers and storage devices are configured in a ring or loop. The drawback is performance. The bandwidth is shared by devices in the loop. In this respect, an FC-AL is similar to a token ring. When a node needs to communicate with another, the transmitting node arbitrates for control of the loop (hence, an "arbitrated" loop). If the loop is not in use, it takes control and notifies the receiving node about the impending communication. The two nodes in the loop take control; they access each other at the full bandwidth of the media (just like a point-to-point connection) for the duration of the data transfer. When the communication ends, they give up control of the loop. The loop is then available for arbitration for any other node that needs to send data.

The nodes in a loop are logically connected in a serial manner. Figure 21-7 shows nodes (servers and storage devices) in an FC loop. The elliptical line shows a logical view of the loop. The distance between two nodes depends on the link type. The hub is transparent to communication between the nodes. There can be 126 nodes per loop.

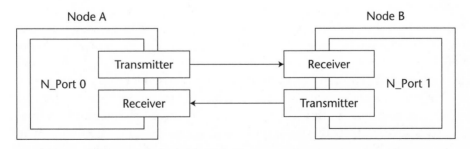

Point-to-Point Topology

Figure 21-6 Logical connection between nodes in a point-to-point topology.

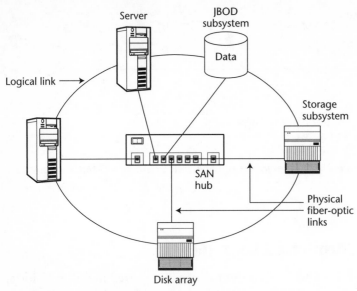

Figure 21-7 FC-AL devices that are physically connected to ports in a SAN hub to form a logical loop.

A loop initialization primitive (LIP) is used to allocate a unique address for each node, to reset a device, or to indicate a loop failure. It is generated whenever a device is added or removed from the loop.

The SAN shown in Figure 21-8 has a failover FC-AL loop. Each storage array and server has two SAN interfaces and is connected to two loops, thus providing redundancy against hub failure.

Bandwidth within a loop is shared. Multiple simultaneous communications are not possible. Figure 21-9 shows the serial-manner communication within a loop. Data flows within the loop from node-to-node until it reaches its destination. The problem, therefore, is that only two nodes can talk at any given instant, and all other nodes must wait and act as repeaters. The advantage is that the hub is cheaper than a switch and is used where cost must be low and low performance is acceptable.

Before the development of stable SAN switches, SAN hubs were the most common FC storage topology. Hubs that cost less than $1,000 were used to connect servers and storage arrays worth $100,000+. Soon, marketing campaigns stressing disruption vulnerability of loops caused large-scale migration from hubs to switches, especially for enterprise HA environments. But, the hub vendors had enough time to ensure nondisruptive behavior and compatibility with several disk arrays. Nevertheless, arbitrated loops are used nowadays to connect NAS disk arrays, JBODs, and internal disks, with a server or RAID-subsystem backplanes.

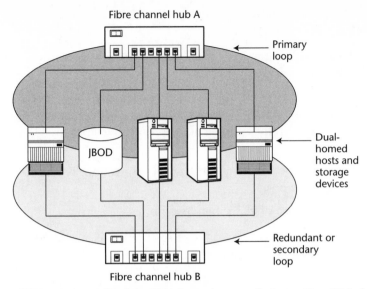

Figure 21-8   Redundant FCAL loops in a small cluster. Two FC hubs provide redundancy for hub failures.

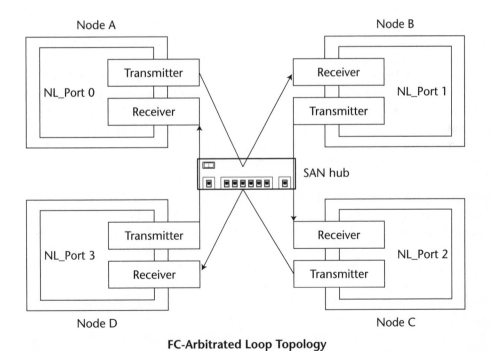

FC-Arbitrated Loop Topology

Figure 21-9   Logical links between transmitter and receiver ports within a four-node SAN loop with speed of 100 MB/sec.

Arbitrated loops offer an economical solution and satisfy a wide range of needs such as the following:

- They provide private and public loop support for several types of nodes and storage devices.

- They increase the total number of loop devices per segment. However, it is common to have two to ten servers where storage arrays are in a loop, except when nodes happen to be housed within a storage subsystem.

- The bandwidth within a loop is shared, but still performance is acceptable for most business purposes.

- They increase the maximum distance between nodes.

Balancing the cost and performance factors has resulted in complex SANs with point-to-point, loop segments, and switched fabrics.

Switched-Fabric Topology

The requirement for a switched-fabric topology is exactly what it sounds like: You need one or more FC switch. All devices (servers, storage, hubs, and so on) must be connected to one or more SAN switch.

An FC fabric is one or more fabric switch in a single or extended configuration. A fabric has higher flexibility and performance. Unlike a loop, a fabric node can be added, removed, replaced, and shut down without disrupting other nodes and has no LIPs. Problems with a device are localized and not transmitted to other fabric nodes. A fabric provides higher flexibility when adding or removing devices or hosts from the fabric. Unlike FC-AL, bandwidth in a fabric is not shared. All device-to-device links are capable of simultaneously delivering the full bandwidth (100 MB/sec for 1 Gbps fibre channel). Data transfer between any two nodes is independent of communication between other nodes. This increases scalability. When you add more nodes, the maximum possible bandwidth increases proportionately.

Figure 21-10 shows a two-switch fabric, with two nodes connected to two ports in each switch. The nodes A, B, C, and D are connected to the four switch ports F_Ports A, B, C, and D. If Node B wants to send data to Node D, the data is first sent to F_Port B in Switch 1. The fabric makes an internal connection by selecting an optimal route between F_Ports B and D. The data is then sent to F_Port D.

FC allows a mix of attachments with different features and speeds. Figure 21-11 shows two fabrics, each consisting of one switch, and communication of node ports with SAN switch ports. Subsequent figures in this chapter show multiswitch fabrics.

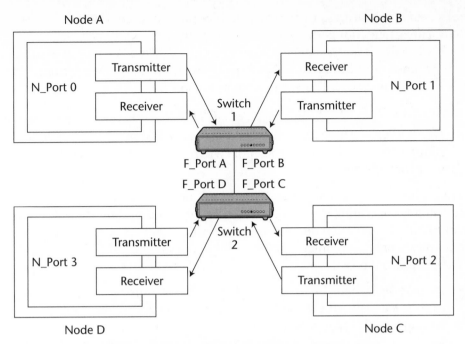

Fabric Topology with 2 SAN switches and 4 nodes

Figure 21-10 Connection between transmitter and receiver ports within nodes and switches in SAN fabric, where each link is at 100 MB/sec.

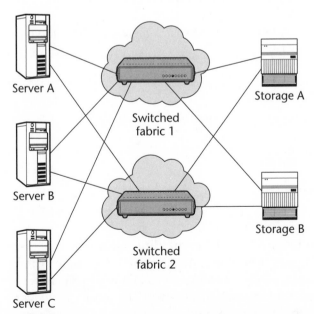

Figure 21-11 A two-switch star fabric prevents the switch from becoming a single point of failure.

SAN zoning is a process by which switch ports or node *world-wide numbers* (*WWNs*) are grouped together so that they can communicate with each other. A WWN is a 64-bit address that is analogous to the MAC address. It guarantees uniqueness within a large SAN fabric. However, it is not used to transport frames within the fabric. There are two types of WWNs:

- *Node WWNs* — These are allocated to the entire adapter.

- *Port WWNs* — These are assigned to each port within an adapter. If an adapter has four FC ports, each port will have port WWNs. These are used for SAN zoning.

Zones allow a finer partitioning of the fabric and are commonly used to separate different operating systems. A fabric can be zoned into functional sets. It simplifies implementation and enhances security. Members within a zone can communicate only with other members within the same zone.

There are two types of zones:

- A *hard zone* is made by assigning switch ID-port number combinations as zone elements. If a device is moved from one port to another, it will end up in a different zone.

- A *soft zone* is created if all zone elements are WWNs, regardless of which port it is connected to.

Zones can overlap (that is, a WWN number or switch port can be members of several zones). However, some SAN switch vendors do not allow hard zones to overlap.

A switched topology is also called *cross-point switch topology*. There are five types of switched fabrics:

- Star fabrics

- Cascaded fabrics

- Ring fabrics

- Mesh fabrics

- Tree fabrics

Star Fabrics

A *star fabric* is one where no two SAN switches are directly cabled. It is also called a *noncascaded fabric*. The simplest type of a SAN fabric is a single switch with ports connected to end nodes (hosts or disk arrays). Figure 21-11 shows a two-switch star fabric. Each switch forms an independent fabric. However, both the fabrics interconnect the same set of nodes. Figure 21-12 shows a star topology with N switches.

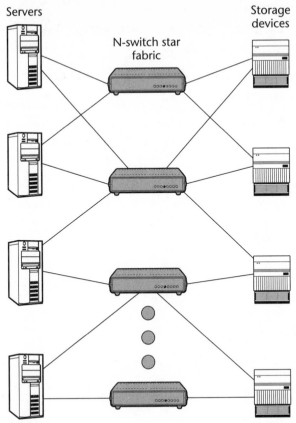

Figure 21-12 A star topology with N switches, with no data traffic between switches.

To maximize performance, no data must be allowed between switches. The goal is to have a single hop between two end nodes that must communicate. However, it is a good idea to connect the switches to create a fabric and share management information but no data traffic. The N-switch star topology has high performance and is simple to manage if you have a few switches.

Cascaded Fabrics

A *cascaded fabric* is one where multiple switches are interconnected within a fabric by one or more interswitch links (ISLs). Switches are connected in a linear array and each switch is connected to a neighboring switch.

Cascaded fabrics have several benefits:

- They have a large port count.
- They have no single points of failure (SPOFs).

- They have longer distance between nodes.
- They are better suited for clustering and disaster-recovery applications.
- They scale easily to accommodate more nodes.
- They can make use of a shared backup and centralized management.
- They provide the foundation for an integrated enterprise-wide SAN.

Figures 21-13 and 21-14 show cascaded SAN fabrics. Figure 21-14 shows a switched fabric, where one SAN switch is a member of an arbitrated loop.

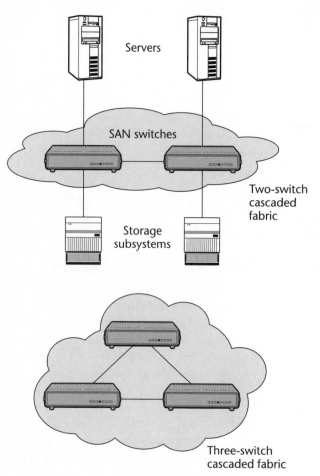

Figure 21-13   Cascaded switched fabric.

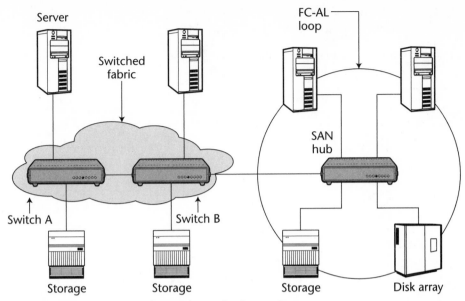

Figure 21-14   Cascaded fabric with attached FC-AL loop.

Figure 21-15 shows a network attached storage (NAS) server as part of the cascaded-SAN fabric that uses disks or RAID volumes on FC-attached devices.

Ring Fabrics

A *ring topology* has a continuous ring of interconnected switches. Each switch is connected to the next, and the last one is connected to the first. The switches can be interconnected in one ring or in two rings. This topology improves resiliency because it has full connectivity and multiple paths. It enables centralized backups and SAN management. Another key advantage is improved scalability because of nondisruptive expansion or changes. Figure 21-16 shows a ring fabric.

Historically the ring topology has been used for token rings or FDDI. These are rings of end nodes, but SAN rings are made of switches (three or more).

The main advantage of a ring is that it can scale infinitely and supports traffic in both directions. The main problem is that the hop counts are very large, especially for communication between diagonally placed switches. This performance problem can be resolved in two ways:

- By placing bisecting links between switches that are not neighbors
- By creating a ring+star topology in which all switches on the ring are cabled to a single core switch placed in the center of the ring

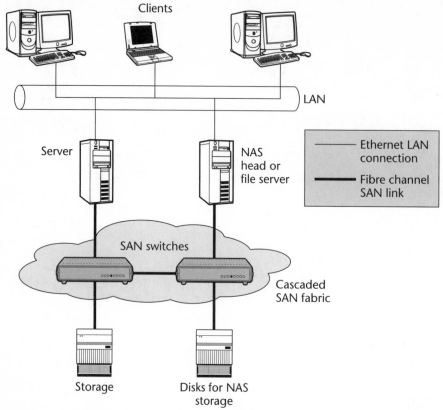

Figure 21-15 NAS and SAN combined in a cascaded fabric.

Data between two non-neighboring switches on the ring go through the central core switch. Two core switches are not required because the ring and core paths provide redundancy. The ring+star topology boosts performance because a maximum of three hops is required between any two end-nodes.

Mesh Fabrics

Similar to a cascaded fabric, a *meshed fabric* is one where all switches are interconnected by ISLs. The topology provides at least two paths between any two switches.

If a switch fails, the standby path gets activated and there is no service outage. Of course, all nodes that are connected only to the failed switch are unreachable, which can be overcome by attaching each node to at least two switches. Thus, any switch, ISL, or link between a node and a switch is no longer a SPOF. Such fault-tolerant fabrics are shown in Figures 21-17 (four-switch mesh) and 21-18 (five-switch mesh).

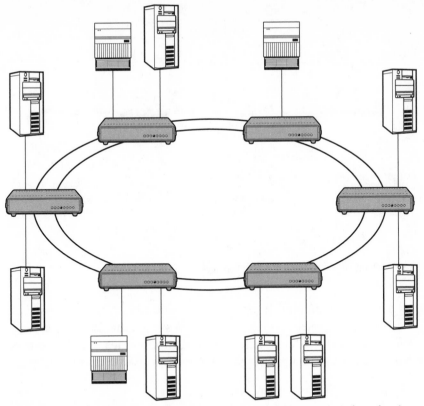

Figure 21-16   Ring fabric. A ring+star topology would have a switch at the ring center and a cable from each of the six ring switches.

Meshed fabric is ideal for situations where data-access requirements are local and distributed. Like cascaded fabrics, it provides a foundation for centralized backup and management and is scalable.

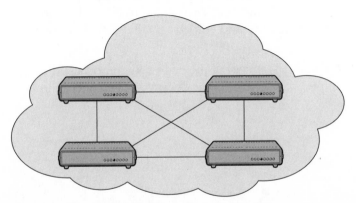

Figure 21-17   Design of a four-switch mesh fabric.

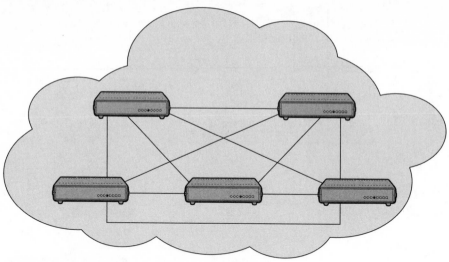

Figure 21-18   Design of a five-switch mesh fabric.

A major disadvantage of a mesh topology is the number of ports consumed by ISLs. In a five-switch mesh, four ports in each switch are used for ISLs, or 25 percent for a 16-port switch. Therefore, mesh topologies should be used when the total number of switches is small compared to the number of ports per switch.

Tree Fabrics

A *tree fabric* is a three-layer configuration of switches with the center layer dedicated as the core or backbone layer and the two outer layers acting as the edge layers. Servers and storage arrays are connected to the edge layer switches.

There are two types of trees based on the number of ISLs:

- *Fat trees* — Here, 50 percent of the switch ports in the edge switches and 100 percent in the core switches are dedicated to ISLs. They provide many-to-many connectivity and enhance availability, as shown in Figure 21-19.

- *Skinny trees* — More than 50 percent of the edge-switch ports and several core-switch ports are available for devices. This is shown in Figure 21-20.

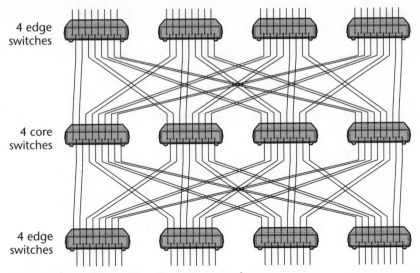

Figure 21-19 Connections for fat tree topology.

The various SAN topologies (point-to-point, arbitrated loop, and fabric topologies) are often combined. For example, four storage devices and two hosts may be connected to a SAN hub to form an FC-AL. One of the hub ports is then connected to a fabric switch, which makes the loop a part of a larger SAN. The host may have a second fiber HBA to form a point-to-point connection with a disk array. A third FC HBA on the host may connect it to a SAN fabric.

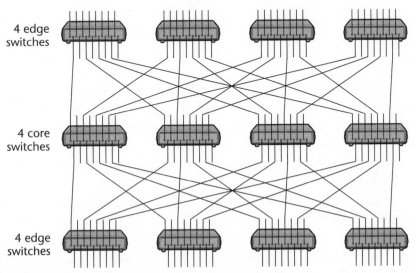

Figure 21-20 Connections for skinny tree topology.

Best Practices

Here are some best practices for configuring SAN topologies:

- If you have various switches and directors from different vendors, they may not all participate to provide a unified virtual storage view. Test your hardware with the virtualization software.

- SAN switches are built with application-specific integrated circuit (ASIC) chips. Each ASIC controls the operation of two, four, or eight ports. Connect server-storage pairs to ports within the same ASIC. This enables faster server-storage communication than that between ports on different switches or even different ASICs.

- When beginning with a simple one- or two-switch SAN, reserve two ports per switch for future SAN expansion.

- If you are building a tree topology (edge and core switches) and most connections are localized to a single hop at the edges, place directors at the edges and switches at the core.

- Meshes are best used when the number of ports per switch is much higher than the number of switches in the fabric.

- For ring topologies, bisect the ring with ISLs to reduce the maximum hop count.

- With ring topologies and high traffic along the ring circumference, consider a core switch to make it a ring+tree topology.

Key Points

Following are some key points discussed in this chapter:

- FC provides a more robust, flexible, fast (100 MB/sec in each direction), and highly available solution for attaching servers and storage devices. It can connect a large number of devices with any-to-any accessibility over a longer distance (10 kilometers). However, it is more expensive.

- There are three types of SAN topologies: point-to-point topology between two devices (host or storage), a fibre channel–arbitrated loop (needs a hub), and a fabric (with one or more SAN switches).

- The drawback with using a hub is that only one pair of devices can communicate at a time in the loop, while other devices are waiting.

With a switch, all devices can be simultaneously engaged in transferring data.

- SAN directors and switches can be used for fabrics. Small SANs have few devices and one or two switches. Large SANs have hundreds of nodes. You can start with a one- or two-switch SAN topology and expand it to an N-wide star, ring, ring+star, mesh, or tree topology.

Configuring
a SAN

The shortest way to do many things is to do only one thing at a time.
— Richard Cech

A phased deployment of SAN is best. Start small, especially if SAN is a new technology to most IT folks in your company. An added advantage is that you have a better chance that your SAN will be optimized for your needs. Every IT environment is unique, and so it is not easy to predict a large-scale SAN setup that will best meet your needs. Although getting started with SAN is no riskier than any other IT projects, it must be carefully managed. The steps suggested in this chapter will provide an understanding of the process of building a SAN. The stages you choose depend on a lot of factors: your budget, user needs, amount and significance of data, and degree of resiliency you want to have.

This chapter describes SAN design phases, where you gather requirements and data, architect a solution, and implement the SAN phases (where you construct the SAN fabric and later evolve it into a resilient, disaster-tolerant, enterprise-wide solution).

SAN Design Phases

SANs are designed to satisfy certain business and technical goals. The needs must be coupled with the existing environment to yield an architecture that has the right mass storage and servers connected using an appropriate topology. During design phases you decide on various SAN aspects such as topology, kind of storage, HA configuration, and heterogeneous platform support.

This section describes the following phases:

- *Phase 1* — Gather requirements.
- *Phase 2* — Gather existing environment information.
- *Phase 3* — Select a mass storage solution.
- *Phase 4* — Connect storage and servers.

Phase 1: Gather Requirements

In this phase, you must collect and document all requirements (such as a list of heterogeneous servers in the SAN, amount of required storage, backup strategy, and HA and DR requirements).

Most SAN implementations have a common set of business and technical goals. The business goals include high performance, high availability, improved DR, lower installation costs, reduced ongoing cost of storage management, ease of data migration, and better RAS (reliability, availability, and serviceability). The technical goals include better security, ease of management, improved backup, and data recovery.

Phase 2: Gather Existing Environment Information

During this phase, you gather information on the following:

- Number of servers in the SAN
- Available throughput
- Total size of storage for each server
- Number and size of LUNs for each server
- Existing fiber cables and storage systems that must be used in the SAN, as well as new ones that must be purchased

Phase 3: Select a Mass Storage Solution

Various factors influence the storage that must be selected for the SAN. These factors are storage throughput and size; HA and DR implementation; and type of servers that will use the storage, connectivity, scalability, backup scenarios, and target applications.

Phase 4: Connect Storage and Servers

In this phase, you connect the servers and storage to make a SAN fabric, providing for HA and scalability. These are explained in the section "SAN Implementation Phases," later in this chapter.

Example of SAN Design Phases

The following example illustrates typical SAN design stages.

Example Phase 1: Gather Requirements

A SAN must be implemented to address the high I/O wait. There are two data warehouse servers that need the highest bandwidth to a resilient, fast storage subsystem. The SAN must provide data to a Web farm and to QA and test servers. The SAN must be scalable. It must be easy to add or remove storage subsystems or servers from the mix. It should be serviceable without ever having to take the subsystem off-line. All links must be redundant between the servers and storage. It must also be capable of remote data replication for DR.

Example Phase 2: Gather Existing Environment Information

In this phase, you must gather information about the current data center and application status. Here are some examples of what you must understand and document:

- The existing environment has a Web farm that shares a NAS-based directory for Web pages.
- The data warehouse servers need the highest throughput with the storage subsystem.
- There are also a number of QA and test servers that need access to data that is modified by the data warehouse server. A copy of the data is made every night for use by the test servers. The new SAN subsystem must be able to make the copy internally without burdening the servers or network.
- A database cluster relies on fast access to shared storage.

Example Phase 3: Select Mass Storage Solution

A single high-end storage subsystem with the following features is selected:

- All volumes are protected by hardware RAID-0 or RAID-5.
- The SAN supports a NAS head that shares a portion of the data over the LAN.
- The disk array has eight or more fibre channel ports for attaching SAN fabrics or servers.
- Adding more disks is an online change.

- All components (such as fans, disks, power supply, and adapters) can be changed without taking down the subsystem.

- It has a cache, with read-ahead capability that makes an intelligent guess of what data will be required by the server, fetches it, and keeps it in cache for a quicker reply.

- The disk array comes with data-replication software that can be used to sync data to another subsystem over a dedicated fiber link or over the enterprise IP WAN.

Example Phase 4: Connect Servers and Storage

Figure 22-1 shows the SAN configuration with servers and storage array. The data warehouse servers are directly connected to the disk array. Each has two links to the array. This yields a bandwidth of 200 MB/sec between the server and array in each direction. The database cluster and NAS head have redundant links and switches. Since the QA and test servers do not require high throughput, they are connected via a SAN hub.

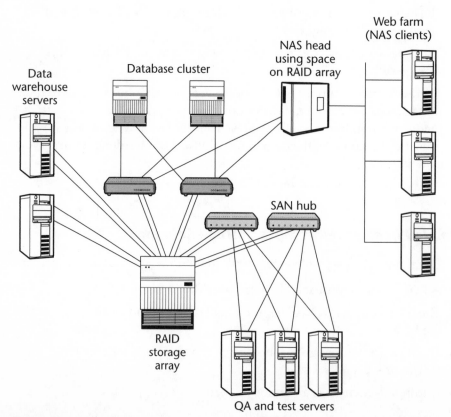

Figure 22-1   Design of a SAN.

SAN Implementation Phases

The configuration of an initial SAN evolving into a larger, enterprise-wide setup follows the three phases outlined in this section:

- *Phase 1* — Create local SANS
- *Phase 2* — Build the enterprise-wide SAN
- *Phase 3* — Protect the SAN data

Phase 1: Create Local SANs

Start with a single switch or hub. You can connect servers and storage devices (RAID subsystem, JBOD, and so forth) to it. If you want to connect existing SCSI arrays to your new SAN, you need a SCSI-to-fibre channel protocol converter or gateway. In a small setup such as the one shown in Figure 22-2, a SAN provides faster data access, ease of adding or removing hosts or storage from SAN, and protection of your hardware investments because it is easy to scale it up to meet increased needs.

Other departments or geographical areas can do the same. The end result could be a number of small SAN islands.

Phase 2: Build Enterprise-Wide SAN

The different SAN islands can be linked together using a switch, as illustrated in Figure 22-3. Although the maximum distance for fiber-optic connections is 10 kilometers, it can be increased using cascaded switches or extenders. This is discussed in Chapter 23.

The various departments or facilities can share valuable storage resources. A backup tape library at one facility can be used to back up SAN data at remote locations. This enables better disaster tolerance by replicating data to remote sites. IT teams can develop common policies to help manage and use each others' resources.

Phase 3: Protect the SAN Data

Once the facilities are connected and you have a site-wide SAN infrastructure, it is time to add features to protect the data against the following:

- *Component failures* — This is done by adding standby components and links. More details are provided in Chapter 23, "Using SANs for High Availability."

■ *Local disasters* — Data from the local SAN storage must be replicated to remote sites. This is done in various ways, such as the following:

■ Interconnecting the FC ports in the storage devices directly using single-mode fiber cables

■ Using DWDMs

■ Interconnecting SAN switches over IP network or over fiber

These are explained in Chapter 24, "IP-Based Storage Communications," and Chapter 39, "DR Architectures."

Figure 22-4 shows the changes necessary to build some degree of fault tolerance between the sites by using redundant switches and multiple intersite links. Servers and storage arrays have more than one connection to hubs or switches. Multiple paths between sites enable load sharing for intersite data transfer. The enterprise will fully experience the resiliency and data replication benefits of SAN.

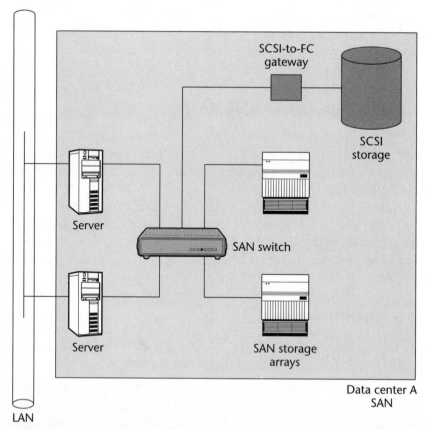

Figure 22-2   A small SAN setup with a single switch.

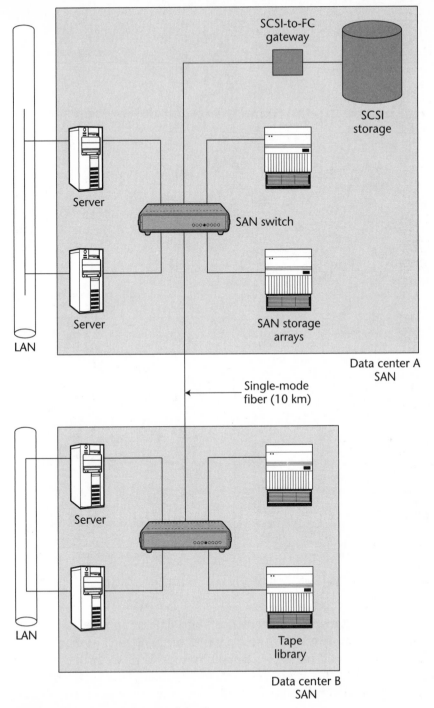

Figure 22-3 Connecting SAN islands.

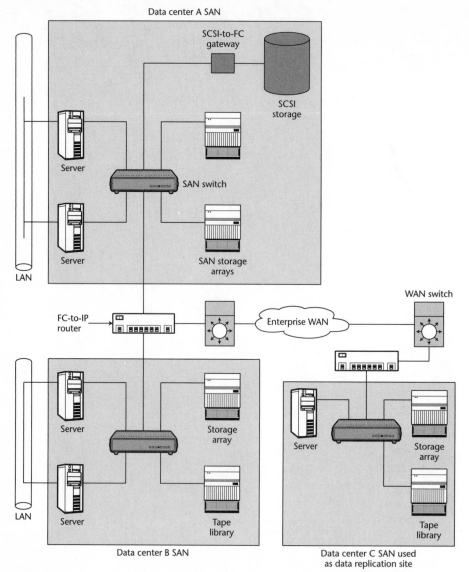

Figure 22-4 Highly available, resilient SAN with remote data replication.

However, there are some risks. Several hosts and data on storage devices are now accessible from all sites. Host and data security, as well as file system integrity, must be carefully managed. Hopefully by this phase of the deployment process, all involved parties have had enough experience with SAN and management software to undertake the challenges of working a diverse, shared environment.

Best Practices for SAN Deployment

Here are some tips for SAN deployment:

- Start with a fabric using a SAN switch or two. Although switches are more expensive, they are scalable and easily integrated into a larger SAN. They provide a quicker return on investment.

- Use hubs for migrating SCSI attachments to SAN, small switches for building storage infrastructures, and large switches for use by entire data centers.

- Maintain up-to-date backups of fabric or hub configuration (such as zoning and private and public loops configurations).

- Evaluate the mission-critical nature of the data and implement redundancy and SAN-based data replication if necessary.

Key Points

Following are some key points discussed in this chapter:

- Because of the fast increase in amount of data, enterprises need consolidated storage design and SANs are a popular strategy.

- When evaluating initial investments in a SAN, keep in mind that the environment will eventually expand to include multiple SANs located at great distances.

- Data on SANs can be protected by implementing device and link redundancy, as well as data replication.

CHAPTER 23

Using SANs for High Availability

You may be disappointed if you fail, but you are doomed if you don't try.
— Beverly Sills

Server and storage arrays in a SAN can be best implemented to increase infrastructure-side high availability (HA). The basics for achieving HA are straightforward. You first need to identify all individual hardware components in a complex system. These are the single points of failures (SPOFs). Then configure redundancy for as many components as possible. To configure redundancy, there must be at least one duplicate or standby component that can do the same task as the primary component. If the primary fails, the standby takes over automatically. This process is called *failover*. It should be transparent to users and applications running on the system.

SANs provide an ideal way to meet the basic requirements of HA and clustering. Because of the any-to-any connectivity, all hosts can access the storage devices. SANs make it easy to configure multiple paths between servers, switches, and storage devices. If one path (cable, host-based adapter, or switch) fails, data can be routed over the alternate path. It is relatively easy to change storage devices or data paths to hosts in a cluster.

Configuring an HA SAN

This section outlines the different levels of HA that can be configured into a SAN. The number of SAN switches, interswitch links (ISLs), and number of paths from server to fabric and storage units to fabric have the most impact on the data availability. SANs can be classified into the following three availability levels:

- *Level 1* — Path-level redundancy
- *Level 2* — Switch-level redundancy
- *Level 3* — Fabric-level redundancy

Level 1: Path-Level Redundancy

It is common for SANs to be initially configured with only one switch. To increase the resiliency of such a configuration, it is necessary to have two or more links from the switch to the storage arrays and to the servers, as illustrated in Figure 23-1.

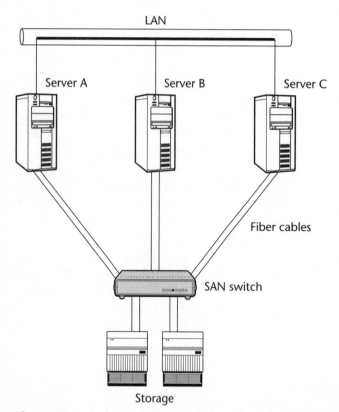

Figure 23-1   A cluster with one switch; each node has two HBAs for path failover.

Server software must be installed on the host to take advantage of multiple data paths to the storage devices. Several vendors such as VERITAS, IBM, EMC, Sun, and HP sell products that provide the load balancing or hot standby features:

- *Load balancing* — All data paths from server to storage devices provide an active I/O path.

- *Hot standby* — If a link from server to storage device fails, it is taken out of service and I/O is dynamically rerouted through the remaining path with no data loss. Under normal conditions, the standby path is not used for data I/O.

An obvious problem with this setup is that the switch itself is a SPOF. This is resolved with having two or more switches.

Level 2: Switch-Level Redundancy

In a two-switch cluster, as shown in Figure 23-2, each switch has the same set of storage devices and servers connected to it. This provides two independent data paths between each server and storage through separate switches. The second path is usually a standby and activates itself if the first path fails. The transfer of activity from a failed path to the standby is transparent to the user. Two SAN zones must be maintained within the fabric.

Although the switches are connected to each other using ISLs, these ISLs should not be used under normal conditions for data transfer. Doing so increases the number of hops from one to two. The ISLs are used for the following tasks:

- They help simplify fabric management by using the same configuration copy for both switches.

- They are used for I/O transfer if two links fail — one from one server to a switch, and the other from the other switch to storage arrays. In that case, the ISL must be used for I/O. The Xs in Figure 23-2 illustrate such path failures that necessitate ISL usage for data transfer. Server A can still communicate with the storage devices by using ISLs to go from Switch 2 to Switch 1, and then to the storage devices.

Level 3: Fabric-Level Redundancy

Just like switch-level redundancy, fabric-level redundancy has separate server-switch-storage paths for data. However, in this case, the switches belong to separate fabrics. There are no SPOFs. The advantages of fabric-level redundancy are as follows:

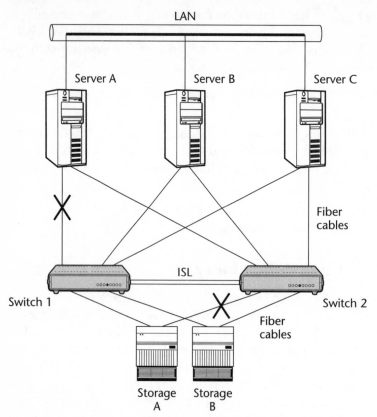

Figure 23-2   Using two switches to set up a cluster.

- It eliminates the risk of outage if the fabric fails. Human errors such as improper switch replacement procedures, erroneous fabric configuration settings, and fabric service failure can take down the fabric.

- The number of total available ports is higher. This, of course, comes at the expense of adding switches.

- Two fabrics allow for nondisruptive firmware and software code updates. Services can be failed from Fabric 1 to Fabric 2 (in Figure 23-3); then you can upgrade firmware in Fabric 1 switches and failback operations to Fabric 1.

Besides building fabric resiliency, the data in the storage arrays must be protected against disk failures using several mechanisms. The volumes in the storage units must be configured as mirrored or RAID-5 volumes. Certain disks must be designated as hot spares to automatically replace a failed disk in a mirrored or RAID-5 volume. The disks must be hot-swappable to allow you to replace failed disks without having to off-line the storage array.

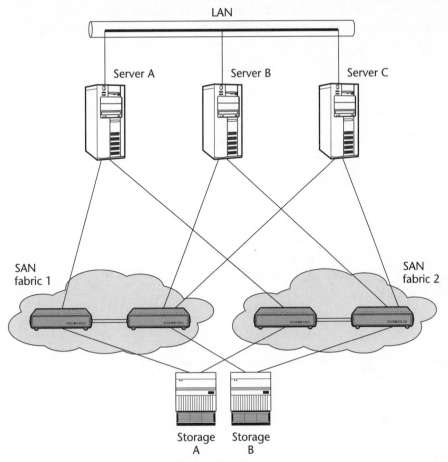

Figure 23-3   Devices connected to two fabrics.

Switch Features for Improving HA and Performance

The operating system and hardware on most SAN switches have several features that enhance HA and performance in the SAN environment:

- *Automatic path failover* — If there are multiple paths between two devices and an active path fails, the switch activates the secondary path without manual intervention or data loss.

- *Load sharing among ISLs* — The load-sharing feature enhances performance of interswitch data transfers.

- *Automatic selection of most efficient route* — In a multiswitch SAN, the fabric uses the fabric-shortest-path-first algorithm to select the most efficient path between two devices that must communicate with each other.

- *Support for high priority protocol frames* — This feature (where certain frames receive priority routing to minimize latency) is of great help to clustering applications.

- *Hot-replaceable components* — Critical components such as cooling and power devices in a switch are hot-replaceable.

Using SANs to Deploy Campus or Metropolitan Clusters

Several SAN features such as high data-transfer rates and native support for up to 10 kilometers make it an ideal choice for implementing a cluster or a remote data-replication site (where servers and storage units must be located across the campus or MAN). There is some safety in distance. Disasters at one end will likely not affect the other end. Figure 23-4 shows an example of a campus or MAN cluster.

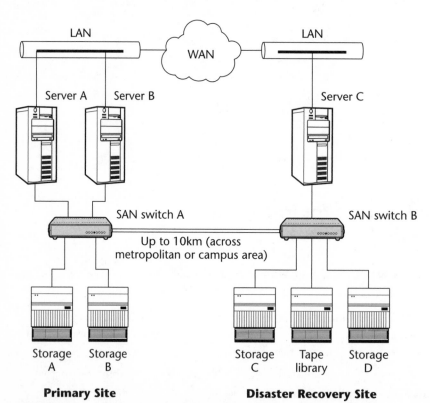

Figure 23-4   Using switches to set up campus clusters where devices can be placed 10 kilometers apart.

In Figure 23-4, area switches (rather than hubs) are used to connect the primary and secondary sites. Unlike hubs (where all data must be transmitted around the entire SAN), area switches localize data transfers. Only data that needs to go to a device located across the campus or metropolitan area is sent across. All data transfers between local devices are kept local. Storage devices can be assigned to servers so that most data transfers are local under normal circumstances. Note that there are two fiber cables or ISLs between the area switches to provide redundancy for communication between the primary and secondary sites.

To cover distances exceeding 10 kilometers, consider implementing one of the following techniques:

- *Repeaters or extenders* — These are used in conjunction with short wavelength (SWL) gigabit interface converters (GBICs). *Link extenders* are small external devices cabled to the switches. Extenders convert the shortwave signals on multimode fiber cable to longwave signals that can be transmitted over single-mode fiber cable. Extenders also boost the power on the laser. At the remote end, another device converts the signals to shortwave laser on multimode cable. Some vendors have successfully tested link extenders for connecting devices up to 120 kilometers.

- *Dense wavelength division multiplexing (DWDM)* — DWDMs are used to connect SANs. They have high bandwidth and low latency but are expensive. The maximum distance is 80 to 120 kilometers. Some vendors allow serial connection between DWDMs to increase the distance, as illustrated in Figures 23-5 and 23-6.

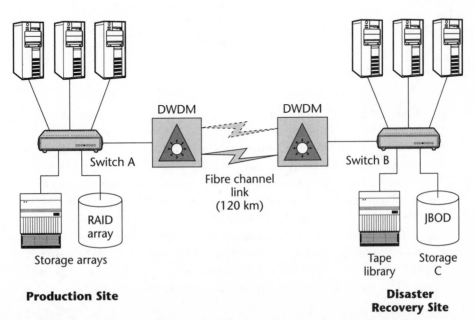

Figure 23-5   A metropolitan area SAN extension to a remote site using DWDMs.

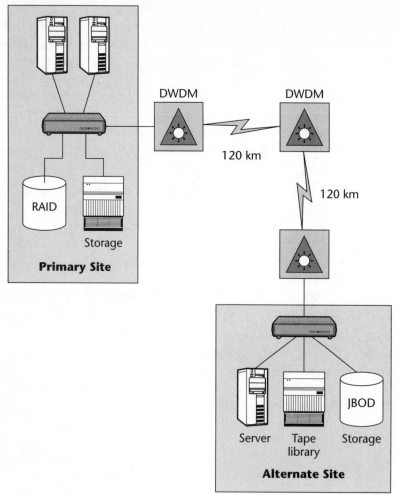

Figure 23-6   Distance increased using chained DWDMs.

DWDMs are usually linked in a manner that avoids any path from being an SPOF, as illustrated in Figure 23-7. If the path between DWDM 2 and DWDM 3 fails, data traffic can still get from Site B to Site C using the alternate path (from DWDM 2 to DWDM 1 to DWDM 3). This redundancy protects against any disruption that can happen in geographical areas outside an organization's control. One of the SAN sites can serve as a disaster-recovery site for the other two. If A and B are primary sites, Site C can act as a hot standby. Data from Site A and B can be mirrored synchronously to C. If either Site A or B goes down, applications from the failed site automatically start up on servers in Site C. This capability is configured using clustering software.

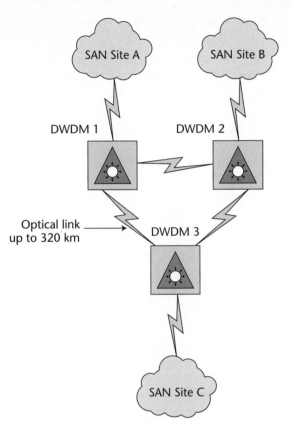

Figure 23-7   A SAN/DWDM-based MAN with redundant paths and business continuance.

- *Extended long wavelength (ELWL) GBICs* — These can be used to extend distances up to 80 kilometers. GBICs can be used in conjunction with external devices (such as extenders) to increase the distances.

The chief drawback is the high cost associated with installing dedicated fiber cables between distant sites.

Key Points

Following are some key points discussed in this chapter:

- To increase resiliency within a SAN fabric, you must provide multiple links from server and storage arrays to the fabric, multiple switches within each fabric, or two or more fabrics connected to the same set of devices.

- Using 1 Gbps fibre channel, the maximum distance between two devices in a loop or the distance from a node to a SAN fabric is 10 kilometers. However, DWDMs, link extenders, repeaters, long wavelength (LWL), or extended long wavelength (ELWL) GBICs are used to increase the reach of SAN switches.

CHAPTER 24

IP-Based Storage Communications

Never be bullied into silence. Never allow yourself to be made a victim.
Accept no one's definition of your life; define yourself.

— Harvey Fierstein

When first introduced into the marketplace, SANs promised ease of installation and management, lower expenses, and improved availability of data from multiple hosts while satisfying the rapidly increasing need for more storage space. However, SANs and fibre channel (FC) failed to keep those promises, primarily in areas such as ease of setup and maintenance and affordability. These problems caused a lower market penetration and a slower-than-expected rate of acceptance for FC and SANs.

The advent of gigabit Ethernet got the entire storage industry thinking about using Ethernet and TCP/IP as a medium for transferring data between storage devices and hosts. The next steps in the evolution of Ethernet technology are speeds of 2 and 10 Gbps. This will add a big impetus to the trend toward storage networking based on IP. Speed is just one of the several factors. Price/performance ratio, reliability and maturity of IP, greater allowable distances, and low cost of new hardware and ongoing maintenance are some merits of IP storage.

Why Use IP Storage?

What exactly is *IP storage*? The term refers to a group of technologies that allows block-level storage data to be transmitted over an IP network. Here are a few key advantages of IP-based storage:

- *No need to build a new infrastructure for data* — IP storage uses existing network infrastructure. Usually there are no new expenses to worry about. Even if a new network has to be set up, building and deploying an Ethernet LAN is much less expensive than installing an FC-based storage network.

- *No additional staffing needs* — IP storage uses protocols that are familiar to most networking professionals. They can set up, upgrade, and manage the network used for data and storage. Little training for the storage administrators is required. Very often, there is no need to hire storage experts.

- *It is possible to back up data to a remote device in another part of the world* — IP allows a user to access storage over long distances, something that FC (limited to 10 kilometers) and SCSI (limited to 25 meters) cannot match. Standard IP routers can be used to extend data access to a WAN or, if transmitted over the Internet, to any location in the world. This helps in setting up an environment that is disaster-tolerant and, there-fore, contributes toward business continuation, issues that have become paramount concerns for all businesses around the world.

- *Storage consolidation* — This is especially important if your storage and servers will be located at offices around the country or world. This advantage is also offered by FC SANs.

Types of IP Storage

There are three main implementations of storage over IP:

- Internet SCSI (iSCSI)
- Fibre channel over IP (FCIP)
- Internet fibre channel protocol (iFCP)

iSCSI

iSCSI is a networking protocol for SCSI traffic over TCP/IP Ethernet. The pro-tocol provides block-level I/O access to storage over existing IP networks. iSCSI-enabled hosts can communicate over IP routers and switches with iSCSI-enabled storage devices. The operating system and applications are unaware of the physical transport devices and media (FC, SCSI, Ethernet, or iSCSI) supporting the storage I/O, thanks to the layers of various SCSI proto-cols. iSCSI disks appear as standard physical disks to the iSCSI host.

The iSCSI standard is being developed by the Internet Engineering Task Force (IETF). SCSI packets are encapsulated in TCP and routed using IP over networks. Figure 24-1 represents how SCSI block-level data is transported within a TCP/IP packet. More information about IETF is available at `www.ietf.org/`.

How does iSCSI work? When an application (or user) on a server sends SCSI data for an iSCSI storage device, the SCSI commands are encapsulated. In some cases, the data should be encrypted; this is necessary especially if the data will have to go over an insecure connection such as the Internet. TCP and IP headers are added to the SCSI packets and the data is transmitted, typically over Ethernet (10BaseT, 100BaseT, or Gigabit) connection. When the packet is received by the storage device, it is decrypted and disassembled. The SCSI commands are sent to the SCSI controller and subsequently to the storage media. The same mechanism can be used to return data in response to requests because of the bidirectional nature of SCSI. This is shown in Figure 24-2. The host and storage device must have adapters and drivers to handle iSCSI protocol. If the storage device is part of a SAN, you need a FC-to-IP router. One such device from Cisco Systems, Inc., is shown in Figure 24-3.

As with any networking protocol, the software that implements the iSCSI protocol over TCP/IP has several layers. These software layers can be run in any of the following three places:

- Operating system of the host computer
- Chip in the iSCSI host-based adapter (HBA) or iSCSI network interface card (NIC)
- Coprocessor that lives on the plug-in board (iSCSI HBA or NIC)

There are two broad product categories that are required to deploy iSCSI. These products can be used at the host computer (initiator) or storage device (target) end.

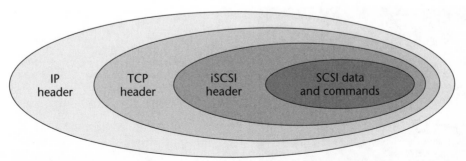

Figure 24-1   iSCSI protocol for transporting SCSI data in a TCP/IP packet.

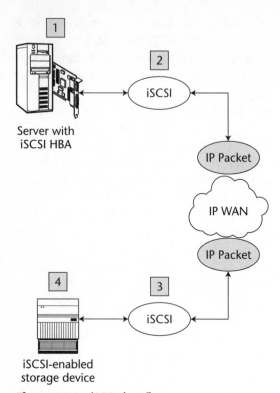

Server with
iSCSI HBA

iSCSI-enabled
storage device

Figure 24-2 iSCSI data flow.

- *iSCSI NICs* — These are traditional NICs with the iSCSI stack running on the host operating system. In some cases, the NICs may run the TCP/IP stack on the board itself. However, the CPU must manage and process the I/O data. Therefore, iSCSI NICs are not the preferred choice for connecting storage and iSCSI hosts.

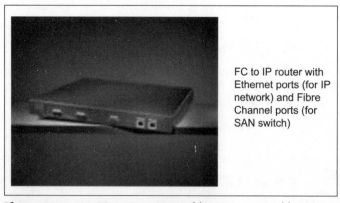

FC to IP router with
Ethernet ports (for IP
network) and Fibre
Channel ports (for
SAN switch)

Figure 24-3 An FC-to-IP router enables IP-connected hosts to access devices in a SAN.

- *iSCSI host-based adapters (HBAs)* — The HBA has a coprocessor that runs the TCP/IP and the iSCSI stacks in firmware. It allows the least load to be placed on the host CPU. The adapter may be configured to appear as a standard SCSI HBA to the operating system. It has an Ethernet port for connection to the IP network. A typical iSCSI HBA is shown in Figure 24-4.

In some cases, the standard network traffic and iSCSI storage traffic can be handled by the same adapter and run on the same Ethernet wire. However, it may result in high loads on the host CPU. Alternatively you could have separate adapters and Ethernet cables for IP traffic and iSCSI storage data.

Fibre Channel over IP (FCIP)

FCIP is a proposed standard to connect geographically dispersed FC SANs using the IP network (MAN or WAN). FCIP enables point-to-point tunnels between SANs. The end result is a single, large SAN. Applications associated with clustering and disaster recovery can use FCIP to copy local data to a remote SAN. Should the local storage array become disabled, an application could use the FCIP link to use the data at the remote site. Remote backups can also be deployed to protect valuable data in the event of a disaster at the primary location.

PCI iSCSI adapter with Ethernet port

Figure 24-4 A pair of iSCSI adapters for connecting hosts or storage arrays to the network.

The specifications for FCIP are also being developed by IETF. The specifications enable transmission of FC data over IP networks. FCIP uses a device (such as a router or switch) to encapsulate FC data frames into TCP packets or byte streams before they can be transported over IP networks. When the data reaches its destination, the TCP frames are stripped off and you again have the FC data frame.

Several vendors such as Cisco, IBM, and Adaptec offer products that use the iSCSI and FCIP protocols. They also sell storage routers such as iSCSI-to-FC storage routers. These are connected to FC switches (SAN) and to the IP network (Ethernet) and enable block-level storage traffic from a SAN to be accessed over an IP network, as illustrated in Figure 24-5. The storage router can have gigabit Ethernet links to an IP or network switch, which in turn is connected to iSCSI-enabled servers. FC links connect the storage router to SAN switches. Data on SAN storage can be accessed by servers across the IP network.

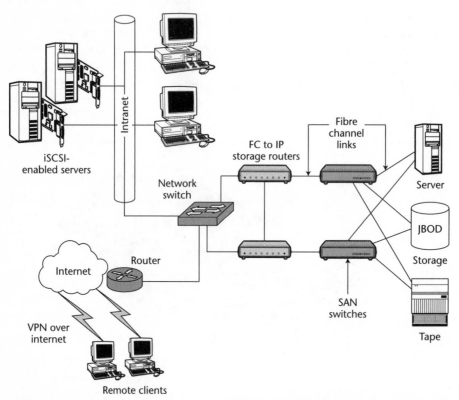

Figure 24-5 FC-to-IP storage routers connect FC devices in a SAN to iSCSI-enabled servers over IP networks.

Internet Fibre Channel Protocol (iFCP)

iFCP also connects FC SANs to IP networks. However, it is just a gateway-to-gateway protocol that combines IP and FC addressing mechanisms to route the FC data frames to their appropriate destination. iFCP provides FC fabric services over a TCP/IP network to devices in a SAN. An IP address is associated with each FC end device. The unique address is used to locate the destination for the data and also helps narrow down the source of a problem.

The specifications for IFCP were originally developed by Nishan Systems of San Jose, California, for some of their products. The specifications have been submitted to IETF for consideration as an FC-to-IP standard.

Extending SAN over ATM, IP, or SONET for Disaster Recovery

We have seen that storage networks within a local or metropolitan area can be linked by dedicated, high-speed pipes. They are well-suited for limited distances. Storage networks outside the metro area are best linked by an IP-based solution. Thus, storage can take advantage of long-haul, fast optical links (used for network traffic and deployed by various data and telecom carriers) to connect disparate storage islands.

Let's consider a local SAN, as shown in Figure 24-6, where local data is mirrored to disks in a remote SAN site. Lets assume that each of the two data centers have disks that have an average seek time of 2 milliseconds. When data is written to the disks, we will first get a response from the local disk, based on average seek time. The response from the remote disks depends on two factors:

- The latency caused by the network equipment used to connect the remote SAN.

- The distance between the two sites. Assuming the sites are connected by 600 kilometers of fiber-optic cable, the latency of the optical signal would be about 5 microseconds per kilometer. For 600 kilometers, the delay would be 6 milliseconds ($5 \times 600 \times 2$) because of the fiber cables.

On top of that, it takes the remote SAN 2 milliseconds to write the data to disk. The average latency for the remote SAN is now 8 milliseconds ($6 + 2$ milliseconds). The overall latency of the configuration is now four times. If you wish to decrease the latency, simply increasing the bandwidth will not help. Latency and bandwidth are separate features. Although both impact the total throughput, they do so in different ways.

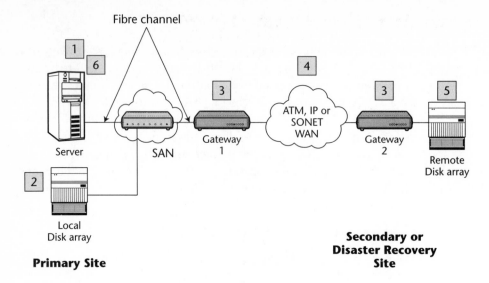

1] Server issues a command to write data to local and remote disk array.

2] Data is written to local disk in 2 milliseconds.

3] Gateways 1 and 2 add to the latency.

4] It takes 5 microsecond/km x 600 km = 3 milleseconds for data to reach
   remote destination.

5] It takes 2 milliseconds for data to be written to remote disk.

6] It takes another 3 milliseconds for the acknowledgement to reach
   the server.

Figure 24-6 Backing data to a remote site and latency introduced by distance and intermediate devices.

Another factor that would affect the previous calculation is the network equipment latency, introduced when FC traffic is encapsulated for transmission over ATM, synchronous optical networks (SONET), or IP. There would be additional queuing delays at each layer or stage within the gateway, depending on the hardware architecture of the gateway. However, a highly integrated chip-based gateway will introduce a latency as small as 0.1 millisecond, but a multiprotocol, large gateway may cause a latency of 0.5 milliseconds or more.

You can use one of the following gateways to connect the FC switch to the WAN.

- *FC-over-IP gateway* — This has a high latency up to tens of milliseconds, but it has the convenience of using standard Ethernet networks (10BaseT to 10 Gbps).

- *FC-over-ATM gateway* — This, like IP, has high latency. The data rates are also low (622 Mbps to 155 Mbps).

■ *FC-over-SONET gateway* — This may appear to be a good choice as it has high bandwidth and low latency. The data rate is up to 2.488 Gbps and is readily available from many telecom carriers, who have SONET as part of their existing infrastructure. FC-to-SONET gateways can be built with integrated chips with low latency.

Figure 24-7 shows how FC-to-network protocol gateways are used to set up a disaster recovery site.

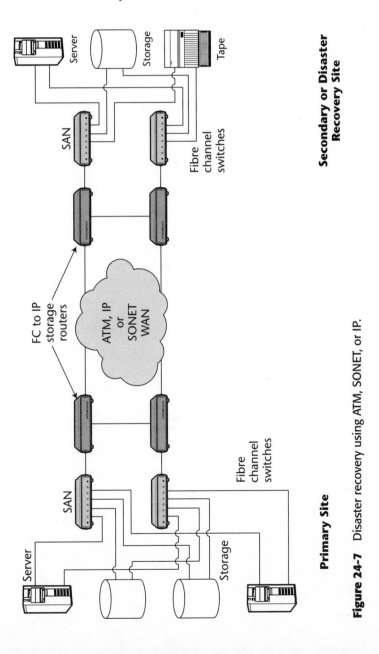

Figure 24-7   Disaster recovery using ATM, SONET, or IP.

Adopting IP Storage

Although IP storage is based on proven technology such as gigabit Ethernet, TCP/IP, and SCSI, it is still in its infancy. As of 2002, the standards were yet to be set by IETF. A few vendors such as IBM and Cisco have some products on the market, but the bugs are still being worked out. Once the smoke clears, IP storage is expected to come on with blazing speed. Only then will many vendors have true and tested products. Until then, everyone is an early adopter of the technology. If you are one of them, you must ensure that the products and vendor you choose will meet your objectives and that your investment will not become obsolete quickly.

Toward that objective, here are some questions to ask your vendor:

- Do I need to make changes to my existing network infrastructure (Ethernet or gigabit Ethernet) to implement the IP storage products?

- Do I need to send my storage and system administrators to any special training before they can deploy the products?

- Do your products comply with the industry standards? If not, do you plan on making them standards-compliant?

- How is the performance, as compared to FC?

- Do you have alliances with major storage or networking vendors? How is the interoperability of your products with network and storage devices from other vendors? What about certifications that demonstrate such interoperability?

- Do you have customers who are successfully using your IP storage devices in a production environment? Can I have their contact information?

Best Practices for IP-Based Storage Networks

Data transfers over IP networks have many exciting possibilities: Some may cause a greater than anticipated impact in the market and some may never leave the confines of the developer. The standards are still being set by the IETF (www.ietf.org/). The fact remains that IP-based storage is flexible and simple and has a low cost of implementation. However, traditional SAN switch-based fabrics are faster but more expensive and complex to implement.

Only a few well-tested IP based storage solutions are available today. Focus on those solutions that are available today to deploy storage networks. Here are a few rules to enhance throughput and ease maintenance:

- Maintain a separate logical IP network for iSCSI or FC-over-IP traffic, but it is not necessary to keep a separate physical network.

- Using VLANs within an existing Ethernet network minimizes potential for bandwidth contention.

- Use dedicated NICs for storage traffic on iSCSI-enabled hosts and storage arrays.

- Deploying iSCSI over gigabit Ethernet minimizes performance problems.

Key Points

Following are some key points discussed in this chapter:

- The traditional ways of direct-attached storage model will be replaced with a consolidated storage network with any-to-any connectivity and enhanced data availability. However, distinctions between SAN, DAS, NAS, and IP storage are blurring. All of these now rise to the challenge of meeting storage demands and offer fault tolerance, speed, and scalability.

- The three types of storage-over-IP solutions are iSCSI, FCIP (fibre channel over IP), and iFCP (Internet fibre channel protocol).

- iSCSI and FCIP are cost-effective solutions because you can use the existing IP network, but performance over IP is an issue.

- iSCSI enables storage access over IP networks for iSCSI-enabled storage devices or for SANs connected to IP networks using storage routes or IP-SAN modules.

- FCIP routers are used to transport FC data over IP networks so that they can be accessed by iSCSI-enabled servers or by another SAN fabric that has an FCIP router.

- Mirroring and data replication to remote storage devices can be done over IP, ATM, or SONET networks using FC-to-IP routers.

- Latency increases regardless of the technology you deploy. Gateway and fiber length contribute to the total latency. Applications that use long-distance links must always consider latency impacts. Adoption of 10 Gbps Ethernet will alleviate some performance problems.

Data Center Clusters

In This Part

Cluster Architecture

Patience is not inactive; on the contrary, it is active; it is concentrated strength.
— **Edward G. Bulwer-Lytton**

A *cluster* is defined as a group of interconnected nodes that work as a single, scalable, and highly available system. Clustering provides a service via a group of hosts primarily to minimize downtime. Other benefits are increased manageability, performance, and SLA compliance. If a clustered node goes down, applications are automatically migrated onto another node. The changeover is ideally transparent to users.

It is important to identify and provide redundancy to complex components. The most complex component within any IT infrastructure is the host. It is composed of several parts, namely, memory, CPU, disks, cables, adapters, fans, power supplies, and so forth. Any of this can fail, and it may take a long time to diagnose, identify, and resolve the problem. The server could be down for the entire duration, which can extend into hours or days. The cluster is used to overcome this problem. A cluster is made up of at least two servers. If an application cannot run on a server (because of software or hardware problems), another member of the cluster starts the applications. The process of migration of a service or application from one server to another within the cluster is called *failover*. Ideally a failover should not require manual intervention and should be quick and transparent to clients.

There are four primary cluster types:

- *Performance cluster* — The emphasis here is on increasing performance (via load balancing), scalability, and availability. They are also called *high-performance computing clusters* (*HPCC*) or *parallel clusters*. The cluster software creates a single system image and splits tasks among all nodes to execute them concurrently. Tasks are coordinated and results are communicated using message-passing libraries. Examples include Oracle Real Application Clusters (RAC) and IBM Sysplex Database Cluster. The cluster is highly available because a node failure does not cause service outage. It is scalable because more nodes can be added to the cluster without incurring service outage to meet increased workloads or boost performance.

- *Failover cluster* — This is the most common type of cluster. If one node in the cluster is down for planned maintenance or because of unexpected glitches, the applications are migrated to another healthy node. The failover duration can vary from a few seconds to several minutes, depending on configuration. The emphasis here is on availability rather than performance.

- *Global cluster* — This is a cluster of clusters and is used to create continental clusters. A cluster at a local site is linked with a cluster at a remote site, usually for disaster-recovery (DR) purposes. This is explained in Chapter 39, "DR Architectures."

- *Load-balancing cluster* — There is no cluster software installed on the nodes. However, a software or hardware load balancer is used to split incoming workload among various identically configured nodes. It increases availability because a node failure does not cause service outage. It is scalable because more nodes can be easily added to the group to boost performance or meet increased loads. This is explained in Chapter 17, "Load Balancing."

This chapter describes failover clusters. There are several types of failover clusters, depending on number of member nodes and whether all nodes are actively providing service or some are waiting for active nodes to fail. Two-node failover clusters are very common. The nodes can be active-active (symmetric) or active-passive (asymmetric). Two-node clusters are simple to implement and manage. Heartbeat networks are configured by directly connecting the two nodes using crossover Ethernet cables. No network hubs are required. This makes the private network less likely to fail.

This chapter also outlines cluster configurations and their relative merits. The inherent flexibility in designing clusters has led to various types of complex cluster configurations for reasons that usually come down to saving money and/or demonstrating creativity. Several machines are linked together to make a complicated configuration. The cable layouts for the service network, private (or heartbeat) network, and disks are complex. Redundant links to shared disks and network further complicate the cabling scheme. At least you must properly label both ends of each cable in such a complex cable mess. Otherwise, tracing any single cable will be onerous and prone to errors.

The following are failover cluster types:

- Asymmetric two-node clusters
- Symmetric two-node clusters
- Complex clusters configurations
  - Many-to-one failover model
  - One-to-many failover model
  - Any-to-any failover model

Asymmetric Two-Node Clusters

The most common clusters have two nodes, configured in an asymmetric or symmetric manner. In an asymmetric configuration, one node runs the critical application. The partner node is simply an idle or passive standby. It only monitors the active partner and is always ready to take over if the active node were to fail. Figure 25-1 shows an asymmetric cluster under normal conditions, and Figure 25-2 shows the status after a node failure.

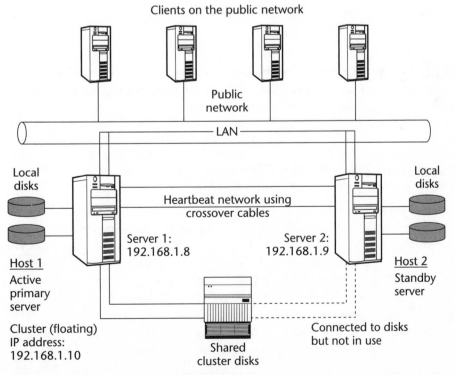

Figure 25-1   Asymmetric two-node cluster.

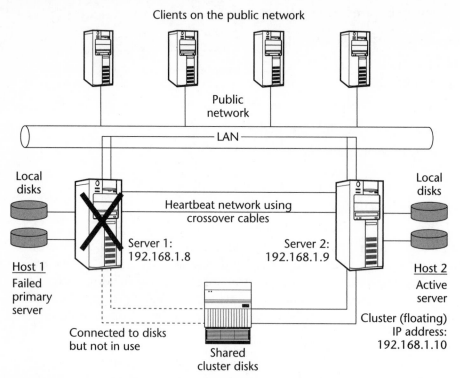

Figure 25-2   Asymmetric two-node cluster with one failed node.

> **NOTE** In a symmetric or asymmetric setup, ensure that there is no client-server relationship between any two cluster members. If there is and the server is down, the client member cannot perform its duties.

Symmetric Two-Node Clusters

A symmetric cluster is similar to an asymmetric cluster. The only difference is that both servers in a symmetric cluster run critical applications under normal circumstances. A symmetric cluster has no idle (that is, standby or passive) server. Both nodes also monitor each other. Should a node fail, the other node takes over the application from the failed node and runs all the cluster applications. Figures 25-3 and 25-4 show a symmetric cluster under normal conditions and after failure of a member node.

The primary advantage of a symmetric cluster is that it enables use of all hardware resources. Both the servers run important applications and provide critical services.

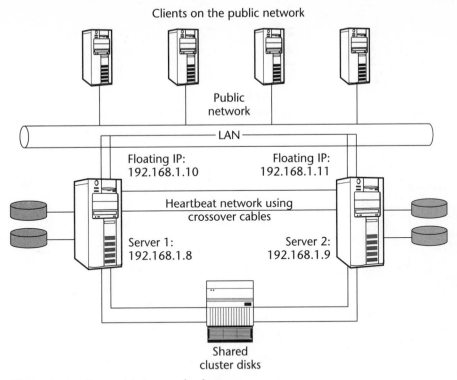

Figure 25-3   Symmetric two-node cluster.

However, there are some downsides to running applications on all cluster members. There is a small possibility that the existence of an active application would use up enough system resources to render the server unable to accept a failed-over application. Well-meaning administrators and users continuously make application- and system-level changes to an active server. Such changes have to be made to all servers that are configured as standbys for the application. If these changes are done carefully, followed by methodical testing, there will be no harm. Otherwise, a standby server may be unable to take over an application successfully during a failover process. If you regularly test your cluster and the applications you run are well tested, the possibility of a takeover failure is low.

The other downside of a symmetric cluster is related to performance. A healthy member that has taken over applications from failed members may exhibit severe performance degradation. Such performance impacts can be resolved by installing extra hardware components (usually memory and CPU) in each server. These downsides to a symmetric configuration are tempered by the fact that the cluster may be running in a failed-over mode during relatively short periods of time, especially over a few months or a year time span.

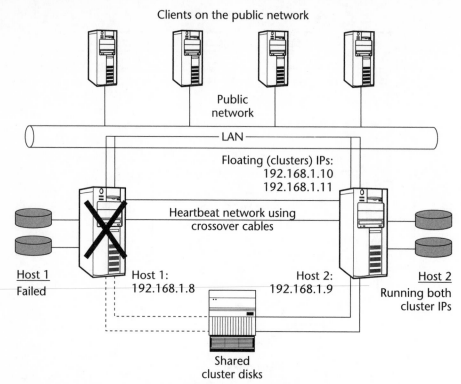

Clients on the public network

Figure 25-4 Symmetric two-node cluster with a failed node.

Complex Cluster Configurations

Almost all clustering software packages allow very complex cluster configurations. VERITAS Cluster Server (VCS) supports up to 32 nodes in a single cluster. But, think about the complexity of a 32-node cluster. It is doubtful if a 32-node cluster even exists outside the labs of the software vendor. Even a five-node cluster can be difficult to implement and manage. In practice, two-node clusters are the most common industry implementations.

Complex clusters with more than two nodes are designed with an initial objective of saving money on hardware purchases. To some extent, complex clusters are the products of creative planning. Prefer simplicity to creativity. Over the long run, the total cost of ownership (TCO) of a complex cluster is high. Configuration, ongoing maintenance, and troubleshooting are complicated. In this section we will describe some configurations with three or more servers. Before that, let's examine some drawbacks of a complex cluster:

- *Complex heartbeat networks* — There are lots of intertwined cables, to say the least. The heartbeat networks require a hub. Each server has two heartbeat NIC ports and, therefore, two connections to the hub. To prevent the hub from being a SPOF, you need two hubs. Besides increasing complexity and cost, you now have more cables and power supply requirements. The hubs increase complexity, setup cost, and power supply requirements. Note that crossover Ethernet cables can be used only for two-node clusters.

■ *Complex storage connections* — All shared disks or subsystems require at least one connection to each cluster server, which is a difficult task with direct-attached SCSI storage and three or more servers. A SAN makes the cabling simpler, at least on paper. But a SAN introduces the switch as a SPOF. Using two switches, like the heartbeat network, adds complexity and cost.

■ *Cluster software setup is difficult* — Each application will have a primary server and a list of standby servers, all of which must be decided during the design phase. If a server, running several applications, goes down, which hosts should pick up the applications without experiencing noticeable performance degradation?

■ *Complicated testing procedures* — You must test all valid permutations of applications and servers. That in itself can be a daunting task. Plus, after changes are done to an application, you must test it again. In an asymmetric pair with one application, there are only two possible states. In a symmetric pair with two applications, there are only four possible server-application combinations. But, in a symmetric three-node cluster with three applications, a server can potentially run any number of the three applications, thereby giving you seven different states that can be tested per server.

■ *Ongoing maintenance problems* — If those who configured the cluster are available to troubleshoot, that would provide the quickest recovery. But you would not want to run critical applications on servers whose maintenance relies on only a few people. Even if you call the vendor with problems, the vendor may be hard-pressed to find someone with experience in complex clusters. Hardware changes are difficult. If you want to unplug a cable, there is a slight risk of unplugging a wrong cable.

A primary feature of complex clusters is whether the storage subsystem connections are point-to-point (as in traditional direct SCSI attachments) or switched (as in SAN configurations), the former being more complicated.

Here are some complex cluster configurations.

Many-to-One Failover Model

The cluster has several primary servers but only one takeover server. The latter is configured to take over applications, if any primary member fails.

In an asymmetric model, the takeover server normally does not run any applications. All other servers run critical applications that are configured to failover to the passive or takeover server if the primary fails. There is no direct relationship between the primary servers. They do not back up or monitor each other. It is only the takeover server that monitors all the primary servers. In the small possibility that all primary servers fail at the same time, the passive server will successfully have to take over and run all the cluster applications. It must, therefore, have enough hardware resources to be able to do so.

In a symmetric model, the takeover server also provides critical services, which are configured to fail over to some or all of the other cluster members. The advantage is that the hardware in the takeover server is being utilized under normal conditions.

The many-to-one model has one advantage. It has only one passive server. However, the model has several demerits, besides the complexity issues detailed earlier. The over-configured takeover server is highly under-utilized most of the time. If the takeover server goes down, the primary servers operate with no redundancy. The uncommon existence and complexity greatly increase the difficulty in troubleshooting and obtaining effective support from your vendor. It also increases the likelihood of operator errors. It is, therefore, highly advisable to stay away from complex cluster implementations. Build two-node clusters. Simplify things.

One-to-Many Failover Model

There is one primary server that provides all the critical services. If the primary fails, all services are moved to several smaller servers. This model is preferred if you have one high-end server that is capable of performing all the tasks. However, you want to build redundancy by utilizing several, existing, low-end servers as passive standbys.

Any-to-Any Failover Model

Some or all of the cluster members run critical applications. All members are configured so that if they fail, the services migrate to any healthy cluster node. All servers must be connected to the shared storage used by any cluster member. SANs make it easy to connect the storage devices to all cluster members. Figure 25-5 shows an example of a SAN-based cluster. SANs offer a far more robust and cost-effective clustering model than the many-to-one or one-to-many models. It is also very easy to add or remove nodes from a SAN-based cluster.

SANs provide an ideal way to set up complex clusters. If that cannot be done, it is best to implement two-node clusters for the sake of simplicity.

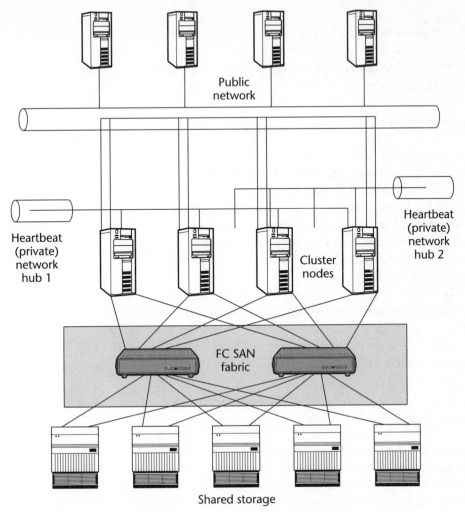

Figure 25-5 SAN-based cluster with any-to-any application failover.

Failover Policies

This section reviews different policies that can be enforced for applications to switch from one node to another.

Failover Pairs

In a two-node cluster, failover policy is simple. The only option after a node failure is for the application to migrate to the other node. In a cluster with three or more nodes, failover pairs can be defined for each application by explicitly assigning two nodes that are eligible to run each application. The two nodes in effect make a two-node cluster, but the large cluster provides the flexibility of replacing a node in a failover pair in the event that a node must be taken out for an extended time (for example, for maintenance or OS upgrade).

This model is good for heavyweight applications such as databases.

N+1 Policy

One node in the cluster is assigned as the hot, standby server. Each clustered application has two eligible nodes on which it can run: the *preferred node* (one default node for each application) and the *standby node* (one node for all applications). It takes over the clustered application from any node that fails.

The advantage is that during failure of a single host, the clustered application from the failed host will not affect other nodes running clustered applications. The standby node must have enough hardware resources to run any application (in the cluster).

This model is good for databases and other resource-hungry applications.

The problem with the N+1 model is that multiple node failures result in several applications running on the standby node. Besides, during scheduled maintenance, the standby server is in use and cannot be dedicated for use by applications on a failed node. The capability of this model to handle multiple-node failures is limited.

N+M Policy

This model has N number of primary nodes (hosting applications) and M number of standby, spare nodes. The spares, under normal circumstance, do not run any applications. If a primary node fails, the application switches to any of the spares not already in use. If all spares are in use, it then selects the spare based on preassigned criteria (such as the spare with the least load or least number of applications).

Like the failover pair and N+1 models, this is best suited for resource-intensive applications.

Failover-Ring Policy

Each node in the cluster runs one or more clustered applications. If a node fails, all applications running on a failed node move to the next node in sequence.

Let's consider a cluster with nodes 1, 2, 3, and 4, forming a ring in that order. Each of the four nodes has a primary application. If node 1 fails, node 2 will run two applications, while nodes 3 and 4 will run one application each.

Should node 2 then fail, node 3 will run three applications and node 4 will run one application.

Since multiple failures cause an uneven distribution of applications, this model is not suited for resource-hungry application such as databases. This is best suited for lightweight applications such as DHCP and Web sites with low traffic.

Random Policy

In a large cluster (or even in four-node clusters), it may be error-prone and cumbersome to predefine failover targets. It is then best to allow the cluster software to select a node randomly (from the pool of all healthy nodes) for switching applications from a failed node.

Since several applications may get bunched on a single node, the random model is not good for heavyweight applications. This model is best suited for clusters that must host several small applications.

Best Practices

This section describes best practices for configuring clusters:

- The first important decision is "to cluster or not." The primary criteria are critical nature of the services and the cost of the servers. If the servers are inexpensive and are, in fact, nothing more than "commodity systems," they can operate as stateless service providers and need not be clustered. Web servers are a good example because they can be inexpensive servers. Several Web servers can be easily load balanced. If a server fails, the services are still provided by the remaining server. You may need to install the OS, HTTP server software, and relevant Web content files on a new server and deploy it. It is crucial to have such commodity systems in hand. On the other hand, critical services such as messaging, financial transactions, and databases run on high-end servers. Installing, configuring, and tuning high-end servers cannot be done in a few hours. They must, therefore, be clustered.

- Which is better, asymmetric or symmetric clusters? Asymmetric environments are comparatively more reliable. If the application is mission-critical (for example, Web and database servers for an e-commerce site), asymmetric is a better way to go.

- Set up simple clusters. Managing a cluster with more than four members gets complicated. Split a four-member cluster into two symmetric clusters, each with two nodes. The overall setup will be simpler, easier to configure and maintain, and have higher reliability. Clusters with two nodes are also the most common configurations.

- You must have multiple heartbeat network links, but they must not be on the same multiport NIC. If that NIC fails, all heartbeat connections will die. NICs, cables, and hubs (if used) must be redundant.

- In an asymmetric configuration, do not use the idle server for code development or tests. Resist the temptation even for quick, nonintrusive tests. Protect an idle standby server as you would protect the active server. The less the idle server does, the better is its ability to accept applications at an inopportune time. Few folks should have accounts on the cluster systems. Do not give away root or administrator logins except to cluster or host management.

Key Points

Following are some key points discussed in this chapter:

- Two-node clusters can be configured as an asymmetric (active-passive nodes) or symmetric (active-active nodes) pair.

- Two-node clusters are preferred over complex clusters with more than two nodes. A four-node cluster is far more difficult to build and maintain and has a higher total cost of ownership than two clusters each with a pair of nodes.

- SANs provide an effective and reliable way to build clusters with more than two nodes.

Cluster Requirements

*One never notices what has been done; one can
only see what remains to be done.*
— Marie Curie

This chapter covers software and hardware requirements that must be met before a cluster can be implemented. The cluster software you select must satisfy certain requirements. If an application cannot run on a server (because of software or hardware problems), the cluster software must be able to switch the applications to another node. The process of migrating a service or application from one server to another within the cluster is called *failover* and is a basic cluster requirement. A failover should be automatic, quick, and transparent to clients. Several other activities that accompany a failover are described in this chapter.

You must make various hardware and operating system–related changes before deploying cluster applications. The SCSI IDs of host-based adapters (HBAs) in a SCSI chain must be different. If the cluster must share or export certain directories (using NFS or CIFS) for clients to mount and use the directories, the file system and device drivers that manage the shared directories must have identical driver-related parameters on all cluster members. Most of the commands in this chapter pertain to the Solaris operating system and are provided as an illustration. Cluster concepts and requirements explained in this chapter are generic and apply to all platforms.

If you manage several clusters (or even one cluster), implement a standard procedure for all cluster configuration issues. For example, when you change an adapter SCSI ID on one of two hosts in a cluster, do so on the host that has a higher suffix in the host name (assuming the host names have a suffix). This makes it easy to remember which host has a nondefault initiator ID.

Document all cluster-related changes (for example, boot PROM settings, major and minor numbers of drivers, logical volumes, and disk partitions). It can assist system administrators in quickly troubleshooting cluster problems.

Required Hardware Cluster Components

A cluster is made up of at least two servers and several other components that will be discussed in this section. Necessary cluster components include the following.

Servers

The fundamental requirement when designing a cluster is a pair of nodes. Nodes that run a clustered application or provide service are referred to as active or *primary servers*. If the primary node fails, the clustered application or service switches to another node. Nodes that do not run any cluster application under normal conditions are called *secondary* (or *idle* or *passive*) *servers*. If a primary server fails, an idle server takes over the applications running on the failed primary. Idle servers are also called *takeover* or *standby servers*. All servers in a cluster can run critical applications. It is not necessary to have idle servers in a cluster. The primary servers can be configured to take over applications from any other failed primary server.

All servers in a cluster must be the same platform and run the same operating system version and patch releases. They must be configured with the same version of the cluster server software and be capable of running the same applications and executables. They must offer similar performance. Although not necessary, the nodes ideally have the same number of CPUs, amount of physical memory, NICs, disk adapters, and other hardware resources.

Private (Heartbeat) Networks

This is a dedicated network connecting all the cluster hosts. The *heartbeat network* is used by cluster software to query the status of each server. The back-and-forth heartbeat packets contain an "I am fine! How are you" message, cluster state information, commands directing a server to change states, and other cluster-related data. If a cluster member fails, the heartbeat protocol notifies other servers about the event. No assistance from external sources is required for this notification.

Heartbeat networks are separate from public networks. In a two-node cluster, private networks can be set up using two crossover, twisted-pair Ethernet cables. For clusters with three or more nodes, it is necessary to use a network hub or switch to build the heartbeat network, as shown in Figure 26-1. Two hubs or switches are used to prevent a single point of failure (SPOF). Hubs add complexity and expense, require power supplies, and introduce failure points. Therefore, they should be avoided for two-node clusters and used for clusters with three or more nodes.

It must be pointed out that hubs offer two distinct advantages. First, they can be monitored by some network management software for link or device failures. Second, if a host fails, the other hosts connected to the hub do not receive and log network errors, thus avoiding performance degradation, excessive logging, and other minor nuisances.

Some clustering software uses a vendor-proprietary protocol over private networks. VERITAS Cluster Server (VCS) uses Global Atomic Broadcast (GAB) and Low Latency Transport (LLT) over heartbeat networks, while many other products use IP-based protocols over heartbeat networks.

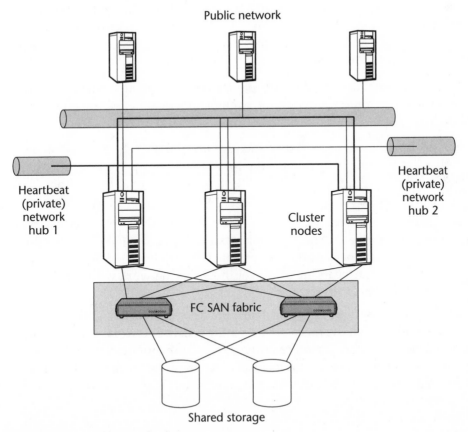

Figure 26-1   A three-node cluster.

When a server stops sending heartbeats, it is assumed to have failed. While this is a genuine problem, there can be other situations that indicate that a node has failed, including the following:

- *Heartbeat network interface card (NIC) failure* — All NICs used for heartbeat links must fail before the server is assumed dead. The odds of such an event is greatly reduced if separate NICs are used for heartbeat networks instead of using multiple NIC ports on a single adapter.

- *Failure of all heartbeat cables* — All cables connected to a cluster node fail.

- *Hub failure* — This can be a potential problem if a single network hub is used for all heartbeat links. To eliminate the hub from posing as an SPOF, redundant heartbeat networks must be connected to separate hubs. Crossover cables used in two-node clusters are an ideal solution, because they do not require a hub.

- *Failure of processes that manage heartbeats* — The clustering software should start and run redundant heartbeat managers. If a heartbeat-manager process stops, it should automatically be started by a partner process running on the same host. VCS software runs two daemons, namely, had and hashadow, that manage heartbeats and monitor each other. If one dies, the other restarts the dead process.

As we have seen, dedicated heartbeat networks have their share of problems. If these problems raise some level of paranoia, there are alternative heartbeat solutions:

- *Disk-based heartbeats* — A disk slice or partition on a shared disk can be used to communicate heartbeat information between the cluster hosts. Each host writes temporarily to the slice, which is read by all other hosts in the cluster.

- *Public-network–based heartbeats* — The public or service network can be used for heartbeats. Some clustering software allows the use of the public network for heartbeats if all private network links are down. In such a scenario, heartbeats are sent over the public network with a lower priority than regular IP packets.

- *Heartbeats based on SLIP or PPP networks over serial lines* — This is preferred only if the hosts do not have available network ports. Serial line-based protocols require far more tedious configuration and management than IP-over-Ethernet links. Again, consider this option only if Ethernet ports and adapters are unavailable.

Administrative (Maintenance) Network

An *administrative network* is one to which each node is attached for administrators to log in for maintenance and other tasks. IP addresses configured on the administrative network are not managed by cluster software.

Although you could configure some cluster software without an administrative network, it is strongly recommended that you have one. The maintenance IP address is tied to the host and usually resides on the public network. Each host in the cluster has one administrative IP address. Even if a host dies, its administrative IP does not migrate to another server. In other words, it is permanently bound to a particular NIC in the host. System administrators use the IP address as a guaranteed path to the server.

Note that this IP address is not used by cluster applications that are configured to failover between servers. The IP address is also not managed by the cluster software. It is the host operating system that sets up and manages the administrative IP address.

Public or Service Network

Users and clients use the *public* or *service network* to communicate with the cluster servers. Each active server has one or more IP addresses on the public network. The IP address is used by applications. If the server fails, the IP address and associated hostname migrate or failover to another node in the cluster. Clients and users continue to access the application or service through the same IP address and do not know which server is providing the services.

These IP addresses are called "virtual IP addresses" because they are not bound to any host. Only one host in the cluster owns a virtual IP address at a time. The cluster software manages ownership of the virtual addresses. When you connect to a virtual IP address, you do not know which server you connect to, nor is it important. The IP address enables you to connect to a service and receive responses for all requests. That is what matters.

Shared Disks

In an asymmetric cluster, the *shared disks* are physically accessible by both servers, although only one server (the active server) is using it. The clustering software manages any disk ownership issues and conflicts. To protect against disk failures, the data on the shared disks must be on parity-based RAID or mirrored volumes. To protect against controller failures, the disks must be accessible over two separate controllers, at minimum. Although disk and controller redundancy are not clustering requirements, they help by increasing data availability.

Some types of cluster software uses a disk configuration called "shared nothing" (rather than shared disks). The data on one server is replicated to another remote server over a network link. At the remote site a hot standby host is ready (with up-to-date data) to start applications if the primary site fails. Such configurations have complexities caused by additional network dependencies and are only a small part of a comprehensive disaster-recovery (DR) solution. Such configurations are described in Chapter 39, "DR Architectures." However, if the servers are close enough for SAN-based or direct-attached storage, then shared disks provide a more reliable solution.

Adapter SCSI ID Requirements

When connecting SCSI devices in a chain, each device must have a unique SCSI ID. SCSI protocol supports two device classes:

- *Initiators* — An initiator is usually a host device capable of initiating SCSI requests and operations. The default SCSI-initiator ID for most platforms is 7.

- *Targets* — A SCSI target is a device that responds to SCSI operations. Disks and tapes are common examples. Targets need an initiator to function and should not use ID 7 if it is used by host initiators. Narrow SCSI targets have IDs from 0 to 6, and wide SCSI targets have IDs from 0 to 6 and 8 to 15. A target ID is set by hardware (for example, jumpers and switches) on the device or by its position in the host bay or storage enclosure.

If a SCSI chain is connected to only one host, the SCSI adapter (initiator) can retain the default ID (usually 7). No changes are required. However, if a SCSI chain is connected to two adapters and if both adapters have the same ID as shown in Figure 26-2, there is a SCSI-ID conflict. To resolve the conflict, one adapter can be left at the default ID and all other adapters in the SCSI chain must be modified to separate IDs. No adapter or disk in the chain can have the same SCSI ID. For example, in a two-adapter SCSI chain, one adapter ID must be changed (for example, from ID 7 to 6). Note that SCSI device drivers are programmed to respond to requests in a certain priority order: 7 to 0, followed by 15 to 8. It is better for performance reasons to use high-priority IDs for adapters and low-priority IDs for targets such as disks and tapes.

You must change an adapter ID before connecting the adapter to the devices. If a SCSI chain has devices with the same ID, the host in the chain cannot configure the SCSI devices. Before changing an adapter ID, shut down the server and disconnect the SCSI devices. Then power on the server and change the SCSI ID of an adapter. Finally, shut down the server, connect the shared SCSI devices, and power on the server.

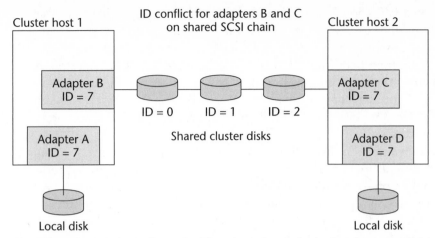

Figure 26-2   SCSI ID conflict caused by adapters B and C having the same ID (7). Either B or C must be changed.

Local Disks

All software (except data essential for cluster services) must be placed on *local* or *private disks*. They are "local" in that they are accessible by one and only one server in the cluster. In other words, only one host should be able to see the drives. They can be either housed inside the server or attached to an HBA in the server.

Examples of data that must be placed on the local disks are the host operating system, swap space, drivers, application binaries, and configuration files. The issue of configuration files for operating system and applications requires special attention, because it must be done manually.

Should the data on private disks be mirrored? The answer is that it is preferred, although not an absolute requirement. This applies to swap space as well. After all, the goal is to provide as much redundancy as possible. If a copy of a mirrored local file system fails, the host will continue its usual operation. There will be no failover and, therefore, no downtime associated with failover process (brief outage during which application switches to the other system).

Cluster Software Requirements

So far, I have explained the hardware requirements of a cluster. But there are several software requirements that must be stated. Application binaries must be installed on each host. These binaries must be of the same version and must run identically on each server.

An interesting choice that arises during an HA design phase is whether application binaries should be placed on the shared or local drives. If you install applications on the private disks, each server has an individual copy of the application and configuration files. The application administrators must then ensure that any configuration changes are made to all cluster servers. However, if you install applications on shared drives, the obvious advantage is that you must maintain only one copy of application and all associated configuration files.

The disadvantage to this is that it is impossible to safely upgrade an application. With multiple application copies on local disks, you can upgrade the application on one server and test the new version by failing over the application to this freshly upgraded server. If all works fine, you can go ahead and upgrade the installation on other servers. If the upgraded application or service fails on the newly upgraded server, you can fail back to the previous server and retry the upgrade.

Your final choice will depend on the number of servers, your willingness to maintain multiple application copies, and the frequency of application upgrades.

The most cost-effective approach for increasing an application's availability is to use failover clusters. A typical failover cluster is composed of multiple systems attached to a set of shared disks connected to a shared SCSI or FC Bus. The systems monitor each other using private heartbeat networks, point-to-point serial connections, shared-disk regions, or public-service or IP networks. If any system in the cluster fails, any remaining cluster is capable of taking over the services of the failed node. The take-over is transparent to the clients accessing the data or using the services.

Before getting into the details of the selection criteria, it is best to understand what data integrity is about. *Data integrity* is the process that guarantees that the data is accurate and up-to-date. This seems like a simple goal, but in a cluster environment it is difficult to guarantee. Data integrity is of high importance, far more importance than availability.

Let's see what happens in a nonclustered environment. A node mounts a file system and accesses the data. The data can then be read and modified. In the interest of enhancing I/O performance, the node caches two things into memory:

- *Copies of data that has been recently modified or accessed* — The most up-to-date version of the data is the combination of what is cached in system's memory and the on-disk data.

- *The metadata of the file system* — The metadata describes how the file system blocks, files, inodes, and so on are organized. You can think of this as the table of contents or index of a book. File systems get confused if their metadata is messed up. If a host crashes without giving the in-memory cache a chance to flush itself to disk, the host will detect that a file system is messed up once it is rebooted. The host will then attempt to scan or check the file system and, if unsuccessful, it will fail to mount the file system. It will be reported as being corrupted and must be manually checked before it can be mounted.

Let's take an example of two nodes, node A and node B, that access a shared disk. Data integrity problems arise if both nodes start using the same file system on the shared disk. Let's assume that we do not have a cluster file system model. Under normal conditions, only one node uses the data.

Two problems arise if both nodes concurrently access the same file system. The first is inaccurate data reported by the cluster nodes.

For example, let's say you have $1,000 in your bank account. It's payday and after work you head to the bank to deposit your $1,000 pay. Your deposit transaction is handled by node A, and total account balance of $2,000 is stored in its cache. Then you withdraw $400 for the weekend family trip. So far, node A has not flushed its in-memory balance of $2000 to disk. The withdrawal transaction is handled by node B, which retrieves the $1,000 balance from disk, gives you $400, and keeps the balance of $600 in cache. Then node A flushes its in-memory balance of $2,000 to disk, followed by node B doing the same with its in-memory balance of $600. Finally, you have $600 in the bank. The shared disk records this as your final balance and your weekly earning has fallen through the cracks.

The second problem is file system corruption. If two nodes, A and B, mount and access the same file system, they cache and modify the file system metadata. Later, when node B is ready to update the file system metadata on disk, it finds that the metadata on disk is different from what it had retrieved some time back. Node A has changed the disk metadata. This forces node B to crash.

Making multiple nodes properly access the same data requires a cluster file system. The true contents of a cluster file system consist of data being cached on each node's memory plus the on-disk data. A few database implementations such as Oracle Real Application Cluster (RAC) and Informix Extended Parallel Server (XPS) and some clustering software such as Sun Cluster or IBM Highly Available Clustered Multiprocessing (HACMP) allow multiple cluster hosts to access the same data on disk using a *distributed lock manager* (DLM). Unless you deploy such a configuration, you must ensure that a file system can be used by only a single node at any point in time. Now, this sounds simple, but there are situations where it is difficult to prevent inaccurate data or a corrupted file system. A good clustering software must provide several ways to ensure data integrity.

If you are evaluating cluster software, be sure to know how it protects you from the following situations:

- System crash
- System hang
- Planned maintenance
- Heartbeat link failure
- Cluster startup problems

System Crash

One of my customers with two high-end Sun servers in a VCS cluster suffered server crashes a few times because of CPU cache panic errors. After replacing a number of CPUs and applying kernel patches, the problem stopped. Server crashes always happen. Some of us may have experienced it more times than others. It is important to understand how a cluster behaves in response to a server crash. Almost all cluster implementations will initiate a failover of services from the crashed system to other systems. But some cluster software provides ways to distribute the services among several cluster members based on system capacity and current system load.

System Hang

This presents a serious challenge to all cluster developers. Computers sometimes lock up and become unresponsive. Just as mysteriously as they lock up, they sometimes unlock and start responding to client requests after a period of time. This can occur on any platform or operating system. If a system is hung, it will stop responding on all heartbeat channels: serial lines, shared-disk–based heartbeats, private Ethernet networks, and so on. It does not matter how many heartbeat communication media have been set up.

If node A in a two-node cluster (node A and node B) is hung, node B will get no heartbeat response and conclude that node A has gone down. Node B will commence to mount the file systems and start the database and other services formerly served by node A. Subsequently node A could unlock and start I/O to the file systems. This results in a situation where two systems are simultaneously accessing and modifying the same file system, thus creating data-integrity problems.

How cluster software handles a system hang is a decisive test. Some software will not take over services running on a system that suddenly stops responding on all heartbeat channels. If a system does take over services of a hung system, it must ensure that the failed system cannot access the shared disks if it were to mysteriously come back. This is done by I/O fencing, exclusive disk reservations, and I/O barriers. You must understand cluster software responses to system hangs.

Planned Maintenance

Almost all clustering software allows for planned maintenance such as software or hardware changes and upgrades on a system. All applications on a system are switched over to other systems before it is taken down for maintenance or upgrades. Most clustering software does not care if systems have different hardware resources (memory, CPU, and so on), but what about operating system and cluster software versions? If it is necessary for them to be all the same version, then it would be necessary for you take down all systems at the same time. Can you afford the downtime? For how long? Beware! You do not have the luxury of upgrading one system now and testing the effects of the upgrade to your environment before upgrading all systems.

Heartbeat Link Failure

Typically, private Ethernet networks are employed for heartbeats. These are set up using crossover cables for two-node clusters or an Ethernet hub for clusters with three or more nodes. But the Ethernet adapter, cable, and hub can fail. If so, each node will think that the other node has failed, whereas in reality they are still up and running all cluster applications. The cluster gets "partitioned" into small clusters. Since each node is left to decide on its own, both of them, in the interest of high availability, start applications running on the other node. Both nodes start accessing the same data, thereby leading to data-corruption problems.

To overcome this problem, the cluster software you select must offer several mechanisms for heartbeat communications. Most cluster software allows you to use shared-disk regions, serial connections, the public IP network, or PPP links for heartbeat communications.

Cluster Startup Problems

At one of my previous workplaces, the week-long Christmas shutdown was used for physical site maintenance. We had a two-node database (nodes A and B) cluster that was powered off. Unfortunately the database users were not notified and could not afford the downtime. They made special arrangements for one cluster system to be powered up. The DBA killed all cluster daemons and brought up the database outside of the cluster software on node A. When regular power was restored, node B booted up, but its cluster daemons did not get heartbeat responses from node A. Node B then started up the database on its own and caused database corruption. We had to hit the backup tapes. That was several years ago, the vendor was a small company, and it was the first release of the cluster software.

Nowadays most cluster software will not automatically start up applications unless it can communicate with and get the application status on all systems that are eligible to run the application. There is a likelihood that the applications will not start on system bootup. That is better than starting the application and risking data integrity. When you are comparing cluster implementations, you must understand whether starting cluster services will start applications or not.

The situations mentioned in this section may be rare (and that's good!), but they can happen. The cluster software you select must be able to handle any problems gracefully in a predetermined manner without data corruption. Remember, it is your data on the line!

What Happens During Service Failover

Failover can take a short amount of time, from a few seconds to a few minutes. During this window, services are unavailable and client applications hang. Ideally the failover process should be quick, transparent to clients, and require no human intervention. As part of the failover process, the following elements must be transferred from a failed primary to a standby server:

- Ownership of shared disks
- Network identity
- Cluster services

Ownership of Shared Disks

The shared disks are physically connected to all cluster hosts but logically accessible by only one host. The cluster software prevents all other hosts from accessing the data. During failover, the disk ownership is moved from the failed server to one that is taking over. The file systems are unmounted on the failed server. If disks are part of a disk group or volume group, the file system is exported from the failed server and imported by the takeover server. The file systems are then mounted on the takeover server.

Network Identity

Clients in the network contact a particular IP address to obtain the services. In other words, each cluster service is tied to an IP address that provides the service. Therefore, the IP address on the public network must migrate from the failed primary to the takeover server. Moving the IP address from one server to another within the cluster is the easy part. The complication arises when client machines need to contact the IP address that has just moved to a new home.

Every machine has a 48-bit media access control (MAC) address. It is a hardware address in hexadecimal digits separated by a colon (:) or a dot. This hardware address uniquely defines each node in a network and directly interfaces with the network media.

The first 24 bits are assigned to each hardware manufacturer or vendor. For example, the first 24-bit string, 00:02:55, is assigned to IBM and 08:00:21 is assigned to Sun Microsystems. The last 24 bits are used to identify each NIC port in the vendor systems. Each NIC port, therefore, has a unique MAC address and usually also has IP address configured by the operating system.

Clients use address resolution protocol (ARP) to determine the mapping between MAC addresses and IP addresses. When a node has to send data to another node, it uses ARP to get the MAC address of the target node. The MAC address goes into the packet header so that the data can reach the correct hardware destination. The MAC address is also cached on the client node for anywhere between 30 seconds to a few hours to avoid repeated ARP requests on the network.

Here is a problem. When a failover occurs, the IP address moves to another host with a different MAC address and the clients that have cached the MAC-IP combination now have stale data. When the cache expires or the client host detects that the MAC-IP pair is invalid, it sends an ARP request to get the new combination. Until then, clients will be unable to contact a failed-over IP address. System administrators must tune the ARP expiration to a value low enough for client applications to tolerate time-outs or delays caused by stale ARP data.

There are some mechanisms to eliminate the ARP cache time-out problem. Some servers broadcast their MAC-IP pair to all listening network members as soon as a new IP address is configured on it. Some of the listening network members are intelligent enough to refresh the cache as soon as they see an ARP broadcast, but some are not. Moreover, some hosts do not broadcast their MAC-IP pair upon activating a new IP address.

You can also change the MAC address of a NIC adapter. Any bit location in the MAC address can be incremented or decremented by one and then used for NICs that own the cluster IP address. Ensure that no other host on your network is using the chosen MAC address.

When a primary fails, the takeover server gets the IP address as well as the MAC address from the failed primary. The advantage is that the MAC-IP mapping remains the same and there are no ARP-related time-outs. But, there are a lot of conditions.

The NIC card on a failed primary must revert to its original MAC address once its cluster IP-MAC address pair fails over to another host. Also, when a host boots up but does not own the cluster IP address, its NIC must come up with its original MAC address. Since the MAC address of an NIC port is tied to an IP address, the port must have only one IP address (and no virtual IPs) on it. The port, therefore, can have only one application on it.

Cluster Services

Application services (such as database instances, NFS services, and Web services) are stopped on the failed primary and then started on the standby after it assumes the proper IP address(es) and disk ownership.

Cluster Installation Checklist

Cluster hardware and heartbeat communication must be configured before it can monitor and manage applications. The following list includes tasks that must be performed in the order mentioned:

1. Ensure that no two devices (disks or adapters) within any SCSI chain shared by two or more hosts have the same ID. If so, there will be a SCSI ID conflict and the host operating system will be unable to configure the SCSI device. If two adapters have the same ID, you must manually change the ID on a host.

2. SCSI devices must be correctly terminated.

3. All node members must run the same operating system version. For Microsoft Windows servers, they must have the service pack.

4. Cable the shared disk devices.

5. Identify NIC ports that will be used for private and public networks. Ports for public network can be aggregated by network teaming for enhanced throughput and failover.

6. Set up private network hardware. Use crossover cables for two-node clusters and network hubs for clusters with three or more nodes. Private heartbeat NICs must be set to specific speed and half-duplex. Use of Auto for port speed can cause problems in some cluster failover software.

7. Configure the heartbeat processes over the private network.

8. If you want disk-based heartbeats, identify partitions to be used for heartbeats and include them in the heartbeat configurations.

Key Points

Following are some key points discussed in this chapter:

- A cluster has servers (active or passive), heartbeat cables, and hubs (if necessary) for private network, connections to the public network, and shared and private disks.
- During failover, the ownership of the shared disks, cluster IP address, and applications move the failed server to the takeover cluster member.
- When connecting shared SCSI devices, each device, including the HBAs in the chain, must have unique SCSI IDs.

CHAPTER 27

Designing Cluster-Friendly Applications

When you do the common things in life in an uncommon way, you will command the attention of the world.
— **George Washington Carver**

This chapter describes how to design applications or modify existing ones to work properly in a cluster. A well-designed cluster-aware application reduces the amount of planned and unplanned downtime experienced by the user. Planned downtime is caused by scheduled backups, software changes, and hardware maintenance. Unplanned downtime is caused by hardware failures, software bugs, and power or network outages.

There are certain key requirements for an application to work properly within a cluster. Such applications include the following features:

- They should be stateless (such as Web servers and VPN servers).

- They should have built-in recovery features (such as databases, file servers, mail servers, and print servers).

- They must be able to handle server panics and reboots gracefully. If a server crashes, the application must be able to stop itself elegantly within a short time and then start itself on another server. In-flight transactions that were interrupted by the server panic must automatically continue after the application starts itself on the other server.

- They should not use host-specific identifiers such as hostname (output of uname –n command on UNIX operating systems), MAC (link-level) address of the network adapters, hostid, or SPU (System Processing Unit) ID of the server.

This chapter describes how the following objectives can contribute to a cluster-friendly application:

- Automating operations
- Controlling application failover time
- Reducing data loss during failover
- Minimizing application failures
- Designing node-independent applications
- Minimizing planned downtime
- Restoring client connections

Automating Operations

The first rule for guaranteeing high application availability is to avoid manual intervention. It must be possible to start, stop, and monitor the application without assistance from an operator. If an application cannot run on a server, it must quickly start on another server in the cluster. If starting an application requires a GUI interface or executing an interactive script, it may take hours to get someone to log in to the system and do the necessary work. If the system cannot be remotely accessed, someone must physically get to the office or data center. The hardware may be in a far-away site, in which case it may be difficult to find someone with required application expertise quickly.

The procedures for starting up and stopping any clustered application must be well defined and fully automated. The procedures must also be based on commands that can be easily scripted. The script must not require user intervention to complete successfully. Network monitoring software must be able to use the scripts to start or stop an application automatically upon detecting conditions such as finding certain predetermined entries in log files. The application must have a robust monitoring script that determines if it is running on a node or not. The script must invoke itself every so often (for example, every minute) to verify that the application is active and running as normal. The monitoring script could be as simple as running a `ps -ef` command on UNIX servers to check for application-related processes or running certain monitoring scripts included with the application software.

If a clustered application is not running on a cluster node, it must determine the nature and cause of failure and try to recover from it on the same host. Restarting an application on the same host reduces the disruption in service experienced by clients.

If an application must switch to another cluster node, end users must be insulated from the outage during the failover period. Consider the following issues:

- If possible, warn users of an impending failover process and slight delays.

- When a client session is lost, an application must attempt to reconnect without user intervention.

- Standby systems must have enough reserve capacity to reduce performance degradation experienced by users.

Controlling Application Failover Time

What steps can reduce the failover duration? If an application must switch to another cluster node, there are several things that can be done to quickly restore service for end users. Here are some rules to increase failover speed:

- *Keep nondata file systems on local disks* — Nondata file systems include application binaries and other software that are not constantly updated by cluster applications. The file systems on shared disks must be checked for inconsistencies before they can be mounted. This is especially necessary if the server that owns the shared file systems crashes. To reduce the time for data checking, it is necessary to keep only the necessary data on shared disks. Another advantage of keeping applications on local disks is that they can be subjected to a rolling upgrade if necessary.

- *Use raw volumes or journaled file systems* — Raw volumes have access speeds that are faster than most file systems. Raw volumes are also not subjected to potentially long file system checks if the server owning them crashes. If file systems must be used, consider using journaled file systems. They have better run-time performance, as well as robust and quicker recovery from a host crash, when compared to a nonjournaled file system.

- *Run application on multiple active servers* — In failover clusters, one server runs an application and is switched to another server if the active server fails. In case of multiple active servers, two or more servers run the application. If an active server fails, the other server in the cluster does not have to start the application. There are several complex issues that arise when two servers must run the same application and access the same data. In this discussion we will focus on the following two examples:

- The simplest design is to have the application running on two servers in a master-slave relationship. Only the master provides service to network clients. If the master fails, the service is transferred to the slave, which then begins to provide service. The slave does not have to start the application, which hastens the failover process.

- The application runs on both servers and provides service to network clients. Both servers access the same shared data. Some clients connect to one application server and other clients connect to the second application server in the cluster. If one server fails, clients must switch from the failed server to the other server. However, the duration of outage is minimized because the server does not have to start the application.

Reducing Data Loss During Failover

Although it is impossible to prevent some data loss during an application failover, certain steps can be taken to minimize it. If a host crashes, application in-memory data (subjected to writes) is lost. To reduce the loss, it is necessary to keep the in-memory data to a minimum. Another advantage is that a node can quickly start a clustered application during failover because it does not have to read and initialize a lot of data from disk to memory. These advantages must be weighed against run-time performance degradation caused by being forced to write data to disk constantly. Data that is used as read-only can be stored in-memory without any concern for data loss.

Most databases permit logs to be stored in memory temporarily. When the in-memory logs grow to a certain size, they are written to a file on disk. Increasing the size of in-memory logs increases run-time performance. However, it will also increase the amount of completed-transaction data lost because of a host failure. Minimizing the size of in-memory logs reduces the amount of data loss caused by a host failure. Another advantage of smaller log sizes is that they can be replicated more frequently to offer a higher level of disaster recovery.

Design transactions that are restartable. When a host fails in the middle of a transaction and the application must switch to another node, the transaction must be able to restart where it left off. There must be no need for the user to start the transaction all over again. This makes the application more robust and reduces the impact of a failover to a user.

One way to do so is to checkpoint transactions to disk. A transaction that appears simple may consist of several database calculations. The application must record the results at certain intervals to disk. If the host fails, the on-disk data can be read by another host to restart the transaction where it was interrupted. It is important to balance checkpoint frequency with performance. If you checkpoint too frequently, the application slows. If you do not checkpoint often, the application will take longer to return to the state where it was interrupted. Ideally an application must provide ways for the end user to customize the checkpoint frequency.

Minimizing Application Failures

Applications should be designed to recover from system resource problems or software bugs. Lack of hardware resources such as memory, disk space, and swap space lead to process failures.

Most applications have several processes, all of which ideally must be configured to monitor each other. If one process fails, another process must also be able to restart the failed process. For example, some databases have one or more listener processes. If the latter fails, the database must be able to start it locally without affecting other database processes. If it is not possible to restart the failed process for any reason, the application must at least be designed to stop itself cleanly, without necessitating any application recovery.

Applications must be designed so that monitoring software (such as IBM's Tivoli or HP's OpenView) can detect failures of the entire application or individual components of the application. If the failure is not automatically detected, it might take several hours for users to identify the failure and take corrective action. Scripts for starting, stopping, and monitoring the application must be noninteractive (not require user interaction) so that monitoring software can execute the scripts if necessary.

Designing Node-Independent Applications

In this section, we will discuss ways to design an application that is independent of node-specific attributes such as `hostid`, `hostname`, and the MAC address of network adapters. This is important because the application must successfully switch between cluster nodes and clients should not notice any difference, regardless of the cluster node running the application.

Application must use floating IP addresses. Network clients should never access the cluster application using the server's maintenance (or fixed) IP address. They must use the floating IP address. Each instance of an application must have a unique IP address tied to it. The IP address must move to the server that runs the instance of the application. This is "application-centric" thinking as opposed to "host-centric."

Applications should use the Unix `gethostbyname()` function with caution because the response may change when the application migrates to another server. Also, the `gethostbyaddr()` functions will return different answers if called with the maintenance or fixed IP address. However, both functions can be used if DNS is configured with the floating IP addresses and corresponding names, which are unique.

Applications must be designed not to use the UNIX `uname()` or `hostname()` command because they return the official system names, which are tied to the fixed IP address. Some applications use the `uname()` command to verify that they are running on the appropriate host. This is not appropriate in a clustered environment. Instead the application must verify the name of the host on which it is running against a previously configured list of cluster hosts where it can potentially run.

Use fixed port addresses for clustered applications that must bind to a socket. Configure all cluster servers to use the same fixed port. If a port number is not specified, the service will be dynamically assigned a random port number. The problem is that a different port number will be assigned to the service when it restarts on another server. This will confuse the clients that are accessing the service. On UNIX servers, port assignments must be specified in `/etc/services`. This will help keep track of the port and ensure that someone else does not inadvertently use the same port number for another service.

Design the application so that it does not rely on the MAC address, `hostid`, SPU ID, or any other unique hardware ID in nonvolatile memory.

Minimizing Planned Downtime

When designing applications for server clusters, the chief concern is often to avoid service outage caused by an unexpected failure. However, if it takes a week or even a few days to upgrade the server operating systems or applications to a newer version, there is bound to be a conspicuous impact on operations or sales.

Planned downtime is a scheduled nonoperation of a server. The downtime could be for hardware replacements, application upgrades, or system upgrades to a new operating system release. Adherence to the following conditions reduces the amount of planned downtime:

- *Design applications that can be dynamically reconfigured* — It must be possible to reconfigure the application without having to shut it down. Changing tablespace sizes for a database, adding application-level users, and changing operation-system or kernel-related parameters must be possible without having to off-line the application.

- *Design for "rolling upgrades"* — The application and the cluster software must be designed to accommodate different versions of the application, operating system, and the cluster software itself. This will enable a "rolling upgrade." When an application, OS, or cluster software must be upgraded, it would not be necessary to do so on all nodes at the same time. That would require the applications to be shut down, doing the upgrade, and starting the application, thus causing downtime. In a "rolling upgrade," the application is taken off-line on a server while other servers provide the service. The software on the server is then upgraded and the application is brought up. Later, another server is upgraded. The application is available at all times. Another advantage is that it provides a way to test a new release before committing all servers to it. The only requirement is that the environment must accommodate different software versions on different nodes.

■ *Maintain same data format across versions* — There are two disadvantages of changing the data format and layout in a new release. First, a rolling upgrade of the application is not possible in the cluster. After an application is upgraded on one server, the data format is converted by the application as soon as it is started on the server. Thereafter, other cluster members cannot use the data. The second problem is that the process of format transformation is time consuming (especially for large amounts of data), and it requires downtime. Therefore, new releases of the application must be able to use the same data layout and format.

There must be well-documented procedures to be followed during a planned downtime. The procedures must be created with a goal to eliminate application downtime. Operators must be capable and trained in using the procedures.

Restoring Client Connections

An important objective of a client application is to reconnect to a service that has restarted on the same or another server transparently and quickly. After a clustered service fails and restarts, it is important that client sessions reconnect to the service. A traditional aftermath of service failover is that users should log in again or restart their session. But a well-designed client application must transparently reconnect to the new service. Depending on the cause of the service failure, the service may restart on the same or another cluster member. Client applications must, therefore, be designed to also differentiate between situations where a failed application has restarted on the same or another server in the cluster.

There are a number of techniques that client applications can use to decide when and how to reconnect to a newly started service:

■ *Client applications that continuously retry* — After experiencing a service outage, the client application constantly attempts to reconnect to the service. As soon as the service is brought online, the client re-establishes the link and continues on where it was interrupted. No manual or user intervention is required. The user will notice the service outage during the time it takes for the application to restart.

- *Client applications that reconnect to another server* — This is possible only if the cluster includes active instances of the same application on multiple servers. If a client loses connection, it then connects to another server in the cluster. Users experience a brief duration of service outage. The client application must make a decision on how long to retry reconnection attempts to the same server before trying another server. The answer primarily depends on two factors: the amount of time it takes for the application to restart itself locally on a server and the amount of time users can suffer service outage. The necessity to provide service from the same server (to preserved session status, in-flight transactions, and so forth) must be balanced by the need to restore service quickly by connecting the client to another server (so user suffers a very brief service outage).

- *Queue up user requests* — Request queuing is useful only if the client application is not interactive and users do not expect responses from the server. For noninteractive client applications, requests can be queued up when service is unavailable. As soon as the service is brought online, the requests are transmitted to the server. The queuing system ensures that messages and transactions are delivered to the server.

Key Points

Following are some key points discussed in this chapter:

- The objective of developing applications for a cluster is to eliminate or decrease the amount of planned or unplanned downtime that clients will experience.

- Applications must have noninteractive and completely automated procedures for starting, stopping, monitoring, and managing applications. It must be possible to reconfigure applications without a need for restarting them.

- Servers must be aware of application states on other servers and be able to continue processing transactions where they were interrupted on a failed server.

- Cluster applications must be designed for rolling upgrades, which, in turn, requires that the cluster allow different versions of the application to run on different nodes.

Network Design, Implementation, and Security

In This Part

Network Devices

*Life must be lived and curiosity kept alive. One must
never, for whatever reason, turn his back on life.*
— Eleanor Roosevelt

During the 1970s and 1980s, the networking industry developed several products and technologies to glue the growing number of LAN segments. This chapter provides an overview of different network devices and how they join various LAN segments in an orderly way.

Network Devices

Let's first examine the components of an internetwork infrastructure:

- *Hubs* — A hub connects individual devices (such as PCs, printers, servers, and laptops) to make an individual LAN or a LAN segment. All devices in a LAN segment belong to the same subnet and share the hub's bandwidth. LANs are the unit building blocks of an internetwork. Figure 28-1 shows a hub-based LAN segment.

- *Switches* — Much like a hub, a switch connects hosts, but the total bandwidth of the switch is not shared by the ongoing communications. Figure 28-2 shows devices interconnected by a switch. Each active connection occurs at the full switch bandwidth, made possible by better electronics that can create individual communication channels operating at full speed. Switches are faster, more expensive, and more complicated to set up than hubs. But, switches do not use IP addresses and are, therefore, not capable of guiding packets through large networks.

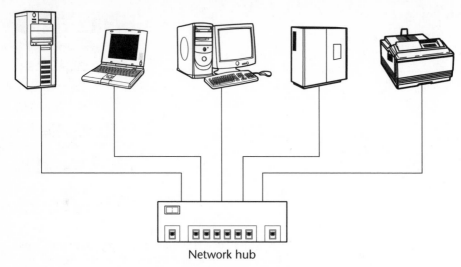

Figure 28-1   A LAN with devices connected by a hub.

■ *Routers* — These are intelligent devices that guide data packets between LANs and networks. Just like hubs or switches have ports to connect individual hosts, routers have ports to connect individual LAN segments, as shown in Figure 28-3. Based on the packet's destination IP address, routers move data packets between LAN segments by figuring out the optimal path that a packet must take through the maze of various LANs.

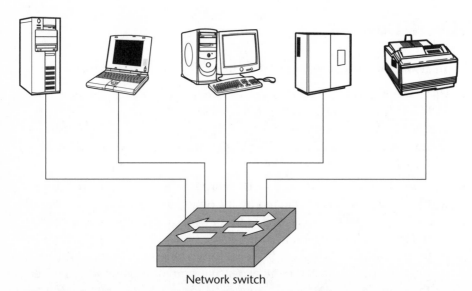

Figure 28-2   A LAN with hosts and printers interconnected by a switch.

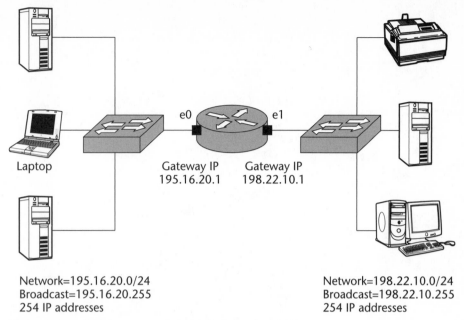

Network=195.16.20.0/24
Broadcast=195.16.20.255
254 IP addresses

Network=198.22.10.0/24
Broadcast=198.22.10.255
254 IP addresses

Figure 28-3 A router connecting two independent LANs.

NOTE In the seven-layer network architecture (the OSI Reference Model), hubs operate at layer 1 (physical layer), switches at layer 2 (data link layer), and routers at layer 3 (network layer).

- *Firewalls* — These are special routers that filter data based on source and destination addresses, port numbers, content, and so forth. They help preserve important data within a network and keep malicious, unwanted packets away. Each packet going through a firewall is intentionally checked for compliance against preprogrammed policies before being let through or being denied. Figure 28-4 shows a firewall with routers filtering data to and from the intranet and the DMZ servers.

  Every corporation with Internet access must have a firewall to protect against external threats. Internal firewalls are also being implemented to shield against internal threats. A firewall can be a specialized hardware that sits between the internal network and Intranet. A router can also be programmed to perform all duties of a firewall.

- *Access servers* — These are installed and managed by Internet service providers (ISPs) at their data centers and are used by small office and home users to dial in and connect to the Internet. Figure 28-5 shows a remote user connecting to the Internet by dialing into an Internet service provider's access server and then connecting to his corporate intranet through a virtual private network (VPN).

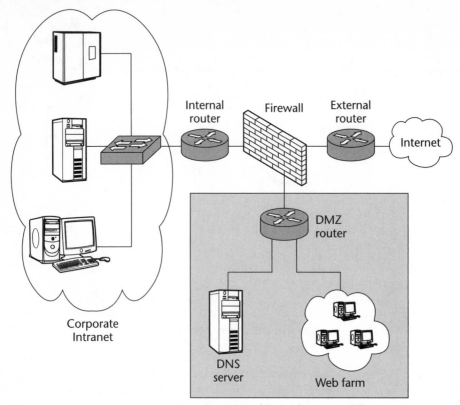

Figure 28-4   A firewall shielding the intranet and DMZ.

■ *Multilayer switches (MLS)* — Normally, switches work at layer 2 of the
OSI model (using flat MAC addresses) and routers at layer 3 (using
hierarchical IP addresses and routes). But, there are several switches
that do both. They have IP routing capabilities built into the hardware.
They filter and forward packets based on the MAC and IP addresses.
Some manufacturers sell an optional *routing switch module (RSM)* to
include routing capability into a switch. These switches are known as
multilayer switches (MLS). The technology is called *IP routing, shortcut
routing, high-speed routing,* or *layer-3 switching*.

MLS switches first determine the best route to each destination using
layer 3 protocols. The route is stored for future use. Packets that need
to use the stored routes are transmitted via the switches to the destination (rather than through the routers). This removes the router bottleneck. MLS can deliver ten-fold increase in throughput, especially at
high-traffic LAN segments. Switches will not replace routers in the
foreseeable future, but there is a distinct trend of welding switching and
routing technologies together.

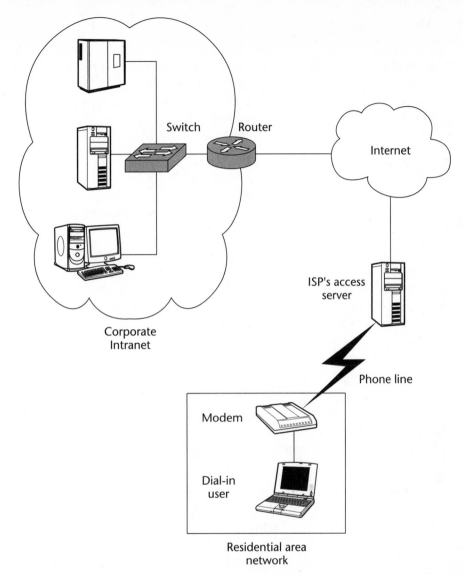

Figure 28-5 Remote dial-in users connect to an ISP's access server to get to the Internet.

These devices combined with WAN telecommunication links make up the Internet infrastructure. The common glue for the disparate devices are the network protocols, with the most popular being transmission control protocol/Internet protocol (TCP/IP). This chapter is the first of several that describe the network technologies, topologies, and protocols.

Hubs Versus Switches

Hubs and switches are similar in many ways. Both contain connection ports into which twisted-pair RJ-45 connectors (similar to phone RJ-11 jacks) plug. They can be administered remotely. Either can be used to create a LAN, and they funnel messages to the network backbones.

There are salient differences between hubs and switches, however:

- *Shared or dedicated bandwidth* — The main distinction is how they operate. Hosts in a hub-based network share the full bandwidth, but a switch is capable of creating independent full-speed connections for any two devices on the LAN that must communicate. Each connection operates at the full switch bandwidth.

- *How they handle signals* — A hub acts like a repeater. It takes an incoming frame and retransmits it to all other attached hosts. Each hub port has a single host connected to it. Hubs are dumb devices and cannot learn. Switches examine incoming frames and immediately transmit them to one or more other ports. This process is very fast. Each switch port can have a single host or a LAN segment connected to it. Switches learn media access control (MAC) addresses and build a content-addressable memory (CAM) table.

- *Cost* — Switches are more expensive than hubs for the same number of ports because they have more powerful hardware and software capabilities. Switches have more memory, a CPU, and a complete suite of software tools to manage them. Hubs have a trimmed-down version of the firmware code.

Like switches, bridges are also layer 2 devices. They learn MAC addresses, filter and forward frames, and can be used to segment LANs. However, they usually have 16 or fewer ports. Much of the functionality of bridges has been moved to routers.

Just as routers have replaced bridges at layer 3, switches (as their cost continues to fall) may eventually replace hubs at layer 2, but that has not happened yet. Hubs, it must be pointed out, have become smarter, less expensive, and easier to set up and manage. As more and more LANs are being set up, network managers continue to deploy hubs as an easy and inexpensive way to connect printers, low-traffic servers, PCs, and management consoles. The number of installed hubs is increasing mainly because of cost and simplicity.

Routers

Many products, technologies, and protocols go into making a network or internetwork. The list seems endless — switches, access servers, firewalls, FDDI,

ATM, Token Ring, Ethernet, topologies, leased lines, DSL, OC, and so on. The one product that glues them all together is the router.

A *router* is a network device that forwards packets of information from one network to another using a predetermined optimal path. Figure 28-6 shows the different levels of work done by a switch and router. Switches move frames within a LAN at layer 2 using MAC addresses. Routers move packets between LANs at layer 3 using IP addresses.

Figure 28-7 shows hubs, switches, and a router in a typical network within an office building. The switches on each floor in Figure 28-7 could be replaced by routers.

Figure 28-8 shows how routers connect LANs. Routers are the basic fabric of the Internet. They are more sophisticated than hubs or switches.

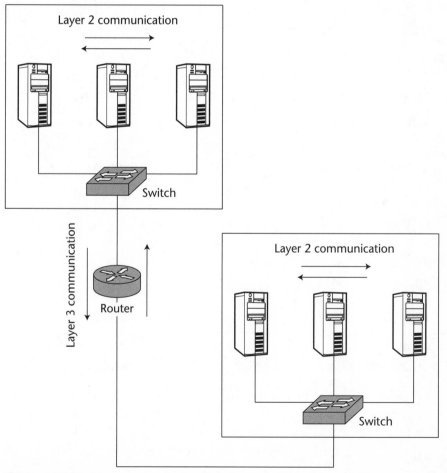

Figure 28-6 Layer 2 communication is between hosts within an LAN segment. Layer 3 communication is between LAN segments.

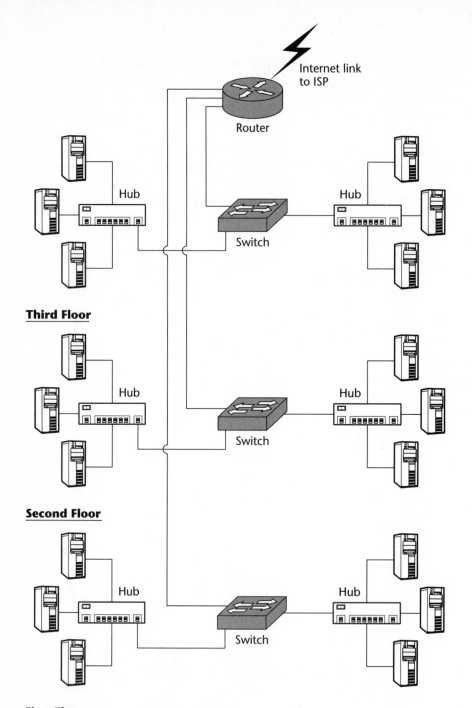

Figure 28-7 LAN segments on each floor are interconnected by switches.

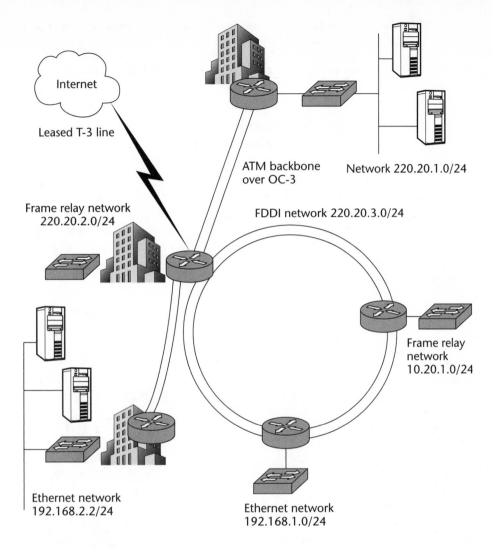

Figure 28-8   Different LANs are connected by routers.

Routers operate at layer 3 of the seven-layer OSI Reference Model. Keep in mind the following characteristics of routers:

- Routers forward packets from one LAN to another and, therefore, must understand all network protocols (such as Appletalk, DECnet, IP, Token Ring, and so on). Routers enable LAN-to-LAN and LAN-to-WAN connectivity.

- Routers keep a table of network addresses and know which path to take to get to each network. Routing is essentially finding a path between a source and a destination. Each router must discover, verify, and maintain all the valid paths in its routing table and then select the best path between two points for packets that need to travel across the maze of routers. Routing is complex because there are several intermediary routers that a packet must traverse on the way to its destination. Figure 28-9 shows a few candidate paths and best path for packets between headquarters and manufacturing plant.

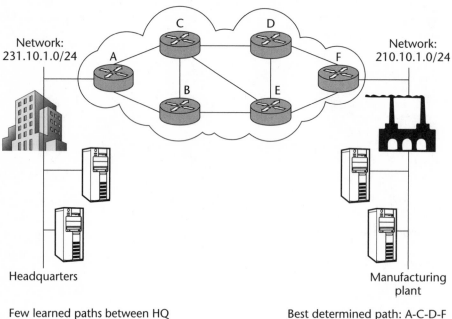

Few learned paths between HQ and manufacturing plant:
1. A-C-E-F
2. A-B-E-F
3. A-C-D-F
4. A-C-B-E-F
5. A-B-C-D-E-F

Best determined path: A-C-D-F
Routed protocol: IP
Number of metric hops: 3

Figure 28-9 Routers determine valid routes and the best route between source and destination.

■ Routers filter data based on a set of access control lists (ACLs). Unlike switches that forward all data, routers selectively drop data that is harmful.

■ Routers are able to block broadcasts. Thus, they can enforce security and assist in bandwidth control.

■ Routers are used for LAN segmentation. This increases modularity in network setup.

Data is encapsulated and de-encapsulated within data packets as the packet makes its way from router to router toward its destination host. The first router in the path (router A in Figure 28-9) encapsulates the data before sending it to the next. At each router, the packet is partially de-encapsulated to expose the destination address. If the router is not the last one (routers C and D in Figure 28-9), the data frame is encapsulated and forwarded to the next router. If the router is the last one in the path (router F) to the destination host, the data is encapsulated in the destination LAN's data-link frame type for delivery to the protocol stack on the destination network.

A router is far more complex than a hub or switch. It must keep a table of network addresses and all valid paths (or *routes*), as well as the best path between any two networks. There are three types of routes:

■ *Static routes* — Routes that a network administrator manually enters into the router.

■ *Dynamic routes* — Routes that a network routing protocol adjusts automatically for topology or traffic changes.

■ *Default route* — A route that is manually entered by the network administrator for the router to forward its packet to when a static or dynamic route does not exist.

Routes periodically broadcast route updates to all neighboring routers. Each router listens for such broadcasts and then updates its routing table. If the destination network is connected to the router, the router then knows which port to forward the packet to. In most cases, the destination network is a remote network. The router determines the path of least resistance for each destination and then forwards the packet to another router that happens to be in the best path.

Network Cables

The most significant fact about LAN cables is that they run over two types of physical media:

- *Copper media* — Examples are coaxial and twisted-pair cables. The vast majority of installed LANs today use copper cables.

- *Fiber media* — This is also called *fiber* (or *glass,* for short) and makes up the high-speed network backbones.

NOTE Wireless communication is also becoming mainstream with laptops now being sold with integrated wireless fidelity (WiFi) ports.

The following sections describe various cable media and distance restrictions.

Coaxial Cables (Copper)

The early LANs used thicknet coaxial cable. They were expensive and difficult to configure. In the mid 1980s, they were replaced by thinnet coaxial cables, which had a distance limitation of 185 meters when used for 10 Mbps Ethernet. Repeaters were used to amplify signals and increase the maximum length possible. Nonetheless, the topology was not suitable for a large number of hosts and was difficult to manage and prone to large-scale outages.

Figure 28-10 shows an example of coaxial cable.

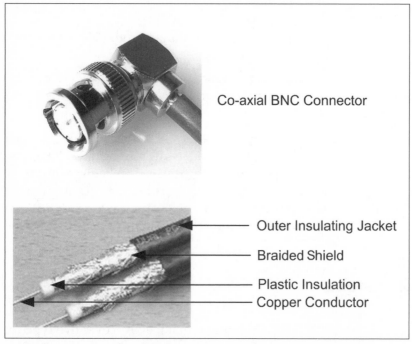

Co-axial BNC Connector

Outer Insulating Jacket

Braided Shield

Plastic Insulation

Copper Conductor

Figure 28-10 Coaxial BNC connector and layers within a coaxial cable.

Twisted-Pair Cables (Copper)

In the 1980s, network hubs were introduced. They brought modularity into network design that was not there with coaxial cables. Hubs also solved many setup and LAN management pains and started a new cabling type called *twisted-pair*. However, this type of cable has a short operating length of 100 meters, but that could easily be extended using hubs. For example, to cover a length of 400 meters, you could install three intervening hubs.

Twisted-pair cable is faster and requires less copper and shielding than coaxial cables. Twisted-pair cables support data rates of 100 Mbps. The connectors at the end are typically RJ-45 (rated jack), transparent, and look like RJ-11 telephone jacks.

To reduce crosstalk and electromagnetic interference (EMI) between pairs of wires, two insulated copper wires are twisted around each other. Each connection on twisted-pair cables requires both wires. The reliability and speed depends on the quality of copper in the wires, insulation around the wires, quality of the connectors, and how tight the copper wires are twisted.

Twisted-pair cables are commonly used to connect hosts, printers, and so on to hubs or switches. Following are the two types of twisted-pair cables:

- *Shielded twisted pair (STP)* — This type has two twisted pairs of cables with a shielded insulation. Each bundle is wrapped in a foil shield to prevent EMI. STP is more expensive and less commonly used than UTP. It is used in areas with high EMI.

- *Unshielded twisted pair (UTP)* — This type has four twisted pairs of cables but no shielded insulation. Interference and signal loss is prevented by a tight twisting of the copper wires and by having more pairs. UTP is reliable, less expensive than STP, and has gained popularity in recent years.

Table 28-1 shows the various UTP cable types. The higher the category number, the higher the speed. Category 5 (Cat5) cables are the most common. Figures 28-11 and 28-12 show examples of UTP and STP cables.

Fiber-Optic Cables (Glass)

Fiber is used to interconnect routers and switches, as well as to create uplinks and network backbones. However, it is also common to connect servers requiring the high bandwidth provided by fiber-optic cables to a gigabit switch directly. Someday all copper cabling may be replaced by fiber, right up to the desktop, but fiber is expensive and requires more protection on the outside than copper cables. However, it can sustain high-speed over long distances and is not subject to EMI. Because fiber-optic cables are not free from interference, light can travel inside them for miles without loss of amplitude.

Table 28-1   UTP Cables with Four Twisted Pairs

UTP CABLE	DESCRIPTION	USE
Category 1 (Cat1)	Old telephone lines.	No longer used for networks or telephones.
Category 2 (Cat2)	Old telephone lines.	No longer in use.
Category 3 (Cat3)	16 MHz. Has three twists per foot of cable.	Used for new telephone lines, 4 Mbps Token Ring LANs, and 10 Mbps Ethernet LANs.
Category 4 (Cat4)	20 MHz.	Used for 16 Mbps Token Ring.
Category 5 (Cat5)	100 MHz. Eight twists per foot of cable.	100 Mbps. Commonly used for Ethernet LANs.
Enhanced Category 5 (Enhanced Cat5)	200 MHz. Like Cat5, it has eight twists per foot, but the wires are made of higher quality copper.	Twice the rate of Cat5 cables.
Category 6 (Cat6)	Each pair is insulated with foil and the four pairs are together wrapped in polymer.	Has a rating of up to six times that of regular Cat5.

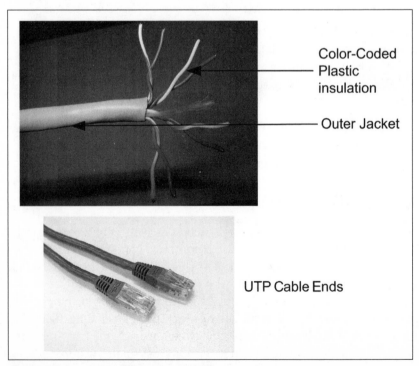

Color-Coded Plastic insulation

Outer Jacket

UTP Cable Ends

Figure 28-11   UTP cable and connector.

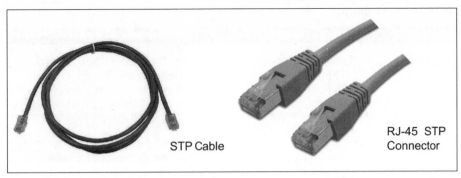

Figure 28-12　STP cable and connector.

The path that light takes within the fiber-optic cable is called the *mode*. A light signal can propagate through the core of the optical fiber on a single path (called *single-mode fiber*) or on many paths (called *multimode fiber*). The most important difference between the two types is the diameter of the core through which light travels. Whether you use single-mode or multimode fiber depends on the distance that must be covered. For up to 10 kilometers, multimode works well. If the devices are farther apart, you need single-mode fiber. The fiber-optic cable types and features are compared in Table 28-2.

Single-mode fiber has the advantage of high information-carrying capacity, higher efficiency, low attenuation and dispersion, and greater distance. However, multimode has the advantage of low connection-and-electronics cost, which may lead to lower system cost.

Table 28-2　Fiber-Optic Cable Types

FEATURE	SINGLE-MODE FIBER	MULTIMODE FIBER
Number of light modes	Allows one mode of light to propagate through the fiber.	Allows multiple modes of light to propagate through the fiber.
Source of light	Uses solid-state laser diodes as light-generating devices.	Uses light-emitting diodes (LEDs) as light-generating devices.
Core diameter (data carrying axis of the cable)	8 to 10 microns (about the diameter of a hair).	62.5 microns.
Bandwidth	Higher bandwidth than multimode. Optical carrier levels transmit up to 4 Gbps.	Bandwidth up to 100 Mbps.

(continued)

Table 28-2 *(continued)*

FEATURE	SINGLE-MODE FIBER	MULTIMODE FIBER
Distance	Greater distance than 1310-multimode. A 1550-nanometer wavelength fiber can cover up to 60 kilometers.	Used for shorter distances. A nanometer multimode fiber can cover up to 10 kilometers. High-powered emitters can travel up to 100 kilometers.
Used for	Used for long-haul connections such as WAN connections and campus backbones.	Commonly deployed for short-distance connections. Used to connect devices and hosts within a LAN segment or data center.

Although fiber-optic cables are capable of carrying terabits of data per second, the available signaling hardware and connectors can manage merely a few gigabits per second. Fiber speeds for multimode (used for LANs and MANs) are about 100 Mbps and single-mode (used for WANs) up to 40 Gbps.

Within a network in a building, the backbone could be made of fiber-optic cable. The fiber backbone connects the switches or hubs in different floors by making a network trunk called the *riser*.

Fiber-optic cable is made up of two strands in separate jackets: one for receiving and the other for transmitting data. Each strand has a glass or plastic core surrounded by more glass (called *cladding*). The strands use photons of light (instead of electrons) for sending and receiving information. The core provides the wave path for pulses of light traversing over the glass threads. The cladding consists of reflective glass that refracts light back to the core. Each strand is further covered by a group of fibers (which enhance the suppleness and strength), and finally by an outermost plastic jacket.

Figure 28-13 shows the ends of various fiber-optic cables. Each cable end is fitted with a plug that can be inserted into a network adapter, hub, or switch. In the United States, most fiber cables use a square SC connector that locks into place when inserted into another fiber cable or host. Cables used in Europe and Asia use a round ST connector. The connectors make an optically pure connection to the glass fiber and provide a window for laser transmitters and optical receivers.

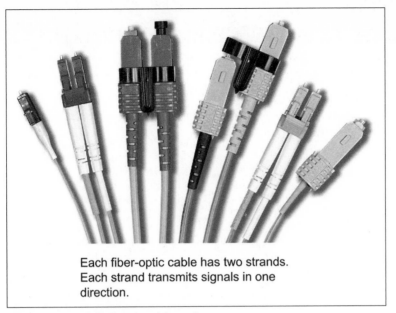

Each fiber-optic cable has two strands.
Each strand transmits signals in one
direction.

Figure 28-13 Fiber-optic cable ends.

Key Points

Following are some key points discussed in this chapter:

- A network requires many types of devices — hubs, switches, routers, firewalls, access servers, and multilayer switches. All hosts connected to a hub share the hub bandwidth, but a switch provides full bandwidth simultaneously to all links. A router forwards data packets between different networks and joins the various devices.

- Network cables are made of copper or fiber. Copper-based cables are coaxial cables, as well as shielded and unshielded twisted-pair cables. Fiber cables have speeds of several terabits per seconds, are interference-free, and are used commonly for network backbones and connecting high-end, bandwidth-hungry servers.

CHAPTER 29

Network Protocols

Tell me and I forget. Teach me and I remember. Involve me and I learn.
— Benjamin Franklin

There are many network equipment vendors, and it is necessary that they all build networks whose devices can mutually communicate. Therefore, in 1984, the International Standards Organization (ISO) met and developed a model for all network communication known as the open systems interconnection (OSI). It is regarded as the primary architecture for intercomputer communication and networking. The main purpose of the OSI model is to describe the software functions and hardware specifications required to move data from one host to another through the network medium.

Table 29-1 describes this seven-layer OSI model. Each protocol (such as TCP, UDP, and IP) described in this book will be identified as belonging to a specific layer within in the OSI model.

Main advantages of the OSI model are as follows:

- It provides a common framework for network and computer vendors for their products, protocols, devices, and internetworking technologies.

- It defines a common interface for communication between protocols, devices, and technologies from different vendors.

- It divides the multifaceted networking aspects into less-complex stages.

- It helps engineers to focus development efforts on modular functions.

Table 29-1 The Seven-Layer OSI Model

LAYER NUMBER	NAME	ENCAPSULATION	DEVICES	EXAMPLES OR PROTOCOLS	DESCRIPTION
7	Application	Raw data	N/A (software-based)	HTTP, FTP, remote login, e-mail, SNMP, DNS	Consists of network applications (not user applications such as spreadsheets or word processors) such as SNMP e-mail. Controls and defines protocols for exchange of information between users and systems.
6	Presentation	Raw data	N/A (software-based)	`.txt`, `bin`, `.cmd`, `bmp`, `.gif`, or `.html`, `.ebcdic`, `.jpg`	Formats data for screen display or printing. Defines the representation of data so that it is exchanged between printers, firewalls, or applications in an understandable manner. Examples include data compression, encryption, and decryption at VPN interfaces.
5	Session	Raw data	N/A (software-based)	NFS, SQL, NetBIOS, RPC, LDAP, operating systems, Web browsers	This layer manages the data for each application. It sets up, manages, and terminates dialog sessions between presentation layer entities. The session consists of service requests and responses between applications located in different devices.
4	Transport	Segments	N/A (software-based)	TCP (connection-oriented), UDP (connectionless), ICMP	Controls the transfer of data between the two end stations by managing frame size, quality, and reliability. It sequences the packets before transmission and acknowledges receipts of each packet.

(continued)

Table 29-1 *(continued)*

LAYER NUMBER	NAME	ENCAPSULATION	DEVICES	EXAMPLES OR PROTOCOLS	DESCRIPTION
3	Network	Packets	Routers, hosts	IP, Internetwork packet exchange (IPX)	Routes packets between LANs. Learns IP addresses and builds a metric-based routing table for each destination network. Uses a store-and-forward algorithm to forward data to each destination. Calculates optimum routes for data packets and controls link congestion. Devices are identified by logical addresses (IP or IPX).
2	Data Link	Frames	Switches, bridges	Ethernet, Token Ring, Frame Relay, ATM, FDDI	Helps frames travel over LANs. Packages data for transmission. Learns MAC addresses and uses cut-through, store-and-forwards, or fragment-free algorithms to forward data to hosts. Deals with data corruption through checksums and negotiates use of shared media. Identifies devices by MAC addresses, vendor codes, or serial numbers.
1	Physical	Bits	Hubs, repeaters, cables	Cables (twisted pair, fiber-optic, coaxial), serial links, connectors, NICs, dial-up, wireless, fiber-optic	Sends and receives signals over the wires. Establishes physical connection between devices and network. Specifies the physical/mechanical characteristics of data-carrying media. Amplifies signal to each port.

Users enter their information at layer 7 using applications such as e-mail and FTP. As the request or information goes down from layer 7 to 1, each layer adds its own header information. This process is called *encapsulation*. Each layer is said to encapsulate the information it receives from the higher level.

At the physical layer (layer 1), data is represented in binary 0s and 1s. The binary data is converted to electrical signals and transmitted across the network media. At the receiving end, the signals are converted to 0s and 1s at the physical layer (layer 1) and then passed to the data link layer (layer 2). The layer 2 header information generated by the sending machine is removed. The information moves all the way from layer 1 to layer 7. Each layer removes its header information and passes in to the next layer. Finally the application data is delivered to the receiving machine's application layer (layer 7).

Note that layers 1 through 4 are in hardware and layers 5 through 7 in software. An easy way to recall the names of layers 1 to 7 is to remember the initials in "Please Do Not Throw Sausage Pizza Away." If you want to reverse that (go from layer 7 to 1) remember the initials in "All People Seem To Need Data Processing."

Transmission Control Protocol/ Internet Protocol (TCP/IP)

TCP/IP is a set of network protocols that enable hardware with different platforms and operating systems to exchange data in an orderly manner. Just as a German person and a Spanish person cannot communicate if they do not know a common language, a system that runs TCP/IP cannot communicate with another that runs only Novell's IPX. Computer vendors around the world agreed to make their hardware TCP/IP-aware so that it can communicate with others.

TCP/IP is the protocol that binds the devices, forming the Internet infrastructure. TCP handles messaging and IP takes care of addressing. The primary TCP/IP components are as follows:

- *Transmission control protocol (TCP)* — TCP is responsible for verifying the correct delivery of data sent from one node or network to another. It adds support to detect errors or lost data in the intermediate network during transfer. In case of failures or incomplete transmissions, it initiates retransmission until the data is correctly and completely received.

- *Internet protocol (IP)* — IP is responsible for moving packets of data from node to node, based on an IP address. A range of IP addresses is assigned to each organization or company, which, in turn, assigns groups of their numbers to departments. IP operates on gateway machines or routers by allowing movement of data between internal networks and also to networks around the world.

■ *Sockets* — This is the package of subroutines that provide access to TCP/IP on most systems.

Individual nodes, printers, or network devices are first interconnected to form a local area network (LAN). TCP/IP enables the devices to communicate among themselves and with those in other LANs around the world.

TCP and UDP as Transport (Layer 4) Protocols

The layer 4 protocols (primarily TCP and UDP) ensure that the data reaches the destination intact and in the right order. All IP messages travel using either TCP or UDP protocol, but not both. TCP is used for critical packets such as secure shell (SSH) and FTP. UDP is used for less-critical messages such TFTP and SMTP.

TCP and UDP essentially do the same thing: They transport IP packets. Table 29-2 shows some salient differences between TCP and UDP.

Table 29-2   TCP versus UDP

FEATURE	TCP	UDP
Reliability	More reliable because it checks with the receiver to ensure that packets were received. Lost packets are retransmitted.	Less reliable. Does not verify delivery with the receiver. Used for messages where a slight delay (caused by retransmission of failed messages) is acceptable.
Overhead	Has more overhead because it goes to great lengths (three-way handshaking) to verify accurate delivery.	Generates less overhead traffic and, therefore, preferred for video, graphics, and so forth.
Level of control applied during message delivery	TCP is connection-oriented. It does a three-way handshake and windowing. It requires acknowledgment (ACK) an message from the receiver acknowledge successful to completion after transmission of each packet.	UDP is connectionless. It does not use acknowledgements or windowing. It is a "best effort" protocol. It sends the data and hopes it will succeed. But it compares checksums of sent and received packets and, if they do not match, the message is retransmitted.
Speed	Slow and causes more network traffic.	Faster and more efficient.
Examples	HTTP, FTP, SSH, telnet, DNS for server-to-server lookups.	TFTP, DNS for client-to-server lookups.

Ports

A *port number* is an endpoint to a network connection and is used by clients to locate a particular server program on a computer on the network. There are several assigned port numbers. The Internet Assigned Numbers Authority (IANA) (www.iana.org/) controls the assignment of port numbers, and they adhere to the following system:

- *Well-known ports (ports 0 to 255)* — These lower port numbers are assigned to public applications such as telnet, e-mail, HTTP, SNMP, FTP, NetBIOS, and DNS.

- *Well-known ports (ports 256 to 1023)* — These are assigned to different organizations and companies for the application network traffic. Any organization that wants a port number in this range must file a request with the IANA.

- *Registered ports (ports 1024 to 49151)* — These are assigned dynamically by network traffic generated by the user applications. In other words, these ports can be used by programs executed by users.

- *Ports 49152 to 65535* — These are dynamic and/or private ports.

Table 29-3 lists common IANA-assigned ports. Ports are used to name the ends of logical connections that sustain long-term conversations.

Table 29-3 Frequently Used and IANA-Assigned TCP and UDP Ports

TCP PORT NUMBERS		UDP PORT NUMBERS	
APPLICATION	PORT NUMBER	APPLICATION	PORT NUMBER
Echo	7	Echo	7
Ftp-data	20	DNS	53
FTP	21	BOOTP	67
SSH	22	TFTP	69
Telnet	23	NetBIOS	137–139
SMTP	25	LDAP	389
DNS	53	Mobile IP	434
Finger	79	Who	513
NNTP(news)	119	Talk	517
NetBIOS	137–139	Routed	520

Table 29-3   *(continued)*

TCP PORT NUMBERS		UDP PORT NUMBERS	
APPLICATION	PORT NUMBER	APPLICATION	PORT NUMBER
LDAP	389	Kerberos	749, 750
Kerberos	543, 544, 749, 750, 754	NFS	2049
NFS	2049	NFS lock manager	4045

Key Points

Following are some key points discussed in this chapter:

- The seven-layer OSI model has helped network vendors develop protocols and products that can communicate with each other.
- TCP and UDP are the primary data carriers.
- Communication among devices is based on ports that allow a client to locate a specific service on another network device or host.

IP
Addressing

*Have a heart that never hardens, a temper that
never tires, a touch that never hurts.*
— Charles Dickens

At layer 2 of the OSI model, devices communicate using a physical or hardware-based MAC address, but at layer 3 all hosts must have a software address. Routers use the software address to determine the next destination for the message. Configuration and proper running of this layer take up the lion's share of a network administrator's time.

In TCP/IP the software address is referred to as the *Internet* or *IP address*. Each IP address (for example, 188.23.16.12) is made up of four bytes, also called *octets*. Table 30-1 shows the various classes of IP addresses. The class is based on the first byte.

All addresses are assigned to organizations by the Internet Assigned Numbers Authority (IANA), which ensures that there is no duplication of IP addresses (except for reserved IPs). Corporations can get IP addresses from the IANA. The larger the corporation, the more IPs they will need. ISPs buy a lot of IP addresses from the IANA and resell them to individuals and small companies.

When the machine encounters the IP address, it immediately converts it to binary. As shown in Figure 30-1, each of the four bytes has 8 bits. Each bit is set to 0 or 1. The decimal value of the bit starts at 1 on the right side and doubles as you move left. They are 1, 2, 4, 8, 16, 32, 64, and 128. If all bits are on (set to 1), the octet is 255. Figure 30-1 shows the 0 and 1 bit values for 255 and 172.

Table 30-1   IP Address Classes Are Determined by the Value in the First Byte

IP ADDRESS CLASS	FIRST BYTE (DETERMINES CLASS)	FOUR BYTES OF AN IP ADDRESS = NET ID + HOST PORTION			
Class A	Network portion				
	Binary: 0xxx xxxx	Net ID	Host	Host	Host
	Decimal: 1–126				
Class B	Network portion				
	Binary: 10xx xxxx	Net ID	Net ID	Host	Host
	Decimal: 128–191				
Class C	Network portion				
	Binary: 110x xxxx	Net ID	Net ID	Net ID	Host
	Decimal: 192–223				
Class D (used by OSPF, EIGRP, and so on)	Network portion				
	Binary: 1110 xxxx	Net ID	Multicast group	Multicast group	Multicast Group
	Decimal: 224–239				
Class E	Network portion				
	Binary: 1111 0xxx	Reserved for research and future use			
	Decimal: 240–247				

Binary Values in a Byte:

Example 1: 255

1	1	1	1	1	1	1	1
128	64	32	16	8	4	2	1

With all 8 bits set to 1, number = 128 + 64 + 32 + 16 + 8 + 4 + 2 + 1 = 255

Example 2: 172

1	0	1	0	1	1	0	0
128	64	32	16	8	4	2	1

With bits set to 1 as shown above, number = 128 + 32 + 8 + 4 = 172

Example 3:

Decimal: 172.14.122.16
Binary: 10101100 . 00001110 . 01111010 . 00010000

Figure 30-1 Numbers and IP address in binary and decimal notations.

Table 30-2 shows the reserved IP addresses that can be used for internal networks as nonroutable addresses. These will never be sold by IANA. Anyone is allowed to use one of these addresses as long as the address is not exposed to the Internet.

IP addresses have a network and host portion as shown in Table 30-1. The bits in the host portion determine the host IP address, but all the bits cannot be 0s or 1s. If all the bits are 0, it becomes the network address. If all the bits are 1, it becomes the broadcast address for the network.

Class A addresses are of the *N.H.H.H* format, where *N* is the network portion and a number between 1 and 126. The *H* in second, third, and fourth octets is used for the host portion. There are 126 Class A networks. All have already been given away by the IANA to different organization and corporations. In the address, 20.12.1.1, 20.0.0.0 is the network address and 0.12.1.1 is the host portion of the address. Each Class A network has enough IP addresses for about 16 million hosts.

Table 30-2 Reserved IP Addresses

CLASS	RESERVED IP RANGE
Class A	10.0.0.0–10.255.255.255 (127.x.xx is reserved for loopback and self-diagnostic purposes)
Class B	172.16.0.0–172.31.255.255
Class C	192.168.0.0–192.168.255.255

Class B addresses are of the *N.N.H.H* format, where *N* is the network portion and *H* is the host portion. The first *N* is from 128 to 191. Each Class B network has more than 65,000 hosts and is still difficult to manage. Figure 30-2 shows an example of a class B network.

Class C addresses are of the form *N.N.N.H* and the first octet includes from 192 to 223. Each Class C network can accommodate 254 hosts. For the full Class C network 195.2.8.0, the number 195.2.8.0 is the network address, 195.2.8.255 is the broadcast address, and the addresses in between — namely, 195.2.8.1 to 195.2.8.254 — are used as host IPs. Figure 30-3 shows an example Class C network.

When you do a Boolean AND of a subnet mask with any address (network, host IP, or broadcast address) within the subnet, you will get the network address of the subnet. This is because the subnet mask has 1s for all the bit positions making up the network address. Routers and hosts determine their own network address by doing a Boolean AND of their own IP address and the subnet mask. Table 30-3 illustrates this for a /28 network, or subnet mask being 255.255.255.240. Recall that in Boolean AND, 1 AND 1 yields 1 but 1 AND 0, 0 AND 1, and 0 AND 0 each yield 0.

Let's recap a few points. We already know that the default mask for a network identifies how many bits are used for the network portion within an IP address. Table 30-4 shows the default subnet size for a "Classful Addressing Scheme."

Example of a Class B Network 183.66.0.0

	Network portion		Host portion		
	183	66	0	0	Network address

Binary:	10110111	01000010	00000000	00000000	0
			00000000	00000001	1
			00000000	00000010	2
			•		
			•		
			11111111	11111110	65535
			11111111	11111111	65536
Subnet mask =	255	255	0	0	

Broadcast address

Network ID = 183.66.0.0

Host address = 183.66.0.1 - 183.66.255.254

Total number of hosts (including network ID and broadcast) =
$2^N - 2 = 2^{16} - 2 = 65536 - 2 = 65534$

Broadcast ID = 183.66.255.255

Figure 30-2   Class B network example.

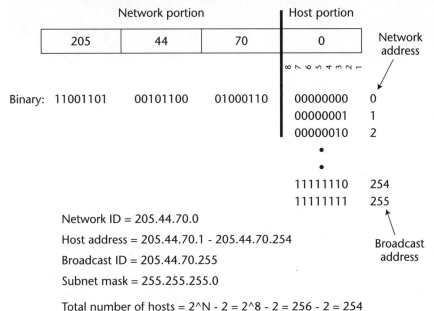

Figure 30-3   Class C network example.

For Class A networks, the first octet is used by the network portion and the other three octets are used by hosts. That would allow you to set up more than 16 million hosts within a Class A network. Even in a full Class B network, where the third and fourth octets are used by hosts, there would be more than 65,000 hosts within a subnet. Similarly a Class C network (where only the fourth octet is used for host portion) is capable of 256 hosts (including network and broadcast addresses). Some mechanism has to break these large networks into smaller, more manageable pieces. Also, we do not want to waste large IP ranges for networks that do not have so many hosts. Enter subnet masks.

Table 30-3   IP Address and Subnet Mask = Network Address

IP ADDRESS	SUBNET MASK	NETWORK ADDRESS (BOOLEAN AND)
1101 0010	1111 1111	1101 0010
0000 1100	1111 1111	0000 1100
1101 1000	1111 1111	1101 1000
0101 0011	1111 0000	0101 0000
210.12.216.83	255.255.255.240	210.12.216.80

Table 30-4 Default Subnet Masks for Different Classes

CLASS	NUMBER OF BITS IN THE DEFAULT MASK	DEFAULT NETWORK MASK	EXAMPLE OF IPs IN THE REPRESENTATION	NUMBER OF NETWORKS
Class A	/8	255.0.0.0	24.0.0.0/8	16 million
Class B	/16	255.255.0.0	141.62.0.0/16	65,536
Class C	/24	255.255.255.0	210.23.12.0/24	256

Subnet Masks

Subnetting is a technique of dividing a full Class A, B, or C network into smaller networks. It defines how 1 or more bits are taken from the host portion and added to the network portion. Following are the advantages of this technique:

- *Saves IP addresses* — Avoids the need to assign an entire IP range within a network to one location.

- *Simplifies network management* — Smaller, independent subnets can be created by routers. Internal networks can be restructured without impacting DMZ or external networks.

- *Reduces network traffic* — Links with high network traffic can be isolated to a subnet. Examples are NFS and backup subnets. NFS client (such as a filer) interfaces can be on a one subnet and backup server and dedicated client NICs on another.

- *Improves security* — It is easy to keep DMZ and front-facing networks separated from internal networks.

Subnetting requires taking a bit from the host portion and giving it to the network portion. The more bits we steal from host portion, the more the number of subnets. But more subnets come at the expense of IPs that would otherwise be used for hosts. Each new subnet requires two IP addresses: one for the network ID and the other for its broadcast ID.

What would happen if we do not subnet? The answer is illustrated in Figures 30-4 and 30-5.

Four Networks with Separate Class C Addresses

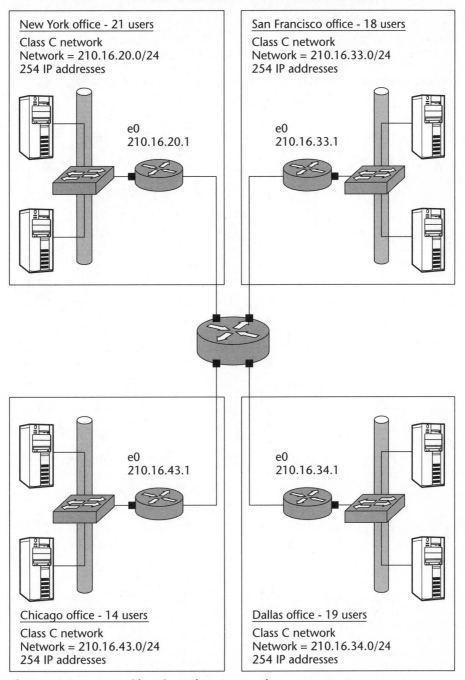

New York office - 21 users

Class C network
Network = 210.16.20.0/24
254 IP addresses

e0
210.16.20.1

San Francisco office - 18 users

Class C network
Network = 210.16.33.0/24
254 IP addresses

e0
210.16.33.1

e0
210.16.43.1

e0
210.16.34.1

Chicago office - 14 users

Class C network
Network = 210.16.43.0/24
254 IP addresses

Dallas office - 19 users

Class C network
Network = 210.16.34.0/24
254 IP addresses

Figure 30-4   Layout with various Class C networks.

**Subnetting a Class C Network 210.16.20.0/24
into 8 Subnets (4 out of 8 shown below)**

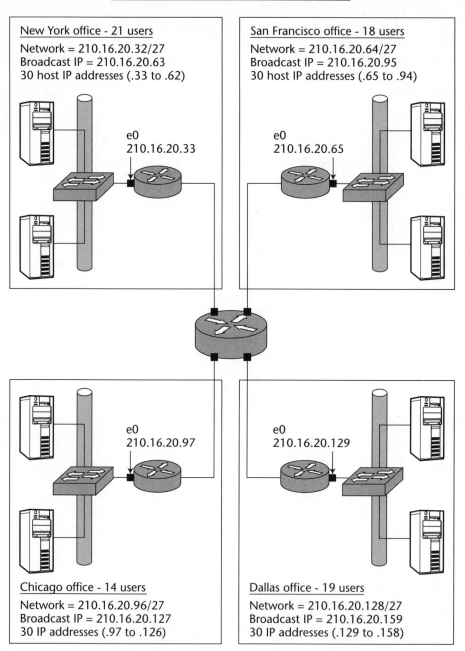

New York office - 21 users
Network = 210.16.20.32/27
Broadcast IP = 210.16.20.63
30 host IP addresses (.33 to .62)

e0
210.16.20.33

San Francisco office - 18 users
Network = 210.16.20.64/27
Broadcast IP = 210.16.20.95
30 host IP addresses (.65 to .94)

e0
210.16.20.65

e0
210.16.20.97

e0
210.16.20.129

Chicago office - 14 users
Network = 210.16.20.96/27
Broadcast IP = 210.16.20.127
30 IP addresses (.97 to .126)

Dallas office - 19 users
Network = 210.16.20.128/27
Broadcast IP = 210.16.20.159
30 IP addresses (.129 to .158)

Notes:

Subnet mask = 255.255.255.224
Each subnet has 30 assignable host IPs (including router IP)

Figure 30-5 A Class C network subdivided into eight subnets.

Class C Subnet Masks

To divide a Class C network (with 24-bit mask of 255.25.255.0) into subnet-works, you must increase the mask to 25, 26, 27, 28, 29, 30, or 31 bits.

Let's divide a full Class C network into two subnets. One bit must be stolen from the host portion and added to the mask to make it 255.255.255.128. Figure 30-6 shows the IP ranges for both subnets.

Table 30-5 shows the effect of taking bits 1 through 8 from the host portion and adding them to the mask.

Figure 30-7 shows a Class C network split into eight subnets, which requires three bits ($2^3 = 8$) from the host portion. This adds 224 (or 128 + 64 + 32) to the default mask. Five bits are left for the host address, which allows a total of $2^5 = 32$ addresses per subnet. The first subnet in Figure 30-6 extends from 210.24.55.0 to 210.24.55.31.

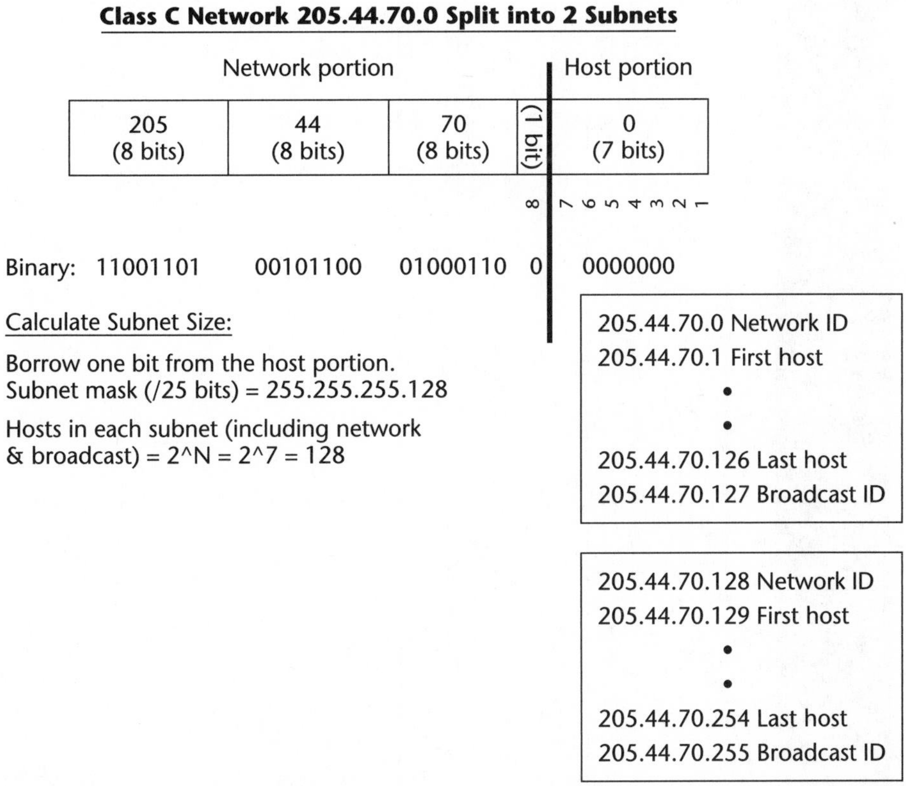

Class C Network 205.44.70.0 Split into 2 Subnets

Network portion				Host portion
205 (8 bits)	44 (8 bits)	70 (8 bits)	(1 bit)	0 (7 bits)

Binary: 11001101   00101100   01000110   0   0000000

Calculate Subnet Size:

Borrow one bit from the host portion.
Subnet mask (/25 bits) = 255.255.255.128

Hosts in each subnet (including network & broadcast) = $2^N = 2^7 = 128$

205.44.70.0 Network ID
205.44.70.1 First host
    •
    •
205.44.70.126 Last host
205.44.70.127 Broadcast ID

205.44.70.128 Network ID
205.44.70.129 First host
    •
    •
205.44.70.254 Last host
205.44.70.255 Broadcast ID

Figure 30-6   A class C network divided into two subnets.

Table 30-5   Class C Subnet Masks

NUMBER OF BITS STOLEN FOR NETWORK MASK	TOTAL BITS IN NETWORK MASK	VALUE OF LAST BIT IN SUBNET MASK	NETMASK	TOTAL NUMBER OF SUBNETS	IP ADDRESSES (INCLUDING NETWORK BROADCAST) = 2 ^ (HOST BITS)
0 (full Class C)	/24	0	255.255.255.0	1	$2^8 = 256$
1	/25	128	255.255.255.128	2	$2^7 = 128$
2	/26	64	255.255.255.192	4	$2^6 = 64$
3	/27	32	255.255.255.224	8	$2^5 = 32$
4	/28	16	255.255.255.240	16	$2^4 = 16$
5	/29	8	255.255.255.248	32	$2^3 = 8$
6	/30	4	255.255.255.252	64	$2^2 = 4$
7	/31	2	255.255.255.254	N/A	$2^1 = 2$

Class C Network 210.24.55.0 Split into 8 Subnets

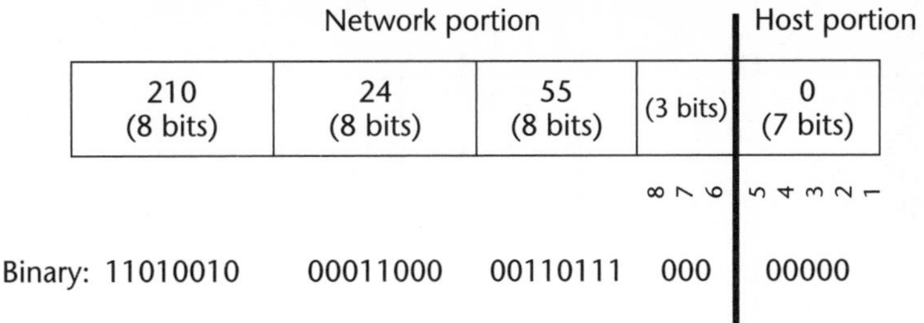

	Network portion			Host portion
210 (8 bits)	24 (8 bits)	55 (8 bits)	(3 bits)	0 (7 bits)

8 7 6 | 5 4 3 2 1

Binary: 11010010   00011000   00110111   000 | 00000

Calculate Subnet Size:

Borrow three bits from the host portion.
Last octet = 128 + 64 + 32 = 224
Subnet mask (/27 bits) = 255.255.255.224

Total number of hosts (including network
and broadcast) = $2^N = 2^5 = 32$

Subnet	NetworkID	First IP	Last IP	Broadcast
1	210.24.55.0	210.24.55.1	210.24.55.30	210.24.55.31
2	210.24.55.32	210.24.55.33	210.24.55.62	210.24.55.63
3	210.24.55.64	210.24.55.65	210.24.55.94	210.24.55.95
4	210.24.55.96	210.24.55.97	210.24.55.126	210.24.55.127
5	210.24.55.128	210.24.55.129	210.24.55.158	210.24.55.159
6	210.24.55.160	210.24.55.161	210.24.55.190	210.24.55.191
7	210.24.55.192	210.24.55.193	210.24.55.222	210.24.55.223
8	210.24.55.224	210.24.55.225	210.24.55.254	210.24.55.255

Figure 30-7   A class C network divided into eight subnets.

All subnets within a network need not have the same size and subnet mask. Variable length subnet masks (VLSMs) is a technique of creating subnet masks of different sizes within a single Class B or Class C network. A single Class B or C network can have a /25 subnet with 128 IP addresses, a /27 subnet with 32 IP addresses, and a /29 network with eight IP addresses.

Class B Subnet Masks

The default Class B subnet mask has 16 bits and a value of 255.255.0.0. Bits 1 through 7 from the 16 bits (in the third and fourth octets) in the host portion can be taken to split a Class B subnet mask. Table 30-6 shows the effect of increasing the mask from 255.255.0.0 to 255.255.254.0.

Table 30-6 Class B Subnet Masks

NUMBER OF BITS STOLEN FOR NETWORK MASK	TOTAL BITS IN NETWORK MASK	VALUE OF LAST BIT IN NETWORK MASK	NETMASK	TOTAL NUMBER OF SUBNETS (INCLUDING .0 SUBNET)	NUMBER OF IP ADDRESSES (INCLUDING NETWORK AND BROADCAST)
0 (full Class B)	/16	0	255.255.0.0	1	65,536
1	/17	128	255.255.128.0	2	32,768
2	/18	64	255.255.192.0	4	16,384
3	/19	32	255.255.224.0	8	8,192
4	/20	16	255.255.240.0	16	4,096
5	/21	8	255.255.248.0	32	2,048
6	/22	4	255.255.252.0	64	1,024
7	/23	2	255.255.254.0	128	512

IP Version 6

All the content in this chapter so far has been for IP version 4 (IPv4). The chief limitation of IPv4 is the shortage of IP addresses for all devices connected to the Internet.

IP version 6 (IPv6) is the next generation Internet protocol proposed by the IETF (www.ietf.org/) in November 1994. It was approved as a standard in 1998. IPv6 is also known as next generation Internet protocol (IPng). It is installed as a normal software upgrade and is interoperable with the current IPv4. It is architected to run well on high-performance networks such as ATM and low-bandwidth networks such as wireless.

Table 30-7 compares IPv4 and IPv6.

Table 30-7   IPv4 Versus IPv6

CONSIDERATION	IP VERSION 4	IP VERSION 6
Running out of IP addresses	IPv4 is a four-field, 32-bit address and can support 4 billion addresses, 75% of which have been used up. Anyone applying for addresses now gets a fraction of the remaining Class C space.	Ipv6 is a 16-field, 128-bit addressing scheme for individual interfaces or sets of interfaces.
Inefficient routing	Internet backbone routers have multiple entries for the same ISP or corporate network, thus resulting in slow, inefficient routing.	The hierarchical addressing scheme enables faster transmission because the routing tables are smaller. The streamlined header design (header compression) reduces latency and packet loss.
Guarantee of packet arrival	IPv4 is a best-effort transmission with no guarantee of a packet's arrival at its destination.	IPv6 includes guaranteed and selectable quality of service (QoS) for transmission over the Internet.
Security	IPv4 packets are not natively secure. IPSec (or IP Security, a set of protocols that support secure exchange of packets over IP) solves it. However, it does not work for NAT addresses.	The IETF has mandated IPSec security as a native feature within IPv6.

(continued)

Table 30-7   *(continued)*

CONSIDERATION	IP VERSION 4	IP VERSION 6
Mobility	IPv4 has problems with mobile devices and nodes and has limited support for them.	Each IPv6 mobile node has a home address independent of its physical whereabouts (care-of address). Other IPv6 nodes cache the care-of addresses and directly forward messages there.
Auto-configuration	IPv4 address configuration is complex. DHCP tried to solve it, but it is not a universal solution for all devices.	IPv6 has transparent self-configuration using router discovery without the use of a stateful configuration protocol.

IPv6 defines the following three types of addresses:

- *IPv6 unicast address* — A unicast address identifies a single interface. A packet sent to a unicast address goes to that interface tied to the IP address. There are three types of unicast addresses:

  - *Global unicast address* — Used for point-to-point communication.

  - *Link local unicast address* — This address is used for packets that must be kept local within a LAN segment or link. Routers do not forward these packets.

  - *Site local unicast address* — Packets with these addresses are kept within the intranet and the edge routers do not forward them to the external network.

- *IPv6 multicast address* — This identifies a multicast scope, which can be node-local, link-local, site-local, or global. A packet sent to a multicast address delivers copies of the packet to all interfaces within that multicast group.

- *IPv6 anycast address* — This identifies a group of interfaces belonging to one or different hosts. A packet sent to an anycast address is delivered to any single interface within that group (usually the closest interface is the recipient).

IPv6 addresses are assigned to interfaces, not nodes. A node is identified by the unicast addresses of any interface. A single interface can be assigned multiple IPv6 addresses of any type. IPv6 has no broadcast addresses. IPv6 unicast address format is explained in Figure 30-8.

IP Version 6 Global Unicast Address Format

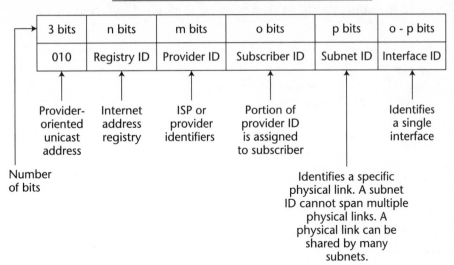

Figure 30-8   Format of an IPv6 address.

IPv6 addresses (128-bit) have four times the number of bits as IPv4 addresses (32-bit). The number of addresses in IPv6 is 4 billion times 4 billion times 4 billion (2^{96}) times IPv4 size (2^{32}). This works out to be 340,282,366,920,938,463,463, 374,607,431,768,211,456 addresses.

This is an enormously large address space. Theoretically this will provide 665,570,793,348,866,943,898,599 addresses per square meter of Earth's surface or more than 10^8 addresses per person on Earth. About 15 percent of the space has already been allocated, which means 85 percent is available for future use.

IPv6 provides a new IP format to provide enough addresses for the long term. At the same time, it optimizes the model for performance, robustness, security and ease of management.

Key Points

Following are some key points discussed in this chapter:

- IP version 4 offers Class A, B, C, D, and E addresses.

- Each network can be split into subnets, which are a group of devices that can communicate directly at layer 2.

- Communication between subnets occurs at layer 3 and requires an intervening router.

- Each subnet has a mask that determines the number of IP addresses within it. Subnets within a particular network need not have the same mask.

- Most of the addresses within IP version 4 have already been allocated and are complex and natively insecure. IPv6 provides a completely different addressing scheme that has adequate IP room for the long term in a secure and robust IP space.

CHAPTER 31

Network Technologies

New knowledge is the most valuable commodity on Earth.
The more truth we have to work with, the richer we become.

— Kurt Vonnegut

A *network* is a collection of user nodes (such as computers and printers) and interconnecting devices (such as switches and routers) that enable communication over various transmission media. There are a few fundamental requirements for a network to exist:

- There must be at least two devices.

- There must be some connecting medium (such as copper cable, fiber-optic or glass cables, or wireless media).

- There must be an underlying technology and protocol that define the hardware standards and rules of communication.

Chapter 28, "Network Devices," explained cable specifications (such as Cat5 and fiber) and physical media used for data transfer. Network technologies describe what makes use of the underlying media capabilities. This chapter provides the basics of LAN and WAN technologies. Ethernet is the most popular networking technology, but there are many others such as ATM, FDDI, and Token Ring.

LAN Technologies

Network technology is implemented at the data-link layer (layer 2) of the seven-layer OSI model. (See Chapter 29 for more on the OSI model.) For better speed and data integrity, it is important that the network technology is well-matched to the physical medium (layer 1).

Following are the industry-leading network technologies:

- Asynchronous transfer mode (ATM)
- Digital signal (DS) and T and E carriers
- Ethernet
- Fiber distributed data interface (FDDI)
- Synchronous optical network (SONET) or optical carrier (OC)
- Token Ring

Asynchronous Transfer Mode (ATM)

ATM is a cell-switching and multiplexing technology that combines two key benefits:

- *Circuit switching* — Providing guaranteed capacity and constant transmission delay.
- *Packet switching* — Providing flexibility and efficiency for intermittent traffic.

ATM divides digital data into 53-byte cells and transfers them over a physical medium (usually fiber-optic cables). The 53-bit cell has 5 bits of header and 48 bits of data. The header contains the source of the transmission. Individually a cell is transmitted asynchronously relative to other related cells and is queued before being multiplexed over the physical path. Each cell passes through ATM switches. The switch analyzes the header information before sending the cell to an output interface that connects the switch to the next appropriate switch in its path to its destination.

ATM operates over fiber cables at different speeds from 51 Mbps to 622 Mbps, as shown in Table 31-1. Its high speed and capability to transfer sound and video with integrity over large distances have increased its popularity around the world. ATM is designed to be implemented by hardware (rather than software), and, therefore, even higher switch speeds are possible.

Table 31-1 ATM Categories and Speeds

CATEGORIES	SPEEDS
STS-1	51.8 Mbps
STS-3c	155.5 Mbps
STS-12c	622.1 Mbps

ATM is asynchronous transfer and it differs from synchronous transfer modes, where time division multiplexing (TDM) techniques are used to preassign users to time slots. TDM is inefficient because if a user's time slot comes up and the user has no data to send, the time slot is wasted. ATM time slots, however, are made available on demand.

ATM has built-in and inherent support for data, video, and voice. Following are the main features of ATM:

- It segments data at high speeds into fixed 53-byte cells.

- It has the benefits of circuit switching, packet switching, and scalable bandwidth.

- It is used in high-bandwidth environments such as corporate backbones, campus backbones, and intersite WAN links.

- It has native support for data, video, and voice.

Digital Signal (DS) and T and E Carriers

DS technology is the transmission of messages based on DS0, which has a rate of 64 Kbps and has bandwidth equivalent to one telephone channel. DS-0 forms the unit for T-carrier systems in North America and E-carrier systems in Europe. DS1 is used in the T-1 carrier and has 24 DS0 signals transmitted using *pulse-code modulation* (*PCM*) and TDM. DS2 is the four DS1 signals multiplexed together. DS3 is the signal carrier in T-3 transmission and is equivalent to 28 DS1 signals (or 44.736 Mbps). Table 31-2 shows various T- and E-carrier levels and speeds.

Table 31-2   DS Categories and Its Derivatives (T and E Carriers)

NETWORK	DIFFERENT CATEGORIES	DS-0 MULITIPLES	SPEEDS
Digital signal (DS) or T carrier	DS0 or T0	1	64 Kbps
	DS1 or T1	24	1.54 Mbps
	DS1C or T1C	48	3.15 Mbps
	DS2 or T2	96	6.31 Mbps
	DS3 or T3	672	44.73 Mbps
	DS34/NA or T34/NA	–	139.26 Mbps
	DS4 or T4	–	274.18 Mbps

(continued)

Table 31-2 *(continued)*

NETWORK	DIFFERENT CATEGORIES	DS-0 MULITIPLES	SPEEDS
E carrier	E1	32	2.04 Mbps
	E2	128	8.45 Mbps
	E3	512	34.36 Mbps
	E4	2,048	139.26 Mbps
	E5	8,192	565.15 Mps

Various T-carrier categories are configured as multiples of T-0 channels. Each T-0 channel has a transfer rate of 64 kbps. A T-1 link has 24 T-0 channels, thus providing you a speed of 1,536 kbps (64 kbps × 24 channels).

T-3 connections are often used by ISPs to create backbones and to connect to the Internet. T-3 lines are made of 672 T-0 multiplexed channels, thereby providing a total bandwidth of 43.008 Mbps (64 kbps × 672 channels).

The E-carrier system is the European digital transmission format formulated and named by the Conference of European Postal and Telecommunication Administration (CEPT). It's the equivalent of the North American T-carrier system format. E-2 through E-5 are carriers in increasing multiples of the E-1 format. The E1 signal format carries data at a rate of 2.048 Mbps and has 32 channels (each rated at 64 Kbps).

Ethernet

In 1973, during his work at Xerox PARC, Robert Metcalfe developed a network technology that soon became Ethernet. In 1999, he said in an interview, "At that time (in 1973), we needed something that could connect hundreds of computers, printers, and file servers in the whole building with acceptable speed." Soon after inception at Xerox, the networking technology expanded to include large parts of the Xerox campus and wider geographical areas. It was embraced and further developed by Cisco, HP, and Intel.

Ethernet is the most widely installed LAN technology. Ethernet specifications are described in the Institute for Electrical and Electronics Engineers (IEEE) 802.3 standards. Other LAN technologies such as FDDI and Token Ring have challenged Ethernet. But the electronics used for Ethernet devices are less expensive and its large installed base provides the economies of scale.

There are various Ethernet-based data transfer rates. At inception, the speed for Ethernet-based data transfers was 10 Mbps. The next speed reached was 100 Mbps, also called fast Ethernet or 100BaseT. Ethernet transmission speeds of 1 Gbps are possible on fiber-optic or copper twisted-pair cables. Currently products to enable Ethernet speeds of 10 Gbps are being developed and marketed by several network vendors.

Hosts and other devices in an Ethernet segment communicate by contention. Each device sends its message frame. If the frame collides with another frame, the frames are aborted and the hosts wait for a random time interval and then resend the frames. In order to reduce the percentage of collisions (and subsequent aborts and resends), Ethernet uses an algorithm called the carrier sense multiple access with collision detection (CSMA/CD). The algorithm tries to sense if the segment is free and, if so, devices are allowed to send frames. Should a collision happen anyway, the colliding frames are aborted and resent later.

The clear drawback is that a lot of bandwidth is wasted because of collisions and retransmissions. It is estimated that only 37 percent of the wire speed is effectively utilized. This inherent bandwidth wastefulness is more than compensated for by ease of manufacturing, simplicity, and low cost.

Ethernet nomenclature seems puzzling unless you know the underlying reasons. Figure 31-1 describes the conventions used for Ethernet networks.

Table 31-3 shows the different Ethernet designations. There are three Ethernet speeds: Ethernet (10Mbps), fast Ethernet (100 Mbps), and gigabit Ethernet (1 Gbps and 10 Gbps). There are two basic media: BaseT ("T" stands for "twisted pair," which uses copper) and BaseF ("F" stands for "fiber-optic," which uses glass).

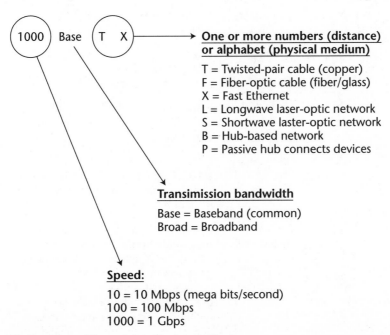

Figure 31-1 Ethernet naming conventions.

Table 31-3 Ethernet Designations: Ethernet, Fast Ethernet, Gigabit and 10 Gigabit Ethernet

DESIGNATION	SPEED	DISTANCE	DESCRIPTION
10Base-2	10 Mbps	185 meters	Operates over coaxial thinnet cables. Popular in the 1980s.
10Base-5	10 Mbps	500 meters	Operates over coaxial thicknet cables. Popular in the 1970s.
10Base-36	10 Mbps	3,600 meters	Operates over multichannel, broadband coaxial cables.
10Base-T	10 Mbps	100 meters	Operates over twisted-pair (copper) cables.
10Base-FB	10 Mbps	2 km	Used for LAN backbones and runs over fiber optic.
10Base-FP	10 Mbps	500 meters	Uses fiber-optic cabling. Links computers into a star topology without using repeaters.
100Base-FX	100 Mbps	15 km with single-mode fiber	Uses two strands of multimode fiber-optic cable per link. Installed sometimes as network backbones.
100Base-T	100 Mbps	100 meters	Uses UTP cables.
100Base-T4	100 Mbps	100 meters	Operates over four pairs of UTP cables.
100Base-TX	100 Mbps	100 meters	Operates over four pairs of Cat4 twisted-pair cables. Commonly installed for host-switch connections.
1 Gigabit Ethernet	1 Gbps	Up to 15 km	Used primarily over fiber for long distances and over copper for short connections.
1000Base-CX (1 Gigabit Ethernet)	1 Gbps	25 meters	Operates over two pairs of STP cables (copper). Used for inter-rack and short-haul data center interconnections.
1000BaseFX	1 Gbps	2 km for multimode and 15 km for single-mode fiber	Operates over single-mode or multimode optical fiber cables. 1000Base-SX uses short wavelength laser over multimode fiber, as opposed to 1000Base-LX, which uses long wavelength laser over multimode and single-mode fiber.

Table 31-3 *(continued)*

DESIGNATION	SPEED	DISTANCE	DESCRIPTION
1000Base-TX	1 Gbps	100 meters	Uses four pairs of Cat5 UTP cable. It is less expensive than gigabit Ethernet over fiber.
10Gigabit	10 Gbps	Multimode fiber supports 300 meters, single-mode fiber up to 40 km	Runs over optical fiber cables.

Gigabit Ethernet and ATM operate over a variety of fiber-optic cables and are the main contenders to replace FDDI as the backbone. Ethernet, however, enjoys a few inherent advantages. Network managers like gigabit Ethernet for two reasons: Their staff is familiar with Ethernet technology and it is compatible with wide-installed 10 Mbps and 100 Mbps fast Ethernet segments. Gigabit Ethernet was originally designed for LANs, but it also performs very well for WAN configurations.

Fiber Distributed Data Interface (FDDI)

FDDI is a standard for transmitting data over fiber-optic lines using the Token Ring protocol. It provides a speed of 100 Mbps and has dual-ring architecture for redundancy. The maximum distance is 2 kilometers and is sometimes used for corporate and carrier backbones.

In 1987, the ANSI published the first official FDDI standard. When it was introduced, FDDI was the first major fiber-based technology to operate at 100 Mbps. It has for years been used for installing network backbones to interconnect LANs, but it can also be used for connecting individual high-traffic hosts to the backbone. FDDI can extend up to 100 kilometers using extenders. This is possible because of token-passing and fiber's inherent long-distance support. However, most of the FDDI networks today are confined within an office campus or building.

FDDI networks contain two Token Rings for improved speeds (of up to 200 Mbps) and redundancy. High availability is important because network backbones are mission-critical. Each station is connected to both rings. Under normal circumstances, only the primary ring is active. The secondary ring is idle, transmitting only the minimum amount of frames to test its health. If the primary ring fails (because of link or node failure), the secondary ring gets activated. Figure 31-2 shows how the ring wraps around and isolates a failed node. Thus, the FDDI ring keeps itself intact.

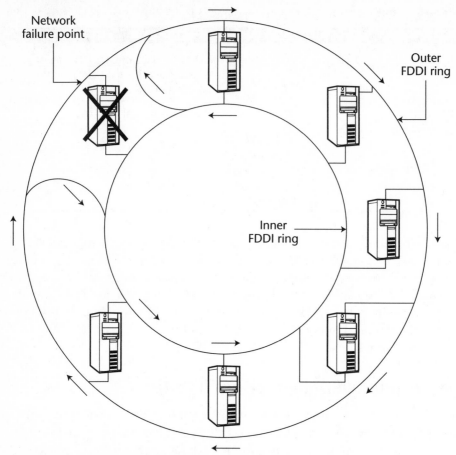

Figure 31-2   Dual-ring redundancy in an FDDI ring.

While FDDI is fast and reliable, it is expensive to install. Another implementation of FDDI uses copper-based STP or UTP cabling instead of fiber and is called copper distributed data interface (CDDI). Like FDDI, CDDI provides a data rate of 100 Mbps using redundant dual-ring architecture. However, CDDI transmits over short distances of only 100 meters.

Despite the early success and market penetration in network backbones, FDDI (or CDDI) has now faded away. Gigabit Ethernet and ATM have become the preferred technology for network backbones.

Synchronous Optical Network (SONET) or Optical Carrier (OC)

SONET is an ANSI standard specifying the physical interfaces for data transmission over fiber-optic cables. It was proposed by Bellcore in the mid-1980s and is now part of ANSI standards for connecting fiber-optic transmission systems. The international standard of SONET is synchronous digital hierarchy (SDH). Together, SONET and SDH ensure that existing transmission systems can take advantage of optical media and optical networks can interconnect in a harmonious manner.

SONET defines a base rate of 51.84 Mbps (optical carrier-1 or OC-1) and a set of multiples of OC-1, as shown in Table 31-4. Raw wire speeds of up to 40 Gbps are possible.

The OC levels form the foundation for physical layers for other network technologies such as broadband integrated services digital network (ISDN) and ATM. Most intercity ISP links are OC-12, OC-24, or OC-48 trunks running ATM. UUNet, one of the largest Internet backbone providers, has more than 60,000 miles of OC-48 between important cities such as New York, Chicago, and Atlanta.

Token Ring

A Token Ring network is a LAN where all hosts are connected in a logical ring. Each frame is transmitted from host to host in a round-robin manner as if the hosts are connected to a ring cable, until it gets to its destination. Physically, however, the hosts are connected in a star topology.

The Token Ring protocol is the second most implemented protocol after Ethernet. However, the cables, connectors, and network adapters are all different from what you would use for a Ethernet segment. The access concentrator for Token Ring networks is called a media access unit (MAU). (It is a hub or switch for Ethernet LANs.)

Table 31-4   Speeds for Different Optical Carrier (OC) levels

OC LEVELS	SPEEDS
OC-1	51.84 Mbps
OC-3	155.52 Mbps
OC-9	466.56 Mbps
OC-12	622.08 Mbps
OC-24	1.24 Gbps
OC-36	1.86 Gbps
OC-48	2.48 Gbps
OC-96	4.976 Gbps
OC-192	9.953 Gbps
OC-256	13.92 Gbps
OC-768	40 Gbps

A Token Ring LAN uses a deterministic method called token passing to allow host access to the physical network. It is a binary (0 or 1) token passing scheme. In token passing, each host must wait for its turn to get the token before it can use the shared LAN. The more hosts in the token network, the longer each host must wait for its turn to use the cable. This wait-for-your-turn policy helps avoid two hosts from initiating delivery at the same instant within the LAN. However, if there is a lot of data, deliveries will be initiated faster than the frames can locate their destinations. Such a situation leads to congestion within the ring.

A good analogy is a traffic signal, found before entering a highway. Each vehicle must wait at the traffic signal for its turn. If there are too many vehicles, the wait period will be longer. But, once a vehicle is given a green light, it quickly accesses the highway, where it can race to its destination despite congestion (if any).

This is how token passing works:

- Empty information frames are always circulating around the ring.

- When a host has to send a message, it takes one of the empty frames, inserts a token flag of 1 (the flag is a binary 1 that tells other hosts that the token is not empty), destination address, and the message.

- Each host in the ring examines the destination information in the frame. Once the right host gets the frame, the host copies the message from the frame and changes the token back to 0.

- When the frame gets back to the originator, it sees that the flag in the frame has been altered to 0 and that the message has been copied. It then removes the message from the frame.

- The frame continues to circulate as an "empty" frame, ready to be used by any other host that has a message to send.

This token-passing algorithm has many advantages. There is no media contention or collisions. Once a frame gets the token, it is in control of the ring. There is no collision or need to retransmit. All these make for utilization of the raw wire speed. The advantages of Token Ring over Ethernet are more pronounced for LAN segments with several devices. Token Ring can use up to 75 percent of the bandwidth (compared to 37 percent maximum utilization for Ethernet segments).

The transfer rate for IBM Token Ring (published in the IEEE 802.5 specification) is up to 16 Mbps. Although this is low, remember that Token Ring has far higher bandwidth utilization than Ethernet. Also, a 100 Mbps Token Ring specification is now being developed.

The advantages of Token Ring when used for large LAN segments also contribute to its biggest disadvantage. Most LAN segments being installed are small. Even large organizations set up numerous small LAN segments and attach them to a LAN backbone. Ethernet performs well for small segments. Another drawback is the high cost of manufacturing Token Ring adapters, connectors, and MAUs. Therefore, Token Ring has far smaller installed base than Ethernet.

Usage Trends

The trend is obviously toward faster speed over cheaper cables. The most common implementation outside fiber-cable–based backbones is 100BaseT Ethernet using Cat5 cables. The top contenders for network backbones are ATM (fiber), FDDI (fiber), and gigabit Ethernet (copper and fiber).

For the high-speed corporate backbones, ATM is preferred for networks that must transfer lots of multimedia data. For intranet backbones, gigabit Ethernet is gaining popularity because of its 1 Gbps speed and compatibility with existing 10/100BaseT Ethernet networks.

For higher transfer rate requirements, optical carrier (OC) and SONET are becoming more prevalent. FDDI is losing ground. ATM is gaining popularity for multimedia-rich LANs.

WAN Technologies

WAN technologies are used by ISPs to enable subscriber dial-ins and by corporations to connect those working from home or remote offices. There are two primary types of WANs:

- *Dial-ins* — This type is used to establish point-to-point connection between a user and a service-provider location. The connection can be established or disconnected whenever the user so wishes. Following are the popular dial-in technologies:
  - Analog dial-in modems
  - ISDN
  - Digital subscriber line (DSL)
    - Symmetric DSL
    - Asymmetric DSL
    - DSL lite
  - Cable modem
  - Satellite connection
- *Trunks* — A trunk is a high-bandwidth point-to-point connection between two sites. Its main purpose is to connect users at a remote

location to a central site. Traditionally T-1, T-3, or Frame Relay has been used, but now newer technologies such as virtual private networks (VPNs) are taking over. Following are some WAN trunk connections discussed later in this chapter:

- Leased lines such as T-1 and T-3

- Frame relay

- VPNs

The phone companies have switching offices and those at home must connect to a neighboring switching office to get to the WAN. The connection between the neighborhood phone switching office and the home is called the *last mile*. The term is not literal, because the distance to the nearest phone switching office could be several miles.

The last decade has seen a phenomenal increase in the number of dial-ups from home, not only for Web surfing but also for telecommuting. The large number of "last miles" has attracted many vendors and shaped technologies such as ISDN, DSL, and cable (see Figure 31-3).

WAN Dial-In Technologies

Dial-in connections enable a user to connect to the local ISP and Internet.

Dial-Up Modem

Most telephone lines going to homes are analog. Therefore, they require modems to transmit digital signals over analog wires that are designed for voice and not data. The problem with such modems is that the connections are at 28 kbps or 56 kbps — far slower than the standard 10 or 100 Mbps in the offices.

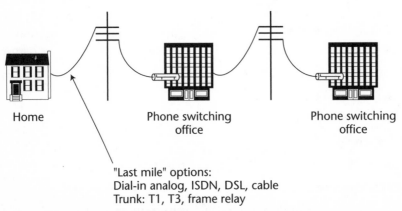

Home

Phone switching
office

Phone switching
office

"Last mile" options:
Dial-in analog, ISDN, DSL, cable
Trunk: T1, T3, frame relay

Figure 31-3 Connections for home users.

ISDN

ISDN is a communication protocol offered by phone companies to allow voice and data to be carried simultaneously over existing phone lines. It was developed in the 1980s to provide faster dial-in for home and small-business subscribers.

The chief improvement over regular analog/modem lines was that it was the first digital line to the home and all voice traffic was converted to digital. ISDN uses a customer premise equipment (CPE) to convert signals instead of modems.

There are two basic types of ISDN service:

- *Basic rate interface (BRI)* — BRI is meant for individual users. BRI consists of two bearer channels (B channels) with a bandwidth of 64 kbps each, and one data channel (D channel) with a bandwidth of 16 kbps. This gives a total of 144 kbps.

- *Primary rate interface (PRI)* — It is intended for small business users requiring higher throughput than BRI. It competes with dedicated T-1 links. A PRI connection comprises 23 B channels and one 64 kbps D channel. The total bandwidth is 1,536 kbps.

ISDN service has largely been replaced by broadband technologies such as DSL and cable modem. These are faster, are easier to install and maintain, and cost less than ISDN. Still, ISDN has its place as a backup to dedicated lines and in locations where DSL and cable modems are still unavailable.

DSL

DSL is a high-speed Internet connection that utilizes the same wires as a regular phone line. DSL assumes that user downloads will be three or four times larger than uploads to the Internet. Therefore, it divides up the available frequencies in the data line in that proportion. It is fast for downloads (receiving data from the Internet) but slow for uploads (sending data over the Internet).

DSL requires a special modem to split the signal between the upstream and downstream channels.

DSL has several advantages:

- You can use phone line for conversation while the DSL modem is actively transferring data.

- The speed of a DSL modem (1.5 Mbps) is much higher than that of a dial-up modem (128 or 56 kbps). It is a dedicated connection for each customer back to the DSL access multiplexer (DSLAM).

- DSL uses the same wires as regular phone and, therefore, requires no new wiring.

But DSL has it shares of woes:

- *Speed* — Uploads to the Internet are far slower than from the Internet.
- *Distance limitation* — The customer must be within 3.4 miles of the company office (CO), as shown in Figure 31-4. Even when within this limit, users at the outer fringes get poor transfer rates.

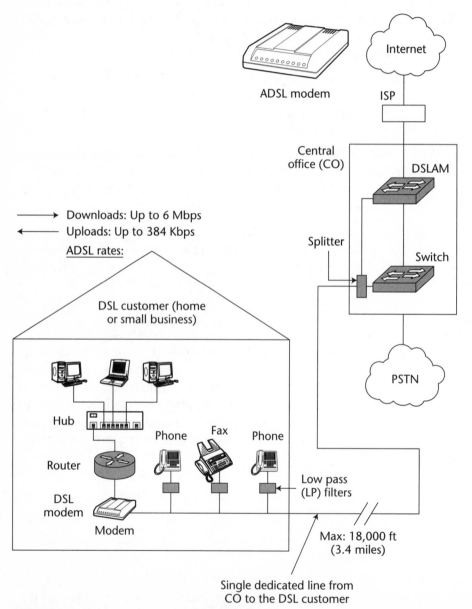

Figure 31-4 DSL customer and central office (CO).

Figure 31-4 shows that DSL requires two pieces of equipment: a DSL modem at the customer's site and a DSLAM at the provider's site (CO).

There are a few types of DSL:

- *Asymmetric DSL (ADSL)* — Most homes and small businesses are connected by ADSL. It can handle up to 6 Mbps for downloads from the Internet and up to 640 kbps for uploads.

- *DSL lite or G.Lite* — This is low-cost and slower version of ADSL. The splitting of channels between those for uploads and downloads is done at the CO and not at the customer home or business. Download speed is between 1.5 and 6 Mbps, and upload speed is between 128 and 384 Kbps, depending on the type of installed modem.

- *Very high bit-rate DSL (VDSL)* — This is a fast connection but works only over a short distance.

- *Symmetric DSL (SDSL)* — This connection, used mainly by small businesses, doesn't allow you to use the phone at the same time, but the speed of receiving and sending data is the same and up to 6 Mbps.

- *Rate-adaptive DSL (RADSL)* — This is a variation of ADSL, but the modem can adjust the speed of the connection depending on the length and quality of the line.

Cable Modem

A television brings news and various entertainment and educational programs for millions of households. Service to television is provided by a cable provider, who allows hundreds of channels to each customer. The same television channel provider often offers Internet connection for laptops, PCs, and other computers within each home. You may or may not use it, but most cable modems or set-top boxes nowadays contain a LAN port for data.

A cable modem is a device that connects to a television via a coaxial cable and also has a network port to connect directly to an Ethernet (10BaseT) port in a PC or to a router port that, in turn, connects to a hub or switch.

Most cable companies nowadays have a fiber-optic cable that goes from the company's office to different neighborhoods. Then the fiber is terminated and signals move on to a coaxial cable for distribution to each of the customers' homes.

The coaxial cable is capable of providing bandwidth to several television channels and data. It has more than 1,000 MHz. Each television channel is given a 6-Mhz slice on the cable. Downstream data (such as Web downloads) is also given a 6-MHz slice, and upstream transfers (such as sending e-mails or using FTP to send a file) are given a 2-Mhz slice on the cable bandwidth. The cable is, therefore, capable of accommodating more than 100 channels.

Table 31-5 shows the advantages and disadvantages of using a cable modem.

The cable modem communicates with a cable modem termination system (CMTS) at the local cable television office. All cable modems on the line communicate only with the CMTS and not to other modems that share the line. Figure 31-5 shows the architecture inside a cable modem. The CMTS provides the same service as the DSLAM in a DSL system.

The sudden growth in cable subscribers has led to different modem types from several manufacturers. However, the CableLabs Certified Cable Modems protocol (formerly known as Data Over Cable Service Interface Specification, or DOCSIS) has provided a standard for modem manufacturers, thus reducing the incompatibilities between modems and service providers.

Satellite Connection

In areas where DSL and cable are not available, satellite comes to the rescue for those in need of speed. It requires a dish antennae (shown in Figure 31-6) bolted somewhere high on the roof.

When data over satellite was introduced, there was one-way transmission (downloads only). Data from the consumer to the Internet (such as sending e-mails and FTP uploads) were done over regular phone line. Now two-way connections are common. Different ISPs offer satellite-based connections in different regions of the world.

Table 31-5   Advantages and Disadvantages of Cable Modem–Based Internet Connection

ADVANTAGES OF CABLE MODEM	DISADVANTAGES OF CABLE MODEM
If more and more power users are slowing the connection for others, it is easy for the cable provider to add a new channel and split the user base.	All cable modem users in a local area share the same network loop (and, therefore, same bandwidth) that runs through the neighborhood. As more and more users are added to cable, the transfer speed declines steadily.
The connection to the Internet is continuous. The actual bandwidth for data over a cable television line is up to 27 Mbps for downloads and up to 2.5 Mbps for uploads. There is no performance degradation due to increased distance.	If the television channel provider has a slow 1.5 Mbps T-carrier system to the Internet, that could become a bottleneck.

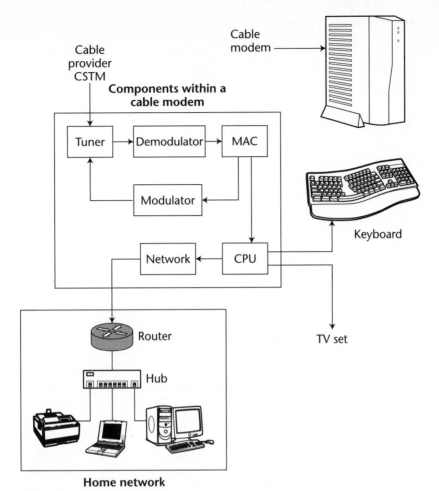

Figure 31-5 Cable modem connections.

Satellite used to
transmit data

Dish for satellite-based
Internet connection

Figure 31-6 Satellites are used to transmit and dish antennae to receive data.

WAN Trunk Technologies

Trunks are high-bandwidth, point-to-point links. They exist between buildings, campuses, cities, or even between continents. They are different from dial-in WAN technologies:

- The links are dedicated circuits. No one needs to dial in when the service is required or hang up when not needed.

- These are high-capacity links. Each connected site has several users and servers.

Following are some WAN trunk technologies discussed here:

- Leased lines (T-1, T-3, E-1, E-3, optical carrier)
- Frame relay
- ATM
- VPNs

Leased Lines (T-1, T-3, E-1, E-3, Optical Carrier)

A T-1 (trunk level 1) line gives you a secure and direct voice and data connection to another office location or an ISP. A T-1 line consists of 24 individual digital channels, each delivering 64 Kbps for a total of 1.544 Mbps in bandwidth. Each 64 Kbps channel can be configured to support voice or data. Some ISPs are connected to the Internet via T-1 lines.

The four most common uses of a T-1 line are as follows:

- From one point to another (often referred to as a private line)
- From one point into a secure carrier network (as with frame relay)
- From one point into the public Internet
- From one point into a carrier's voice network

T-3 is the successor to T-1 lines and has a bandwidth of 45 Mbps. Because of the high bandwidth and expense of leasing T-3 lines, they are leased as fractional T-3 lines. E-1 and E-3 lines are used in Europe.

Small and mid-sized business can live with T-1 and T-3 links. However, large enterprises, ISPs, and phone operators have optical-carrier (OC) links. As of this writing, ISPs in North America are offering T-1 leased lines at $400/month, T-3 at $2,500/month, and OC-3 at $9,000/month.

Other technologies described here (such as frame relay, ATM, and VPNs) require a link such as T-1, T-3, E-3, OC-3, OC-92, or OC-196 (See Figure 31-7).

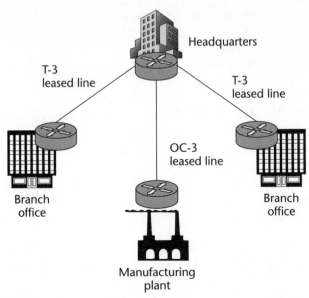

Figure 31-7 Leased lines connections to remote sites.

Frame Relay

Frame relay connects multiple locations by switching packets over phone circuits and infrastructure provided by telephone companies. The infrastructure is leased by the frame-relay provider and shared by several of its customers (see Figure 31-8).

Frame relay places data within variable-sized units or frame. Following are the primary benefits of frame relay:

- *Reliability* — Each customer is a permanent virtual circuit (PVC) that is a dedicated, continuous connection.

- *Cost efficiency* — The customer does not have to pay for a leased line. Customers are charged on the level of usage and requested quality of service (QoS) within the frame relay cloud.

Frame relay combines the functionality of a private network with the cost-savings of a public, shared network.

ATM

ATM is a data-link technology that is specified at layer 2 of the OSI model. The transmissions do not use packets but cells. A *cell* is a fixed-length message unit.

In ATM's case, each cell size is 53 bytes. Ethernet and frame relay use variable-length message units. Ethernet packets can range from 64 bytes to more than 1,500 bytes — about 30 times larger than ATM cells.

ATM's small and fixed-size cells provide a few outstanding advantages:

- *Highly controllable* — The receiving station can process the cells as they come in because it knows the start of each cell.

- *Speed* — The fixed cell size allows ATM to predict where each header and data starts within a cell, thereby speeding operations. The raw wire speed utilization of ATM is well above Ethernet's 35 percent and Token Ring's 75 percent. This makes it ideal for optical-fiber network backbones. Most intercity WAN links use ATM over OC-48 or even OC-768 (4 Gbps).

ATM (like gigabit Ethernet) is designed to run cables that follow the SONET specification. SONET, in turn, is an ANSI standard for interfaces for fiber-optic cables. The various speeds over fiber are called optical-carrier (OC) levels and they go from OC-1 (52 Mbps) to OC-768 (40 Gbps).

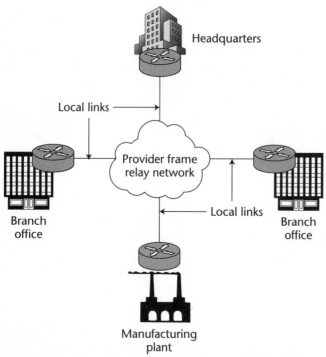

Figure 31-8 Frame-relay connections over a shared infrastructure.

VPNs

VPNs are an extremely affordable and scalable alternative to owned or leased lines (T-1, T-3, or OC). They are dedicated to one company. A VPN is set up over the public network such as the Internet. It enables a remote user (at home or at a remote office) to connect to the corporation's internal servers securely without using a leased line. Figure 31-9 shows a VPN configured over a pre-existing Internet connection.

VPNs use encryption and other security mechanisms to establish a connection (usually over the Internet) and to ensure that only authorized users can access the network and the in-transit data cannot be intercepted. Encryption encodes the data before sending it over the Internet. Once it reaches the destination, the receiving station must use the correct key to decode it.

VPNs are getting very popular because of their convenience in setting up, geographical reach, use of existing Internet links, and cost savings. Of course, it requires add-on modules to a router or new hardware at each end, but this cost is made up by not leasing lines for each site.

VPNs are discussed in more detail in Chapter 35, "Internet Access Technologies and VPNs."

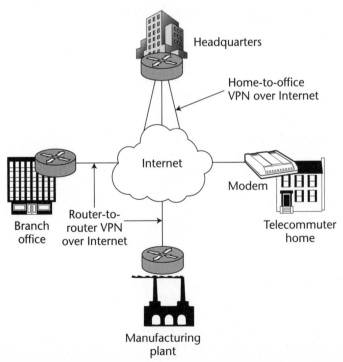

Figure 31-9   VPN provides a secure connection over an otherwise untrustworthy network or Internet.

Key Points

Following are some key points discussed in this chapter:

- The popular network technologies include ATM, T and E carriers, Ethernet, FDDI, SONET (or optical carrier), and Token Ring. ATM and optical carrier are widely used for fast WAN links.

- Ethernet is the most popular networking technology because of its good balance of speed, cost, and ease of installation. Ethernet is a well-accepted standard for server, interswitch connections, and switch-to-router connections. Gigabit Ethernet is being deployed for backbones and bandwidth-hungry servers. Indications are that 10 gigabit Ethernet will soon be available.

- Ethernet is followed by IBM's Token Ring in popularity. Its main advantage is that it avoids collisions and the payload utilization is higher (75 percent compared to Ethernet's 35 percent).

- Token Ring has a speed of 4 to 16 Mbps and FDDI 100 Mbps. However, Token Ring is fast fading off from new installations.

- FDDI, ATM, and gigabit Ethernet over fiber-optic cables are commonly used for corporate backbones and high-speed WAN links.

CHAPTER 32

Network Topologies

To be nobody but yourself, in a world which is doing its best, night and day, to make you everybody else, means to fight the hardest battle that any human being can fight — and never stop fighting.

— e. e. cummings

The word *topology* comes from the Greek word "topos," which means "place." Topology is the description of the physical layout of a place. In networking, it means the pictorial layout of a network, including hosts, other devices, and lines that connect them.

Networks can be defined by protocol (for example, an IP network or AppleTalk network), by the physical and logical connections (such as ring or star topology), or by geography (for example, a local, metropolitan, or wide area network). In spite of the specific criteria used to move data between devices or LAN segments, network infrastructures, in general, follow a hierarchy that extends from the physical layer up through the end-user application.

Architecture-Based Network Topologies

Topologies are logical arrangements and need not be physically cabled as shown in topology diagrams. A ring topology is shown as a logical ring, but physically it is cabled like a star topology. Following are examples of the various architecture-based network topologies:

- Bus topology
- Tree topology

- Ring topology
- Single-star topology
- Hierarchical-star topology
- Wireless topology
- Point-to-point topology
- Mesh topology

It is important to distinguish between intra-LAN and inter-LAN traffic. LANs are interconnected using routers. Based on a packet's destination IP address, the packet travels from router to router until it reaches its last destination router, which usually happens to be inside an office building or campus. Then it must hop out of the router's cloud and look at the wall plates and ports to find its destination host. This stage requires making the transition from the destination host's IP address to the host's physical address, also called the *media access control (MAC) address*. The transition is done via hubs and switches. All hosts, printers, servers, and other devices in a LAN must have a NIC with a unique MAC address. In short, The IP address gets the message over the routers to the neighborhood, and the MAC address gets the message over the hub or switch to the host.

Bus Topology

A *bus topology* is a linear architecture where hosts or devices are cabled directly to a line. All signals propagate the length of the medium and are received by all devices. Each device has a unique identity and can recognize (and accept) signals intended for it.

In the early days of networking, bus topologies were common. A fat coaxial cable called *thicknet* ran through the building. All hosts tapped directly into the cable, which seemed like the network backbone. This is shown in Figure 32-1. As technology developed, a thinner coaxial cable called *thinnet* was introduced. It was cheaper, easier to work with, and less bulky.

The topology and all its trouble remained the same, however. If any part of the network broke down, a number of hosts connected along the cable lost their LAN links. Bus topologies were hard to manage. Adding taps for additional hosts was a lot of manual work. Someone had to crawl into the plenum, find the coaxial cable, make a tap, connect a new cable to the tap, and drop it for the device.

The bus topology has given way to star topology, implemented using hubs and switches. This has provided network architects with a lot of flexibility in configuring logical and physical layouts. The star topology is discussed later in this chapter.

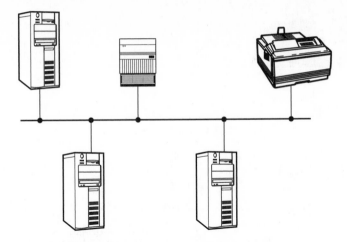

Bus Topology using Thicknet or Thinnet cables

Figure 32-1   Thicknet or thinnet coaxial cable-based bus topology. The bus portion is the common physical path for signals.

Tree Topology

A *tree topology* is similar to bus topology except that tree networks contain branches with multiple nodes. As in bus topology, all signals traverse the entire bus length. The advantage is that it requires less cabling than ring or star topology. However, if any device is broken, the sequence is disrupted and the entire network goes down. Therefore, bus or tree topologies are not used today.

Ring Topology

A *ring topology* includes two or more devices attached along the same signal path, forming a closed loop or ring, as shown in Figure 32-2. A controlling device, called a media access unit (MAU), manages the unidirectional flow of all packets along the ring. Each node in the ring acts like a repeater. Each node has a receiver on the incoming cable and transmitter on the outgoing cable.

FDDI and Token Rings are implementations of ring topology. However, Token Ring has the largest installed base and is described in more detail in Chapter 31, "Network Technologies."

Single-Star Topology

A *star topology* consists of a backbone or central transmission device, to which a number of network lines can be attached. Each line provides a port for attaching a host or device. The transmission device acts like a network concentration point, as shown in Figure 32-3.

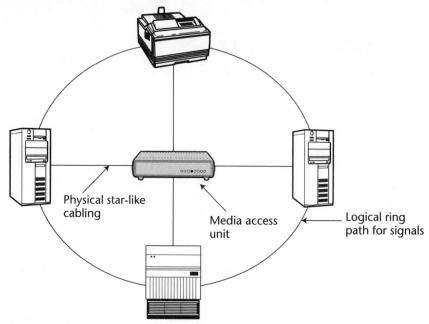

Figure 32-2 Logical arrangement within a ring topology. Devices are physically and individually connected to the MAU as in a star topology.

A star topology is set up using one or more hubs or switches, which have ports for network cables. Following are some advantages of the star topology:

- *Modular design* — It is easier to set up and manage many small segments, as opposed to a large number of interconnected hosts. Adding a host is as easy as plugging a telephone-type connector into a hub or switch.

- *Increased reliability* — Failures are localized within a segment.

- *Improved performance* — User traffic within a segment does not impact others.

A single-star topology uses one hub or switch to form a LAN. This setup is common in small office networks or home networks.

Hierarchical-Star Topology

In a *hierarchical-star topology*, outlying hubs and switches are connected to a master switch (Figure 32-4). This allows a far greater number of hosts to be connected to the network than is possible with a single hub or switch. There is also no need to lay many long cables to connect distant hosts. This topology is closely tied to the geographical or building layout. Each floor can have a single hub or switch, which is connected to the master switch.

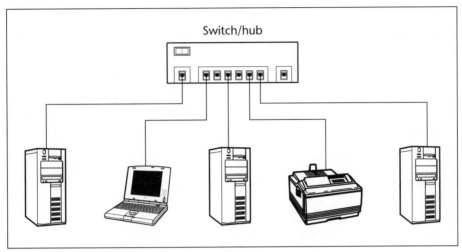

Single-star topology

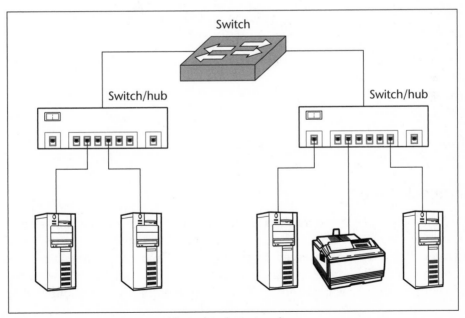

Hierarchical-star topology

Figure 32-3   Single-star and hierarchical-star topologies.

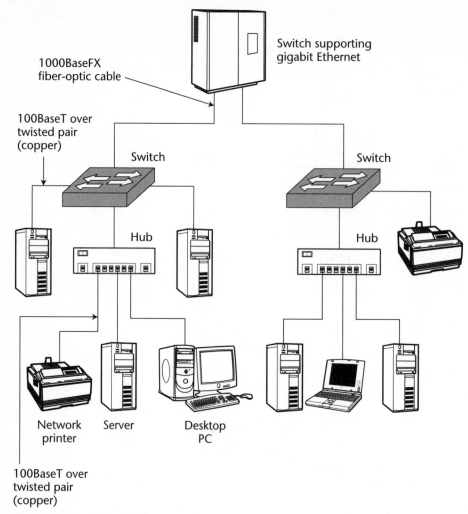

Figure 32-4 Hierarchical-star topologies.

Wireless Topology

A *wireless topology* has geographical areas that are divided into cells. Each cell has a wireless repeater. A mobile device attaches to the network via the cell's repeater. If the device is moved from one cell to another, it maintains network connection via another cell's wireless repeater. Figure 32-5 shows three cells with wireless repeaters and devices such as laptop computers and mobile telephones.

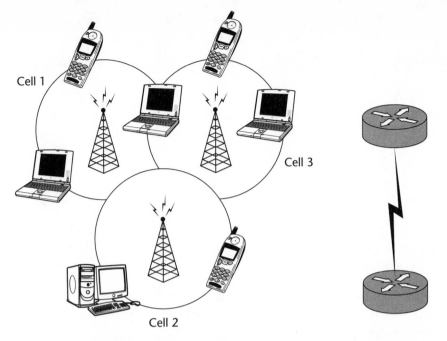

Wireless or Cell topology   **Point-to-Point topology**

Figure 32-5   Wireless and point-to-point topologies.

Point-to-Point Topology

A *point-to-point topology* includes two devices that are directly attached using a point-to-point connection.

Meshed Topology

A *mesh* is where two network devices (routers, switches, hubs, and so forth) are directly connected. A *meshed topology* includes several point-to-point connections between devices. There are three types of meshes:

- *Fully meshed topology* — All nodes have physical or virtual circuits to every other node in the network.

- *Partially meshed topology* — All nodes are connected to a few other nodes but not to all other nodes. Figure 32-6 shows two mesh types.

- *Hybrid topology* — Some parts of the topology are fully meshed and the rest of the topology has nodes connected to one or two other nodes.

Fully meshed topology   **Partially meshed topology**

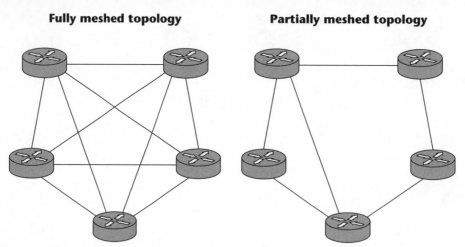

Figure 32-6   Fully and partially meshed topologies.

At first inspection, a fully meshed topology seems like the way it should always be done. It has high availability because of redundant paths and high throughput because of load balancing and one-hop links between any two points. The fewer the hops, the faster the speed. Despite these advantages, meshing must be used selectively because of its high complexity and cost. Each mesh link uses ports that could otherwise be used for networks or hosts. The denser the mesh, the more often devices have to broadcast their services and changes, thus eating into payload bandwidth. Dense meshes make it difficult to pinpoint a bad link or device. A misconfigured device will broadcast indiscriminate messages to devices farther from the source. For all these reasons, only backbones and core layers are fully meshed. Access and distribution layers are partially meshed.

Distance-Based Network Topologies

A topology is a physical arrangement of nodes within a network. A *topology map* represents each node and the media and links between them. Network topologies can be classified by the type of mesh (star, bus) or by the distance they span. There are three distance-based topologies, as shown in Figures 32-7 and 32-8:

- Local area networks (LAN)
- Metropolitan area networks (MAN)
- Wide area networks (WAN)

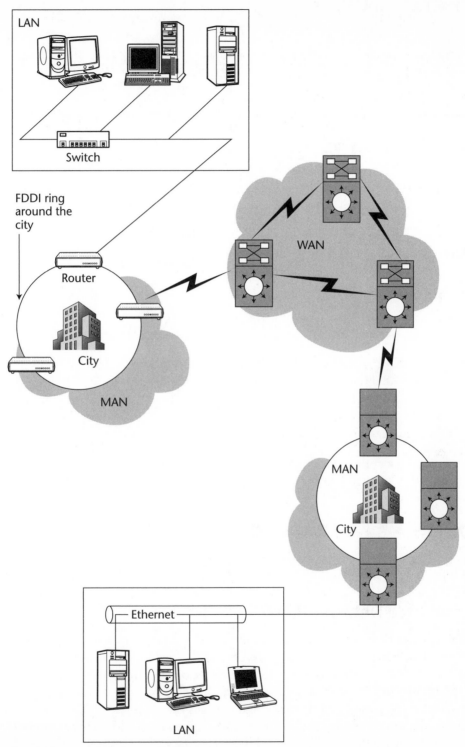

Figure 32-7   LAN, MAN, and WAN.

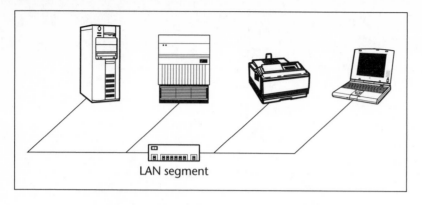

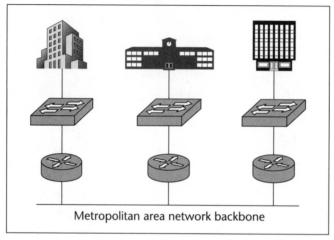

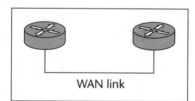

Figure 32-8   LAN, MAN, and WAN devices and links.

Local Area Network (LAN)

LANs are small networks that are limited to the confines of a building, office, or small campus. They are made up of PCs, workstations, servers, printers, and so on and are often connected with copper or fiber links.

The distinction between a LAN segments and a LAN is often blurred. A LAN segment is the basic building block and consists of a number of hosts, servers, and so on, connected by hub or switch. A collection of individual segments within a small office or building is a LAN. The Internet is a collection of many thousands of LANs.

Although a LAN is limited to a small area, it can be extended geographically via MANs or WANs.

Metropolitan Area Network (MAN)

MANs are high-speed networks that extend LANs across a metropolitan area or city. They generally span an area up to 100 kilometers in diameter.

MANs are used where there is a need to extend the reach of LANs to further distances but not far enough to necessitate the use of WANs. They have several LANs interconnected by a high-speed, fiber-optic backbone.

Required services and equipment can be contracted from service providers, or you can lease the fiber cabling from the service provider and build your own private MAN. MANs are typically architected using point-to-point or ring topology, and speeds range up to several gigabits per second.

Wide Area Network (WAN)

WANs connect networks or resources beyond the reach of MANs. As shown in Figure 32-5, WANs connect MANs in different geographical locations and usually provide a conduit to the Internet.

WAN links should not be confused with network backbones. WAN links connect distant sites, but a network or campus backbone is a high-speed (fast Ethernet, fiber-optic) link between neighboring LANs.

WANs are made up of geographically separated network equipment that are owned by telecommunications or network service providers. Each customer can lease an end-to-end connection with some guarantee of uptime and service levels. The service comes with a bill, the amount of which depends on the speed of the line, service level agreement, distance covered, and the level of competition among providers in the area.

WAN links are intercity telecommunications links on intercontinent links strung across the ocean floors. Currently most WAN connections are fiber-optic carrier such as OC-48 (rated at 2.5 Gbps) and OC-192 (rated at 10 Gbps) links. Older WAN links include T-1 (which run at 1.5 Mbps) and T-3 (known as DS3 in Europe and running at 45 Mbps).

Beside the above broad networks, there are several other acronyms that you will hear:

- *Campus area network (CAN)* — A campus is a building or group of buildings within a corporate campus that is connected to form one enterprise network. It consists of several interconnected LANs. It spans over a small geographical area and is usually owned and managed by one organization.

- *Residential area network (RAN)* — This is a LAN within a home, consisting of a modem and one or more hosts. It may also have a router, switch, or hub.

- *Personal area network (PAN)* — This is the set of devices that a person can carry and is part of a wireless network. Common devices include a cellular or mobile telephone, pager, and navigation system (typically satellite-based) within an automobile.

VLAN Concepts

A VLAN is a way of microsegmenting a layer 2 or layer 3 topology into separate broadcast domains. Each VLAN is a broadcast domain (that is, the broadcasts are seen only by the ports within the VLAN). In other words, ports within a VLAN share the same broadcast domain.

A single switch can contain multiple VLANs. Similarly, a VLAN can span several switches. Ports within a VLAN can be dissimilar.

Traffic is switched within a VLAN but routed between VLANs. Ports within a VLAN can switch packets to one another. However, to communicate with another VLAN (that is, another broadcast domain), they require a routing device (such as a router). A separate instance of spanning tree protocol (STP) is run within each VLAN. STP is a self-configuring, layer 2 protocol that is responsible for removing loops in a bridged network and providing path redundancy if the primary path fails.

VLANs are a good management practice. They separate broadcast traffic, restrict problems from having a widespread impact, and improve security. Heavy traffic within a VLAN does not impact other VLANs.

Key Points

Following are some key points discussed in this chapter:

- The most common network topologies are bus, tree, ring, single and hierarchical star, point-to-point, and partially and fully meshed topologies.

- Wireless topologies are rapidly becoming popular and deployed as an alternative to wired connections.

- LANs, MANs, and WANs are based on geographical distances.

Network Design

The tragedy of life is not that it ends so soon, but that we wait so long to begin it.
— **W. M. Lewis**

This chapter takes you through the design of a typical enterprise network. Most networks are hierarchical. Gone are the days of flat, coaxial cable–based LAN segments. As you will see, most networks follow a three-layer design. The focus here is on IP networks. You will need to consult more material if you design for non-IP protocols such as IPX or AppleTalk.

Later in this chapter is an exercise for evaluating an existing network and recommending a new, fast, highly available alternative that accommodates the existing infrastructure. This will prepare you to design LAN/WAN infrastructure in a systematic manner rather than just worrying about switch and router configurations.

Three-Layer Hierarchical Network Design

There are two types of network designs or layouts: flat and hierarchical. A *flat layout* is one where all devices do more or less the same work. As the number of devices in the topology increases, the overhead traffic increases. For small LAN segments, a flat topology is sufficient. But if the number of hosts increases by three- or four-fold, each LAN segment would be flooded with a high proportion of overhead traffic.

A *hierarchical layout* is one where the hosts are split into smaller LAN segments. Traffic from one segment does not interfere with other segments. A layered and hierarchical design model is one of the best practices when designing a network and is recommended by most expert architects. A hierarchical model allows the network to be designed in three discrete layers, each having its own set of components and functions. Such a modular network is scalable and robust. It can effortlessly accommodate most of the expected and unexpected future changes and growth.

A typical hierarchical network includes the following three layers:

- *Access layer* — This consists of hosts and end-user devices such as IP-based phones, printers, and PDAs that are connected to hubs or switches to make LAN segments.

- *Distribution layer* — This consists of switches and routers that are configured to implement security and network policies. They interconnect the access-layer LAN segments.

- *Core layer* — This consists of high-end routers and fast switches. They make up the campus or WAN backbone. This layer is optimized for performance and availability.

Figure 33-1 shows the different devices within the three layers of a hierarchical network. Figure 33-2 shows a three-layer network hierarchy.

Table 33-1 compares the three layers.

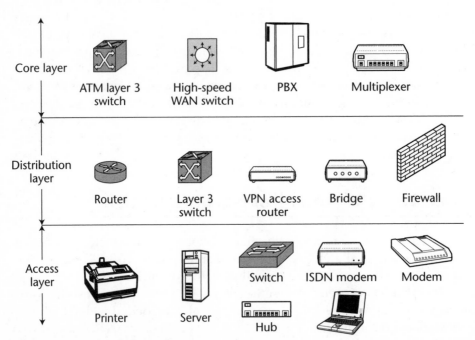

Figure 33-1   Networks devices in each layer.

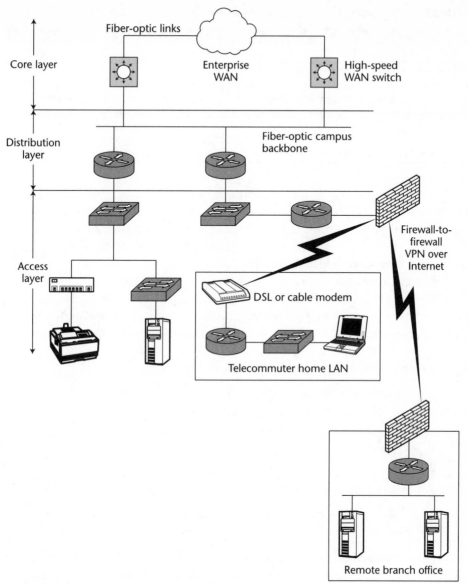

Figure 33-2 Three-layer hierarchical network.

Access Layer

This layer includes devices connected by hubs and switches. This layer is also referred to as the *desktop layer* because it connects hosts, laptops, printers, workstations, and servers to the network using repeaters, hubs, or switches. This layer ensures that packets are delivered to end users.

Table 33-1 Comparing the Three Layers in a Hierarchical Network Design

ACCESS LAYER	DISTRIBUTION LAYER	CORE LAYER
Desktop layer	Workgroup layer	Backbone layer
Connects hosts to switches and provides LAN segmentation	Provides routing, filtering, and WAN access and serves as an aggregation point for broadcast and multicast domains	Transports high volumes of data at high speeds and does no packet manipulation
Switches or hubs	Routers or multilayer switches	Routers or switches

Nodes are connected in a collision domain. A *collision domain* is part of an Ethernet network at layer 1 of the OSI model where any communication is sensed by all nodes within the network. Routers are sometimes used at the access layer to separate and to isolate overhead control traffic within LAN segments and to enforce internal security.

The access layer also includes access servers or routers to connect branch offices using leased lines (such as OC-3, T-3, or T-1) or a shared Frame relay network, as well as to connect telecommuters from homes and remote sites. VPN devices are used in the access layer for users connecting to the intranet from homes using DSL, cable modem, or ISDN.

At the access layer, you can do the following:

- *Configure MAC address filtering* — You can program a switch to permit only certain systems to connect to the LAN.

- *Manage switch bandwidth* — This is done to improve performance. Data is moved from one network to another to perform load balancing.

- *Create separate collision domains* — A switch can create separate collision domains for each connected node to boost performance.

- *Share bandwidth* — You can allow the same network connection to handle all data.

To recap, the access layer provides connectivity to local users via switches and routers and to remote (off-site) users via leased lines or via VPN over Internet connection (DSL, ISDN, cable modem, and so forth).

Distribution Layer

This layer includes routers and layer 3 switches. It is responsible for connecting different LAN segments in the access layer and ensuring that packets are properly routed.

It is at this layer where you begin to exert control over network transmissions, including what comes in and what goes out of the network. You can also limit and create broadcast domains, create virtual LANs (if necessary), and conduct various management tasks (including obtaining route summaries). Traffic from many subnets can be consolidated into a core network connection.

Although the distribution layer is primarily responsible for routing, it also allows enforcement of several policies:

- *Traffic separation* — This layer separates slow-speed local traffic from high-speed backbone traffic. Traffic at the access layer is mostly bandwidth-intensive because of the presence of individual hosts and overhead traffic such as SNMP and routing protocols. Routers keep the traffic local within subnets.

- *Address aggregation* — This serves as the address aggregation point for LANs and switches in the access layer.

- *Quality of service (QoS)* — This reads packets and prioritizes delivery based on preset quality of service (QoS) requirements.

- *Performance increase* — By default, domains are limited within LAN segments, but routers extend the boundaries of broadcast and multicast domains across LAN segments. This increases performance by sending packets as directly as possible to their destinations.

- *Packet filtering* — This creates network boundaries by regulating transmission of packets based on source, port, and destination information. At the distribution layer, you can also create protocol gateways to and from different network architectures.

- *Security features* — This includes encryption for VPN tunneling; traffic-based security using ACLs, and firewall rules, as well as user-based security and authentication using Kerberos, LDAP, and so forth.

Distribution layers that use multilayer switches (MLS) filter and route messages based on MAC and IP addresses. These switches have route-switching modules (RSMs) that perform layer 3 functions such as routing.

VLAN routing is an important function in the distribution layer. There are two routing mechanisms:

- *Static routing* — This is the simpler of the two. It is highly controlled and specified manually by an IT administrator. It is unidirectional and allows traffic from one specified network to another. It is resource-efficient, uses far less memory and wire bandwidth, and does not waste router cycles trying to calculate paths. The network administrator manually enters route information. But, it has some grave shortcomings. It is unmanageable and impossible to keep track of all routing tables. If there is a network failure, an IT administrator must manually log in and update static routes on all devices and hosts.

- *Dynamic routing* — This is preferred over static routing in mid- and large-sized networks. *Dynamic routes* are routes discovered by the network routing protocols and adjusted automatically for traffic or topology changes. There are two types of dynamic routing protocols:

  - *Distance-vector protocols* such as routing information protocol (RIP) and interior gateway routing protocol (IGRP)

  - *Link-state protocols* such as open shortest path first (OSPF) and intermediate system to intermediate system (IS-IS)

At some sites, the distribution layer can be used to allow incoming remote connections and serve as the demarcation between static and dynamic routing protocols.

Core Layer

This layer is the backbone of the network, because it usually is a high-speed switching network primarily dedicated to switching packets as fast as possible. This layer should be optimized for low latency and good manageability.

This layer includes fiber-optic or copper cables, high-speed ATM switches, and gigabit Ethernet switches. This layer should not be used to route traffic at the LAN level, manipulate packets, or be concerned about access list filtering (these are done at the distribution layer). The core layer must be tasked with only high-speed and reliable packet delivery.

ATM, FDDI, and gigabit Ethernet are the key contenders for the network backbones. ATM does all its processing in hardware primarily due to its fixed 53-byte cell size. This results in more than 75 percent raw wire-speed utilization. The technology is architected for T-3 (45 Mbps) and OC levels. OC-48 runs at 2.5 Gbps. ATM is preferred for voice and multimedia applications. FDDI operates at 100 Mbps and has limited backbone installations. Gigabit Ethernet is catching on because of its compatibility with millions of installed Ethernet LANs and familiarity among network managers.

Efficiency is the key word when designing the core layer or backbone. All other layers rely on the core layer. Packet manipulation, security enforcement, and other value-add routing services are best left to the distribution layer, and therefore high-speed switches (rather than routers) with low latency are the preferred devices in the core layer.

Following are important factors in core-layer design and implementation:

- *Load sharing* — Traffic must have multiple network paths to travel.

- *High reliability* — Multiple data paths ensure fault tolerance. If a path fails, data can use the other existing path.

- *Speed and low latency* — The core layer must use high-speed, low-latency circuits and switches that forward packets so that it is not bogged by policy-enforcement overhead. Gigabit Ethernet or ATM switches over fiber optic are gaining popularity. FDDI's limitation is its bandwidth of 100 Mbps.

Benefits of Hierarchical Design

Hierarchical network design has several benefits. It simplifies the task of building a scalable, reliable, and less-expensive network. Following are the primary advantages of hierarchical network design:

- *High performance* — It allows you to architect high-performance networks by localizing high-volume traffic within segments that are adequately equipped to process them quickly.

- *Efficient LAN administration* — It allows you to isolate causes of network trouble quickly and create a trouble-free (as much as possible!) network.

- *Policy creation* — You can create policies and specify filters and rules for each subnet.

- *Scalability* — If the network is divided into functional areas, each area can grow without impacting others.

- *Behavior prediction* — When planning for changes or upgrades, a hierarchical model will allow you to predict network response when subjected to another traffic level.

Campus Network Design

"Campus network" is one of those overly used terms in networking. Its traditional meaning is a high-speed backbone that connects the LANs in buildings located within a radius of a few miles. Nowadays the geographical realm has expanded to include a numbers of LANs that may be housed within a single skyscraper or spread across several miles. Whatever the distance is, a number of campus network designs have emerged. This section describes design components that are common to most campus networks.

The host-switch-router configuration encompasses the access and distribution layers in the three-layer hierarchical network design. These two layers and the hosts they connect are all usually located in the same building or floor. The access layer provides connections to the following:

- Remote sites by VPN over dial-up such as DSL, cable modem, or leased lines (such as frame relay, T-1, or T-3)

- Wireless access to laptops and other devices

- Wired hosts on the office floor or data center

Host-to-Switch Connection

Figure 33-3 shows an office building with multiple floors. Each floor has one switch or hub. More switches or hubs can be installed if you are out of ports for the hosts. As shown in Figure 33-3, the hosts are connected to patch panel using Cat5 UTP. Sometimes hosts are directly connected to the switch. A 100 Mbps fast Ethernet connection is widely used because of its low-cost infrastructure, high speed, and ease of management. Although each port in a switch costs about 30 percent to 50 percent more than those in a hub, switches are becoming more popular because of their dedicated full-bandwidth connections. Recall that hubs share the bandwidth among all active connections.

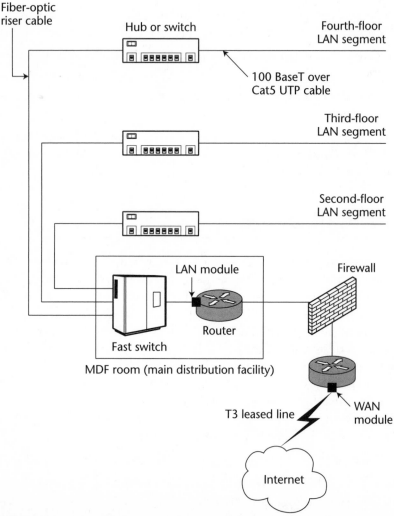

Figure 33-3 Typical hub-switch-router configuration within a building.

A typical host-to-switch topology is made up of the following:

- Network closet
- Patch panel
- Main distribution facility (MDF)

Figure 33-4 shows the *network closet* (also known as *data closet*) with switches and patch panels. A *patch panel* connects hosts to hubs or switches. It has rows of RJ-45 ports that are similar to RJ-11 telephone ports on the walls. Each hub port or switch port has a cable that connects to a patch panel port. Patch panel ports are also cabled to data center cabinets or office area RJ-45 wall ports, which are in turn connected to host NICs. Each office floor can have hundreds of devices.

On the other side, the uplink port of each hub or switch is connected to a large switch or router in the MDF, as shown in Figure 33-4. MDF is a small room containing equipment that terminates telephone wires and data wires leading right up to the hosts. The MDF is typically located in a computer room or a network closet. The riser cables from each floor snake down to the MDF through holes punched in the floors or via the elevator space. The riser cable is usually fiber optic for several reasons:

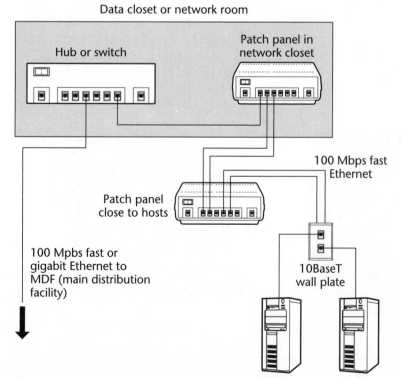

Figure 33-4   Patch panel and hub/switch configuration in an office floor or part of data center.

- The riser cables form a network backbone, connecting different LAN segments and therefore must have higher bandwidth than the 100 Mbps UTP cables used for hosts.

- The riser cables must have long-distance capability, at least up to 100 meters. Fiber optic provides the long-distance capability.

- Twisted-pair cable cannot be used because gravity (given enough time) will straighten out the twists in a vertically hung cable and reduce its electrical insulation. Fiber optic does not have twists and is unaffected by gravity. Fiber-optic cables have better resistance to electrical noise (from large photocopiers, elevators, or heavy machinery) than copper.

The strategy of placing switches or hubs in each LAN segment and connecting those to a central switch or router has clear advantages over having a router on each floor. Switches offer a higher bandwidth, use less subnets and IP addresses, and are cheaper than routers. Figure 33-5 shows a network closet.

The Switch-to-Router Configuration

At some point, users and servers must be routed to the Internet. Internal routers connect to one or more firewalls, which in turn are linked to routers with WAN ports. Each WAN port is connected to a dedicated T-3 link running at 45 Mbps or higher. Many small- or medium-sized businesses do not need or want to pay for the high T-3 bandwidth. ISPs lease a fractionalized T-3 or fiber link, for which customers pay and use a fraction of the total bandwidth.

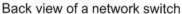

Back view of a network switch   Network or wiring closet

Figure 33-5   Wiring or network closet with rear switch view and patch panel.

Network Backbones

A *network backbone* is a relatively fast LAN that interconnects other LANs. It consists of a number of fast routers and switches, linked by high-speed, fiber-optic cables. These routers and switches move traffic between geographically distant sites and not within a site or LAN segment. (That is done by LAN switches.)

Based on the distance they span, backbones are classified into two groups:

■ *Campus backbones* — These cover a short distance (a few kilometers), usually through underground fiber-optic cables. Figure 33-6 shows a campus backbone connecting three buildings, with a backbone switch in each. The three backbone switches are interlinked by fiber-optic cable and also connected to downstream LAN switches.

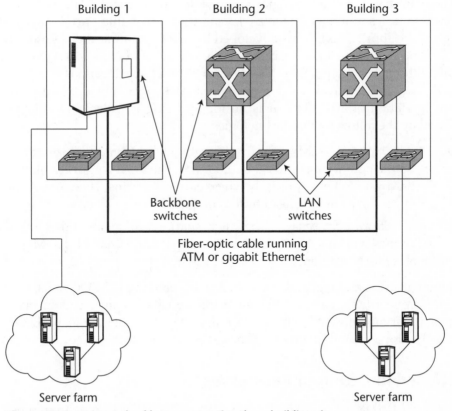

Figure 33-6   Campus backbone connecting three buildings in a campus.

- *WAN backbones* — These are installed and managed by Internet back-bone providers and used by large enterprises, ISPs, and telephone companies. WAN backbones move network traffic between cities. They use high-speed, fiber-optic cables strung underground or on the ocean floors. Sometimes WAN connections are provided by satellites.

Network backbones share a few fundamental features:

- *Main duty is to move traffic* — Backbones do not worry about ACLs, user authentication, port filtering, and so on. They are tasked with moving packets quickly, and therefore most backbones are switched and not routed.

- *They require high-speed devices and links* — Slow routers or switches have no place in a backbone. You need high-speed switches or routers connected by fiber cables operating at least at 1 Gbps.

The main backbone technologies are gigabit Ethernet and ATM. Both use fiber-optic cables running the SONET specification. Most links are OC-48 (running at 2.48 Gbps). SONET was developed by Bell Communications Research for fiber-optic cables and is the basis of Internet infrastructure. All ATM and gigabit Ethernet development is based on the SONET specifications.

FDDI was traditionally used for network backbones, but because of its speed limitation of 100 Mbps, it is no longer being installed and is being replaced by the following two technologies:

- *ATM backbones* — ATM uses a fixed-length packet format instead of variable-length format as used by Ethernet. The fixed-length cell allows the hardware to know precisely where each cell begins. Therefore, ATM generates very low overhead traffic compared to the payload.

- *Gigabit Ethernet backbones* — The quick, sharp rise of gigabit Ethernet backbones is primarily attributable its compatibility with 10/100 Mbps Ethernet LAN segments.

Although ATM and gigabit backbones use the same SONET OC links, they require different adapters and blades in the switches. Many vendors make switches that can house ATM blades (for an ATM backbone) or gigabit Ethernet blades (for a gigabit Ethernet backbone).

Switched and Routed Backbones

A *switched backbone* is a set of high-end switches that collect traffic from other switches. Their main task is bandwidth aggregation (that is, it combines what otherwise would be many hops into one hop through a single backbone network). To do so, the backbone switches have a large dynamic address table or MAC addresses and their respective switch ports.

Switched networks operate using MAC addresses, which have a flat topology (not hierarchical). A MAC address is a worldwide unique serial number assigned to a host's NIC. MAC addresses consist of two parts: the vendor (or manufacturer) code and the serial number of the NIC. Switched networks are flat because they depend solely on the NIC's MAC address and think that all devices or hosts are connected to the same cable. The message unit format at this layer is the *data frame* (or *frame*, for short).

Switched backbones are made up of several high-end switches for two reasons: to provide redundancy and to provide fast throughput rates. Figure 33-7 shows a switched backbone. It is implemented using one of the following technologies: fast or gigabit Ethernet, ATM, FDDI, or Token Ring.

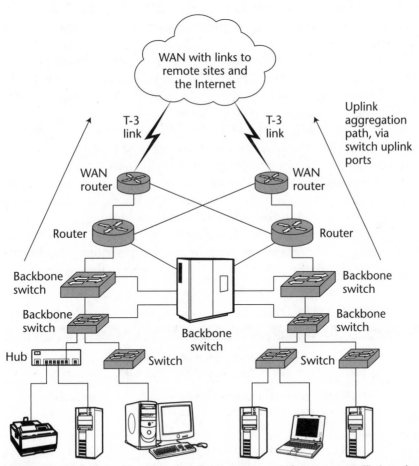

Figure 33-7 Switched backbone. Uplink ports on switches amass traffic into the backbone switches.

How does a switched backbone combine or roll up messages from large numbers of subsidiary switches? This cannot be done by routing because switches deal at layer 2 in MAC addresses only (not IP addresses or routes). The way around the problem is to use uplink ports to connect layers of switches. Figure 33-7 shows how traffic is funneled from hosts to host switches and then rolled up to backbone switches. Once the message gets to the backbone switches, it meets a much larger dynamic address table that helps it find its way. Table 33-2 helps to clarify this.

At layer 2, hosts on the network are identified by their MAC addresses. These are unique to each device and are burned into the NICs. The MAC address is a 48-bit address expressed as a 12-digit hexadecimal number (for example, 08:00:20:9c:91:67). The first six hexadecimal digits contain the manufacturer identifier number given out and maintained by the IEEE. The last six hexadecimal digits are administered by the vendor and represent the network interface serial number.

Routers interconnect LANs. A *routed backbone* is a group of routers that gather traffic from subsidiary switches and LANs and direct the messages to other routers. They use the destination IP address to decide the next hop for each packet. Figure 33-8 shows a routed backbone.

Routers are far more intelligent than switches and, at some level of internetworks, they are a requirement for messages to find their destination. It is, therefore, not possible to do away with routers. However, they are slower and more expensive than switches. Wherever possible, there is a tendency to replace routers, hubs, and so on with switches. At the high end, some routed trunks that do not connect to the outside world and have limited reach can be replaced by switches, thus providing speed, simplicity, and cost savings. At the low end, hubs can be replaced by access switches, providing the advantages of higher bandwidth. But switches are more expensive than hubs.

Table 33-2 Connecting Layers of Switches

START	USING	END
Layer 3: Data packets	Uses routers and network addressing to direct packets. Examples include AppleTalk, IP, and IPX.	Routed networks
Layer 2: Data frames	Uses MAC addresses to direct frames over switches using technologies such as Ethernet, ATM, FDDI, and Token Ring.	Switched networks
Layer 1: Signals (bits)	Uses physical media such as coaxial cables, copper twisted-pair cables, fiber-optic, and wireless.	Cables (copper or glass)

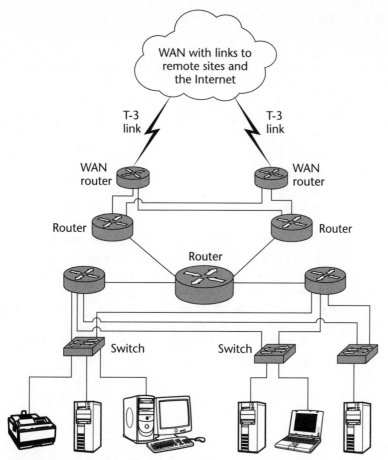

Figure 33-8 Traditional routed backbones will always be required for outside world connections.

Enterprise Network Design Phases

This section presents a systematic, four-phase network design process for meeting business and technical objectives. It builds a hierarchical network. The four phases are as follows:

- *Phase 1* — Identify the customer's technical and business objectives.
- *Phase 2* — Evaluate the current network.
- *Phase 3* — Design a new network.
- *Phase 4* — Document your findings and proposed design.

Phase 1: Identify the Customer's Business and Technical Objectives

This phase requires you to speak with various members within the corporation (up and down the food chain) to get their goals and what's on their minds. At the end of this phase, you will have a document with all requirements and current pain points. This phase is not about the current network configuration; that will be done in the next phase. Some requirements such as scalability, availability, security, and performance are universal. You might as well bring these up in your meetings. Focus on the following.

Business Goals

For the network design, some of the business goals could be to reduce telecommunication and network costs, decrease communication costs, increase corporate revenue, and increase employee productivity by making it easy and secure for them to log in remotely from home, hotel, airport, or any wireless hotspot. The existing customer team must be able to provide better service. Partners, vendors, and some key clients must have VPN capabilities to log in to the corporate intranet to access certain specific applications. There must be a robust disaster-recovery plan.

Technical Goals

The business requirements must translate into technical requirements for the project to be successful. If you cannot translate a business goal into a technical goal, then the network design cannot meet the business goal. Here are some examples:

- Increasing revenue is a perennial business goal and your network design may help to some extent (the sales and executive team have to do their part as well). All you can do is make data easily accessible to sales staff and keep a robust VPN system.

- In the long run, you can reduce telephone bills by enabling voice over IP (VoIP) telephone systems between the headquarters and the branch offices.

High Availability

If the customer wants "four nines" or "five nines" uptime, then redundancy and load balancing are a must. Technologies such as HSRP (hot standby router protocol) and spanning tree are essential. You must identify the application, servers, and LAN segments that must be up at all times. What is the cost of downtime? That will decide how much the customer is willing to pay to avoid outages and build robustness and redundancy.

Scalability

This is another universal requirement. It means that if the number of employees, partners, or clients were to suddenly increase ten-fold, the customer should not have to redesign the network and replace all devices and cables. Instead, the customer should be able to add more equipment (switches, routers, cables, patch panels) to the existing mix. Since the future is unknown and businesses plan to grow like there is no tomorrow, scalability is often a top requirement.

Performance

No business likes to have its employees sitting around waiting for the screens to load data. If an e-commerce site is slow, shoppers will click away. In today's Internet age, Web surfers hate to wait. In general your Web page must fully load in 20 seconds, or your visitor will start doing something else on the screen.

Network performance is a broad and complicated topic. If your client tells you, "It should be fast enough so the employees and clients do not complain," that is the client's goal. As a LAN/WAN designer, your goal is to get the capacity utilization, throughput, and latency.

Capacity utilization is the portion of the raw bandwidth used as a percentage of the wire speed. Ethernet networks can utilize only 37 percent of their bandwidth; the rest is taken up by collisions caused by their CSMA/CD algorithms. Token-passing such as Token Ring, FDDI, and CDDI can use up to 75 percent for payload data. You need management tools such as CiscoWorks or Tivoli to get current utilization before deciding on boosting network bandwidth. The capacity of a 100 Mbps link is 100 Mbps, but the throughput or capacity utilization is only 37 Mbps.

Latency is another performance parameter, especially over long distances or protocols such as voice over IP and videoconferencing. Delay caused by distance cannot be avoided. Adding more wire capacity or raw bandwidth may help at times, but the bottleneck could be the application. Compressing the data before transmission (especially at the VPN endpoint) would improve performance. Other helpful technologies are traffic shaping and QoS (quality of service).

Security

This topic is becoming more important by the day. Determine the sensitive data servers and applications. Create high-security segments for such servers. Identify servers that must go on the DMZ. Identify whether the client is using proxy services on their external firewalls.

Now you need to document these findings and refer to them again and again during the entire process. It is a living document. You will find new things, and your document must be changed accordingly.

Phase 2: Evaluate the Customer's Current Network

You should develop a strategy to understand an enterprise network. It is a tall order and, like many tasks that seem like a mountain, it must be divided into manageable portions.

You must also uncover the potential problems in the existing design and identify solutions to existing problems. Recall the needs identified in Phase 1 because you must look for ways to introduce solutions to meet those needs.

As a first step, you must get network diagrams. All enterprises have some level of network documentation. Getting them and understanding them is a good start. Some parts of the network will have no diagrams. Researching them and making up-to-date diagrams is the first step. Figure 33-9 shows a diagram of an enterprise's existing network. You should make both logical and physical diagrams of the existing infrastructure:

- *Logical diagrams* depict the flat or hierarchical nature of the network and show the logical architecture.

- *Physical diagrams* show the cabling between the physical devices, their physical location within a building, and geographical information such as building, city, and country.

The diagrams should also include the WAN links, VPN devices, authentication servers, and edge devices (such as firewalls, routers, and switches).

Network behavior is determined by a few key devices such as firewalls and routers. You need to get log-in access to these devices. Understand their setup and characteristics and document as much data as possible about these key devices (such as names, number of interfaces, MAC addresses, number of ports, and attached subnets).

Phase 3: Design a New Network Topology

As previously described, a topology is a conceptual arrangement of network devices and connecting lines between them. This phase designs the new network layout. You do not have to decide on the device model and type, but you do have to decide on the types of interconnecting devices (hub, switch, router, or firewall), size and scope of each network segment, and interconnection between them.

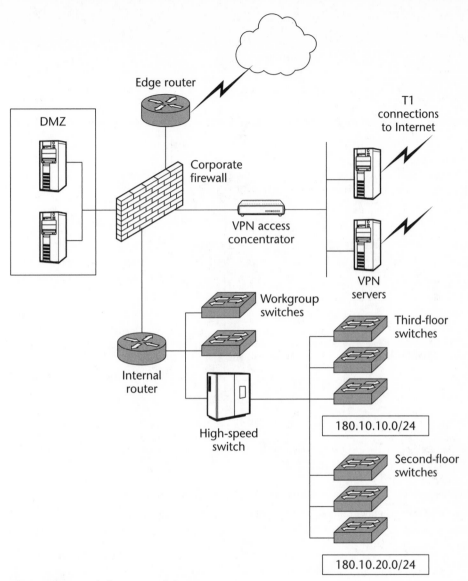

Figure 33-9   Existing network layout.

One of the best practices in network design is to use the three-layer hierarchical design described earlier in this chapter. Since network outage is a no-no, redundancy must be designed into the network. Figure 33-10 shows a three-layer network with redundancy at the access, distribution, and core layers. Such a design boosts performance and scalability.

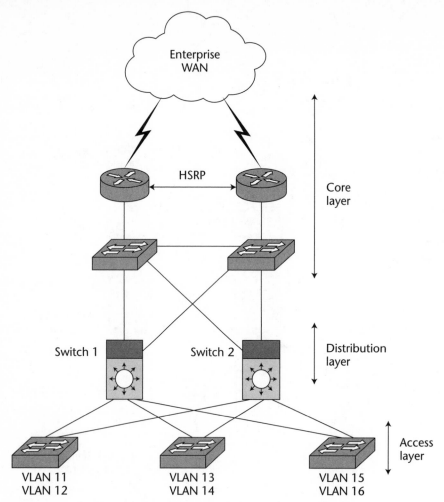

Figure 33-10   Highly available three-layered network architecture.

Figure 33-11 is a proposed network design. The core layer has redundant routers and firewalls. There are two sets of load-balanced Web servers, each feeding off different load balancers. The Web servers access a clustered pair of database servers. The campus backbone has two high-speed switches that connect the LAN segments in different buildings. The firewall connects to different VPN servers via a VPN access concentrator. The section "Best Practices for Network Design" later in this chapter describes some essential ingredients of a good network design.

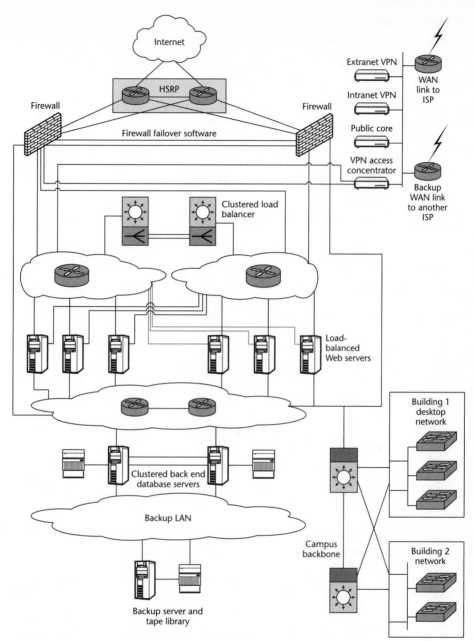

Figure 33-11   Proposed network layout.

Phase 4: Document All Findings and Proposed Design

Now that the network has been designed, the importance of a well-written proposal cannot be ignored. It does not have to be daunting; the readers are looking for a short but exact description of what is being proposed and why.

Sometimes the client will have a request for proposal (RFP) that lists the required format. If not, develop a document that includes the following:

1. Executive summary

2. Objective of the project

3. Scope of the project (what is intended and what is outside the project)

4. Business and technical requirements

5. Existing network infrastructure (including logical and physical diagrams)

6. Shortcomings in the current networks (gap analysis)

7. Proposed design including logical and physical diagrams

8. Advantages of the proposed design

9. Risks involved

10. Cost of implementing the proposal

11. Cost/benefit analysis and ROI

These sections will help make a comprehensive document.

Best Practices for Network Design

All network designs have a few common objectives:

- They must be fast, secure, and scalable and be able to accommodate future growth without requiring an overhaul.
- They must be robust, reliable, and highly available.
- There must be enough redundancy that service will be always available, despite device failures.

These goals cannot be achieved unless they are included in initial network design. The best practices in this section aim to meet the above goals:

- *Replace hubs with switches* — Traditionally hubs had a place in the wiring closet and routers in the data center. But client-server applications and multimedia-rich traffic demand greater bandwidth. Replacing hubs with high-speed switches provides the following benefits:
  - The capability to increase bandwidth to the hosts.
  - The capability to deploy bandwidth-hungry services safely (such as multimedia and large databases).
  - The capability to implement VLANs to organize hosts into logical workgroups that are independent of wiring closets and physical

whereabouts. This increases flexibility by reducing the amount of work involved in moves, adds, and changes.

- The capability to lay the roadmap for future upgrades to fiber-based ATM or gigabit Ethernet switches.

- *Divide network into small LAN segments* — Splitting a shared LAN into LAN segments reduces the number of users contending for bandwidth. The rule is to keep subnets with as few hosts as possible. It helps localize traffic within a segment. High user, voice, and video traffic on a segment does impact the neighboring segments. Also, faults and problems within a segment are confined within the segment. Segmentation makes it easier to add, remove, and troubleshoot network devices.

- *Implement three-layer hierarchical design* — It allows for graceful changes and adding more devices in the future. Robustness and availability can be implemented at each layer. Network traffic is also separated by LAN segments. It also adds scalability. If the number of users increases (tenfold, for example), it is easy to add more switches at the distribution layer.

- *Use VLANs to enhance flexibility* — With VLANs, a user can be moved to anywhere in the enterprise without having to change the static IP address of the user's devices as long as the VLAN number remains the same. This makes it easy to add or move devices and contributes to increased scalability and ease of management.

- *Use hot standby router protocol (HSRP) for routers* — This increases availability by having a standby, redundant router.

- *Use spanning tree protocol (STP) for switches* — This increases switch availability because it guarantees a layer-2 path between two devices. STP enables an active path between two nodes and a redundant path will be activated if and when the active path dies. In Figure 33-10, switch 1 provides the active path for VLANs 11, 13, and 15 by acting as the root bridge. Similarly switch 2 is the root bridge for VLANs 12, 14, and 16. Under normal conditions, each switch services different VLANs and share the network load (three VLANs per switch). If one switch fails, the other switch takes up the load of all six VLANs. This design boosts performance and availability of the network.

- *Using backup WAN links* — When it comes to WAN links, a network administrator is less in control than with LANs. WAN links are leased from a service provider. Select a trustworthy WAN provider with a competitive SLA. Get statements about the WAN's reliability, availability, and scalability (RAS). A failsafe strategy is to get a backup WAN link (T-1, frame relay, fiber) from another service provider. A weak point to note is that WAN service providers lease capacity to each other, either directly or through third-party companies. This makes it difficult to judge if different WAN links are or will be truly diverse. They may share the same cable or telecommunication facilities somewhere in the connection.

Key Points

Following are some key points discussed in this chapter:

- This chapter introduced and discussed the three-layer hierarchical design, namely access (hosts and LAN segments), distribution (routers), and core layer (campus backbones and WAN links).

- Network architectures with switched backbones have better performance. ATM and gigabit Ethernet are chief contenders at the backbone layer.

- An enterprise network design requires four phases: objective determination, current network evaluation, design, and documentation.

- A good network architecture requires an upfront and thorough evaluation of the business and technical goals, as well as the benefits and shortcomings of current network. The evaluation is followed by a network architecture that optimizes performance, can be expanded to meet growth, is reliable, and is easy to manage. A three-layer design with redundancy will help meet most required goals.

CHAPTER 34

Designing Fault-Tolerant Networks

I will prepare and someday my chance will come.
— Abraham Lincoln

A *fault-tolerant network* is one that has high uptime, made possible mostly by having redundant components. Failure of any network device does not bring the network or service to a halt. The failure is transparent to users and other devices. This chapter describes various approaches you can take to make your network resilient to device or link failures.

Importance of Highly Available Networks

Network-based computing has become a vital business tool. Uninterrupted availability of data and network services is critical for business operations. Applications such as e-commerce and enterprise resource planning (ERP), as well as several other rapidly growing business tools, need quick access to data and servers over the network. For some companies (such as a Web-based retailer), the network is virtually the entire business infrastructure.

Because of the rapid growth of information on the Internet and company intranet, customers and employees have become dependent on data available on the Web. It has become an important channel for marketing, public relations, product information and distribution, and customer support and communication. Additionally e-mail has become the preferred channel of intraenterprise and external communications. Unlike voicemails, e-mails do not have an incremental cost of usage, support automated responses, and can send the same message to a broad audience.

ERP databases have become the most important and up-to-date repository required for critical business decisions. Several network-based applications are being deployed to improve the efficiencies of sales, customer support, and human resources. These applications require access to each other and to ERP databases to achieve enterprise application integration (EAI).

Besides data, several other applications (such as streaming media, Internet-based call centers, voice, and Unified Messaging) use an IP-based network. This will lead to a converged or multiservice network, which will be far more mission-critical than any single service network. It will support emerging communication services such as video-on-demand, voice over IP (VoIP), multimedia conferencing, and streaming live audio and video for remote events.

As more and more services are consolidated onto a single network infrastructure, the availability of the network becomes critical to the entire organization. If e-mail and voice use the same infrastructure, the redundancy between these two means of communication is lost unless the network itself guarantees availability.

Although some organizations may not be quick to deploy all mission-critical applications over a network infrastructure, it is clear that high network availability is becoming a basic requirement.

Implementing High-Availability Networks

This section describes ways to improve the availability of host connection and the entire network. High availability (HA) can be achieved by introducing the following:

- Fault-tolerant devices
- Redundant network interface cards (NICs) in a host
- Redundant network topologies

Availability through Fault-Tolerant Devices

One way to implement highly available networks is to use extremely fault-tolerant network devices throughout the network. Each key component within the device has a backup. For example, a fault-tolerant switch has redundant power supplies, fans, switch processors, switch fabrics, and multilinked connections. This approach can result in high mean time between failures (MTBF). However, there are a number of drawbacks in trying to achieve network HA only through device-level fault tolerance:

- Duplicate components within a device add to the equipment cost.

- Device firmware must be intelligent enough to detect and replace a failed component.

- Redundant or duplicate components often run in a hot-standby mode and, under normal conditions, do not contribute to the performance of the entire device.

- The network may be made of several fault-tolerant devices, but each device is a single point of failure (SPOF). Network devices reside in a physical environment that requires human operators, electrical power, and environmental control. The operation of each device and interaction with other devices is governed by internal firmware, software, and configuration parameters. Imperfections or failures in any of these factors can cause entire devices to fail. Such an event cannot be overcome by component-level redundancy or fault tolerance.

Availability through Redundant NICs in a Host

There are some simple ways to implement redundant network connectivity for a host:

- Use multiple NICs in a host to connect to the same network.

- Connect a host to more than one network.

- Do both of these.

Figure 34-1 shows a two-node cluster. Each node has two NICs. The redundancy protects against failures in the NIC, the system board containing the NIC, and the cable from the NIC to network hub or switch. You must configure both NICs as an active/passive pair, with the passive NIC attached to the same network as the primary. The passive NIC should not be on the same system board or controller as the primary NIC. This will protect against the possibility that system board or controller failure can bring down all NICs simultaneously.

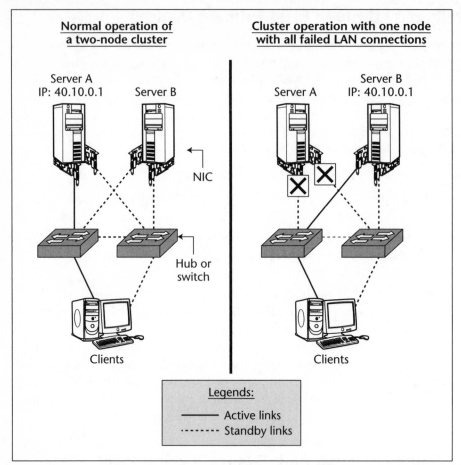

Figure 34-1 IP address fails over to an alternate host if all LAN connections for active cluster members fail.

Some clustering software includes an automatic network IP address failover mechanism. VERITAS Cluster Server (VCS) software has an agent called Multi-NICA, which supports asymmetric redundant NIC pairs. If the active NIC fails, the IP address fails over to the standby NIC on the same host. You can write a script that runs every so often and monitors the output of a `netstat` or `ping` command and, upon finding an unresponsive network link, activates the standby NIC. However, home-grown scripts and software have their share of woes. Typically homegrown software is not tested extensively. Innovation and creativity are important, but scripts that are not well-tested but used on production servers can lead to unforeseen problems. Support is limited to the developer's availability and willingness to troubleshoot problems.

Some cluster software offers a feature called *subnet-failure detection* and consequent IP migration to another host in the cluster. As shown in Figure 34-1, if all NICs in server A fail, all connections to server A are severed and its IP address migrates to an NIC in server B. Clients will again connect to the IP address, which happens to be on server B now.

Interface trunking is another way to implement NIC redundancy. It has the advantage of improved bandwidth between host and the network. Trunking enables a group of network links between two devices to be coalesced into a single virtual interface with the capacity of the individual links. Trunking improves network performance, just as RAID-0 or striping increases I/O performance. All links are active. Multiple cables must run between the host and switch, as shown in Figure 34-2. Both the switch and the host must support trunking software. Just like the redundant NIC case, the trunk has a single IP address. The trunking software transparently handles any NIC or cable breakdown. The failure is masked from users and applications.

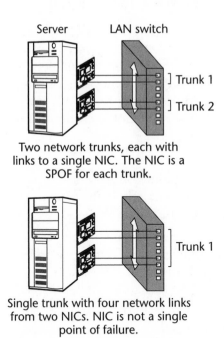

Two network trunks, each with
links to a single NIC. The NIC is a
SPOF for each trunk.

Single trunk with four network links
from two NICs. NIC is not a single
point of failure.

Figure 34-2   Two examples of trunked network interfaces.

While trunking increases redundancy and performance, the NIC can be a single point of failure (SPOF) if all links in the trunk are tied to the same physical NIC. The performance advantage of grouping multiple pipes together is realized only if a single connection causes a bandwidth bottleneck. An NFS server can suffer from a bandwidth bottleneck if multiple NFS client segments come into a switch. The aggregate read/write requests to the NFS server may be higher than the capacity of a single network link or even higher than the capacity of the internal bus of the switch. Running multiple links from the server to distinct switches helps alleviate network congestion.

Common implementations of network trunking are Adapter Teaming from Intel, Sun Trunking Software from Sun Microsystems, and Multi-mode Trunk implemented from Network Appliance. Understand that the warm feeling you get from bundling multiple pipes together helps the clients only if your servers are network-bandwidth limited.

Availability through Redundant Network Topologies

Another approach to building highly available networks is by providing redundancy at the device level in the topology rather than within the host or network device. Following this approach, you must configure redundant network devices and links (configured to automatically failover from primary to secondary device or link). Network services would be interrupted briefly during the failover from active to standby. Therefore, it is important to ensure that the failover time is acceptable (usually a few seconds).

This approach has several benefits:

- Problems and changes in the firmware, configuration parameters, and software within a device can be dealt with separately in the primary and backup paths without interrupting network services.

- The primary and backup devices can be located in separate physical areas. This reduces the chance of service interruption caused by problems in the physical environment.

- Since redundancy is introduced by a backup device, the requirements for fault tolerance at the component level can be partially relaxed. This reduces the cost of each network device offsetting the expense of redundant devices.

- The primary and secondary paths can be configured to share run-time load during normal operations. This increases aggregate performance and capacity.

The key to eliminating network failures is understanding the network topology being used, identifying the SPOFs, and removing the failure points from the configuration. There are several types of network topologies, and each has its own SPOF. The campus network shown in Figure 34-3 has single points of failure: the NICs within the servers, the access layer switch, the multilayer switch (in the distribution layer), and the router (in the core layer). Figure 34-4 shows a highly available network with a backup for every link or device between the servers and the client at the remote site.

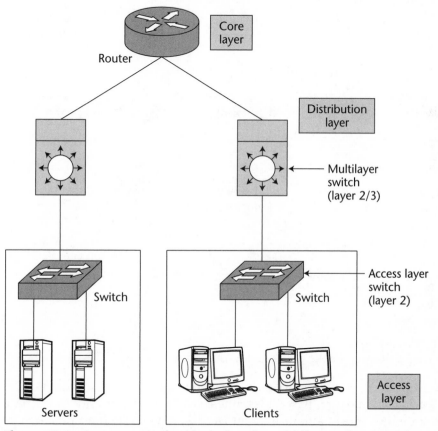

Figure 34-3 Campus network with single points of failure at the access layer switch, multilayer switch, and router.

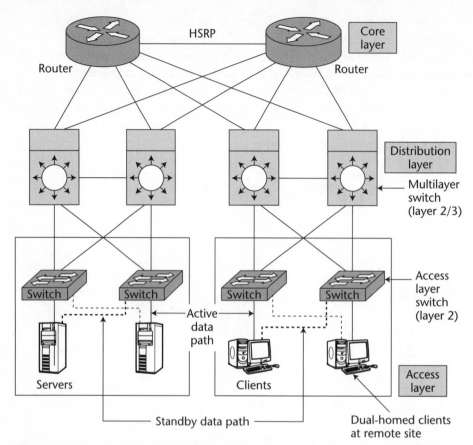

Figure 34-4 Campus network with redundancy at each layer (access, distribution, and core) due to failover devices.

Best Practices

You must evaluate your network topology and identify (and plan to eliminate) SPOFs using redundant NICs, cables, hubs, switches, or concentrators. These network devices must be fault tolerant (that is, have redundant power supplies, fans, switch processors, and so on) and allow online maintenance.

Removing the SPOFs and setting up servers for failing over IP addresses from a failed NIC to another NIC within the same server or another server are the initial steps toward improving network availability. A successful implementation of a highly available network involves a right combination of the following considerations:

- *Failure diagnosis and management* — All faults must be carefully diagnosed. You should make adjustments to prevent recurrences of the same types of faults. An accurate event correlation requires that the time on all network devices be synchronized with a central time server.

- *Device-level reliability* — An appropriate level of fault tolerance must be configured on all network devices, the degree of which can be in proportion to the impact of the hardware failure. Core and distribution switches (which form the backbone of corporate networks) require a greater degree of fault tolerance than switches connected to end-user workstations.

- *Network-level redundancy* — Configuring redundant network devices ensures uninterrupted services despite a hardware or nonhardware failure of a device. Wherever active/passive redundant pairs are set up, the failover from an active to a standby device should take just a few seconds. The design should allow a failed device to be serviced without need to take the device off-line.

- *Load sharing among redundant devices* — Study the network traffic loads and patterns to decide if the redundant devices should also be used under normal operations. If necessary, use the secondary paths or devices to share the network traffic. This improves network performance under normal circumstances and when a minimum number of ports and links are idle. However, the disadvantage of an active-active pair is the high load on the surviving device in case of a failure.

- *Operational practices* — Hardware failures are not the only reason for network outages. Nonhardware failures also cause network downtime. These failures can be avoided by following some guidelines in software version and device configuration control. There should be proper cabling in the computer room and wiring closets. Maintain tight security and user access privileges. Invest time in regularly inspecting your physical site. These steps will provide measurable reduction in failure rate.

- *Documentation* — You should have detailed and clear documentation of the current networking environment. There should be ongoing plans and work done to improve network availability. Step-by-step procedures for replacing failed parts or network devices should be well-documented and understood by all.

Highly available networks can be configured and maintained, but it takes careful investigation and planning.

Key Points

Following are some key points discussed in this chapter:

- With the emergence of multiservice networks that support data, voice, and streaming media applications over an IP infrastructure, the need for fault-tolerant networks has never been so critical.

- Reliability and high-availability features have become pressing goals for all IT designs. You can take several steps to increase network availability.

- Resilient networks are designed by understanding the topology, identifying single points of failure, and removing them as far as possible.

- NICs within a server can be set up as active-active or active-standby pairs.

- Failover management software is required to migrate the services and floating IP address.

- Trunking is used to group several network links into a single virtual network interface, which can be configured to use only one IP address. Link failures are handled transparently. Performance increases as all links are active.

Internet Access Technologies and VPNs

Don't go around saying the world owes you a living.
The world owes you nothing. It was here first.
— Mark Twain

The preceding chapters on networking describe how networks function and data flows. Starting from the host and UTP cables, the message travels to the hubs to switches to routers and finally to its destination across the street or in another part of the world via satellite or fiber-optic cables on the ocean bed. Private networks have been established over the otherwise wild and untrusted Internet. Businesses, commerce, documentation, news, and so on have taken no time to move to the Internet. Most corporations around the world have moved almost all their financial and business data online in an attempt to make data readily available.

In this interconnected world, almost all communications are two-way. If your network can get to anyone outside your company for business, anyone can get back to your company as well. Not everyone is as busy as those scurrying hastily around downtown Manhattan or Tokyo. Some people around the world who have lots of free time are motivated by the prospect of making money by selling stolen data, defacing other corporations, and telling others about successful break-ins. In response to the open threats, the industry has come up with a wide diversity of security technologies.

Managing a safe network is like managing a store. You must build a large parking lot for others to use and a friendly storefront inviting them to come in. You must let everyone in to see and touch the goods you sell. But you must also identify the bad guys and stop them from entering your store.

Three network technologies try to balance the contradictory goals of easy access and tight security:

■ *Access servers* — These are hardware devices that accept connections from remote modems over normal phone lines. They are also known as *communication servers*. They are equipped with hardware and software to make them behave like normal internetworking devices accepting connections from modems connected to serial phone lines. Figure 35-1 shows access servers located at a remote office and at the corporate headquarters.

They are the Internet's version of front-end systems used in WANs. They provide remote users (telecommuters, small remote office, and mobile workers) with a way to link to the corporate intranet.

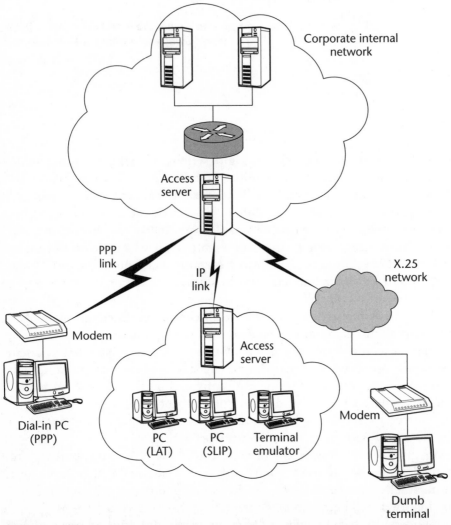

Figure 35-1 Remote access servers connect different corporate offices over the phone line.

- *Virtual private networks (VPNs)* — These are secure, dedicated channels that work over an existing, public network such as the Internet.

- *Firewalls* — These are special routers that are dedicated to intercepting between a public network such as the Internet and the private network. This topic is discussed in Chapter 36.

Access servers and VPNs enable connections from remote users. Firewalls do nothing to enable connections, but they audit incoming and outgoing traffic to check if traffic should be allowed free passage or blocked.

Virtual Private Networks (VPNs)

The corporate landscape is rapidly changing. To stay competitive and on the leading edge, corporations must contact vendors around the world, find ways to sell to remote geographical markets, and have development and support centers wherever they find the best talent for less money. All this has led to several requirements, one of which is to maintain low-cost yet highly secure communication among the geographically dispersed offices and employees.

One solution is to use leased lines (such as T-3, OC-3, or frame relay) to connect to a corporate WAN. But, as the number of sales offices and telecommuters increases and they spread out to more far-flung areas, maintaining leased lines gets very expensive. They are also inflexible and difficult to set up. As you expand your network with more and more leased and shared lines, you increase your potential security risks.

Enter VPNs. A VPN is a secure connection between two private LAN segments at distant sites over a public network such as the Internet. Instead of using dedicated, leased lines, a VPN uses a virtual connection through the Internet between the sites, which may be a corporate internal network, remote office, or at an employee's home. The data going over the connection is encrypted. VPNs are negatively impacting the leased-line market.

A well-architected VPN provides the following benefits:

- It extends geographical reach and provides global telecommuting opportunities.

- It provides a highly secure connection. Remember that data in transit through the Internet is vulnerable to many threats such as spoofing, sniffing, session hijacking, and main-in-the-middle attacks. The VPN connection must, therefore, include measures to be secure from attacks and data tampering.

- It reduces total cost of maintaining WAN connectivity. Unlike VPNs, leased lines require expensive hardware, access modems, cables, and in-house equipment. VPNs are estimated to be 30 percent to 80 percent less expensive than private WANs, primarily because of the low cost of Internet connectivity versus the cost of leased lines and equipment. This is also because of the economies of scale provided by the Internet.

- It increases employee productivity by providing an easy, quick, efficient means of connecting to the intranet.

- It provides faster return-on-investment (ROI) than traditional leased lines.

The primary objective of a VPN is to extend private, network-like trust relationships across an economical public network without sacrificing security. There are two types of VPNs, as shown in Figure 35-2:

- Remote-access VPN
- Site-to-site VPNs
  - Intranet-based VPN
  - Extranet-based VPN

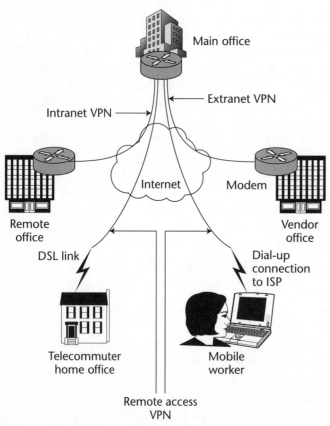

Figure 35-2 Three main VPN types.

Remote-Access VPN

Remote-access VPN is a secure and scalable encrypted tunnel across a public network such as the Internet. It is also called *virtual private dial-up network (VPDN)* and is a user-to-LAN connection.

A good example is a company with many traveling salespeople and telecommuters who must safely connect to the intranet from anywhere in the world. The employee first establishes a connection to the Internet via DSL, cable modem, ISDN, or using dial-up analog modems. Then he or she uses VPN client software to establish a secure tunnel to the corporate internal network. Figure 35-3 shows how a business traveler accesses the corporate internal LANs (using a software VPN client on a laptop) over the Internet, without which there would be no VPN infrastructure.

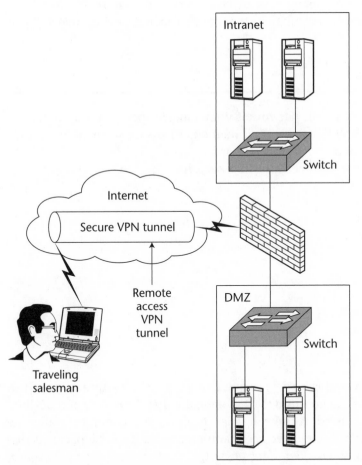

Figure 35-3   A remote employee uses VPN over the Internet to access corporate networks.

Site-to-Site VPNs

Intranet-based and Extranet-based VPNs are examples of site-to-site VPNs. *Site-to-site VPNs* are encrypted, secure channels of communication between two fixed sites over a public network such as the Internet. They have rich VPN services such as QoS (quality of service) and IPSec (IP security) to increase security and reliability between the sites. (IPSec is discussed in more detail later in this chapter.)

Following are some distinctions:

- *Intranet-based VPN* — Intranet-based VPNs connect remote offices and the main office to form a private, corporate network.

- *Extranet-based VPN* — A corporation can establish a VPN with partners, clients, and vendors, where the partner's LAN communicates with the corporate network using a secure channel over the Internet. This enables the various companies to work in a shared environment.

VPN Security

Data in transit over a public network is vulnerable to spoofing, alteration, and being corrupted. A VPN uses several methods to ensure security of the data when it is moving over the public network.

The following are used to ensure VPN security:

- Firewalls
- Encryption
- Data integrity
- IPSec
- AAA server
- Authentication

Firewalls

At most sites, a firewall is a prerequisite to a VPN. A firewall restricts which protocols and ports can go through. It makes sure that the source and destination networks are trusted. A firewall inspects all packets coming through the VPN tunnel to verify if they have been tampered with. If so, the packet is discarded and the sender is asked to retransmit.

NOTE Firewalls are discussed in detail in Chapter 36.

Encryption

Encryption is a technique by which data, before being sent over, is encoded in a manner in which only the receiving station can decode it. There are two common types of encryption: public-key encryption and symmetric-key encryption.

Public-Key (Asymmetric) Encryption

Public-key encryption was invented in 1976 by Whitfield Diffie and Martin Hellman. Hence, it is also called *Diffie-Hellman encryption*.

Each machine involved in mutual communication has two keys: a private key and a public key. The *private key* is kept local to each machine and never shared with anyone. The *public key* is, however, publicly shared with every host or user in the world.

The sending machine encrypts the message using the recipient's public key. When the recipient gets the encrypted message, it decrypts it using its own private key. The message cannot be decrypted without the private key. Therefore, it is important to never share the private key. This process is shown in Figure 35-4.

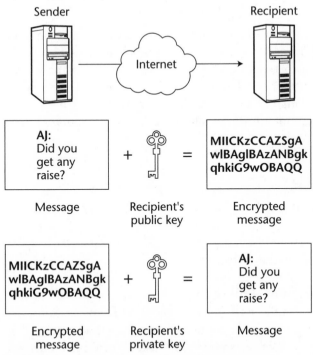

Figure 35-4 Asymmetric or public-key encryption.

The public and private keys are related such that only the public key can be used to encrypt messages and only the corresponding private key can be used to decrypt it. Also, it is impossible to deduce the private key if you know the public key. The problem with this method is that the sender must know the public key of the recipient before the message can be encrypted and transmitted.

This technology is also called *asymmetric encryption* because it uses two keys instead of one key (*symmetric encryption*). A popular public-key encryption is Pretty Good Privacy, available at www.pgp.com.

Symmetric Encryption

Each machine has a *secret key* that it uses to encrypt a message before sending it over the network to another machine. The secret key is also called the *symmetric key* because it is the only one involved in encrypting as well as decrypting the message. After encrypting the message, the symmetric key is encoded using the receiver's public key. The receiving host uses its private key to decrypt the symmetric key and then uses the symmetric key to decode the message. Figure 35-5 illustrates the process.

Data Integrity

Encryption and decryption addresses the problem of eavesdropping (someone else getting and understanding the data). But it does not address two problems: data tampering and impersonation. Data integrity mechanisms within VPN systems address the problem of data tampering and ensure that the data is not altered while it is in transit over the public Internet. Most VPN systems use one of the following technologies to ensure data integrity: one-way hash functions and digital signatures.

One-Way Hash Functions

A *hash function* takes an input file and generates a fixed-length output value. The output value is unique for each input file (that is, if the input file is altered by even 1 bit, the output value will change). This calculation is easy, but it is impossible to reverse-engineer the output value to give you the input file. That's why the algorithm is called "one-way."

The recipient, after getting the input file, calculates the hash value of that input file and compares it with the hash value it received from the sender. If the two hash values are identical, the recipient is assured that the input file has not been altered during transit. Some examples of hash algorithms are MD-5, RIPE-MD-160, and SHA-1.

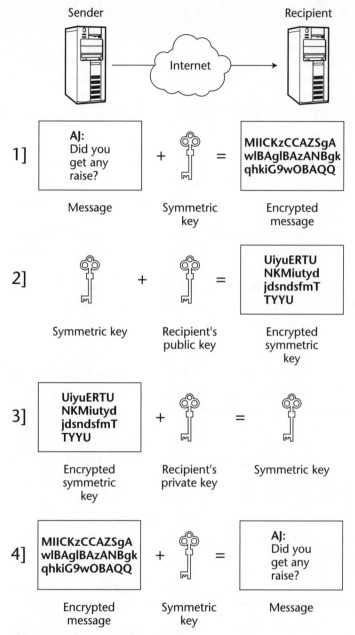

Figure 35-5   Symmetric encryption.

Digital Signatures

A *digital signature* is a digital code attached to an electronically transmitted message that uniquely identifies the sender. Its purpose is to guarantee that the individual sending the message is really who he or she claims to be. It is also used to verify that the data has not been altered.

A digital signature is essentially a public-key or asymmetric-key encryption in reverse. The sender attaches his or her signature along with the document. The signature is an encryption of the one-way hash value of the content of the document using the sender's private key. The sender sends the document and the signature. Since the document itself is not encrypted, this cannot be used for sensitive data.

The recipient uses the sender's public key to decrypt the signature and gets the one-way hash value of the content of the document. Separately the sender also calculates the hash value of the received document using the sender's procedure. If the two hash values match, the recipient is sure that the document contents have not been altered in transit. If they do not match, either the content has been altered or the private or public keys do not belong to the same person (or have themselves been tampered with). The message is then discarded and the sender is asked to resend. This is illustrated in Figure 35-6.

In short, a digital signature is used to guarantee that the message sender really is who he or she claims to be and to guarantee the integrity of received data.

IPSec

Internet protocol security (*IPSec*) provides encryption algorithms and a more comprehensive authentication process. It encapsulates a packet by wrapping another packet around it and then encrypts the entire packet. The encrypted stream then travels across the otherwise unsafe Internet.

IPSec has been widely deployed by VPN hardware vendors and service providers, but it can be used only for systems that are IPSec-compliant. Also, all devices must use a common key for encryption, and the firewall on both sides of the VPN tunnel must be configured with similar security policies.

IPSec has two encryption modes:

- *Tunnel* — The header and the payload data of each packet are encrypted.
- *Transport* — Only the payload data is encrypted.

IPSec can be used to encrypt data between various devices (such as between two routers, between a PC and a router, or between a router and a firewall).

AAA Server

AAA stands for *authentication* (who you are), *authorization* (what you are permitted to do), and *accounting* (what you actually did). When a request to establish a VPN session comes in, the request is sent to an AAA server. The server authenticates the user and authorizes it for certain tasks. The accounting data is useful for reporting, billing (if the user is billed for the session time), and for later audit of activities.

Authentication

Besides AAA servers, there are a few other common technologies used to authenticate VPN users.

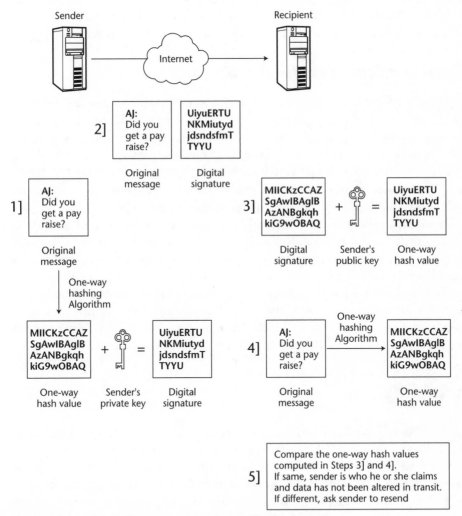

Figure 35-6 Digital signatures are used to verify data integrity.

Password-Based Authentication

This is the most common authentication used in computer systems, and it is also the weakest. All you do is type your login name and password and wait. Passwords are easy to steal or guess. The server maintains a list of valid login names and passwords. All you have to do is type the right combination.

Token-Based Authentication

Many VPN systems support SecurID by Security Dynamics. It is a token that provides a one-time password, which is generated by encrypting a time stamp with a secret key. The password is valid for a short time (30 to 60 seconds).

Digital Certificate–Based Authentication

A *digital certificate* is an electronic document issued to an individual by a *certificate authority* (CA) that can vouch for an individual's identity. A certificate contains a public key, user-specific information, issuer's information, and a validity period. This information is used to create a message digest, which is encrypted using the CA's private key to get a digital signature for the certificate. The digital signature can be used by servers and clients to authenticate each other (that is, verify that they are who they claim to be).

The client digitally signs a randomly generated piece of data and sends both the certificate and the signed data across the network. The server uses techniques of public-key cryptography to validate the signature and confirm the validity of the certificate.

Client authentication based on certificates is part of the SSL protocol. To authenticate a client to a server, the client digitally signs a randomly generated piece of data and sends its certificate and the signed data across the network. The server authenticates the user's identity on the strength of this evidence.

Tunneling

Most VPNs rely on tunneling to establish a private network across the Internet. *Tunneling* is a process of placing an entire packet within another packet and then sending it over a network to the other end of the tunnel, where the outer packet is removed. The ends of the tunnel are called *tunnel interfaces*.

The fact that you can place a packet inside another has some interesting outcomes. A VPN tunnel can send a packet with a nonroutable, private IP address across the Internet after placing it inside a packet with a routable address. Packets with protocols not supported by the Internet (such as NetBEUI) can also be safely sent across the Internet inside IP packets.

Tunneling requires three protocols:

- *Passenger protocol* — This is the protocol of the original data that must be transported through the VPN. Examples include IP, IPX, and NetBEUI.

- *Encapsulating protocol* — This is the protocol (GRE, IPSec, L2F, PPTP, or L2TP) that makes up the outer packet. The same encapsulating protocol must be supported on both tunnel interfaces. (L2F, PPTP, and L2TP are discussed in more detail in the following section.)

- *Carrier protocol* — This protocol is used by the network (usually the Internet) that the information travels over.

Tunneling is like a gift delivery. The gift may be gardening equipment such as shovels (passenger protocol) that are well-wrapped and nicely packed in a large cardboard box (encapsulating protocol) and then delivered by the postal mail system (carrier protocol) to your home address. When you receive the box, you remove the box (encapsulating protocol) and use the real goods inside. Figure 35-7 shows a VPN tunnel between two sites.

Remote-Access Tunneling

Remote-access VPN depends on PPP as the carrier protocol over the network. Following are common encapsulating protocols used for remote-access VPN tunnels:

- *Layer 2 forwarding (L2F)* — L2F uses any PPP-supported authentication scheme. This protocol was developed by Cisco.

- *Point-to-point tunneling protocol (PPTP)* — PPTP was jointly developed by members of the PPTP Forum, which includes 3COM, ECI Telematics, Lucent, Microsoft, and US Robotics. It supports 128-bit and 40-bit encryption schemes. Like L2F, it supports any PPP-supported authentication scheme. The problem with PPTP is that it can support only one tunnel at a time for each user. However, its successor, L2TP, can support several, simultaneous tunnels for each user.

- *Layer 2 tunneling protocol (L2TP)* — L2TP combines the features of L2F and PPTP and was jointly developed by Cisco, the Internet Engineering Task Force (IETF), and PPTP Forum. L2TP is included in Microsoft Windows 2000 and it supports IPSec for data encryption and integrity. L2TP can be used for both site-to-site VPNs and remote-access VPNs.

Site-to-Site Tunneling

In *site-to-site tunneling*, the passenger protocol is encapsulated using generic routing encapsulation (GRE) protocol or IPSec and is then transported over the network to the other end of the VPN tunnel.

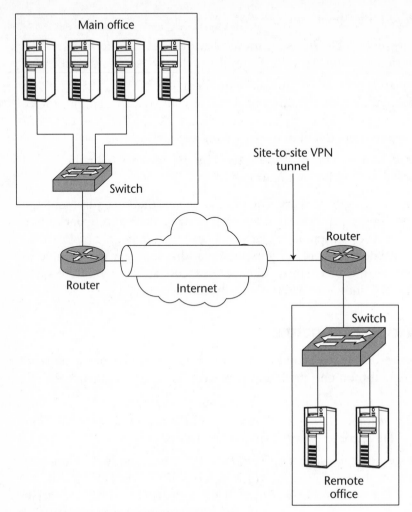

Figure 35-7   VPN tunnel between two sites.

Key Points

Following are some key points discussed in this chapter:

- Mission-critical applications are being deployed across the Internet, and lack of security can jeopardize the business success.

- VPNs can play a major role in mitigating this problem. Corporations have started to use VPNs as a low-cost, secure, and flexible way to keep their employees and remote offices connected to the main office. They have become an alternative to expensive, hard-to-scale leased lines.

Firewalls

*Advance, and never halt, for advancing is perfection. Advance and
do not fear the thorns in the path, for they draw only corrupt blood.*
— Kahlil Gibran

A firewall in a building is a structure that prevents fire from spreading from one area to another. In networks, a *firewall* is a device that sits between the two networks (such as corporate network and Internet) and inspects every incoming and outgoing message to decide whether it should be allowed through or discarded.

Let's see how a company with 1,000 employees can use a firewall. The company will have 1,000 laptops (or desktops), a few Web servers, one or two FTP servers for customers to download documents and software, and internal servers for Payroll and HR. The company has a connection to the Internet via a T-3 line. Without a firewall, all of those computers will be directly accessible (using FTP, telnet, SSH, Web, and so on) to anyone in the world who wants to guess login names and passwords. If any employee makes a mistake and leaves a security hole, hackers can exploit the hole and get to the machine. There are many hackers running automated scripts to scan and report open vulnerabilities.

A firewall makes the landscape very different. A firewall is placed at every incoming Internet connection. Firewalls have preprogrammed and manually specified rules. A rule can be like this:

Out of all the computers in the company, only two specific servers are
allowed to receive and process Web requests on port 80 from the Internet.
Incoming Web requests to all other servers are denied by the firewall.

Firewalls give a great amount of control to how employees can use the internal servers and how those outside can access the corporate servers.

Firewalls use one or more of the following three methods to control traffic:

- *Packet filtering* — Each incoming and outgoing packet is inspected against a set of requirements or rules. Packets that satisfy all the criteria are allowed to go through. All other packets are discarded. The criteria to allow or deny access are based on source and destination names or IP addresses, ports, and protocol (TCP, UDP, ICMP, SNMP, and so forth).

- *Proxy service* — Firewalls often work as a proxy server. A *proxy server* is an application that acts as an intermediary between two end systems. Proxy servers operate at layer 7 (the application layer) of the OSI model and they are also, therefore, referred to as *application-layer firewalls*.

  A proxy service must be run on the firewall for each Internet application. You set up an HTTP proxy for Web services, an SMTP proxy for e-mail, and so on.

  A Web proxy server, for example, is used to retrieve Web pages from the Internet for internal requests. The internal machines are never allowed to go out to the Internet to get data. Similarly external users are never allowed to access the internal servers. The firewall intercepts each incoming request, gets the data from the internal server, and forwards it to the requestor.

  Proxy servers increase the efficiency of Internet access. They cache (locally store) all data that it has retrieved for requestors. Data is kept locally for a certain period of time (10 minutes, 2 hours, or any other period). Future requests for the same data, if found in the cache, are answered instantaneously from cache without contacting the remote server.

- *Stateful inspection* — The firewall looks at certain characteristics of each packet leaving the firewall-protected network and adds those to a database of trusted information. Characteristics of each incoming packet are compared to the database, and if the comparison yields a reasonable match, the message is allowed through. Otherwise, it is discarded.

DMZ Areas

A *demilitarized zone* (DMZ) is just a network subnet that contains servers that you want more open access to than the internal networks. This is shown in Figure 36-1. Think of the DMZ as the front yard of your house and the house as the internal network. You would place things in your front yard that others can come and see. Remember, it is vulnerable and someone can damage it. Therefore, you must have enough backup provisions to rebuild the damaged area.

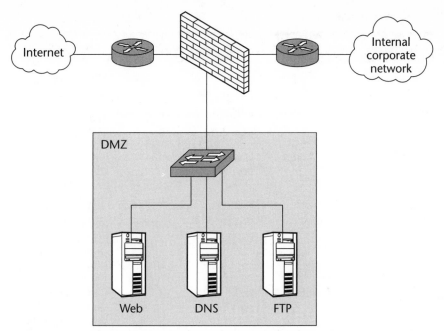

Figure 36-1   Firewall delineating the internal, external, and DMZ networks.

All corporations have a DMZ area, where they keep various hosts such as their Web servers, FTP upload and download servers, and front-end e-commerce servers for online business.

Firewall Rules or Filters

Firewalls use a set of rules to decide if each packet should be allowed through or discarded. Each incoming or outgoing packet is tested against each rule, starting from the first rule in the set (top-down order). Each rule has an ALLOW or DENY flag at the end. If the message meets any one of the specified rules, it is then handled accordingly: either allowed through or denied further progress. The last rule in the set is the *clean-up* or *drop-all rule*, based on the policy that, "What is not expressly permitted is implicitly prohibited." The last rule discards all packets that have not met any of the previous conditions for being allowed through.

Table 36-1 shows a simple set of firewall rules. "Internal" is defined as subnets in the corporate network, and "External" is the Internet. (An easy way to define "External" is all subnets except those that are internal.) DMZ-DNS, DMZ-FTP, and DMZ-WEB are servers in the DMZ area. Figure 36-2 shows a firewall between external and internal networks that use a set of rules to forward or discard packets.

Table 36-1 A Simple Ruleset

RULE NO.	SOURCE	DESTINATION	PROTOCOL	ACTION	COMMENT
1	Internal	Any	HTTP (TCP port 80, 443)	ALLOW	Allow outgoing Web requests.
2	Internal	Any	SSH (TCP port 22)	ALLOW	Allow outgoing SSH requests.
3	DMZ-DNS	Any	DNS (UDP port 53)	ALLOW	Allow DNS servers in DMZ to send DNS requests.
4	External	DMZ-FTP	FTP (TCP ports 20, 21)	ALLOW	Allow Internet users to FTP servers in DMZ area.
5	External	DMZ-WEB	HTTP (TCP port 80)	ALLOW	Allow Internet users to WEB servers in DMZ area.
6	Any	Any	Any	DENY	Clean-up rule to discard all other packets.

The decision to allow or discard a packet could be based on any of the following criteria within a rule:

- *Source or destination IP addresses* — Packets coming from or destined to a certain IP address or a range of addresses are allowed through or discarded.

- *Source or destination domain names* — Because IP addresses can change and they are difficult to remember, domain names are also used in rules. You can have a rule to allow or block traffic to a certain domain name. Also, incoming traffic from a certain domain on the Internet can be denied or allowed.

- *Service protocol* — A protocol is a way to access a service. Rules use protocols to allow or deny passage to packets. Some common protocols used for firewall rules are as follows:

  - *File transfer protocol (FTP)* — This is used to download and upload files from one server to another.

  - *Hyper text transfer protocol (HTTP)* — This is used for transferring Web pages.

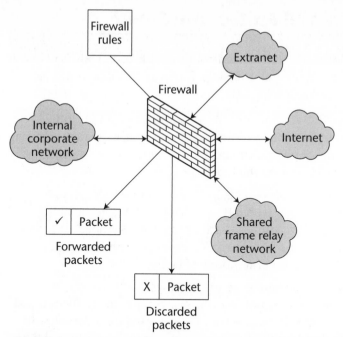

Figure 36-2   Rules used to forward or discard packets between the external and internal networks.

- *Internet control message protocol (ICMP)* — This is used by a router to exchange the information with other routers.

- *Internet protocol (IP)* — IP is the main delivery system for information over the Internet.

- *Simple mail transport protocol (SMTP)* — This is used to send text-based information (e-mail).

- *Secure shell* (ssh) — This is used to log on to a remote UNIX machine.

- *Transport control protocol (TCP)* — TCP is used to break apart and rebuild information that travels over the Internet.

- *User datagram protocol (UDP)* — This is used for information that requires no response and confirmation after each delivery. It is primarily used to transfer streaming audio and video files.

You may set up a rule to allow incoming traffic with a certain protocol to access certain corporate servers and ban that protocol for all other hosts.

- *Ports* — Services are made available by a host using numbered ports. For example, Web services are commonly configured on Port 80, secure HTTP or HTTPS on port 443, and e-mail services on port 25. A corporation may have a rule to block incoming FTP requests (which are on port 20 and 21) to all servers except one FTP server located in the DMZ.

What Does a Firewall Protect You From?

There are many, many inventive ways that devious people use to find and abuse vulnerable machines. After a firewall is installed, it must be customized to protect you effectively from the following:

- *Application or operating-system backdoors* — Some installed programs have little-known features that allow for remote access. Some programs or operating systems have bugs that can be used to create a backdoor (or hidden access) to log on to the machine.

- *Denial-of-service (DoS) attacks* — This is a widely known problem but is difficult to protect against effectively. The hacker slows and disables a server by consuming its resources (such as memory, kernel data structures, bandwidth, or CPU cycles) to an extent that legitimate users are denied service. There are several modes of DoS attacks:

  - *SYN flood attack* — The hacker sends a request to the server. When the server responds, it cannot find the system that made the request. In the meantime, the server has reserved a kernel data structure for the request. By flooding the server with such unanswerable session requests, a hacker can slow the server to a crawl or crash it. This type of attack can be done from a slow PC with a modem connection against a fast site. It is an example of an *asymmetric DoS attack.*

  - *Using server's resources against itself* — The hacker uses forged UDP packets to connect the echo service on one machine in the victim's network to the charged service on another machine. The effect is that the network's bandwidth is consumed and thus slows or denies access to other users.

  - *Bandwidth consumption* — A hacker consumes a network's entire bandwidth by generating a large number of packets (such as ICMP ECHO packets) that are directed toward the network. The hacker need not be operating from a single machine but can coordinate different machines on several networks to achieve the same effect.

- *E-mail bombs* — The hacker sends the same e-mail thousands of times within a small interval of time to overload the e-mail server and network until the server is unable to accept any more e-mails. This can also be used as a personal attack to fill someone's e-mail inbox and slow his or her desktop.

- *Macros* — A *macro* is a script file containing application commands that can be run to simplify complicated procedures or automate tasks. Hackers write their own macro that is run from within an application that they have somehow got control of. The macro can be used to destroy or crash the computer.

- *Redirect bombs* — Intruders use ICMP to change or redirect data packets from a server to another router that is unable to deal with the packets. The network is therefore clogged and brought down with misrouted packets. This is a type of denial-of-service attack.

- *Remote login* — You will find many attempts to log in to your computer using SSH, telnet, and Windows Terminal Services. If hackers can connect to your computer, they will do what is possible: view files, steal data to sell to other interested parties, or run programs to damage your computer.

- *SMTP session hijacking* — SMTP is used to send e-mail over the Internet. Intruders get access to a list of e-mail addresses and send junk e-mails to thousands of users by using an unsuspecting SMTP server as the e-mail originator. This makes it impossible to trace the actual sender of the e-mails. Some e-mails sent in this manner contain links to Web sites. If a user accidentally clicks on the link, he or she thereby accepts a cookie that provides a backdoor to the computer.

- *Source routing* — Packets travel through the Internet to their destination using routers along the path. The source of the packet usually specifies the path that the packets must take. Intruders make their own packets containing malicious data, appearing to have originated from a trusted source or even from an internal corporate network. Most firewalls can disable source routing.

- *Viruses* — This is the most familiar threat to computers. A *virus* is a small program that attaches itself onto another program such as a spreadsheet or document. When the program is opened, the virus executes itself and spreads to other systems using network protocols. The impact can be devastating. It can spread quickly to all networked machines, use stored e-mail addresses to send itself to those addresses, and wipe the hard disk.

Some of these can be contained by a firewall, and others are difficult or impossible to filter using a firewall. E-mail spams get through the firewall. Antivirus software must be installed on each host.

Global Addresses Can Hide Internal Networks

Firewalls can be used to conceal internal network topologies from the Internet. There are two types of IP addresses:

■ Routable (or public) IP addresses such as 160.50.0.0

■ Non-routable (or private) IP addresses such as 192.168.0.0 or 10.0.0.0

This is done mainly to conserve IP addresses. There are simply not enough IP addresses in IP version 4 to allocate a unique number to every networked device in the world. It is possible to run an internal network using private addresses, as shown in Figure 36-3.

As packets are sent through the firewall to the Internet, network address translation (NAT) overwrites the internal, private IP address with a public IP address taken from a pool of available, public addresses. NAT maps each outbound connection to a public address. NAT can work in several ways:

■ *Static NAT* — This maps a private IP address to a certain public address on a one-to-one basis. The mapping is predetermined and used in every case. This is useful when a device must be accessible from the outside.

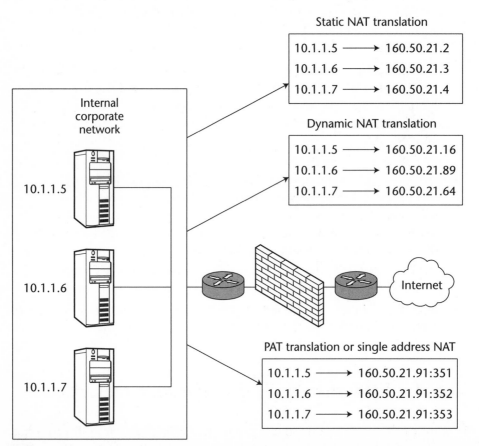

Figure 36-3 Internal, private addresses can be translated to public IP address on a one-to-one basis or a many-to-one basis.

- *Dynamic NAT* — A private IP address maps to the first available address in the public IP address pool. There is no predetermined one-to-one mapping. A certain host will get different public addresses each time it tries to access the outside world.

  Once the connection is terminated, the public address is returned to the available pool for reuse by the next outgoing connection. NAT is therefore able to hide internal addresses, but it does not reduce the number of required public addresses.

- *Overloading* — This is a form of dynamic NAT that maps multiple internal IP addresses to a single, external IP address by using different ports. This is called *port address translation* (*PAT*), *port-level*, *multiplexed NAT*, or *single address NAT*. It makes it possible to run an internal network using one public IP address. All internal addresses are translated to one public address but with different port number assignments. Besides conserving public IPS, PAT enhances security by hiding all internal hosts behind a single address and making it impossible for intruders to identify individual hosts behind the firewall.

Firewall Best Practices

Following are some best practices for using firewalls:

- A sure protection you can offer is to block everything, but that makes the connection unnecessary. An effective way to set up a firewall is to block everything and then open up incoming and outgoing traffic as required. Incoming requests (such as FTP, Web services, and so on) must be opened to certain servers within the corporate network. Outgoing messages (such as e-mails, `ping`, and Web page requests) must be allowed to go through. Apply antispoofing rules on all firewall interfaces.

- Once you have set up your firewall, you must test it. One great test is to go to `www.grc.com` and try their free Internet security verification, Shields Up!, to detect vulnerabilities in your network. You will get immediate feedback on your configured level of security.

Key Points

Following are some key points discussed in this chapter:

- A network firewall is a device that is logically situated between the two networks and inspects every incoming and outgoing packet to decide whether it should be permitted to go forward.

- Firewalls use packet filtering, proxy services, and stateful inspection to make the decision.

- Firewalls protect internal networks from viruses, attacks, redirect bombs, and other threats from the wild Internet.

- Firewalls conceal internal, hidden IP addresses using NAT or PAT.

Network Security

Courage is being scared to death but saddling up anyway.
— John Wayne

The networks of today are more extensive in their geographical reaches and the communities they connect. They are more complex to manage and yet more fundamental to the organization's success. They support a wide variety of services: voice, video, data, wireless, Web services, and all applications. They are also more open and connected to the untrusted public networks. In fact, the line between private and public networks is hazy and feeble. Employees, partners, and customers need various levels of access to data from remote locations over the Internet. All this has increased the need for robust and comprehensive security. This chapter describes security implementations.

> **NOTE** More security issues are discussed in Chapter 35, "Internet Access Technologies and VPNs," and Chapter 36, "Firewalls."

Everyone has a different idea of what security should be and what degree of risk is tolerable. However, a crucial point to remember when building an IT network is to define what security means to your corporation. A corporate-level security policy is crucial to establishing an effective barrier to intruders. A *security policy* is a set of guidelines adopted by the corporation to protect users, systems, and data. It serves as the fountainhead for architecting the network, implementing security, and resolving conflicts.

TALES FROM THE TECH TURF: RESUME OF A VIRUS AUTHOR

In September 2004, a German firewall company named SecurePoint hired an 18-year-old employee who had written several variants of the Sasser and Netsky worms. These worms disabled several hundreds of thousands of computers worldwide in 2004 and have been among the fastest-spreading worms of all time. The new employee had been charged with computer sabotage and faced three to five years in prison. The hiring brought protest from several organizations and network security experts, who have expressed concern over where to draw the line between the Internet underworld and those who have the onus of shielding against them.

Going through the entire process of developing a security policy is not enough. Threats change, vulnerabilities change, business needs change, and the effectiveness of existing defenses change. All of these must be routinely re-evaluated to pull off a network security policy that is realistic, enforceable, and, at the same time, does its job.

The world of computers has drastically changed over the past 30 years. Thirty years ago, most computers were centralized and locked in data centers. You either had a terminal wired to the mainframe or you were out. Threats were rare, and break-ins and data corruption were easy to identify and prevent. They were usually caused by disgruntled employees.

Now all systems are connected to the Internet. The Internet is the world's biggest and boundary-less network of networks. While it is necessary to be connected for sharing information, it has allowed for a proliferation of malicious code that could damage any device with even a slight vulnerability. Hacker tools and tutorials are freely and widely available on the Internet. It does not require any level of expertise to scan for susceptible hosts. All it requires is time and a malicious intent.

It is therefore critical for corporations to ensure that their networks are safe and to minimize the risk of intrusions both from inside and outside the organization. Although no network can be 100 percent safe, a secure, hard-to-break network will keep everyone but the most determined hacker out. The topic of network security is a very vast one, and there are several books and Web sites dedicated to this subject. This chapter will review some basic tenets of network security.

Computer Viruses

A *computer virus* is an unauthorized software program or part of a program that has been introduced into a computer or network. Its intention is to destroy or change data, delete files, fill up all available disk space, and do other damage. Depending upon the purpose of a particular virus, the reformatting of the infected hard drive may be the only method of eradication. Of course, this will result in data loss. You cannot get the data from backup tapes unless you are sure when the damage started and have older backup data.

Computer viruses are becoming more and more common. The number of viruses being detected is ever increasing. The loading or copying of unauthorized software onto PCs and other machines is one of the easiest ways for viruses to attack a computer, a system, or a network.

Internet Worms

An *Internet worm* is a program or algorithm that replicates itself over a computer network and usually performs malicious actions, such as filling up the disk space, consuming all the processing resources, deleting files, and possibly shutting down the system. Internet worms are a primary threat to any IT infrastructure. The Sobig and Blaster worms that occurred at the same time in 2003 are estimated to have caused losses of over $2 billion.

Following are some examples of Internet worms:

- The *Sobig worm* is a network-aware, mass-mailing program that sends itself to all e-mail addresses it finds in files with the following extensions: `.dbx`, `.txt`, `.html`, `.txt`, `.wab`, and `.mht`. The worm uses its own SMTP engine to propagate. It also tries to create a copy of itself on available network shares but fails because of bugs in its own code. The spoofed and "Send To" addresses are both taken from the files found on the computer. The worm uses settings of the infected computer to check for and contact an SMTP server.

- The *Blaster worm* exploits a distributed component object model (DCOM) remote procedure call (RPC) vulnerability on port 135 on Microsoft platforms that are not properly patched. It does not have a mass-mailing capability.

- The *Codered worm* was one of the first worms to receive attention outside the network security community because of its speed and effectiveness in spreading. It exploits a vulnerability in Microsoft Internet Information Services (IIS).

- The *Loveletter* or *"I Love You" worm* uses very effective social engineering and Visual Basic to spread to several e-mail inboxes.

- The *Lion worm* uses a known flaw in Linux Berkeley Internet Name Domain (BIND).

The most common methods used to defend against worms are reactive (such as virus scanning and software patching). They provide no hope against fast-spreading and zero-day exploit worms. Proactive defense mechanisms are necessary to prevent damages from Internet worms:

- *Intrusion detection systems (IDS)* — These are best thought of as a combination of network sniffer and virus scanner. Each packet is scanned against a signature database for suspicious behavior or content. It filters away suspicious traffic to an isolated network for manual examination and alerts internal users and administrators.

- *Intrusion prevention systems (IPS)* — These systems react to dangerous operating system requests by querying the user for authorization, outright denial of the request, or terminating the offending program. They also trigger alerts and log all suspicious actions. They operate from predefined rules that outline all legal and illegal behavior.

- *Firewalls* — These test packet headers against a set of rules such as source or target IP addresses or ports. They do not test the contents of the packet. This is *packet filtering*. Another mechanism called *stateful inspection* monitors all incoming and outgoing requests and responses. It allows incoming packets only if they are in response to internal requests or destined for appropriate IP addresses and ports. (See Chapter 36 for more information on firewalls.)

- *Antivirus heuristics* — Antivirus products keep a database of malicious code patterns created by studying known viruses and worms. Heuristics allow antivirus programs to detect new threats and prevent damage from worms or viruses that are not in their database.

- *Integrity checking* — Integrity checkers use a trusted baseline of files and keep cryptographic hashes of known good versions of files. The baseline is used to make integrity comparisons at any time and restore files that may have been modified by a worm.

- *Stack-guarding* — Stack-guarding technologies attempt to make programs resistant to buffer-overflow attacks.

The Security Philosophy

Security is not a one-time implementation. Even in the past, kings had soldiers parading their palace gates 24×7. Even if the army had no future battle plans, they still exercised often and cleaned and tested their guns regularly. The new-world order is no different.

The different security tasks are shown as a wheel in Figure 37-1. The wheel signifies that the tasks must be done endlessly. Following are the phases:

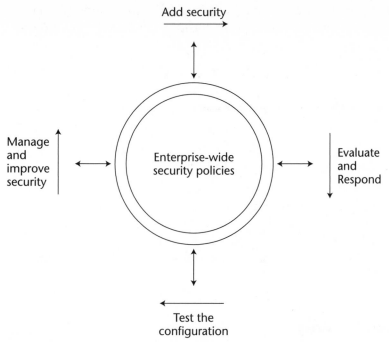

Figure 37-1 Security is not a one-time undertaking. It needs continual monitoring and improvement.

- *Add security phase* — You must install hardware- and software-based mechanisms to prevent intrusions and safeguard the data when it is traveling over untrusted networks. A very underestimated (and yet powerful) aspect of protection is physical security such as video cameras, motion sensors, and different ways of reading badges. Some badges have prerecorded parameters (such as palm prints), and when the person scans a badge, the parameters must match before access is permitted. On the network side, layers of security must be installed.

- *Evaluate and respond phase* — The network and the edge devices must be monitored to see what type of scans, viruses, and threats are out there. You must know your enemy before you can effectively start preparing safeguard measures. Network monitoring packages must be evaluated well before implementation.

- *Test phase* — It is time to think like your enemy. Try to break the security. Get third-party tools and security consultants to attempt to break in. This is not a time to find flaws or evaluate different teams of people but to evaluate the configuration. Be objective and separate the humans (security implementers) from the machine (security devices).

- *Manage and improve phase* — Once you have tested the configuration, the findings must be used to improve the setup. Then start the monitoring again.

Security is a never-ending process of finding flaws and incremental improvements.

There are two basic types of network security:

- *Traffic-based security* — This security configuration is part of the infra-structure built by the network administrators. The underlying policies and setup are usually hidden from the network users.

- *User-based security* — This determines whether a user can log in or not to a system or applications and what tasks can be done after a success-ful login. The framework is called *authentication, authorization, and accounting (AAA or "triple-a")*, which is designed to be modular and provides flexibility to network administrators for implementing the corporate security policies.

Traffic-Based Security

Traffic-based security is implemented by enforcing access control lists (ACLs) on routers and rules on firewalls. It checks each incoming packet to ensure that it complies with at least one rule for being allowed access. A packet is dis-carded if it does not meet even a single rule for being let in. The list of criteria is the source and destination IP address, port number, and protocol.

Access List Security

All routers have an access control list (ACL), which, like a firewall, can screen out packets based on their characteristics.

Here is an example of an ACL of a router:

```
access-list 101 permit tcp 0.0.0.0 255.255.255.255 122.120.1.6 0.0.0.0
eq 80
access-list 101 deny ip 0.0.0.0 255.255.255.255 122.130.1.6 0.0.0.0 log
```

The following statement adds an explicit deny:

```
access-list 101 deny ip any log
```

Router ACLs can be used to improve performance by isolating traffic or restricting access and traffic (much like a firewall). This is shown in Figure 37-2.

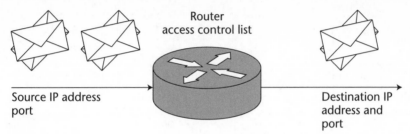

Figure 37-2 A router ACL uses source and destination IP addresses and ports to allow or deny passage.

Firewall Security

A firewall restricts traffic and protects the internal servers in many ways:

- It uses address translation to hide internal host identity.
- It uses proxy services to prevent internal hosts from having to go out to the Internet for data.
- It uses packet filtering to allow through packets whose characteristics (port, source address, destination address, and so on) match a rule that would allow them to go through.

Firewall inspects each packet that originates from or goes to the networks connected to its interfaces. The CPU-based packet inspection and processing on the firewall slow the traffic, as shown in Figure 37-3.

User-Based Security

User-based security is concerned with people, not devices or hosts. All of us are familiar with login security for hosts and applications where you are asked for login name and password. Login/password controls are placed on all servers, devices, and applications. Once a user logs in (is authenticated), each account is also assigned a certain privilege (authorization) on what activities he or she can do.

User-based security is used to do the following:

- Grant access to employees on servers and devices
- Allow network administrators to log in to network devices with different levels of privileges
- Grant accounts to remote employees of the enterprise network
- Allow ISPs to create an account for each subscriber

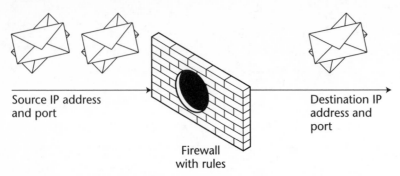

Figure 37-3   A firewall allows some packets to go through, based on source and destination IP address and port.

WAN connections, access servers, and dial-in protocols are all part of a robust user-based security system because users frequently need to dial in from a remote site or home.

Local User–Based Security

This is login access to a local PC, a UNIX system, a network device, or an application. Most user databases are stored in an active directory, NIS or NIS+ database, or simply on local disk. Figure 37-4 shows a client authentication by a Web server. The Web server keeps a database of users and passwords and authorizes users for the pages that he or she can view.

Remote User–Based Security

When a subscriber dials into an ISP for Internet connection, he or she is greeted by an access server. An ISP computer room has several high-density access servers to handle calls from thousands of subscribers. An access server looks like a PC with no monitor. On one side it has IP ports, and on the other side it has ports to accept incoming phone connections. Access servers must contact a central user database for user authentication.

TALES FROM THE TECH TURF: WHERE'S MY IM

In late 2001, a Web site for university students deployed an Instant Messenger (IM) service. The users had message boards and e-mail services. Just after classes were over for the day, the students got on the IM server and used it so much that it slowed the IM services to a crawl. E-mails would get through quicker than IM. The firewall was the bottleneck. It was set to process a few thousand sessions, but IM raised the bar to more than 100,000. The firewall memory was not enough to process so many sessions. This problem went undetected during tests. They had to replace the firewall boxes with ones with more RAM.

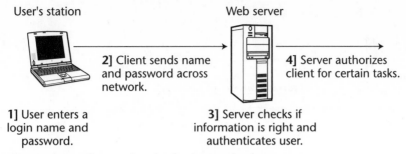

User's station

Web server

2] Client sends name
and password across
network.

4] Server authorizes
client for certain tasks.

1] User enters a
login name and
password.

3] Server checks if
information is right and
authenticates user.

Figure 37-4   Client authentication by a Web server.

AAA Model

AAA (or triple-a) is a key component of user-based security. The three acronyms are in order of what happens when a user logs in, making the concept easier to grasp and remember:

- It first checks if the entered login name and password is valid. If so, the user is *authenticated* and let in.

- Then the server decides what portions of the application the user can use. This is *authorization*.

- The server also keeps a log or *account* of all user activities.

The AAA model allows network administrators a high degree of control in enforcing security policies. Most AAA parameters can be implemented for each LAN segment, each user, and for each protocol (IP, IPX, or NetBEUI).

Authentication

Authentication is validating a user's identity to allow or deny login. In other words, "I need to know who this person is and I will see how he or she proves it to me." This is often done by the all-too-familiar login name and password. The process relies on each user having a unique set of criteria for gaining access. The AAA server compares a user's authentication credentials with a stored database of credentials. If the credentials match, the user is granted access to the network. If the credentials are at variance, authentication fails and access is denied.

There are several types of access:

- Network administrators log on to a router or switch to change configurations.

- An employee on the intranet is authenticated by a router to access a protected host to run an application. The router contacts a security server, as shown in Figure 37-5.

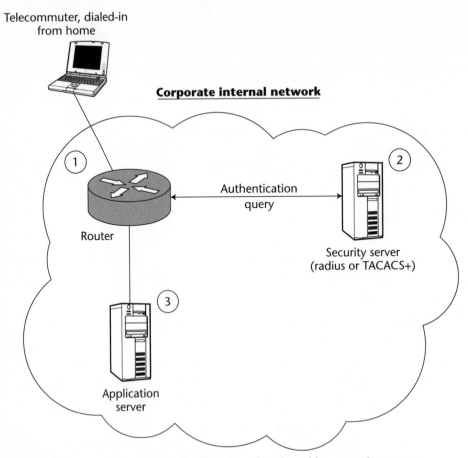

Figure 37-5 User's access to applications is authenticated by a security server.

Figure 37-6 shows a dial-in ISP subscriber. The access server accepts the call and verifies user authentication from a security server (which has a user database) before allowing the user access to the router and the Internet.

Authorization

Authorization controls the services that a user can access. In other words, "Now that I know who you are and I know your rights, I will allow or disallow activities." After logging into a device, for example, the user issues commands. The process of user authorization determines whether the user has the authority to run those commands.

Authorization is more complex than authentication. After successful authentication into a device, the security server provides the device with user-specific information: what commands the user can run, which networks he or she can access, which applications can be started, and the level of access within each application.

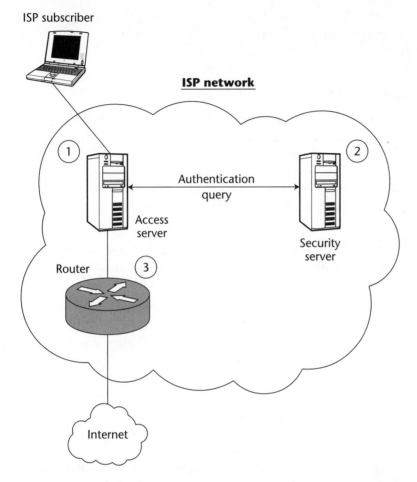

Figure 37-6   A dial-in subscriber's login is verified against a security server.

Authorization helps enforce security policies. It determines what activities, resources, and services a user is allowed. Without a centralized database of permissions for each user for each device, it would be impractical to manage the database effectively. User permissions would be spread across hundreds or thousands of devices, hosts, and so forth.

Accounting

Accounting does not allow or deny anything. It just keeps a current record of all user activities and consumed resources. In other words, "I am going to log all your activities, in case someone asks that of me later." It records the amount of data transferred, length of connection, what was done and when, and so on. Many ISPs bill the subscriber a flat, minimum charge, plus a charge for number of actual hours. Many server collocation and Web-hosting sites bill clients on the amount of network traffic. The data is also used for studying utilization trends, performance analysis, and capacity planning.

AAA Implementations

Authentication, authorization, and accounting services are often provided by an AAA server, or software on a shared or dedicated device to perform these three duties. AAA servers are manufactured and sold by several corporations. Several types of devices (such as access servers, routers, switches, hosts, and firewalls) can be configured as clients. The clients query one or more AAA security servers to validate user requests. The servers operate on one the following protocols:

- *Remote authentication dial-in user service (RADIUS)* — This is used mainly for authentication and is an IETF-blessed industry standard. It is a popular dial-in password protocol.

- *Terminal access controller access control system (TACACS+)* — This is a Cisco-proprietary protocol and has all features of RADIUS (such as dial-in security), along with greater levels of authorization and accounting for each user or device. It is commonly used in Cisco environments for managing users on Cisco switches, routers, access servers, PIX firewalls, and so forth.

- *Kerberos* — This was developed at MIT and is an emerging secret-key authentication protocol. It uses data encryption standard (DES) as its cryptographic algorithm. It is gaining popularity in environments with sensitive data. Microsoft and Sun have included Kerberos in their operating systems. Its primary benefits are its compatibility with several other security protocols and that it does not transmit passwords over the network. Instead, it passes tickets. However Kerberos is more difficult to configure and manage. A free implementation of Kerberos is available at `http://web.mit.edu/kerberos/`.

Key Points

Following are some key points discussed in this chapter:

- The first step in effective network security is to develop a corporate-level (and yet detailed) policy. This takes time and involves technical, management, and executive time. Success depends largely on support of the upper management and employee awareness.

- Effective network security consists of traffic- and user-based security.

- Traffic-based security deals with network devices and is enforced via configurations such as router's access control lists (ACLs) and firewall rules.

- User-based security deals with users who must log in and is enforced via security servers such as AAA servers. The latter controls access to computer and network devices (authentication), enforces policies (authorization), and logs usage and provides information needed to bill for actual services (accounting).

- Common AAA protocols are RADIUS, TACACS, and Kerberos.

Disaster Recovery

In This Part

Disaster Recovery

*We are nothing but a minor surface nuisance,
and the planet will be fine long after we are gone.*
— George Carlin

Today almost all businesses have most of their information online for obvious reasons such as accessibility, ease of backups, and manageability. As we have seen in the previous chapters, various layers of protection can be configured to save the data. Setting up a highly available (HA) cluster protects against server or OS failures. RAID protects from disk failures. Backups are a basic way to protect against storage-array failures. However, backup media and servers can be destroyed by sabotage or by man-made or natural disasters such as floods, earthquakes, fires, and smoke. This chapter describes strategies for protecting systems and data from a regional disaster.

A *disaster* is defined as an extended outage of mission-critical applications and data because of a lack of network- or computer-processing capabilities. If the outage does not cause loss of revenue, it may take a couple days of outage to qualify it as a disaster. This is an extreme case. For several businesses such as e-commerce sites, hospitals, and airlines, even a few hours of outage constitutes a disaster. In these days of Internet-accelerated business practices, the demand for 24 × 7 availability and online operations must be met by businesses that wish to remain successful. Gone are the days when small periods of prescheduled downtime were acceptable for maintenance or backups.

The key to disaster recovery (DR) is planning and identifying an optimal recovery procedure that incurs minimum delay. DR planning involves configuring a remote standby site that can take over mission-critical applications and operations within a reasonable time if disaster strikes the primary site.

A good DR plan is a difficult goal to achieve. The main obstacle arises from the fact that you do not really know what catastrophes you are planning for. At the same time, you hope the events you are trying to protect against never happen. Yet, you may be required by your customer-service agreements to provide some level of DR. The nature of several businesses requires them to be ready to respond quickly and recover from disasters. You must also choose which disasters to protect against, and the amount of downtime allowed for the recovery process. These decisions will impact the design and cost of your DR plan. However, if a properly designed plan saves your business in the face of a disaster, you will want it at any cost.

When Bad Things Happen to Good People

Everyone knows it happens. A flood in Chicago in 1992 disrupted operations in 400 data centers. The World Trade Center (WTC) bombing in New York in 1993 disabled several critical data centers of multinational companies.

Downtime is expensive. Reports have shown that the hourly cost of downtime ranges from several thousand dollars to millions (for financial institutions) of dollars. There are various not-so-obvious costs associated with downtime, including the following:

- Missed sales
- Cost of time and material for hardware repairs
- Reduced reputation for customer service and reliability
- Loss of goodwill and reputation among customers
- Idle employees and lost productivity
- Missed service level agreements (SLAs) and penalty payments
- Legal ramifications and liabilities

Even a small period of downtime has a severe impact on profit and public perception. However, if you compare the cost of downtime to that of protecting your data, the cost of data protection does not seem expensive.

Table 38-1 shows some broad and varied causes of disaster. Some of these may be a familiar concern. If so, you need a DR plan for your computing site. The familiar disaster causes are the ones you would like to protect against, and they would be a factor when designing your DR plan.

Table 38-1   Causes of Disaster

DISASTER	CAUSES
Natural calamities	Storm, tornados, fire, earthquake, flood, high winds, heat
Man-made	Wars, military operations, vandalism, bomb threats, explosions, disgruntled employees, malicious destruction, data or computer theft, viruses, human error
Accidents	Plane crash, radiological accidents, explosions, office accidents, plumbing leaks
Technical breakdown	Hardware or software crash or failure, telecommunications outage, interruption of building operations and services, power outage, sprinkler failure

Here are some natural causes and man-made causes of disasters:

- *Fires* — A serious fire creates a myriad of problems (the most disastrous being injuries or loss of lives). Fires cause water mains to leak. This can flood data centers and entire floors. Smoke can travel to upper floors. Entire buildings or parts of them must be closed to everyone during or immediately after a fire. The secondary site must be far enough away so it is protected from the impact of the fire at the primary site. If a fire destroys the physical work area of the users, you must plan for space and workstations for users at the secondary or DR site.

- *Flood* — A broken water main or a broken pipe on a higher floor can cause a flood. Water can easily run down through ceilings and floors. Various natural events such as tornados, hurricanes, heavy rains, and flash floods can deposit too much water for the sewers and ground systems to absorb. That excess water can enter buildings and computing sites.

- *Earthquake* — If you are in an earthquake-prone area, you should locate the fault lines. When selecting a secondary or DR site, ensure that it is far from fault lines, especially those close to the primary site.

- *Site-wide power failure* — A power outage for a short time can be addressed by using a good uninterruptible power supply (UPS). A power failure for an extended period would qualify as a disaster. In that case, it would be necessary to move the users and operations to a DR site. But, before doing so, ensure that the power is available at that DR site. A rolling blackout may follow you.

- *Terrorist attacks* — Several institutions and banks in metropolitan areas such as Boston and New York have their DR sites in remote, unmarked locations that would be less likely to be terrorist targets.

TALES FROM THE TECH TURF: POWER PLAY

At a customer site, there were several servers in rows of cabinets. At one time, both power supplies in a certain server went bad. The bad power supplies in the host unfortunately took down the primary and redundant power distribution units (PDUs) in the data center, which caused all of the cabinets to lose power. Unfortunately most of them were not on a UPS. The fuses on the PDUs were eventually replaced and power was restored. However, the problem resurfaced and all cabinets lost power for a second time. To determine the exact cause of the problem, someone brought an ampmeter and measured the current in all cabinets. The source was narrowed down to a bad server. It was disconnected and placed in a corner for hardware replacements. The process took most of the afternoon.

- *Software, operating system, or application errors* — An improperly coded application or data corruption have the potential to render the data at the primary site unusable. If so, the data at the DR site can be used, provided online data replication procedure has not copied the corruption to the DR site. If the worst has happened, tape backups are your only recourse.

- *Hardware failures* — The primary site could be inaccessible because of complete network outages or failure of one or more critical components. Hardware redundancy protects against device or host-level failures, while a DR site is required to protect against a site-wide outage.

- *Operator or human errors* — The outage at a site could be caused by a mistake or inexperience on the part of operations personnel or by intentional malice of certain employees. Operator errors have been found to be the most common cause of downtime. Employee training and well-documented operating procedures help decrease the possibility of human errors.

High Availability (HA) and Disaster Recovery (DR)

Although HA and DR may have some similarities, they are certainly different, and they address separate problems. Table 38-2 lays out the distinction between HA and DR.

Table 38-2 Differences between High Availability and Disaster Recovery

	HIGH AVAILABILITY (HA)	DISASTER RECOVERY (DR)
When to use it	To protect against host failures.	To protect against loss of an entire physical site or facility.
Configuration	Hosts are connected by heartbeat cables. They have shared storage and they use the same network and subnet.	Nothing is shared. The primary and secondary sites have independent servers, data storage, networks, and so on. Therefore, there are no distance limitations. Data from the primary site is replicated to the secondary site.
Location of servers	HA servers are usually in the same data center, sometimes even in the same cabinet (bad idea because the network or power failure in the cabinet would take all redundant servers), or just a few meters apart in different cabinets or on different floors. If they are farther than that, you could run into length (disk or heartbeat cable) limitations.	The primary and secondary sites are several kilometers apart. If they are far enough apart, the chances a disaster would impact both sites is decreased.
Process of recovery	The recovery process in a cluster is simple. If a server fails, applications failover to the other healthy members in the cluster automatically with no impact on clients or users. After a failed server is repaired, it can be easily brought back into the cluster as a standby or active member.	Recovery is complicated. After a disaster, it may be impossible to ever make the site the same as before. If the disks and data are destroyed, new disks will have to be set up and data restored from secondary site over the network or by using backup tapes.
Effect on clients	Clients and users do not feel the impact of a server failure. The application failover process from failed server is transparent to users.	If the primary site fails, all clients and users feel the effect. It may be necessary to relocate all users to the secondary site.

Five Phases of DR

Planning how to recover from a disaster may appear to be a sprawling task. You must cover not only the hardware, software, and other computing resources, but also the entire business operation including clients, network, user desktops, Internet connection, phone lines, and anything else required for a smooth transition in the event of a natural or man-made disaster. The initial task of computer and data recovery expands to be a business recovery task.

The high-level steps outlined in this section will help you set up a DR program. These are broad phases. The amount of time and work required in each phase will vary from site to site.

Following are the five phases:

- *Phase 1* — Find the funds.
- *Phase 2* — Assess existing environment and risks.
- *Phase 3* — Create DR procedures.
- *Phase 4* — Test the procedures.
- *Phase 5* — Adjust your DR plan to site changes and technical advancements.

Phase 1: Find the Funds

This is easier said than done. Everyone appreciates the need for a DR plan, but the benefits of DR programs are realized only during a disaster. What if the disaster never happens? All the money and time involved in configuring the program would be in vain. People will point out that they do not live in a hurricane-prone state such as Florida or along a fault-line in California. The second problem is that a DR plan usually does not seem as urgent as day-to-day business tasks.

You must take a different approach. Sell a DR program as you would sell life insurance. Most people have life insurance because it gives them peace of mind knowing that if something fatal were to happen to them, presumably their family would not be in financial trouble.

A DR plan provides the same advantage. If your business has a disaster and faces unexpected, extended downtime, your business can use the DR plan to quickly recover mission-critical applications and services, thus avoiding the high cost associated with downtime.

This leads us to the second strong reason why businesses worldwide need a DR plan. When they determine the hourly cost of downtime, businesses consider several things such as lost productivity of employees, lost sales, cost of trying to recreate data, cost of missed SLAs, and time involved for an event's post-mortem and meetings. More importantly there are softer costs such as reduced employee morale and customer confidence. Compare the estimated cost of downtime and the cost of implementing a DR plan. Chances are good that the cost of downtime will be far greater than the cost of protecting the data.

A failsafe way to get the approval of senior management and DR funds is to understand what to worry about and expound those concerns. Senior management must feel understood. Your solution must address these worries. The following are common DR problems that keep senior management worried:

- DR is important, but who will do it? It is a program that does not generate revenue.

- Will the DR plan keep pace with the raw growth?

- How much will it cost? With all the push for lower headcounts, can we pull this off?

- If the work gets too thick midway, will the DR project go to the back-burner and get extinguished?

- In operating in a DR mode, will the project-management team have enough steam? They seem too stretched in normal day-to-day operations.

- How much DR is enough? If there are multiple disasters in a wide geographical area, will there be ample capacity to address them all?

These concerns do not make planning easier, but once you address them, you know the DR project stands a chance of funding. Then you are ready to go to the next step.

Phase 2: Assess Existing Environment and Risks

Planning how you will recover from a disaster may seem to be a huge, sprawling undertaking because you must cover not only your client-server environment, but also the entire business. This includes LANs, Internet connectivity, workgroup recovery, telecommunications, and desktop network. Your IT network is scattered across the organization. In the early days of computing, DR was planning for computer systems, but now it cannot be separated from business recovery planning. Computing has spread the length and breadth of each organization. The business folks do not have the background or mindset to put together a business recovery plan. It is the job of an IS manager.

Feeling overwhelmed? You should. There are hundreds of considerations, and the extent of your attention to detail will determine the degree of final success or failure.

The work is not insurmountable, though. You begin by pinpointing the risks and getting a lay of the IT land. Make a list of the disasters your business is susceptible to such as earthquakes, fires, viruses, hackers, operator errors, malicious employees, hardware or software failures, and natural calamities. The top disasters should get more attention. Then map the impact of the disasters to the business and operations. Make a list of applications, data, and servers expected to be available at the DR site. Conduct a business-impact analysis. Develop your "what-if" scenarios. Find out from users how long they can afford to have the applications and data down. Identify business areas that would suffer the greatest financial pain in the event of a disaster. Finally, assemble a DR team and assign responsibilities to each member.

Phase 3: Create DR Procedures

In this phase, you establish the actual procedure for the aftermath of a disaster. This phase will take the most work and time. The DR procedure should clearly document how to deal with various failures that can devastate your IT infrastructure (such as complete loss of servers, data, routers, bridges, communication links, and so on). This includes non-IT equipment (such as office space, fixtures, cables, and telecommunications support).

As you look for ways to deal with such losses, you will often find that there are no workarounds or shortcuts. The current setup may not have allowances for site failures or an entire configuration outage. These were just not included when the environment was patched together. Before you determine and document a DR process, you must rearchitect configurations that do not have site-wide redundancy. This chapter describes ways to design disaster-tolerant solutions.

The DR procedure should also specify who arranges for repairs or reconstruction and how the data is recovered at the primary, secondary, or DR site. You must also create a checklist to verify if everything has been restored to normal status.

At the end, the DR plan must be complete, comprehensive, and current. By "complete," I mean it must be detailed enough to include each recovery step. In times of stress and when the right people are not around, it must serve as a step-by-step how-to. It must be comprehensive and include all items within the data center and out, all critical components, and all business units. Finally it must be current. Corporations buy servers, downsize and upsize IT environments, expand LANs and WANs, upgrade servers and applications, add new software, and so on. The DR must be updated all the time. Otherwise, it will be a DR document for a corporation that does not exist.

Phase 4: Test the Procedures

Testing is the most practical way to find flaws in the DR program and resolve them before a disaster strikes. Everyone would look foolish if the DR program did not work when it was called upon to save the company. However, testing a DR plan is expensive. Effects are widespread and it takes everyone's time, but it is the only way to discover flaws and ensure that it works when things are helter-skelter.

There are several prerequisites for a test. First, devise a test plan and decide on the frequency of testing. This depends on personnel turnover and technical changes in the DR procedure, system, and network. We all agree it is difficult or impossible to recreate a real disaster. It is also unwise to flood the data center or set offices on fire. Such acts are dangerous to everyone's well-being and job. Decide on a mock disaster that will not injure anyone. Also, decide on who must be notified. It is unnecessary to inform everyone of the upcoming DR test. Only a few supervisors, managers, and company executives would need to know, since an element of surprise is closer to reality. But those who are in the know should control the emotional stress, disputes, and chaos. Finally devise a way to measure the success of each test.

Pick a weekend and do a full run. Get as many people involved as required. In the middle of the test, remove some people from the building and bring in new ones. Remember that in any disaster some people will leave the site (some may immediately leave), and others will join right in the middle of the chaos. After the test, document the flaws that were uncovered and the lessons that everyone learned.

Phase 5: Adjust Your DR Plan to Site Changes and Technical Advancements

Operating systems, network devices, configuration, applications, and other technologies always change. The DR plan must keep up with these changes. There will be new servers and applications added to the DR plan. Be aware of the latest technological trends, especially those that increase the efficiency of the DR procedure. The time to recover from a disaster is critical. If you decide to employ a new feature, go through the steps outlined here, with emphasis on the testing phase.

Set up regular meetings to review the plan and the documents that describe what must be done during a disaster. The documents should be simple enough for a new employee to understand and act accordingly.

Designing a Disaster-Tolerant Architecture

You must take various steps to ensure that the different aspects of your business are protected. Network equipment (especially the equipment that enables Internet access) must be fault-tolerant. Critical network devices and links must be redundant. To protect against server failures, they must be clustered. A local cluster has all nodes and disks in a single data center. Although this protects against server failures, it will not protect you against failure of the entire data center or physical site. Therefore, such an architecture is not disaster-tolerant.

This section provides some guidelines for designing an architecture that protects you against destruction of an entire data center, building, or physical site. Disaster-tolerant architectures represent a shift from centralized data centers toward more distributed data-processing facilities. The objective is to protect against the loss of an entire data center. Although each design satisfies a particular availability need, there are some basic rules for designing disaster-tolerant architectures:

- *Protecting data and nodes through geographic diversity* — In other words, cluster members and data copies must be located far enough away so that a regional disaster does not destroy all cluster nodes and data. Based on the distance between cluster members, there are campus, metropolitan, and continental clusters. These three types of clusters and their implementations are described later in this chapter.

- *Off-line data replication* — In other words, backup tapes and media must be stored offsite at another data center. The backup tapes must be shipped every day (or at least every week) to the remote site. The remote data center must have enough servers and disks in cold-standby mode in case of a failure at the primary data center. In that case, applications are configured on the servers as quickly as possible and data is restored from backup tapes. The advantage is that the data on tape is always consistent. The process itself is simple, involves low expenses, and is easy to document and execute. The main disadvantage is the data is not as up-to-date as the lost data in the primary site. It is only as current as the most recent backup tape. Depending on the volume of data and complexity of applications, the process of recovery can take anywhere from a day to a week. Business-critical applications require a faster recovery time, within hours or even minutes. Online data replication must therefore be used.

- *Online data replication* — Online data replication is a process that copies data from one set of disks to another complete and independent set of disks located at a separate site and attached to a separate set of hosts. Replication is not the same as mirroring. Mirroring treats the disk sets as a single logical volume, and all data copies are accessible from the same host. Replication, on the other hand, treats the disk sets as separate and independent of each other. The downside of replication is the cost of disks and hosts for each site that must have replicated data. Each replicated disk set is usually a RAID-1 or RAID-5 volume. In return for the added hardware expense, the replicated data gives two consistent and equally viable data sets and, therefore, can quickly recover from disaster or outage at any one site. Different methods used to replicate data are discussed later in this chapter.

- *Alternative power sources for redundant servers and data* — If servers within a disaster-tolerant cluster are at different data centers, they must receive power from different sources or power grids. Within a data center, the UPS for different nodes must be on different circuits. If possible, power to different circuits must be supplied from separate power substations on the grid. This adds protection against sabotage, large-scale outages, and electrical storms.

- *Disaster-tolerant networks* — Fault-tolerant networks may increase availability, but they are not disaster-tolerant if all redundant links or networks devices are located in close proximity. To be disaster-tolerant, redundant cables and links must be installed along physically separate and distant routes. Redundant network devices must also be located in different physical sites.

Online Replication Techniques

Online replication is a method of copying data from one site to another over a dedicated I/O or network link. Replication can be as simple as doing a complete backup (for example, using UNIX commands such as `tar` or `dump`) and then reloading it on another system. On the other extreme, it can be as complex as replicating in-process state or in-memory data to another system over the network.

Data can be replicated synchronously or asynchronously. *Synchronous replication* requires writes to all data copies to be complete and replicated before the next write operation can begin. The advantage is that data at the remote site is always consistent and as current as the primary data. However, this procedure reduces server performance and overall response time.

Asynchronous replication does not require the server at the primary site to wait for data to be written to the remote disk before beginning another write operation. Writes to the remote disk are simply queued into a buffer and later synchronized to the remote disk. Obviously the data on the remote site is not as current as the primary data copy. If the primary site fails and remote data is out-of-sync, applications start at the remote site with data that is not current.

Let's examine some common techniques of data replication.

User-Level Replication

This technique uses utilities such as `rsync`, `ftp`, `scp`, `rcp`, and `rdist` to copy files from one system to another. You can use `cron` to copy all updates at regular intervals.

Here is an example using two UNIX hosts, galileo and hubble. Let's say you need to replicate all updates in certain directories from galileo to hubble. You can use rdist or rsync. Write a script on galileo that rdist can use for specifications and run it periodically on Galileo (can be automated via cron).

```
# rdist  -f   /sync_script
```

This command will copy updates in specified directories to hubble. The script /sync_script on galileo looks like the following:

```
HOSTS = ( hubble )
FILES = ( /bigdir/common  /bigdir/forall   /export/home/ )
${FILES} -> ${HOSTS}
install -o chknfs,numchkowner,numchkgroup ;
notify  senior_admin@yourco.com
```

Although user-level replication of data is quick and easy to set up, it is prone to failures. The copy process may not complete because of lack of space on the target. Also, the data on the target is not always up-to-date. The techniques mentioned in the following section automate the replication process using software- or hardware-based solutions.

Software-Based Replication

Several vendors offer software-based solutions that are less expensive than hardware-based options. VERITAS Volume Replicator replicates data to remote sites over any standard IP network in synchronous or asynchronous mode. Software-based solutions support heterogeneous hardware platforms and, therefore, help reduce vendor-specific storage limitations.

Logical volume mirroring is another effective way of having a remote copy. However, the disk-to-server link must be extended to a site far enough away to be unaffected by a local disaster. Cascaded SAN fabric, fibre-channel repeaters, and DWDMs are some ways to extend cable lengths. For details see Chapter 5, "Network Infrastructure in a Data Center."

Device Driver–Level Replication

Write operations for certain directories and file systems go through a special file-replicating device driver that copies required data to other systems. The device driver is installed and configured on the hosts. The write operation is considered complete only after writes to both local and remote systems are done.

Disk-Subsystem Hardware-Based Replication

Some hardware disk array controllers have a replicating driver that sends data to another disk array. The disk blocks are copied to local and remote arrays concurrently using the controller microcode or firmware. Like device driver–level replication, hardware-based replication causes a serious impact on network and host performance, is expensive, and ties you to a particular hardware vendor. Common industry implementations include EMC's Symmetrix Remote Data Facility (SRDF) and Network Appliance's Snap Mirror.

Database Replication

Most leading database vendors (such as Oracle and Sybase) provide ways to replicate database transactions at the primary site to a database instance running on servers at a remote site. They do not replicate application configuration files or files that are not part of the database or application. Because they run at the application level, they can slow the application.

Transaction-Based Replication

In this technique, transactions coming into a database are also written to another database system. The process is usually managed by the application itself in two phases to guarantee that the transactions get committed to both systems. Transactional replication can be done by either of the following:

- *Transactional processing monitors (TPMs)* — TPMs provide the infrastructure for building and managing complex transaction-processing systems with a large number of clients and multiple servers. The client communicates with a resource-monitoring or router process that routes requests to the appropriate server. Traditionally TPMs have existed in the realm of mainframe computers running applications such as IBM's CICS. Nowadays, distributed TPMs such as Encina, NCR's Top-End, and Microsoft's MTS have demonstrated the suitability of building transaction-based systems using client-server architecture. Also, *object-oriented transactional processing monitors (OTMs)* are being developed. OTMs, although new, are quickly gaining wide acceptance. There are CORBA-based OTMs (such as M3 from BEA Systems), DCOM-based OTMs (such as MTS from Microsoft), and DCE-based OTMs (such as Encina from Transarc Corporation, which is now an IBM subsidiary).

- *Asynchronous queuing systems* — Commercial implementations include BEA Systems' Tuxedo/Q and IBM's MQ Series. The application is logically positioned in front of the database and therefore can direct all incoming writes to databases on multiple systems.

Process-Level State Replication

The previous techniques replicated data to multiple locations. Process replication guarantees you have another server that knows enough about in-memory, intermediate data, and status to take over active sessions from a failed primary server. This gives you the advantage of a very short failover time because clients are redirected to a replicated server.

Best Practices

After a disaster or event that can cause a lengthy downtime, the amount of time needed to recover data and applications is important. The DR procedures must enable quick recovery from any type of disruption.

Understand the major causes of downtime at your site. It is estimated that 40 percent of business disruptions are caused by human errors. Although human errors or the dreaded "rm − r *" scenarios may be impossible to eliminate, the frequency of occurrence can be reduced by better procedures, documentation, and continuous training.

The other causes of downtime are software errors and bugs, power outages, hardware failures, and true, natural disasters (such as fires, earthquakes, and floods). Hardware failures can be managed with redundancy but cannot be completely eliminated. Software and hardware will break, regardless of the measures you implement. Therefore, you need to plan and test procedures that must be followed during disasters and unexpected downtime.

One important and common way to overcome disasters is to retrieve data from backups. Following are some tips to ensure that you have a fail-proof backup strategy. Having an up-to-date and reliable set of backups is your first line of defense.

- Know the nature and significance of your data and the tolerance for its unavailability. Then determine the level of protection to be applied to that data.

- Test the integrity of your backup tapes by running partial or full restores.

- Run full system-level restoration tests on a quarterly basis. Then evaluate the recovery speeds and procedures.

- Plan to centralize backup, if it is not already centralized. A centralized backup reduces management overhead and leverages shared devices such as tape libraries.

- When selecting commercial backup software, examine all aspects of the software: tape formats, service requirements, OS support, compatibility with other vendors, and so forth.

- To ensure backward and forward compatibility, buy technology from companies with proven track records and clear product road maps.

One of the most important tasks when preparing for a disaster is studying the current configuration and deciding whether the architecture of each component will protect it from a site disaster. Do not be disheartened to find that the answer is often "not ready." Various servers, applications, network layout, and so on must be rearchitected. You must set up data replication to a remote site. The farther away the remote site, the safer it is from region-wide disasters. But, there are practical limitations. If cluster members are at remote sites, your configuration is bound by the maximum length of heartbeat links, distance of data from server, and network reliability between cluster members.

Here are some general guidelines for a successful DR plan:

- The DR team needs a lot of time and resources from each area of organization. Management awareness is the first and most critical step. Management must acknowledge the risks of a disaster and support the ongoing efforts to deploy a DR plan. To develop management support, you must first identify possible disaster scenarios. Make a list of top disasters (such as fires, terrorist attacks, loss of key personnel by accidents, hurricanes, viruses, software errors, and so on). Assess the impact of a disaster from both a financial and physical (infrastructure) perspective. Compare the financial and business losses with the costs required to build a DR strategy. Managers are then willing to deploy resources to develop and implement a DR strategy across the organization.

- Ensure that key members of various groups (such as database administrators, network engineers, system administrators, facilities personnel, and senior management) are included in the DR team.

- The DR planning group should provide regular reports to senior management.

- Assign business processes and applications to three categories:
  - *Mission-critical* (outage would cause extreme business disruption and financial losses and harm customer service)
  - *Important* (outage would cause minor legal or financial harm)
  - *Minor* (outage would cause problems with accessing other systems)

Once you have established priorities, dedicate proportionate efforts to developing and implementing a recovery plan.

Key Points

Following are key points discussed in this chapter:

- Unexpected and extended downtime is an expensive nightmare and is caused by human errors, hardware or software faults, natural calamities, and acts of terrorism. Downtime for business-critical applications can cause losses of up to millions of dollars per hour.

- A DR plan should include identifying the risks, creating easy-to-follow procedures, testing the procedures, and keeping up-to-date with technical advancements.

- A disaster-tolerant site is one whose data is replicated to a remote site either synchronously or asynchronously and in which applications continue to be online, even in the event of a complete failure of the data center or building.

DR
Architectures

*We are told never to cross a bridge until we come to it, but this world is owned only
by men who have "crossed bridges" in their imagination far ahead of the crowd.*
— Robert Frost

A disaster-recovery (DR) architecture is a design where servers and data copies
are placed in geographically dispersed locations (for example, in different buildings, in different cities, or on the other side of the world). The distance between
nodes depends on the type of disaster from which you need protection and the
technology you deploy to replicate data. Based on these factors, there are three
types of clusters (illustrated in Figure 39-1):

- Campus (or local) clusters (distance limited to 50 kilometers)
- Metropolitan clusters (distance limited to 100 kilometers)
- Continental (or wide-area) clusters (unlimited distance)

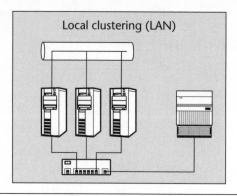

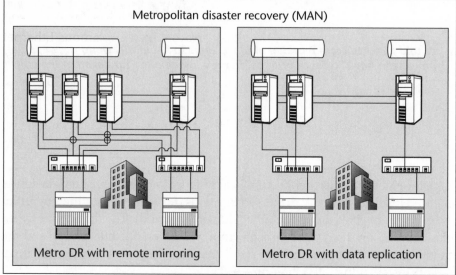

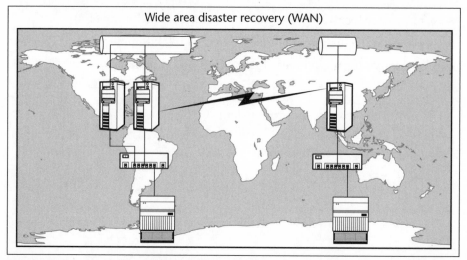

Figure 39-1 DR architectures using data mirroring or replication.

Campus Clusters

Campus clusters are designed so that no single building failure causes the cluster to fail. By definition, a "campus" implies that network, power, and storage access cables can be laid or rerouted without outside permission. The nodes in a campus cluster are placed in adjacent buildings or those that are up to 10 kilometers apart.

Figure 39-2 shows a campus cluster with member servers and disks in separate data centers. All disks attached to fibre channel (FC) switches A and B are accessible by both servers. Logical volume mirroring on the servers is used to keep a mirrored data copy in each data center. For example, storage arrays A and B can be mirrored to arrays C and D. Redundant links must be used to connect the servers, FC switches, and disk arrays. Likewise, campus Ethernet network must be highly available with redundant links between data centers. Power supply to data centers must be from different circuits or sources.

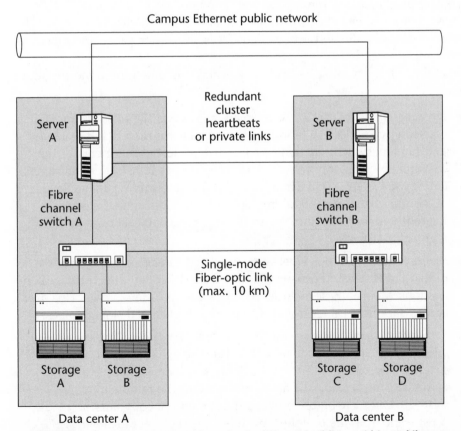

Figure 39-2 A campus cluster with nodes in different buildings within 10 kilometers.

Metropolitan Clusters

A metropolitan cluster has member nodes in different parts of the city or in adjacent cities. The distance separating the nodes is limited by the network and data replication technology available. The distance between the two sites must be wide enough to reduce the likelihood of both sites getting destroyed by the same disaster.

Metropolitan clusters are useful to Internet service providers (ISPs) that have several sites along a fiber-optic network and to application service providers (ASPs) that need to reach customers around the city. Like a campus cluster, a metropolitan cluster is also a single cluster, the main distinction being that the members are farther apart than in a campus cluster. Increasing the distance between cluster members causes problems. The latency caused by the distance interferes with the performance required for heartbeat links. Therefore, heartbeat links should be over dedicated and fast network connections. DWDMs, repeaters, extended long wavelength GBICs, and cascaded SAN fabrics are used to access remote storage. You need dedicated dark fiber links between the two sites to be able to use the entire bandwidth for storage. The maximum distance allowed between DWDMs, FC switch ports, and repeaters depends on the vendor.

Several hindrances must be overcome when implementing a metropolitan cluster:

- *Distance limitations of I/O links* — In an FC-AL topology, the distance between two nodes in a fabric device must be less than 10 kilometers. You can link switches to make a cascaded fabric, but this increases the cost and you gain only an extra 10 kilometers per link. With mainframes, enterprise systems connection (ESCON) directors and repeaters have a maximum distance of 60 kilometers. Yet, these distances fall short of the required long-distance separation to protect at least one site from regional disasters.

- *Right-of-way obstacles* — Fiber-optic links that run beneath the cities are difficult to obtain and expensive to lease for dedicated direct storage connections. Most of these are used by telecommunications traffic. This precludes dark fiber cables from being used as high-speed storage pipes.

- *Performance degradation caused by distance-induced delay (latency)* — I/O write delays are proportional to the intersite distance. Intermediate gateways or extenders add to the delay and increases application response time because the host must wait for the remote mirrored writes to complete before proceeding. If the local copy fails, all reads must come from the remote copy, which further degrades performance. When the failed disk set is brought online, data synchronization further exacerbates performance problems.

Continental Clusters

Unlike campus and metropolitan clusters with single-cluster architecture, a *continental cluster* uses multiple clusters to enable wide-area application failover. As evident by their name, systems in a continental cluster are separated by large distances. WAN connections range from 100 kilometers to transoceanic distances. WAN protocols such as TCP/IP are used for intercluster communications.

The intersite distance is not the only difference between continental and campus or metropolitan clusters. The other distinction is the way data is written to the remote site. In a campus or metropolitan cluster, host mirroring software is commonly used to update the remote disk. In a continental cluster, data at one cluster site must be replicated to storage devices at the other cluster site over the WAN.

There are several ways to replicate data over the WAN. You can use FC-to-IP routers (such as Cisco 5420 storage routers). They enable hosts to access devices in SANs over a network link. You can also use ESCON-to-WAN converters or bridges. The bridges have ports that connect to the storage devices and network switches. Other techniques are described in Chapter 5, "Network Infrastructure in a Data Center."

Figure 39-3 shows typical continental clusters, consisting of a cluster in Dallas (standby) and another in Boston (production). The two clusters can be an active-passive (asymmetric) or active-active (symmetric) pair. Let's assume an asymmetric configuration where the Boston cluster is running mission-critical applications with servers configured as a local cluster. Applications failover from node to node as necessary. The data in Boston is replicated over the WAN to storage connected to hosts in the Dallas cluster. The Dallas cluster is also configured with the same applications as on the Boston cluster. However, the nodes in Dallas do not run the applications under normal circumstances. If none of the servers in the Boston cluster can run the applications, or if there is a site-wide power outage (or any other disaster) in Boston, one of the servers in the Dallas cluster starts the applications. The two clusters can also run in active-active mode, where they monitor each other for failures and data is replicated in both directions. In addition, the cluster servers in Dallas and Boston may run applications that are not part of the cluster configuration.

There are several issues concerning a continental cluster:

- The WAN lines are usually leased from a telecommunications provider. Sometimes they cannot provide a high degree of reliability and performance. The distance imposes a significant time lag or latency, which creates an issue with data consistency between the two sites.

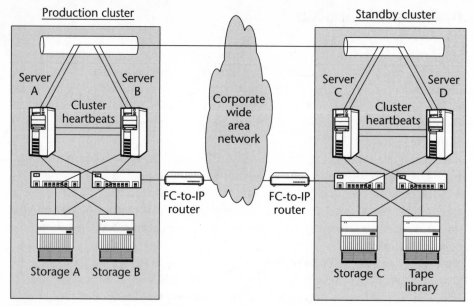

Figure 39-3   A continental cluster with two geographically distant clusters.

- WAN-enabled tools such as transaction processing monitors (TPMs) and data replication tools are required to ensure that the data copies are consistent.

- Because of the distance between the nodes, operational issues such as failover testing and working with staff on the remote site become more difficult.

Key Points

Following are some key points discussed in this chapter:

- Campus and metropolitan clusters have servers that are far apart and data that is replicated to a remote site usually via hardware or software mirroring.

- Continental clusters are usually made up of two or more clusters that are located very far apart and monitor each other. Data at each site is replicated over the WAN to the remote site.

- If a cluster fails, a remote cluster takes over the failed applications.

- Data between two systems can be replicated by user scripts, device drivers, disk controllers, and transaction-based replication techniques.

Future Considerations

In This Part

Voice over IP and Converged Infrastructure

Let us not be content to wait and see what will happen,
but give us the determination to make the right things happen.
— Peter Marshall

In a world where IP networks dominate LANs and WANs and where data storage and voice communication needs grow unabated, it is unavoidable that these forces would converge. This chapter discusses technologies that allow voice and storage communications across the data network. It will briefly look at these key components and later how they can be combined.

A *converged infrastructure* is an IT network that supports various services, the primary of which are as follows:

- Data storage communications
- LAN communications
- Voice communications using telephones

> **TALES FROM THE TECH TURF: DIALING OVER DATA NETWORKS**
>
> In September 2004, Bank of America purchased 180,000 IP-based phones from Cisco Systems, Inc., to replace its copper-wire traditional phone sets. A key motivation was to cut part of the $500 million spent on communication. They planned to replace at least 5,800 desk phones in the near future and use their internal IP network and Internet for voice calls. This represented one of the biggest voice-over-IP (VoIP) phone orders for Cisco. Boeing and Ford Motor have also moved to VoIP phones.

Each service has its own set of set of hardware and protocol requirements such as switches, cables, speed, and type of interfaces. Because of their idiosyncratic requirements, most corporations have a dedicated, supporting network and a dedicated team of people to care for each service.

However, every business today faces an unprecedented challenge to "do more with less." Businesses must keep the networks up and available at all times. Customers and employees must have the flexibility of logging in at any hour and from anywhere over VPNs, and they expect the infrastructure to work. They are expected to generate more business. But, the budget to beef up and maintain the essential networks is continuing to shrink. Headcounts are flat or decreasing. Every technology investment is expected to provide a quick return on investment (ROI) or pay for itself within a reduced time.

This chapter discusses the following major enterprise networks as components of the converged infrastructure:

- *Component 1* — Independent data networks
- *Component 2* — Independent storage networks
- *Component 3* — Independent voice networks

In a converged infrastructure, all these services are provided by a single IP-based network.

Component 1: Independent Data Networks

Almost all large corporations in the world haves offices and business spread over multiple sites. They are all dependent on information. They require a high level of availability, reliability, and ability to scale to a larger size. Loss caused by network downtime exceeds the cost of building a resilient infrastructure. The trends driving to complete resilience on network connectivity are as follows:

- Rapid growth in use of network-based applications that require data from other hosts
- Increase in online data
- Growth of remote offices
- Demand for VPN services

The networks of today are more extensive in terms of their geographical reach, as well as internal and external user groups they connect. Figure 40-1 shows an enterprise network, connecting remote sites and employees. Figure 40-2 shows how the Internet enables communication between different locations of an enterprise and between enterprises.

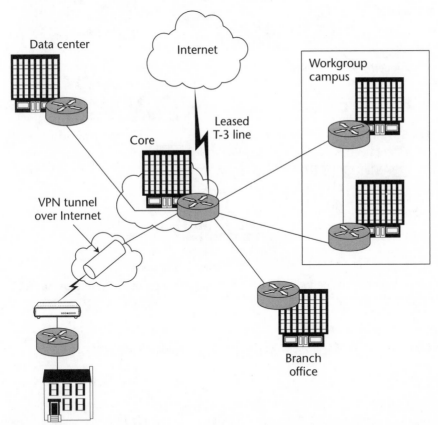

Figure 40-1   Network within an enterprise, connecting remote sites and telecommuters.

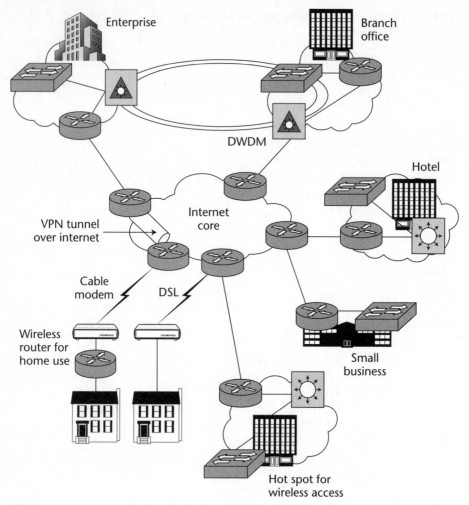

Figure 40-2   Internet is a "network of networks" and connects users around the world.

Component 2: Independent Storage Networks

All enterprises are experiencing an exponential growth of storage. It is estimated that the storage sales worldwide are more than server sales, and the amount of required storage is doubling every year. There are a number of key drivers for this explosive growth:

- More and more data is moving online. Employees and customers expect to view and modify online information.

- 24 × 7 e-commerce and customer care with lower budgets require online access to transactional information, support data, and so on.

- Information stored and moved on the network has been moved to increase employee productivity.

- E-learning and supply-chain information is driving media-rich and storage-hungry content to servers where it can be easily accessed.

Figures 40-3 and 40-4 show the three ways that servers access storage:

- *Direct attached storage (DAS)* — The storage is directly connected by SCSI or fibre channel (FC) cables to the host-based adapters (HBAs) within the server. The storage is captive behind the server. Even if the storage is not used, it cannot be accessed by any other server. This is the traditional way of connecting storage, and most of today's storage is being connected in this manner.

- *Network attached storage (NAS)* — The file server or NAS head export or share its locally attached disks to other servers and clients in the network. It is the only one (out of DAS, NAS, and SAN) that uses the existing IP network.

- *Storage area networks (SAN)* — Most of today's corporations use SAN-based storage for enterprise-level applications. SAN is explained in Part V, "Data Storage Technologies," of this book. The storage devices are all connected to a set of FC switches to form a common pool of storage that can be accessed by any server connected to the set of switches.

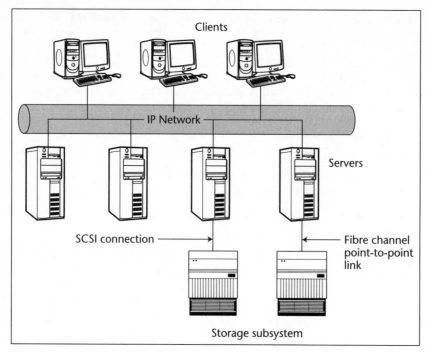

Direct Attached Storage (DAS)

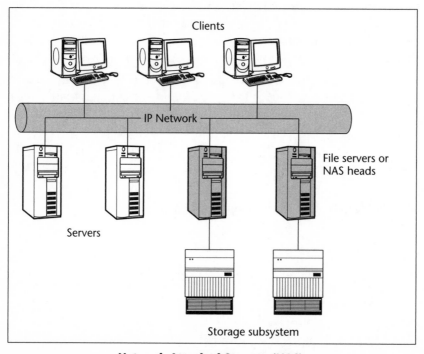

Network Attached Storage (NAS)

Figure 40-3 Direct- and network-attached storage.

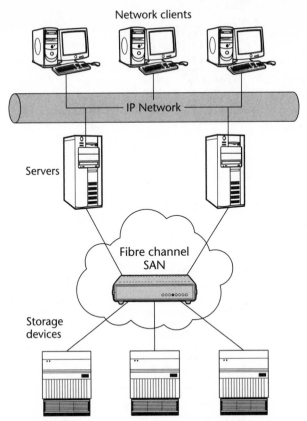

Figure 40-4   SANs using FC switches to connect hosts and storage subsystems.

Component 3: Independent Voice Networks

This section provides an overview of an existing telephone network, including its shortcomings that can be remedied by VoIP. Figure 40-5 shows a telephone network as it exists without modern VoIP equipment. The Public Switched Telephone Network (PSTN) is the oldest network in the world. It has 700 million subscribers worldwide. The connection from the central office (CO) to home is usually analog. Digital devices (such as a fax machine or computer) require an intervening modem for conversion to analog.

Figure 40-5 shows buildings 1 and 2 and the remote branch office having their own private branch exchange (PBX) devices. It connects phone calls coming from the PSTN to the extensions within the organization. Calls from one internal phone to another are kept within the organization without having to use the PSTN. This is possible if the PBXs are interconnected (as shown between buildings 1 and 2 in Figure 40-5). The PBX interconnections are digital (such as T-1 links or channels configured on a TDM backbone). The TDM splits the bandwidth into channels dedicated for voice or data.

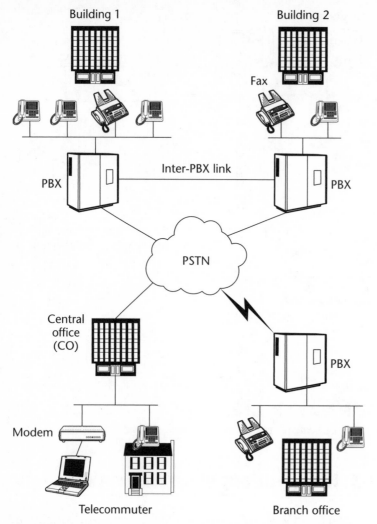

Figure 40-5 Existing telephone network within an organization's sites.

> **NOTE** PSTN and PBX are described in more detail in the following section.

The problem is that the voice-dedicated channels are underutilized most of the time. A study has shown that during a phone conversation, 56 percent of the duration is pause, 22 percent of the time is exchange of essential components of the conversation, and the remaining 22 percent is repetition. An alternative would be to set up a protocol to allow data and voice packets to travel along the same channels. This is possible by VoIP, where voice is encapsulated into IP packets for transmission over IP networks.

Figure 40-6 shows the need to build and manage two parallel networks for telephone conversations and for data. The section "Voice over IP (VoIP)," later in this chapter, explains the convergence of the two networks.

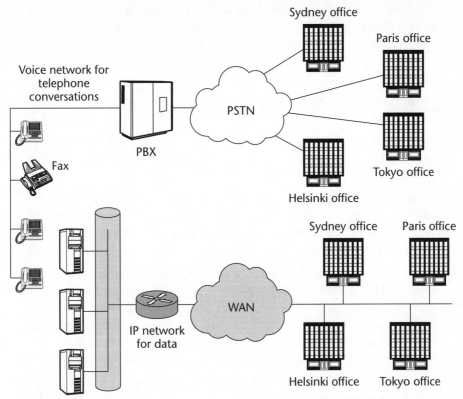

Figure 40-6   Two independent networks: one for telephone conversations and the other for data.

Important Telephone- and VoIP-Related Terms

Before delving into VoIP configurations, a brief introduction with terminology is necessary:

- *Public Switched Telephone Network (PSTN)* — PSTN is the world's collection of interconnected public voice telephone networks. It is also known as the Plain Old Telephone Service (POTS). It is set up and managed by the government and commercial organizations. It has evolved from the early days of Alexander Graham Bell to mostly digital, circuit-switched telephone network.

- *Private branch exchange (PBX)* — This is a device located within an organization that routes telephone calls to internal extensions or to the PSTN. It provides additional features such as voicemail and call-forwarding. A PBX is less expensive than connecting an external line to every telephone. Numbers within the PBX (internal numbers) can be dialed using the last few numbers of the entire phone number and without going through the PSTN. A PBX usually has more than 125 ports.

■ *Key telephone system* — This is used like a PBX in small offices where far fewer phones are required. Each key telephone system supports up to a hundred ports.

■ *Software IP phones* — These consist of a headset that plugs into the USB or serial interface of a PC. The PC needs client software that supports IP telephony.

■ *Hardware IP phones* — These look like regular telephone sets, but they are plugged into a LAN switch. Most IP phones get power from the switch (power over Ethernet or PoE) and encapsulate voice data into IP frames for transmission over the LAN.

■ *H.323* — This was approved by the International Telecommunications Union (ITU) in 1996 as a standard for multimedia and audiovisual transmission across disparate networks. In 1998, it was followed by version 2. It also includes several functions such as bandwidth management, call control, multimedia management, and interoperability between different network types. H.323 has come to be the most popular protocol for VoIP.

■ *Session initiation protocol (SIP)* — SIP is IETF's standard for multimedia communication over IP networks. It is an application-layer control protocol that initiates, manages, and terminates calls between two or more terminals. It is picking up as an alternative to H.323.

Converged Infrastructure

Storage over IP (SoIP) and *voice over IP (VoIP)* are the underlying technologies that make a converged infrastructure possible. IP network speed is evolving from 1 Gbps to 10 Gbps. This advancement leads to progress in storage and telephone technologies. There is a strong incentive to use the network infrastructure for other data, mainly storage and voice. However, not all traffic has the same requirements. Table 40-1 shows the services grouped by their requirements.

Table 40-1   Network Requirements of Different Applications

REQUIREMENT	VOICE	MISSION-CRITICAL APPLICATIONS	FTP	E-MAIL
Bandwidth	High	Moderate	Moderate to high	Low
Sensitivity to random drops	Low	Moderate to high	High	Low
Sensitivity to delays	High	Low to moderate	Low	Low
Sensitivity to jitters	High	Moderate	Low	Low

Storage over IP (SoIP)

The leading protocols that enable storage to unite with IP networks are Internet small computer systems interface (iSCSI) and fibre channel over Internet protocol (FCIP). These have been discussed in Chapters 20 through 24. Here I will just point out how they can coexist to make an end-to-end solution.

The following differentiate the two protocols:

- *iSCSI* — iSCSI is a protocol to encapsulate and map block-oriented SCSI data and SCSI commands for transmission over IP networks. An iSCSI adapter is placed within a server so that it can access storage devices within subsystems that are iSCSI-enabled.

- *FCIP* — FCIP is a protocol to encapsulate FC frames for transmission over IP networks. SANs allow high-speed communication between storage and servers and also eliminate the storage from becoming a data island. This is because servers connected to a SAN fabric can access any storage within the fabric.

Both protocols are compatible with existing Ethernet and IP WAN infrastructures. iSCSI and FCIP hosts or storage can access each other over an IP WAN. In a WAN environment, TCP/IP ensures transmission reliability by reducing network congestion and retransmitting if necessary.

Figure 40-7 shows iSCSI-enabled servers that can access iSCSI-enabled storage devices and those behind a storage router. SAN fabrics that have SAN switches connected to storage routers (or IP-SAN modules) can communicate with each other and iSCSI-enabled servers. This removes the limitation that storage within a SAN fabric can be accessed only by servers in the same fabric.

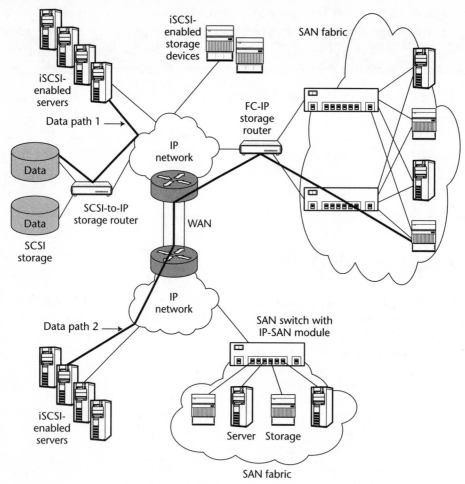

Figure 40-7   iSCSI servers and storage devices and IP-enabled SAN fabrics.

SoIP provides several capabilities:

- Copy data synchronously to storage devices at a remote disaster-recovery (DR) site. *Synchronous access* refers to copying data to primary and DR sites at the same time.
- Copy data to a remote tape drive.
- Interconnect SAN islands across a MAN or WAN.
- Leverage economies of scale and simplify overall architecture by using existing IP infrastructure for storage data.

Figure 40-8 shows a campus network with iSCSI-enabled servers and storage devices that can access each other. The storage devices behind the IP-SAN module switches and storage router can be accessed by any iSCSI-enabled server.

Figure 40-9 shows two remote sites that are connected by a shared dense wavelength division multiplexing (DWDM) network. SAN switches and IP network switches (such as gigabit Ethernet) can be connected to the DWDM, thus using the same network to transport IP and storage data between Data Center 1 and Data Center 2.

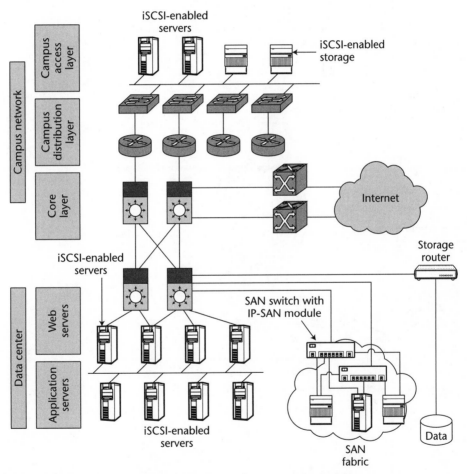

Figure 40-8   IP-enabled storage devices with a campus network.

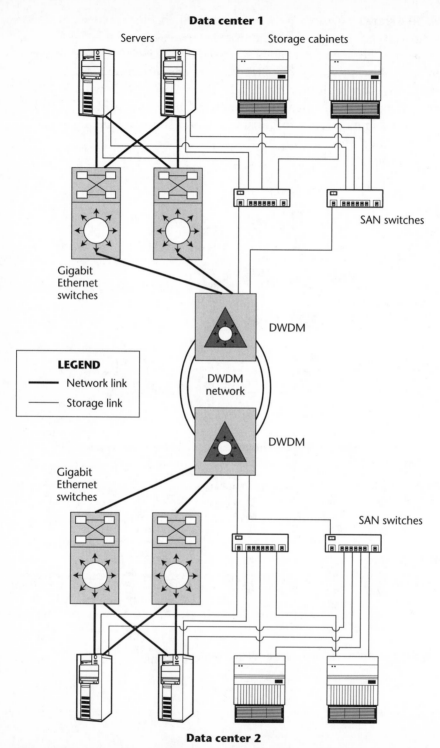

Figure 40-9   Network and storage connection between two distant sites using a common DWDM network.

Voice over IP (VoIP)

Voice over Internet protocol (*VoIP*) is a group of hardware, software tools, and protocol that allow you to use the Internet as the transmission medium for placing telephone calls. It encapsulates the voice data into IP packets and transmits the packets over the Internet (rather than using PSTN). An obvious advantage is that the user does not have to pay a toll or surcharge for the call. All he or she has to pay is the Internet access ISP fee, usually a flat fee per month. This is similar to sending e-mails, where the user is not charged for every message delivered or sent. It is also known as *IP telephony* (*IPT*), or *Internet telephony and voice over Internet.*

Following are some facts about VoIP:

- The per-minute surcharge for long-distance and international calls is decreasing primarily because of the VoIP used by most carriers.

- Telecommunication carriers are moving to an IP-centric world.

- Market research studies have estimated that 10 percent of all calls as of 2005 are being transmitted over VoIP.

- By the year 2007, 7 million IP phones will be installed around the world.

- Research by the Yankee Group estimates the number of VoIP users will increase from 1 million in 2005 to 30 million in 2009.

Most corporations are aware that they will have to move to VoIP sooner or later. They also know that VoIP has been experiencing rapid growth. They are being driven by hopes of reduced communication surcharges, lower infrastructure setup and management costs, and increased productivity through converged applications.

A report by *USA Today* has projected that the VoIP revenues within the Unites States will rise sharply over the next five years, as shown in Table 40-2.

Table 40-2   Projected VoIP Revenue in the U.S.

YEAR	U.S. REVENUE BECAUSE OF VoIP
2003	$10 million
2004	$800 million
2005	$1,700 million
2006	$3,100 million
2007	$4,600 million

Most U.S. cities rely on money they get by imposing taxes on traditional phone bills. As people migrate to VoIP phones that have lower bills and taxes, the cities face a serious threat to their economic stability.

The complexities of building a converged infrastructure and delivering the high quality of service (QoS) required for voice conversation should not be underestimated. The ultimate test of quality — the users' perception — depends on sound planning, high QoS, vigilant monitoring, and quick troubleshooting.

Building VoIP Networks

Transitioning to VoIP is a technically simple concept but has far-reaching impact. The business case for and issues with VoIP are discussed in subsequent sections of this chapter.

The easiest way to deploy VoIP is to replace the PBX units with a VoIP gateway or relay. This is a unit that encapsulates voice data into IP frames and serves as an interface between PSTN telephone calls and IP telephony.

Figure 40-10 shows a voice-enabled router at sites 1 and 2. Phone conversations between the two sites use the IP network. There is no PSTN integration to fret about. This is ideal if you just want to route intersite phone calls within a corporation. The IP phones are connected to the Ethernet ports. Several Ethernet switches provide power over the wires to the IP phones. This feature is called *power over Ethernet (PoE)*, and PoE phone sets do not have any power supply unit. Instead of using IP phones that plug into an Ethernet switch and have the look and feel of a regular phone, you can use software-based IP phones. That way you do not run out of phone ports on the switch. A laptop or PC speaker and microphone can be used as a phone. A headset that plugs into a USB or serial port will also work. You must get IP telephony client software, however.

VoIP phones need to use the PSTN to communicate with phones that are not on the IP network. Figure 40-11 shows a VoIP relay or gateway and a voice-enabled router connected to a PSTN network. A gateway links VoIP calls to the PSTN. The PSTN network is used for two purposes: phone conversations with non-IP phones and for both IP and non-IP phones when the WAN links are down. The router enables the use of the IP WAN for VoIP-to-VoIP calls.

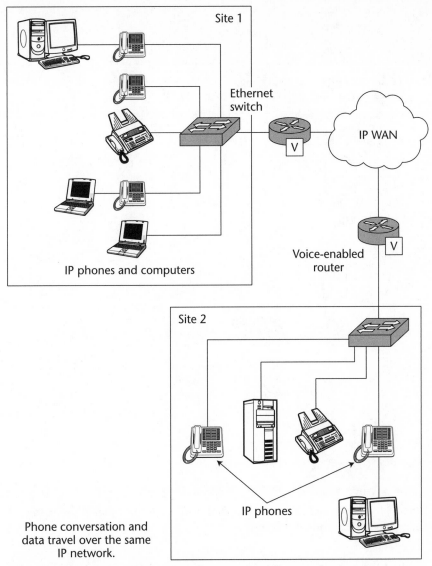

Figure 40-10   Phone conversations between two sites use the IP network.

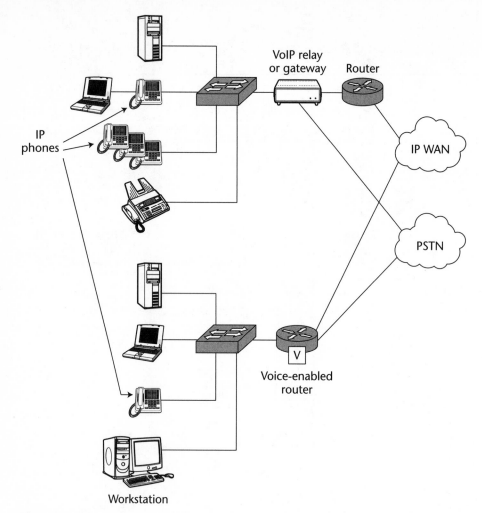

Figure 40-11 IP phones and data are connected to the WAN for communication to other IP phones and to PSTN for non-IP phones.

Figure 40-12 shows the same network as Figure 40-6, except that the voice-enabled router has allowed many users to switch from older-style phones to VoIP phones. All phone conversations are routed through the IP network. The PBX still exists to support the remaining older-style phones and to serve as a hot standby for VoIP services during WAN failures. The PBX routes calls to the branch offices over the IP network.

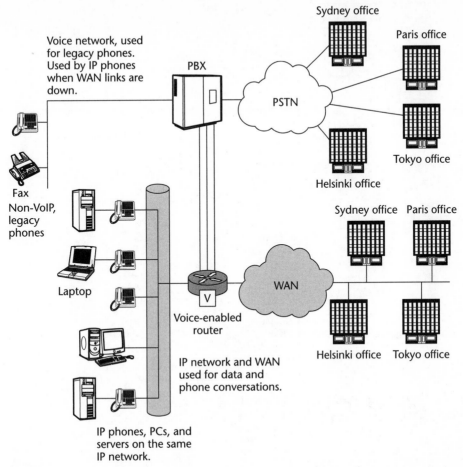

Figure 40-12 IP network is used for data and VoIP phones. The PBX is used by non-VoIP phones.

Figure 40-13 shows a corporation's headquarters and branch office. The headquarters has VoIP phones and regular PBX-connected phones that communicate with other VoIP phones and the branch offices over the IP WAN. The PSTN links are used to communicate with non-VoIP phones and as a backup for the IP WAN.

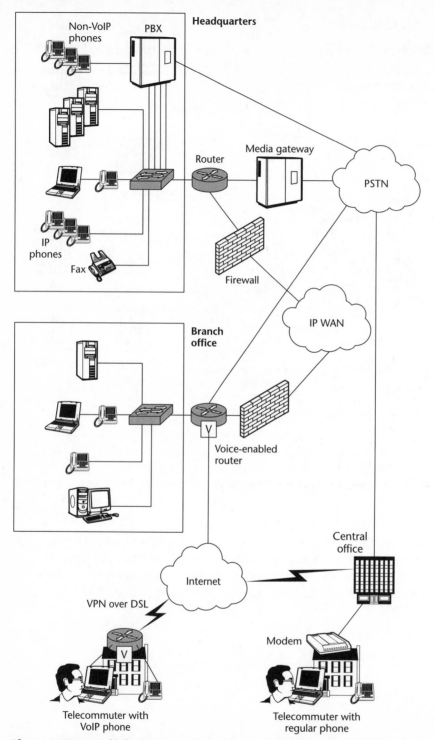

Figure 40-13 Multiple corporate sites with IP- and PBX-connected telephones.

Business Case for Voice over IP

Although the VoIP technology is simple and you may already have most the infrastructure in place, migration requires detailed planning and a hard look at your current environment. It is necessary to build some business justification to get executive sponsorship. VoIP has problems such as clarity of conversation, but it also has the following advantages:

- *Higher user productivity* — Telecommuters and employees on the road can access all phone services regardless of their whereabouts and participate in all business activities. Software-based IP phones allow them to set their call-forwarding to their laptop without incurring toll charges.

- *Enhanced user applications* — Moving phone calls to IP networks removes the media and location-dependency in voicemails, faxes, instant messaging, e-mails, and other productivity tools. All of these can be combined into a single GUI, accessible via a phone or software application. These components of the next-generation call centers can be merged with the Web, making them available from anywhere at anytime. The net advantage is increased level of access to information, improved efficiency, and superior customer interaction.

- *Cost control* — Cost control is not so much about saving per-minute charges for long distance and international calls. Savings, attributable to using the IP network instead of PSTN to transmit voice packets, is elusive. You can sign up for a prepaid domestic calling card for less than 3 cents/minute. Get your friends to use the same carrier and you can frequently call them for free. The major cost savings come from other areas such as integrated voice and data network management, phone moves, adds and changes (this is another MAC address) being made by the network team, and potentially reduced staff needs.

Adoption and use of VoIP by all organizations is unavoidable and simply a matter of time.

Issues with VoIP

With all the advantages listed previously, migration to VoIP should be a no-brainer. In fact, in 2006, more VoIP and IP telephony phones will be sold than analog phone sets. By the year 2007, there will be 7 million VoIP phones installed worldwide. Despite the market momentum, there are some challenges when architecting and implementing VoIP.

Quality of Service (QoS)

"Sorry, I did not hear that; please repeat what you said" is unacceptable, especially when you have a customer who is agitated even before he or she dialed into the call center. Voice conversation requires instantaneous transmission in the correct sequence. Acceptable audio quality over VoIP phones is not automatic There must be some level of guarantee that delay-sensitive voice traffic will be given priority over the typically delay-insensitive data traffic. VoIP conversations will work if you provide ample bandwidth and dedicated, fast pipes, but all this defeats the goals of achieving economies of scale and sharing existing IP infrastructure.

The final test is end-user perception of audio quality, and it is a tough test. But before that, VoIP must meet some International Telecommunication Standards (ITU) metrics that detail how users perceive and understand speech quality:

- *Dial tone delay* — This is the user's wait time after he or she takes the phone off the hook and before he or she hears a dial tone.

- *Call setup time* — This is the time taken for the called party to hear a bell tone after complete dialing.

- *Call-completion ratio* — This is the number of dials that successfully went through versus those that did not go through.

- *Post dialing delay* — This is the user's wait time after he or she completes dialing and before he or she hears the ring on the other side.

Sound waves exist in analog form. They must be digitized before transmissions. Audio compression helps reduce the time taken for transmission, but digitization and compresses lead to new problems, such as delay and jitter. VoIP must effectively deal with the following:

- *Delay or latency* — This is the length of time that a voice packet takes to travel between the two phone sets. A minimum delay is unavoidable because of distance, but VoIP should reduce that and remove other causes of delay.

- *Packet loss* — There is some packet loss caused by conversion of voice data to packets, but VoIP should keep that within acceptable limits. Data packets are transmitted using TCP, which can retransmit lost or collided packets. However, voice packets are transmitted using real-time transport protocol (RTP), which is based on connectionless UDP. In the interest of speed, UDP does not retransmit packets in case they are lost or have a transmission error.

- *Jitter* — This is the time between packet arrivals. This must be consistent to avoid unusually long silence.

It has been estimated that more that three-quarters of the networks in the world are not suitable for VoIP and will need upgrades. To remedy these issues, network switches must be able to detect the presence of a VoIP phone and automatically configure proper packet prioritization. For better performance and bandwidth utilization, the phone set should deal with data compression.

Availability

When you pick up the phone, you expect a dial tone. Analog phones and the PSTN have provided high levels of availability for a long time. Likewise, VoIP service should be always available despite failures of the IP network, PBX, VoIP servers, or network switches. The servers and network switches should be on UPS, and VoIP phones should use PoE (power over Ethernet) from the switch. The entire network should have no single points of failure, enough redundancy to allow maintenance without service disruption, and a reliable configuration at a remote site for extended outages and natural disasters.

Managing a Network of Networks

VoIP cannot ignore the legacy PSTN network because most of the world still uses it. There are several networks that must now be managed together: internal network, access to Internet, remote access (such as VPN networks), PBX network for non-VoIP phones, key systems, analog phones, and connection to PSTN. Because of the increased reliance on a single integrated network, performance and high availability needs are further heightened. The network manager is now a manager of a network of networks.

Toward a Complete Enterprise Convergence

Despite the challenges and problems with VoIP and SoIP, the adoption has a strong drive, primarily because of unification of different networks and the promise of a single all-purpose communication application. Both of these promises are what corporations like, because they can potentially lead to reduced IT costs and increased user productivity. Together they also support the "do more with less" tenet.

Hardware Convergence

Hardware convergence is the union of voice and storage networks into IP networks. The IP networks will need some upgrades to handle voice and storage. Gigabit and 10-gigabit Ethernet will encourage more convergence. Several leading network vendors such as Cisco Systems, Inc., 3Com, Nortel, and Lucent are selling voice and storage products.

As part of a wholehearted move to an integrated network, IT must develop shared features such as single sign-on (a single login and password grants access to several applications and devices), security, and QoS for each service, as well as support for new end-user needs (new VoIP phone, applications, storage devices, and so on).

It is not possible to do away with pure voice and storage networks, however. There will be PBX, analog phones, and PSTN networks for a long, long time to come. Not all storage devices will move to network. Direct-attached SCSI and FC devices will never go away. It would be an unnecessary overhead and a nuisance to keep server OS data remotely across an IP network. Disks are getting cheaper every month, and dedicated links guarantee better availability and performance than what the network manager can ever promise.

Software Convergence

Perhaps the biggest draw toward VoIP is applications than can unite voice and data communications. VoIP can be used as an effective catalyst to lay the foundation for a host of new user applications. Future versions of customer relationship management (CRM) tools will unite these communications into a single Web-based GUI. At a minimum, VoIP users should have access to the following:

- A VoIP user should have application software (on a laptop) and a portable phone set with speaker and microphone. Incoming calls can be taken on the laptop whenever connected to an IP network, regardless of physical whereabouts.

- Call-management services such as call logs, call screening, and recording of conversations should be available to VoIP users.

- Voicemail, e-mail, and faxes should be integrated to a single inbox, which can be accessed and managed from a desktop application or a telephone interface. The inbox should support a mix of media types such as voice message, e-mails, and so on.

Convergence applications can create a higher level of user productivity and enable stronger customer interaction. They must become a component of the VoIP package to be a cause for increased business performance.

Storage devices such as SAN switches, iSCSI server and storage, and storage routers must be managed from a central administrative tool.

Internal Staff Convergence

Network and application convergence will bring many teams together. Network, storage, and phone system administrators, who previously knew each other's e-mail IDs but not their faces, will have to meet often. Duties will be merged and staff shakeout is inevitable.

Vendor Convergence

In the past, there were separate vendors for storage devices, SAN switches, network switches, routers, PBX sets, and analog phones. In the future, the company that continues to exist in this space must provide as many of these devices as possible. The company must get storage, network, and voice technologies under its belt. Again, there will be space for providers of niche technologies, but a larger shakeout and merger is certain.

Clients will prefer a single vendor with network, voice, and storage experience and products. Such vendors will be more likely to reduce the risks of convergence, will stop finger-pointing, and will allow the client to capture benefits of integrated solutions.

Key Points

Following are some key points discussed in this chapter:

- A converged infrastructure is a network that transmits IP data, voice communication (telephones), and storage data. Storage over IP (SoIP) and voice over IP (VoIP) are primary technologies that make a converged infrastructure possible.

- iSCSI and FCIP are two leading protocols for SoIP. By extending storage communication to IP networks, several elusive goals such as remote data replications, disaster recovery, and storage consolidation can be achieved in a reliable manner.

- VoIP allows the use of IP network to make telephone calls, thus bypassing the age-old PBX systems and PSTN. Although toll-saving is the first benefit that comes to mind, application integration, staff reduction, and user productivity are the leading drivers.

- Issues with voice communication over IP networks require immediate attention, such as performance, integration of too many networks into one, and audio quality.

What's Next

*We must be willing to let go of the life we have planned,
so as to have the life that is waiting for us.*
— E. M. Forster

Where is the technological world going? In the 1990s, it was the Internet, telecommunications, and home networking services. Next it was storage and voice over the omnipresent IP networks. This chapter describes a few emerging technologies that promise to break out and capture a place in the data centers worldwide in the coming years.

First is the question of what makes an emerging technology. In short, it must have a set of features that make it easier and less expensive for IT administrators to do what they are already doing. To that end, here are some promising technologies:

- Network convergence technologies
- Storage virtualization
- Embedded systems
- InfiniBand (IB)
- Blade servers
- Bluetooth
- System area network

Some of these technologies have been around for a while, but I believe they will have a disproportionately higher attention and market impact in the future.

Network Convergence Technologies

This is discussed in Chapter 40. Integrating services such as storage and voice into IP networks helps reduce setup and support costs. It enables an organization to use existing networks for applications, storage, and telephone calls. Various service teams can be merged. All this reduces personnel and maintenance costs and avoids pockets of underutilized resources such as network capacity or storage space.

Storage Virtualization

Storage virtualization is the ability to pool the storage on diverse and independent devices into a single view. Features such as mirroring, data replication, and snapshot backups are as important to storage management as the virtualization of data itself.

There are three types of storage virtualization, as illustrated in Figure 41-1:

- *Host-based virtualization* — All storage attached to the host is pooled together for use as logical volumes, and the intelligence to do so lies in the server. Since the server has to process the virtualization tasks, it takes host cycles but does not burden the network, SAN switches, or storage subsystem. An example is VERITAS Volume Manager, which has gained enormous popularity among Sun users.

- *Array-based virtualization* — The intelligence lies within the storage array or subsystem. Each storage subsystem vendor has proprietary subsystem-resident virtualization software. It does not put burden on the SAN switches or host. Since the vendors are best familiar with the array internals, the task of virtualization is best left to them. Examples of such storage are EMC's Symmetrix, IBM's Shark, and Hitachi's Lightning series.

- *Network-based virtualization* — This puts the burden on the network virtualization server, which must provide information to storage devices and hosts on where their data is. The server can quickly become a bottleneck.

Table 41-1 compares the three types of virtualization.

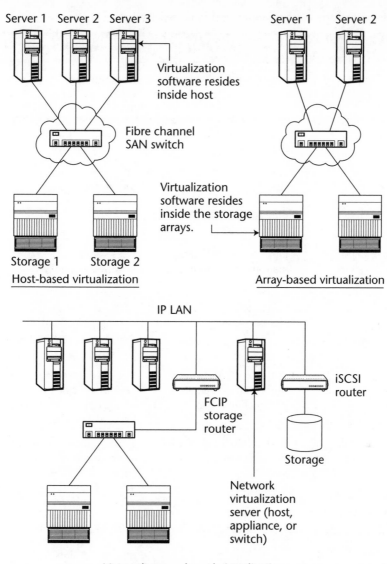

Figure 41-1   Three types of storage virtualization.

Despite the shortcomings mentioned here, storage abstraction is going to create more benefits than problems. Storage is doubling every year. Technologies that can help manage disparate storage devices attached to different host platforms are sorely needed. Eventually these technologies may not exist as separate tools but get integrated within a larger management package.

Table 41-1 Three Common Ways to Configure Virtualized Storage

TYPES OF VIRTUALIZATION	ADVANTAGES	DISADVANTAGES
Host-based virtualization	Independent of storage vendor or storage devices.	Dependent on host OS and must be installed on each host.
	Does not burden network or storage array.	Virtualization is limited to arrays directly connected to the host.
	Fully implemented on the OS and managed by the processing system administrator.	Virtualization uses host resources.
Array-based virtualization	Independent of host platform or operating system.	Uses vendor-proprietary software.
	Fully implemented by storage vendor.	Requires storage managers to get login name and password to the array.
	Virtualized devices are presented identically to all attached hosts.	Requires learning vendor-specific tools and scripts to manage devices within the array.
Network-based virtualization (virtualization server could be a switch, host, or an appliance)	Added functionality to the network server.	Performance is limited by resource such as memory and CPU within the virtualization server.
	Allows storage aggregation over MAN or WAN.	Virtualization server outage would take all storage off-line.
	Storage is managed on the same platform as the virtualization server.	System administrators' access to storage arrays is limited.

Embedded Systems

An *embedded system* is a specialized computer system that is part of a larger machine or system. It usually sits on a single microprocessor board with programs stored in its read-only memory (ROM). Almost all appliances with a digital interface such as microwaves, VCRs, car dashboards, and watches use embedded systems. Many of these embedded systems are so specialized that the entire logic is implemented on-board as a single program, while others include an operating system.

Embedded systems are ubiquitous. However, this technology is going to get more common as complexity increases. The embedded systems within switches, controllers, and adapters will offload work from the operating system, but they will have to get smarter about different possible configurations and working environments. With embedded systems, there is no opportunity to fix bugs or security threats. It must be bug-free and complete from day zero.

InfiniBand (IB)

Non-InfiniBand servers have separate, independent controllers and HBAs for local storage devices, FC storage devices, and the network. *InfiniBand (IB)* offers one type of integrated fabric for all types of communication: storage I/O, interprocessor communication (IPC), and network communication. InfiniBand architecture is a point-to-point, switched interconnect fabric that uses a channel-based message-passing communication.

InfiniBand is used to connect servers with other servers, remote storage, and networking devices. It is also used inside servers in a parallel cluster for inter-processor communication (IPC). Following are key advantages of InfiniBand:

- Organizations that have a densely populated server or blade racks will gain from the small form factors of InfiniBand-based servers and network.

- It has greater performance, lower latency, and faster and easier data sharing than PCI or other local buses. InfiniBand improves the performance of servers by offloading IP tasks from servers. It moves from the load-and-store–based communications methods used by shared local bus I/O to a more efficient message-passing approach.

- It has a high degree of built-in security.

- InfiniBand architecture reduces total cost of ownership by focusing on reliability and ease of management. It uses shared and multiple paths between nodes, thus requiring less hardware that must be purchased.

- Scalability is increased in two ways. The I/O channels are designed to scale without encountering the latencies experienced by shared bus I/O architectures. Second, the physical modularity of InfiniBand avoids the need to buy excess capacity up front in anticipation of future growth. Instead, InfiniBand users can add more capacity when needed without impacting installed services.

The nodes within an InfiniBand network are described in the following list and shown in Figure 41-2:

- *Host channel adapters (HCA)* — These connect CPU and memory modules within a processor node to the data I/O and network I/O fabric. HCAs are present in servers or even desktops and provide an interface to integrate InfiniBand with the operating system.
- *Switches* — These are the building blocks of an InfiniBand subnet.
- *Target channel adapters (TCA)* — These connect the I/O controllers (such as FC, SCSI, and Ethernet) to the InfiniBand switches. TCAs are present on I/O devices such as a RAID or JBOD subsystem.

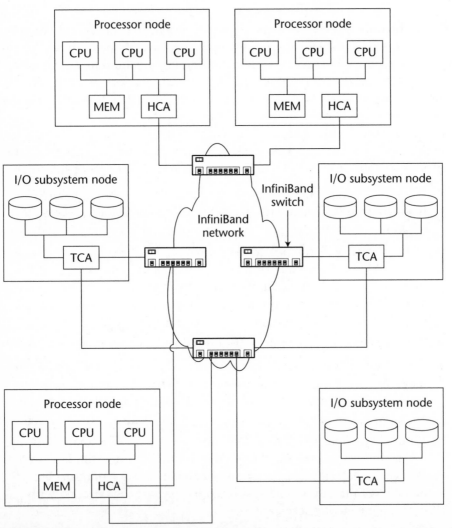

Figure 41-2 Nodes within an InfiniBand network.

Each HCA or TCA has one or more ports and can be connected to one or more switch ports. This allows for multiple paths between a source and a destination, resulting in improved performance and fault tolerance. The storage devices can be accessed and shared by multiple servers. Also, two storage devices can perform I/O on each other without the intervention of any host, other than initiating and managing the operation. Thus, the server CPU is not impacted by subsystem-to-subsystem I/O.

It is easy to scale the network by adding more switches without service disruption. The link speeds for InfiniBand switches range from 2.5 to 30 GB/sec.

Blade Servers

Blade computing introduces a new data center paradigm where various thin compute blades share centralized resources in a single chassis. A *blade server* is a single circuit board populated with components such as memory, processors, I/O adapters, and network connections that are often found on multiple boards. Server blades are built to slide into existing servers. They are smaller, need less power, and are more cost-efficient than traditional box-based servers.

Managing these servers requires the following:

- A virtualized view of the servers and resources it uses (such as storage)

- A high level of security within the server and on the network devices

- Dynamic resource provisioning that is automated as much as possible

- A layout that is easy to scale to meet ever-increasing user demands

Data centers will realize a shift from box-based servers to densely packed racks of blade-based servers.

Bluetooth

Bluetooth is a standard developed in the late 1990s by a group of network vendors. It enables wireless communication between electronic equipment — from laptops and cell phones to PDAs and headphones. The communications do not require direct user intervention. Bluetooth is planned to be a standard that operates at two levels:

- Bluetooth is a radio frequency–based standard and operates at the physical level.

- It also provides agreement at a higher level where products have to agree on when and how data is sent and received and how the communicating parties will be sure that the messages have been properly delivered and received.

TALES FROM THE TECH TURF: DANISH FACTIONS

There is some history behind the name Bluetooth. Harald Blatand (or Herald Bluetooth in English) was the king of Denmark in the late 900s. He united Denmark, parts of Norway and Sweden, and other warring factions into a single kingdom. He later introduced Christianity into Denmark. He had a monument built describing the achievements of his father, his own, and those of his son, Svend Forkbeard. In 986, he had a war with his own son over control of certain parts of his kingdom. Harald was killed in the battle and Svend had the monument buried. About 600 years later, a farmer, curious about a large mound in his farm, rediscovered the stone. Just as Herald Bluetooth had been instrumental in uniting various factions, the Bluetooth wireless technology is expected to allow diverse devices such as phones, automotive parts, entertainment devices, and laptops from many manufacturers to communicate seamlessly.

Hardware vendors such as Toshiba, Intel, Siemens, Ericsson, and Motorola have developed a specification for a very small radio module to be built into equipment (laptop, cell phone, entertainment equipment, and so on).

The art of connecting electronic devices is becoming more and more complex. Bluetooth tries to make the process easier for users of electronic devices. Bluetooth is wireless and automatic and has a number of interesting features that can simplify our daily lives. These devices have the following key features for the users:

- *They are wireless devices* — You do not carry cables when you are traveling. For static Bluetooth devices such as entertainment devices, no wiring needs to be planned or installed.

- *It's low cost* — Bluetooth technology does not add to the cost of the equipment.

- *Minimal or no configuration is necessary* — The devices find each other and do not require user intervention to work.

Figure 41-3 shows a few Bluetooth devices. Bluetooth is designed to transfer small amounts of data between devices rather than to network your office or home. It is architected merely to allow small devices such as cell phones, PDAs, and computers to synchronize files, calendars, address books, task lists, and specific documents. As far as hardware is concerned, each device needs an embedded Bluetooth "chip" or "transceiver" within itself. After five years of introduction, these chips are now available in the market. Bluetooth's distance range is only about 30 feet and the speed is relatively slow and between 1 and 2 Mbps.

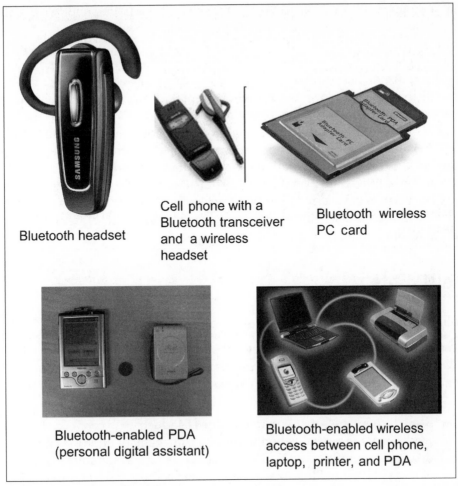

Figure 41-3 Bluetooth devices.

System Area Networks (SANs)

System area networks (*SANs*) represent an area of computer architecture that has evolved quickly during the past 10 years. The term SAN in this section refers to "system" (not "storage") area networks. After various competing standardization efforts starting in the late 1990s, the state of the SAN field became temporarily unclear. However, the technology has emerged with a richer set of features that promise to impact the server and clustering arena.

A SAN uses high-speed connections to attach high-performance computers in a cluster configuration. The configuration delivers very high bandwidth of 1+ GB/sec with very low latency. They are switched, with a typical hub supporting 4 to 8 nodes. Larger SANs are built with cascading hubs with cable length limitations that vary from a few meters to a few kilometers.

Interconnections in a SAN differ from other existing high-performance media (such as gigabit Ethernet and ATM) in several ways. SAN adapters implement reliable transport services that are similar to TCP or SPX, but directly in hardware. SANs have very low error rates. SANs are often made highly available by deploying redundant interconnect fabrics.

SANs provide bulk data transfer through a remote direct memory access (RDMA) mechanism. The performance within a SAN resembles more that of a memory subsystem than a traditional network (such as an Ethernet LAN). The initiator specifies a buffer on the local system and a buffer on the remote system. Data is then transferred directly between the local and remote systems by the network adapters without involving either of the host CPUs. Both read and write operations are supported in this manner.

Key Points

Following are some key points discussed in this chapter:

- The future is hard to guess. Several promising technologies never saw the light of the market. A successful product has two features: It helps people do their work in a less expensive and simpler manner, and it gets the support of various industry leaders.

- Some technologies that will impact the IT industry are converged networks; storage virtualization to ease its management and use; embedded systems; InfiniBand to connect servers, storage, and networks; use of more and more Blade servers in the data center; Bluetooth-based wireless devices; and system area networks (SANs).

Appendix

In This Part

Storage and Networking Solutions

This appendix contains solutions that have concepts covered in several chapters. These are complete end-to-end solutions. Although several figures in the chapters also have end-to-end solutions, these do not readily lend themselves to any single chapter.

Figure A-1 shows two data centers with data replication between them. There are two ways to replicate data:

- Using DWDMs interconnected by fiber-optic links
- Using FC-to-IP router and WAN or MAN links between the two sites

Figure A-2 shows how data in different storage networks can be accessed over the IP WAN. The first storage network consists of a SAN and iSCSI-enabled servers connected to the LAN. The second storage network has NAS, SAN, and several iSCSI-enabled servers.

Figure A-3 illustrates three data replication designs between remote sites: The first shows data replication over shared metro network using FCIP routers. The second uses DWDMs to link remote SANs. The third links data centers using FCIP routers and shared WAN.

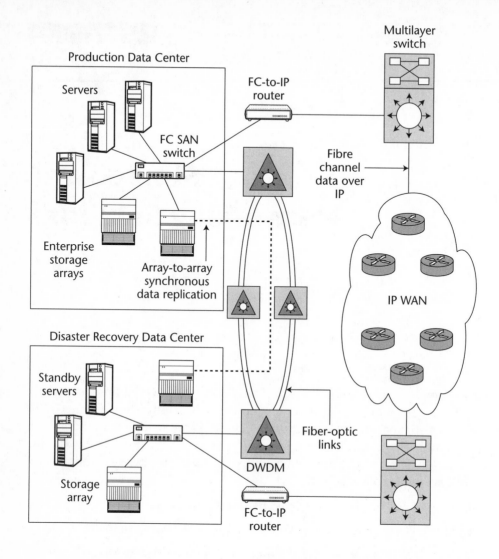

Figure A-1   Data replication to a disaster-recovery data center over IP WAN or DWDMs.

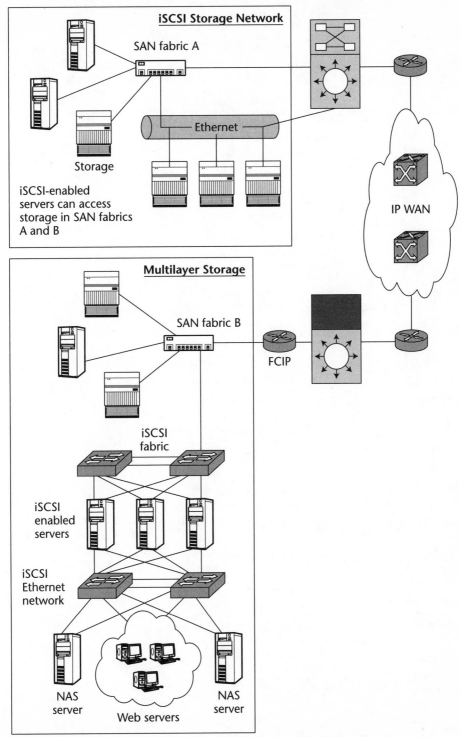

Figure A-2   iSCSI networks can access SAN storage across an IP network.

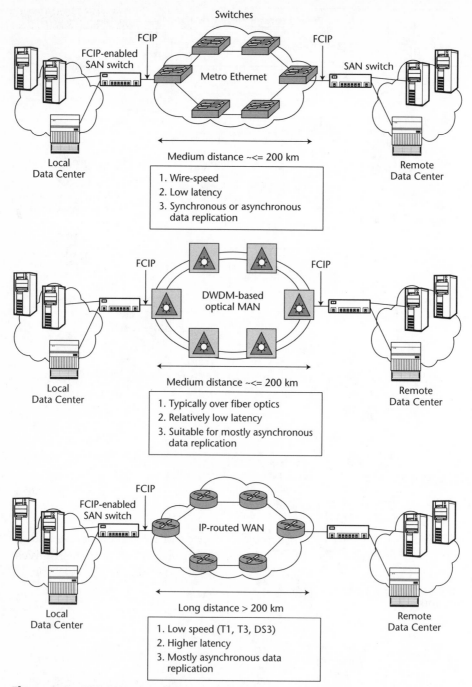

Figure A-3 FCIP SAN extension.

Glossary

It is unfair to expect that all readers will be familiar with all technical jargon used in this book. Therefore, this glossary contains a brief definition of technical terms. Many of these definitions are explained more fully elsewhere in this book.

Numbers

5-Nines — Maintaining availability 99.999 percent of the time.

10 Gigabit Ethernet — Networks with a speed of 10 Gigabit per second (Gbps). It usually uses fiber-optic media. In March 1999, representatives from Cisco Systems and other companies drafted the IEEE 10 Gigabit Ethernet standards.

A

Access control list (ACL) — A persistent list that describes the rights of principals (for example, users and groups of users) to access resources. Access control lists can be assigned to network traffic and ports or data objects such as files. Network ACLs are used to examine each packet to determine whether to forward or drop the packet based on the specified ACL criteria.

Active/passive — A system where one redundant component or server is active while the other is available, but not in standby mode.

Active/standby — A system where one redundant component or server is active and the other is in standby mode, ready to take over with little switchover time. The switchover is quicker than for active/passive systems.

Address resolution — The method of determining a MAC address, given a more abstract WAN or LAN address.

Address resolution protocol (ARP) — This is a protocol to map a higher layer address to a lower layer address. In networking, ARP is used by an IP networking layer to map IP addresses to lower level hardware (that is, MAC) addresses.

American National Standards Institute (ANSI) — Organization that establishes voluntary standards for various technologies such as programming languages, disk properties, backup systems, and telecommunications.

Application failover — Process by which an application is started on its backup server in the event of a failure on its primary server. Not only is the application restarted, but all of its disk resources and the IP address through which clients were accessing it are also migrated over to the backup node.

Arbitrated loop topology — A fibre channel (FC) standard that defines a loop topology where up to 126 devices can communicate with one another using an arbitrated access protocol. This provides a less-expensive way to attach multiple communicating devices in a loop.

Arbitration — The process of selecting one respondent from a group of several candidates that request service at the same time.

Asynchronous data replication — Local I/O will complete without waiting for the remote or replicated I/O to complete. However, it is expected that the I/Os will be processed in the original order.

Asynchronous I/O operation — An I/O operation where the initiator does not wait for I/O completion before proceeding with other work. Therefore, the initiator can have several concurrent I/O operations in progress.

Asynchronous transfer mode (ATM) — A connection-oriented network communications technology that is based on switching 53-byte fixed-length units of data called *cells*. ATM transmission rates are multiples of

51.840 Mbps. SONET uses ATM at transmission rates of 155, 622, 2,048, and 9,196 Mbps, which are called OC-3, OC-12, OC-48, and OC-192, respectively.

Authentication — The process of identifying an individual. It is usually based on a username and password. It merely ensures that the individual is who he or she claims to be but specifies nothing about the access privileges of the individual.

Authorization — This is a process of deciding whether a requestor is allowed to perform an operation or receive some data or service. Access control is an example of authorization.

Availability — The amount of time that a system is available. It is usually calculated as a percentage of an elapsed year. For example, 99.95 percent availability equates to 4.38 hours of downtime in a year ($0.0005 \times 365 \times 24 = 4.38$) for a service or machine that is supposed to be available all the time.

B

Bandwidth — The maximum amount of data (measured in bits/second) that can travel a communications path in a given time. If you think of the link as a pipe, then bandwidth represents the width of the pipe and tells you how much data can flow through it all at once.

Bayonet Neil Councilman (BNC) — A type of coaxial cable connector. Specifications for various BNC style connectors are defined in EIA/TIA 403-A and MIL-C-39012.

Block — The unit of data in which information is stored and retrieved on storage devices (such as disk drives and tapes).

C

Cache — A high-speed memory or storage device used to decrease the time required to read data from or write data to a slower memory or device. *Read cache* holds data in anticipation that it will be requested by a client. *Write cache* holds data written by a client until it can be safely stored on permanent media such as disk.

Campus cluster — A single cluster where the nodes (or hosts) are geographically separated within the limits of an organization's own area and within which it can run cables above or below the ground. Campus clusters are usually spread out in different rooms within a single building or in neighboring buildings.

Cascade — Process of connecting two or more hubs or switches together to increase the number of ports or extend distances.

Cascaded fabric — A topology where one switch connects to another switch with an interswitch link.

Cascading failover — The ability of an application to fail from a primary to a secondary location and then to fail to a recovery location on a different site.

Class of service — A mechanism for controlling traffic in a network by specifying message or packet priority.

Client — The client part of a client-server architecture. A client is usually an application that runs on a PC and relies on a server to perform some operations. A client could be a host or device that relies on another node for some data or service.

Cluster — A group of systems that work together as a single system to provide fast, uninterrupted service. A cluster has enough redundancy of software and hardware that a single failure will not significantly disrupt service.

Cluster quorum — A dynamically calculated majority used to determine if there are enough nodes to start or run the cluster. Cluster quorums help avoid *split-brain syndrome,* which can lead to data inconsistency or corruption.

Continental cluster — A group of clusters that use routed networks or common-carrier networks for data replication and cluster communication to support service failover between separate clusters in different data centers. Continental clusters are often located in different cities or countries and can span hundreds or thousands of kilometers.

Controller — A device that manages the transfer of data from a computer to a peripheral device and vice-versa. For example, tape drives, monitors, printers, and LAN connections all require controllers.

D

Data center — Physically proximate collection of nodes, storage arrays, network equipment, and so on, all in one large, dedicated room.

Data replication — Scheme by which data is copied from one site to another for disaster tolerance.

Demilitarized zone (DMZ) — A no-man's land between the Internet and the internal network. This is one or more network subnet(s) that are not well-managed and limited open connections to the Internet. A firewall or a router protects this zone with traffic-filtering capabilities.

Denial-of-service (DoS) attacks — A type of attack on a network that is designed to slow network with useless traffic.

Dense wavelength division multiplexing (DWDM) — Wave division multiplexing (WDM) is an optical transmission technique where multiple optical signals are transmitted to a single optical fiber using different wavelengths. The term DWDM is often used to describe systems with 16 or more channels.

Digital subscriber link (DSL) — Scheme to send data over copper wires. They are sometimes referred to as *last-mile technologies* because they connect telephone switching stations to a home or office but do not interconnect switching stations.

Distributed lock manager (DLM) — A software mechanism that synchronizes access to shared resources among cooperating processes throughout the cluster.

Domain Name System (DNS) — An Internet service that translates domain names to or from IP addresses.

Dynamic load sharing — Ability to distribute traffic automatically among multiple paths.

E

Enterprise storage connect (ESCON) — A type of fiber-optic channel used for communication between storage subsystems.

Ethernet — The leading networking technology that is based on packetized transmissions between physical ports over many types of electrical and optical media. Ethernet can transport various upper-layer protocols, the most common being TCP/IP.

F

Fabric — A network of one or more fibre channel (FC) switches that are used to link hosts and storage devices.

Fiber — Strands of glass through which data in the form of light pulses are transmitted in fiber-optic cable.

Fibre — Covers all data transmission media types specified in the Fibre Channel Physical Layer standard (FC-PH), such as optical fiber and copper (twisted-pair or coaxial) cables.

Fibre channel (FC) — High-speed data transmission technology among servers and storage devices using SCSI. Three common topologies are point-to-point, arbitrated loop, and switched, usually with speeds of 1 Gbps in both directions.

Fibre channel–arbitrated loop (FC-AL) — A fibre channel workgroup topology supporting up to 126 devices. Media access is performed through arbitration.

Fibre channel over IP (FCIP) — A proposed IETF standard for encapsulating and sending fibre channel packets over an IP network.

Firewall — A combination of hardware and software buffer placed between internal networks and the Internet. It allows only specific kinds of messages to pass back and forth with a goal to protect the internal systems for undesired, malicious traffic.

Frame — The smallest unit of information carrying user data.

Frame relay — A packet-switching method to communicate data that uses available bandwidth only when it is needed. This fast packet-switching method is efficient enough to transmit voice communications with the proper network management.

Full-duplex communications — A pair of nodes can both simultaneously send and receive data to one another, effectively doubling the speed themselves.

G

Gigabit — One billion bits or 1,000 Megabits. It is generally used to refer to bandwidth.

Gigabit Ethernet — Ethernet switching that provides full-duplex non-blocking 1 Gbps throughput. It is typically associated with IP data traffic. It also supports voice, video traffic, iSCSI, and block-level storage traffic.

Gigabit interface converter (GBIC) — A transceiver that converts serial electric signals to serial optical signals and vice-versa. It is often used to connect a fiber-optic system (such as a fibre channel SAN) to a gigabit Ethernet system.

H

H.323 — An International Telecommunications Union (ITU) standard for real-time interactive voice and videoconferencing over LANs and the Internet.

Heartbeat network — A network that provides reliable communication among nodes in a cluster, including transmission of heartbeat messages and signals from each cluster node.

Heating, ventilation, and air-conditioning (HVAC) — This generally refers to the air-conditioning system in the data center.

Hot swap — Changing a system hardware component without shutting down the system.

Hub — A central connecting device in a network that joins communication lines into a star configuration.

I

Integrated services digital network (ISDN) — An international communications standard that allows ordinary phone lines to transmit digital instead of analog signals. This allows data to be transmitted at a faster rate than using a traditional modem.

Internet protocol (IP) — A protocol designed for use in interconnected systems of packet networks.

Internet telephony — Means of transmitting human voice in real time over IP network.

Interswitch link (ISL) — Connection between two switches.

iSCSI — Acronym for small computer systems interface (SCSI) over IP. Used to access block-level storage from IP-connected hosts.

J

Jitter — Variation in the amount of latency among packets being received.

K

Key exchange — A cryptographic process in which two communicating entities establish a shared key in a manner such that a third party who reads all of the communication cannot effectively determine the value of the key.

Key pair — A public key and its corresponding private key, which are together used for public key or asymmetric encryption.

L

LAN-free backup — A disk backup methodology in which a SAN appliance performs actual backup I/O operations to free network devices from data transfers from storage device to backup media.

Latency — The time delay of data traffic through a network or a switch.

Lightweight directory access protocol (LDAP) — An IETF protocol to create, access, and remove objects and data from a directory. It provides the ability to search, compare, add, delete, and modify directory objects. LDAP got its name from its goal of being a simpler form of directory access protocol (DAP) from the X.500 set of standards.

Load sharing — The division of an I/O load or task among several storage subsystem components. This may or may not try to equalize each component's share of the work.

Local area network (LAN) — A network communications system that geographically covers less than 5 kilometers (approximately).

Local cluster — A cluster located in a single data center. This type of cluster is not disaster-tolerant.

Logical unit number (LUN) — An identifier assigned to each disk drive or a logical collection of disks (such as RAID array) so the host can address and access the data on those devices.

Logical volume — A virtual disk or volume set that is made of one or more disks or disk sections.

Long wave — Lasers or LEDs that emit light with wavelengths around 1,300 nm. Long wave lasers are used for long fibre channel links typically with single-mode fiber with a 9-micron core size.

M

Manual failover — Failover requiring human intervention to start an application or service on another node.

Mean time between failures (MTBF) — The average time from start of use to first failure of a device in a large population of identical devices.

Mean time to failure (MTTF) — The average time between two consecutive failures calculated over a large number of failures.

Mean time to repair (MTTR) — The average time it takes to repair a component or system as measured over a large number of repairs.

Media access control (MAC) address — The 48-bit (12-digit hexadecimal) address constructed from the 24-bit IEEE company ID and a 24-bit vendor-specified identifier associated with an Ethernet port. It is also used to construct the Worldwide Name.

Mesh — A cascading subset that defines the physical connections between switches where multiple switches are all connected to each other.

Metropolitan-area network (MAN) — A network that covers the metropolitan area, typically within a radius of about 100 km. MANs use high-bandwidth devices such as DWDM that are commonly used in the wide-area networking environments.

Metropolitan cluster — A cluster that is geographically dispersed within the confines of a metropolitan area and usually has a right-of-way to lay cables for redundant network and data replication devices.

N

Name server — A node that translates device names to IP addresses and vice versa. In a fibre channel network, a name server translates between Worldwide Names and fabric addresses.

Network address translation (NAT) — Provides the ability to map hidden, internal network IP addresses to routable, external IP addresses.

Network attached storage (NAS) — File-oriented and dedicated storage appliances that are connected to the IP network and offer data-sharing services across multiple platforms. They use protocols such as NFS, HTTP, and CIFS.

O

OC-n — A data rate that is a multiple of the basic SONET speed of 51.84 Mbps. OC-3 is 155 Mbps, OC-12 is 622 Mbps, OC-48 is 2,488 Mbps, and OC-192 is 9,953 Mbps.

Off-line data replication — Data replication by storing data off-line, usually a backup tape or disk stored in a safe location. This form of data replication is used for applications where a 24-hour recovery is acceptable.

Online data replication — Process of copying data in real time to another disk subsystem at a remote location. There is a slight delay in copying data because of distance. This is used for applications requiring quick recovery (within a few hours or minutes).

Out-of-band — Use of an alternate or separate channel for a task at hand. This is more expensive, but it ensures that primary applications such as voice and critical applications receive full bandwidth.

P

Parallel database — Databases that use shared-memory, shared-disk, or shared-nothing architectures and leverage the inherent parallelism of these environments to achieve high-end performance and service availability.

Plenum — From the Latin word *plenum,* an area within a data center such as the space between the subfloor and the raised floor that is used to move cooling air to racks.

Point of distribution (POD) — A rack containing network switches, terminal servers, and network cable patch ports.

Power distribution units (PDUs) — An electrical distribution box fed by a high-amp three-phase connector with power outlets and circuit breakers.

Practical Extraction and Reporting Language (PERL) — A scripting language commonly used for creating CGI programs on Web servers because it is more efficient than UNIX shell script programs, especially for very large files.

Private branch exchange (PBX) — A private telephone network used within an enterprise. A certain number of outside lines must be connected to the PBX to make/receive outside calls. Internal extensions can be reached by simply dialing four or five numbers. This is also less expensive than connecting external lines to each phone.

Protocol — A set of rules for using an interconnect or network so that information conveyed on the interconnect is correctly interpreted by all communicating parties.

Proxy — An agent that acts on behalf of some other network element. It intercepts incoming requests from a client application to a real server to see if it can fulfill the request itself. Proxy servers have two goals: improve performance and filter requests.

Public key — A key that is used for encryption and can be distributed widely without impacting the security of the system.

Public Switched Telephone Network (PSTN) — The world's combined public circuit-switched telephone network, consisting of all analog or digital. These could be fixed-line or mobile. This is analogous to the Internet, which is a combination of the world's public IP-based packet-switched network.

Q

Quality of service (QoS) — Refers to the capability of a network to provide better service to selected network traffic over various technologies such as frame relay, ATM, SONET, and Ethernet. The primary goal is to provide priority including dedicated bandwidth, reduced jitter, low latency (required by VoIP), and controlled loss characteristics.

R

Real server — Physical server providing the services behind the virtual server to the clients.

Redundant array of inexpensive disks (RAID) — A group of disks that is configured to appear as a single disk drive to the host. It offers more capacity, faster access, and data protection from disk failures.

Remote failover — Failover to a node at another data center or remote location.

Router — A device connected to two or more networks that decides to which network to send the data.

S

Scalability — The capability of a system to increase connectivity and performance incrementally.

Secure socket layer (SSL) — A security protocol that provides encrypted, authenticated privacy over the Internet to prevent eavesdropping, tampering, and message forgery.

Serverless backup — Data backup process where the device receiving the backup manages and performs actual backup I/O operations, thus freeing the server to perform I/O operations for clients and reducing the number of trips the backup data takes through the server.

Session initiation protocol (SIP) — A proposed standard for configuring sessions between one or more clients.

Shortwave — Lasers or LEDs that emit light with wavelengths around 780 nm or 850 nm. Short wave lasers are used for FC-AL links up to 1 km and are typically used with multimode fiber.

Simple network management protocol (SNMP) — A protocol used to examine and change configuration parameters and counters of network-connected devices. They store information about whether or not a component is operating properly using management information bases (MIBs).

Single point of failure (SPOF) — A component of a cluster or node that, if it fails, prevents access to applications and services. It is becoming the leading protocol for signaling for voice over IP and will replace H.323 in this role.

Split-brain syndrome — Occurs when heartbeat link failure causes a cluster to re-form into two independent server groups, where each group thinks it is the authority and starts up the same set of applications and tries to modify the same data, resulting in data corruption.

Spoofing — Unauthorized use of legitimate identification to mimic a subject different from the attacker. Impersonating, masquerading, piggybacking, and mimicking are forms of spoofing.

Standby — The role of a redundant component that is monitoring its counterpart and is ready to be switched into service if the counterpart fails.

Star — A configuration of computing devices where each device is connected by links radiating out from a central connection point such as a hub.

Storage area network (SAN) — A scalable, high-speed, server-storage infrastructure with any-to-any connectivity for block-level data transfer among all devices.

Synchronous optical network (SONET) — A standard for optical networks that provides modular building blocks, fixed overheads, flexible payload mappings, and a basic bandwidth of 51.840 megabits/second. This is known as OC-1. Higher bandwidths that are n times the basic rate are available (known as OC-n). OC-3, OC-12, OC-48, and OC-192 are currently in common use.

T

Topology — The physical or logical layout of nodes on a network.

Transaction processing monitor (TPM) — Software that allows you to modify an application so that in-flight transactions are stored in an external location until that transaction has been committed to all possible copies of the database or file system. Although this increases the CPU overhead, it also ensures completion of all copied transactions and protects against data loss.

Transmission control protocol/Internet protocol (TCP/IP) — A suite of communications protocols used to connect hosts on the network.

Transparent failover — A client application that automatically reconnects to a new server without the user taking any action.

Transparent IP failover — Moving the IP address from one failed node or another healthy node in the same IP subnet so that users or applications continue to use the same name and address after a failure.

U

U — A unit of measure for the sizing of network equipment. One U is equal to 1.75 inches (44.45 mm) in height. A typical 7-foot rack contains about 6.5 feet of usable rack space, or 45 U tall (1.75 in. $\times$ 45 = 78.75 in.).

Uninterruptible power supply (UPS) — A very large battery capable of sustaining power load for a given amount of time. Some UPSs are capable of generating their own power using gasoline. Used to power devices in the event of an external power grid failure.

V

Virtual local area networks (VLANs) — An administratively defined broadcast domain that enhances performance and security by limiting traffic. Only nodes within a VLAN receive packets that are unicast, broadcast, or multicast (flooded). They enhance security by separating nodes on different VLANs within the same switch.

Virtual private network (VPN) — A secure network that is created over an otherwise unsecure public network such as the Internet. It uses encryption and other security mechanisms to protect the data being transported within its network and allow authorized users to access it.

Virtual server — A logical server in a content switch or load balancer that presents a single IP address, protocol, and port to clients for a particular service. The virtual server, in turn, directs the client requests to services offered by multiple real servers.

Voice over IP (VoIP) — Category of hardware and software that enables people to make telephone calls over the Internet. Voice signals are converted to IP packets and transported over public, shared lines, thus avoiding the traditional Public Switched Telephone Network (PSTN).

W

Wave division multiplexing (WDM) — Method of transmitting data from different sources over the same fiber-optic link at the same time. Each data channel is carried out on its own unique wavelength, resulting in an aggregate bandwidth that increases with the number of wavelengths employed. There are two common types: dense (DWDM) and coarse (CWDM).

Wide area network (WAN) — Special-purpose networks to provide connectivity to multiple locations in different areas.

Worldwide Name (WWN) — The SAN equivalent of a network adapter's MAC address. Each host adapter and switch port in a SAN has a WWN number such as 10:00:00:00:d4:11:cf:10 — 16 hexadecimal digits grouped as eight colon-separated pairs.

Z

Zone — A group of fibre channel NL_Ports and/or N_Ports (device ports) that are allowed to communicate with each other within a fabric (set of SAN switches). Zone membership may be specified by: (1) port location on a switch (that is, Domain_ID and port number); (2) the device's N_Port_Name; (3) the device's address identifier; or (4) the device's Node_Name.

Zoning — The ability to divide a SAN into a number of independent zones for binding targets and initiators. Only elements within a zone can communicate with each other.

Index

Index